Japanese Foreign Policy, 1869-1942

FOREIGN POLICIES OF THE GREAT POWERS
Edited by C. J. Lowe

The Reluctant Imperialists C. J. Lowe
Vol. I British Foreign Policy 1879–1902
Vol. II The Documents

The Mirage of Power C. J. Lowe and M. L. Dockrill
Vol. I British Foreign Policy 1902–14
Vol. II British Foreign Policy 1914–22
Vol. III The Documents

*From Sadowa to Sarajevo: The Foreign Policy
of Austria-Hungary, 1866–1914* F. R. Bridge

The Foreign Policy of France from 1915 to 1945 J. Néré

Italian Foreign Policy 1870–1940 C. J. Lowe and
F. Marzari

German Foreign Policy, 1871–1914 Imanuel Geiss

Japanese Foreign Policy
1869-1942

Kasumigaseki to Miyakezaka

Ian Nish

Reader in International History
London School of Economics

Routledge & Kegan Paul

London, Henley and Boston

First published in 1977
by Routledge & Kegan Paul Ltd
39 Store Street,
London WC1E 7DD,
Broadway House,
Newtown Road,
Henley-on-Thames,
Oxon RG9 1EN and
9 Park Street,
Boston, Mass. 02108, USA
Manuscript typed by Jacqueline Bayes
Printed in Great Britain
by Redwood Burn Ltd,
Trowbridge and Esher

ISBN 0 7100 8421 8

Contents

v

Contents

Contents

Maps

Acknowledgments

Like all authors in this series, I owe a great personal
debt to the late Professor Cedric Lowe, who was the
general editor of this series. Professor Lowe died
tragically after a motor accident at Edmonton, Alberta,
on 26 April 1975. This volume in the series endeavours
to interpret for a non-Japanese readership Japan's
foreign policy from the Meiji restoration until the
Greater East Asian war through the careers and thinking
of those who guided her policy-making.

In the translations at the end, I have tried to
select documents which illustrate the quality of Japan's
thinking on foreign affairs. In the small selection
which space allows, I have tried to uncover the motives
and ideas of the Japanese leaders and the way that they
communicated them to one another. I have in general
avoided documents which are already available in English
translation or in previous documentary collections. I
have been greatly helped by Mrs Toshiko Marks who
checked my translations for me though she is in no way
responsible for the errors and faulty nuances which they
may still contain since communication between the
English and Japanese languages can never be a precise
or unambiguous exercise.

In preparing this manuscript for treatment as one of
the early Routledge typewritten volumes, I am grateful
for the considerate attention of Miss Eileen Wood and
other members of RKP staff. For other services in
connection with writing and re-writing the manuscript,
I would like to thank Mrs M. Bradgate and Mrs I. Capsey.

Foreign Ministers

Date		Foreign Minister	Cabinet
1869		(Lord) Sawa	
1871	July	Iwakura Tomomi	
1871	November	Soejima Taneomi	
1873		Terashima Munenori	
1879		Inoue Kaoru	
1888		Okuma Shigenobu	From 1885 Itō
1889		Aoki Shūzō	Yamagata
1891		Enomoto Buyo	Matsukata
1892		Mutsu Munemitsu	Itō
1896		Okuma Shigenobu	Matsukata
1897		Nishi Tokujirō	Itō
1898	June	Okuma Shigenobu	Okuma
1898	November	Aoki Shūzō	Yamagata
1900		Katō Takaaki	Itō
1901		Komura Jūtarō	Katsura
1906	January	Katō Takaaki	Saionji
1906	May	Hayashi Tadasu	Saionji
1908		Komura Jūtarō	Katsura
1911		Uchida Yasuya	Saionji
1913	January	Katō Takaaki	Katsura
1913	February	Makino Shinken	Yamamoto
1914	April	Katō Takaaki	Okuma
1915		Ishii Kikujirō	Okuma
1916		Motono Ichirō	Terauchi
1918	April	Gotō Shimpei	Terauchi
1918	September	Uchida Yasuya	Hara
1923		Ijūin Hikokichi	Yamamoto
1924	January	Matsui Keishirō	Kiyoura
1924	June	Shidehara Kijūrō	Katō Takaaki
1927		Tanaka Giichi	Tanaka
1929		Shidehara Kijūrō	Hamaguchi
1932	January	Yoshizawa Kenkichi	Inukai
1932	July	Uchida Yasuya	Saitō

1933		Hirota Kōki	Saitō
1936	April	Arita Hachirō	Hirota
1937	March	Satō Naotake	Hayashi
1937	June	Hirota Kōki	Konoe
1938	May	Ugaki Kazushige	Konoe
1938	October	Arita Hachirō	Konoe
1939	September	Nomura Kichisaburō	Abe
1940	January	Arita Hachirō	Toyoda
1940	July	Matsuoka Yosuke	Konoe
1941	July	Toyoda Teijirō	Konoe
1941	October	Tōgō Shigenori	Tōjō
1942		Tani Masayuki	Tōjō
1943		Shigemitsu Mamoru	Tōjō

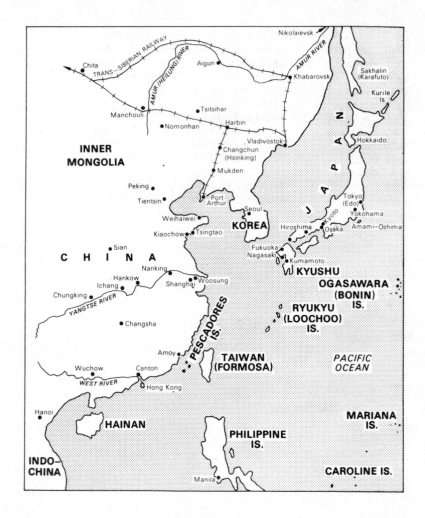

MAP 1 Japan and East Asia

Introduction

'The army has this time really asserted itself at the
Foreign Ministry over China policy.   It looks as
though not only the foreign minister but also the prime
minister are busy waving white flags.' (1)   So wrote
the former foreign minister, Shidehara Kijūrō, from his
retirement in 1935.   Power, as he saw it, was passing
from his old Ministry (Kasumigaseki) to the general
headquarters of the army (Miyakezaka).   This remark
was made with great regret because Shidehara and many
liberals like him inside and outside the Ministry
mourned the fact that Kasumigaseki had a smaller voice
in affairs and were ready to admit that they must bear
some share of the blame for it.
    The story of the Japanese Foreign Ministry contains
many elements of tension.   Among these the tension
between Kasumigaseki and Miyakezaka was by the 1930s
to prove to be the most important one.   But it was not
new and had been present throughout the three-quarters
of a century of its existence which are covered in this
book.   The Foreign Ministry was established soon after
the Meiji restoration.   It rose meteorically like the
Japanese nation-state itself.   But, since Japan's
fortunes seemed to be punctuated by wars and 'incidents',
the Foreign Ministry inevitably found itself confronted
with the dilemma of co-operating with military agencies.
In the course of time, the Ministry, with its liberal,
internationalist approach, came under special attack.
But it did not fall.   Shorn in the 1930s of many of
its privileges and divided within itself, it none the
less survived these tribulations.   And, when the military agencies were destroyed in battle, the Foreign
Ministry (but in the disguise of the Liaison Bureau)
emerged into the postwar era.   We are concerned in this
study with the period of its rise and fall, but not its
rebirth.

1

I have tried to write a history of Japanese foreign
policy with special emphasis on the role of the Foreign
Ministry. I have sought to do this by way of inter-
pretative essays on a selected number of foreign
ministers which focus on the main aspects of policy
which occupied their attention. This approach is
deliberately personal and selective. It is personal
because it has always seemed to me that there has been
a tendency to neglect 'personality' in Japanese foreign
policy studies. Among non-specialist readers overseas, many Japanese foreign ministers have appeared as
'cardboard figures'. I shall therefore be trying to
throw a little light on the men behind the policies.
For reasons of space this book has had to be selective.
I have selected those foreign ministers whose contribution has been greatest in two respects: to the development of the Ministry and to the formulation of policy.
Opinions differ widely on the merits of different
ministers as one might expect. Some of those included
were more important than others and influenced the
diplomatic scene much longer. Some have been included,
I acknowledge, because they are interesting rather than
important. Nor can I say that I like all those selected: in many cases quite on the contrary. But this
is healthy because it is a common mistake for foreigners
to dwell on those Japanese with whom they can identify.

It is necessary to state also what I have not tried
to do. I have not attempted to present a connected
narrative of Japan's foreign relations which would
require a much longer book than this. Nor have I
written at length, except incidentally, on that most
important of themes, the role of the military in foreign
policy-making. The reason is the simple one that much
research and many publications have lately been devoted
to this subject which is properly a part of the history
of the Japanese domestic scene. I am not, therefore,
interested in Miyakezaka for itself but only in so far
as it has an impact on Kasumigaseki.

My choice of foreign ministers has been governed also
by the needs of the series of which this is one volume.
This requires that, alongside the narrative, there
shall appear documents illustrative of the thinking
underlying the development of Japan's foreign relations.
Of necessity, these documents have in the main had to
be translated. I have avoided official diplomatic
documents, treaties, etc., for the reason set out long
ago by Mutsu Munemitsu, a foreign minister who had a
great historical sense: 'Official diplomatic documents
generally contain subtle meanings which do not reveal

their true sense to the outsider.   Thus, if we read
them only, there is quite often a feeling of vagueness.
But in this volume we show the true facts and do not
hide secrets.' (2)   I have therefore sought to go
rather deeper than official diplomatic documents, to
contemporary memoranda or letters which show, as we
hope, the unedited views of the writer.   I have
selected for discussion foreign ministers who did
leave behind some writing, whether in the form of
original papers or published material.   In this way,
I have had as my object to give Western readers some
indication of the motives which underlay the thinking
of what an earlier generation of authors would have
called 'the makers of Japanese foreign policy'.   Only
by studying the original documents can a non-Japanese
begin to understand these motives;   the documents
assist him also to reach his own judgment on how
efficient the Foreign Ministry bureaucracy was and how
far the foreign policies which emerged were based on
rational criteria.

It seems necessary before embarking on a series of
essentially biographical studies to suggest the perspective within which one should see the astonishingly
rapid development of Japan as a nation.   It would not
be unreasonable to divide the history of Japan in our
period into three phases: The Powers versus Japan,
1853-94;   Japan among the Powers, 1894-1931;   Japan
versus the Powers, 1931-45.   In the eyes of some
Japanese, this last period would be regarded as that
of 'the Powers versus Japan'.   It is important by way
of introduction to this volume to examine Japan's
conception of her status in the world during the purview
of this study.
   The Japanese nation grew up in the shadow of Europe.
This statement may seem basically implausible in view
of Japan's geographical remoteness from Europe.   Yet
Japanese of the Meiji period had a deep feeling that
they were 'among the Powers' from 1868 onwards.   Moreover, they felt that they were growing up in a hostile
world of acquisitive naval Powers.   Looking back, it
would appear that Japanese leaders greatly exaggerated
the threat which was posed by the foreign Powers.
Indeed, this threat became something of a national
neurosis.   But it was a valuable neurosis for a new
nation-state which kept the need for national defence
very much before the people and urged on them the
necessary sacrifices.   When one analyses Japan's

situation in the 1870s, it is probable that she was
isolated enough to prevent any invasion by a Western
Power and strong enough to defend her own coasts. To
be sure, Western countries by their 'unequal treaties'
were an obstacle to her national development but not
to her national independence.

After her defeat of China in 1894, Japan's entry
among the Powers took place in three phases. Gradually down to 1910 she became a continental Power in
east Asia. Taking the first step after the war with
China, she established herself on the Asian continent
by the war with Russia. She was, in reality, dominant
in Korea from 1904 onwards; and the annexation in
1910 was only the end of a long process. Moreover she
obtained from the Russian war a well-placed 'sphere of
influence' in southern Manchuria. It took some time
to turn this into an asset: encouraging emigration of
Japanese; obtaining foreign loans; overcoming the
technical difficulties of rehabilitating the railways.
Not to mention the permanent undercurrent of tension
between the army on the spot and the Tokyo civil
government. But Japan gradually established herself
as a continental Power.

From 1910 onwards, Japan became a Pacific Power.
In this progression, the year 1914 was an important
turning-point. Japan jumped into the First World War
with that same mixture of adventure and calculation
which she had displayed in 1904 and was to show again
in 1941. After the initial campaigns in China and
the Pacific had ended in Japan's favour, the Japanese
were to be spectators in the European war down to the
Siberian intervention of 1918. They would not send
troops to the European front; and naval vessels were
only slowly allocated for service in European waters.
At the same time it was recognized as 'a moment of
opportunity' - not only continentally but in the Pacific
area. The area covered by Japan's trade expanded to
the periphery of the Pacific ocean.

By the end of the First World War Japan could legi-
timately claim to be a world Power. It was with great
pride that Prince Saionji commented in 1919: 'Japan
stands among the five Great Powers in the world and has
passed the threshold which allows her to take part in
the affairs of Europe' (Document 20). Japan's new
accession of strength was acknowledged by many outsiders. Thus, the Canadian prime minister in 1921 told
the British imperial conference that 'there were only
three major Powers left in the world: the United
States, Britain and Japan.' In this and other remarks

of the time, it was implied that Japan had grown to her
position by virtue of her naval strength.   But the
measurement of world status purely in terms of naval
strength can be misleading.   Although Japan had
become a Pacific Power and although Japan had unquestionably benefited from the destructiveness of the
First World War to improve her position in the league-
table of world Powers, there were serious weaknesses
in the Japanese state.   Thus, there was strong
evidence that the Japanese army had fallen behind since
1905: 'infantry units [in 1917 still] advanced with
regimental colours unfurled and officers waving swords,
while the cavalry charged in mass formation.' (3)   Second,
there was Japan's economic weakness: after her prosperity of the war years, there was a period of slump
which saw the collapse of many wartime companies and
small banks.   Added to the shortage of vital raw
materials, the severity of the depression also left its
legacy in increased left-wing activity on the political
and industrial front, which, while it was small by world
standards, was a worrying feature for the cabinets of
the day.   For these and other reasons the contribution
demanded of Japan as a new member of the League of
Nations placed her no. 5 in the table.

In the 1920s Japan was among the Great Powers.   She
had achieved this new status by her economic and
military-naval strength and had to be treated as an
equal.   This did not imply that Japan had in this
decade an internationalist approach to affairs or was
ready to collaborate with the other Powers.   Nor was
she prepared to defer to the views of other Powers for
the sake of contriving a united front among them as she
had to some extent done before 1914.   On the contrary,
Japan was determined, especially in China, to go it
alone regardless of the views of others.   She would
pursue her national interests in parallel to, and even
in opposition to, others.   Having reached the heights
of Great Power status, Japan did not find it necessary
to be complaisant, far less to be subordinate, to
other members of the club.

With the Manchurian crisis, Japan came to a major
turning-point.   Her army called the bluff of the
Powers, of the League of Nations, and got away with it.
When Japan recognized Manchukuo and left the League,
she voluntarily went into isolation.   It was not that
she threw down the gauntlet to the world and that the
Powers hastened to pick it up.   By and large, they
wanted to keep Japan within the world community.   The
fact was that many Japanese felt their country no

longer needed to be among the Powers and could more easily continue without the restraints imposed by membership of the world community.   By 1933 Japan had come of age.

As the 1930s advanced, these trends seemed to be confirmed.   The Western world saw Japan as moving slowly away: first, from the League of Nations;   second, towards Germany and Italy;   third, towards freedom of naval building;   and fourth, against China, whom other countries were inclined to support, even if they fought shy of direct involvement in her cause.   Naturally, the Japanese perception of these events was different. At its most extreme, it was expressed through the position of the armed services: that Japan was being held back by the application of the naval ratio formula;   that she was being cold-shouldered by the Powers apart from Germany and Italy rather than the reverse;   and that she was strong enough to stand on her own feet.

It may be helpful to use this introduction also to set the role of the Foreign Ministry in perspective. In Japan there was always a spectrum of views - not necessarily a broad spectrum - about Japan's place in the world.   In this the central ground was generally held by the Kasumigaseki diplomats, but they had fluctuating fortunes in getting their message across. In the Meiji period (1868-1912), the Foreign Ministry began in a modest way, its work being for a long time concentrated on routine aspects of maintaining contacts with foreigners.   On most crucial decisions, the genro were consulted and generally carried sufficient weight to lay down policy.   Over the wars with China and Russia, the Foreign Ministry still ensured that the utmost was done by negotiation and that the ground was prepared diplomatically.

But Japan's victory in two major wars brought about a subtle change in the balance of society.   Hitherto there had been a fair degree of co-ordination between the armed services and the civilian instruments of government like the Foreign Ministry.   Where there had been disagreements, these had been resolved imperceptibly with the help of the Elder Statesmen.   But this co-ordination was about to break up, partly because the gap between the civilians and the military was widening, partly because the mollifying influence of the genro was declining and partly because new agencies like public opinion were coming into play. The war of 1905 left the Japanese army in occupation of Korea and southern Manchuria where its views and those of the Foreign Ministry were poles apart. The tensions generated by these places were to continue and come to a peak over Siberia (1918). The old stability over foreign policy-making was lost. These crises placed great emphasis on national defence and forced the Japanese to re-examine the constitutional aspects of the problem. According to the Meiji constitution (1889), the emperor had the right to formulate and execute foreign policy with the assistance of his advisers. But in the matter of military command and administration, the emperor had prerogatives which were operated through military advisers who were separate from the emperor's civilian advisers and independent of them. With the accretions of time and the success of the army in war, its leaders came to carry more and more weight in the making of Japan's external policy. After the co-ordinating role of the genro ended, the Foreign Ministry was bound to find difficulty in reconciling its position with that of the military. By the 1910s it would not be wrong to portray Japan as having two governments, each with the sanction of the Meiji constitution behind it, a military one and a civilian one. It was in the struggle between these that the Foreign Ministry was to be embroiled for the next three decades.

In the Taishō period (1912-26) the genro lost its influence because of increasing age and the loss of the more illustrious members. The role of the Foreign Ministry certainly increased, as the world entered a period of increasing postwar complexity. This coincided with the growth of political parties. Though this had its beneficial effects in placing financial restraints on potential schemes for expansion, it had also deleterious results in that government was sometimes tempted to use external questions, especially the nakedness of a weak China, for its own electoral advantage. There were often conflicting views within the Ministry; but it generally had its say, even in matters where the army was influential, i.e. the Siberian intervention. In the 1920s the diplomats knew some success in controlling policy and securing friendlier relations with China. But its success was transitory when the military outpointed the Foreign Ministry by provoking a number of incidents, notably the Mukden incident of 1931. For most of the 1930s the Foreign Ministry was fighting a rearguard action to keep a restraining hand on policy. It was too late to speak of its controlling events; it could at best resist the excesses and maintain a superficial internationalism.   On a broad front, its diplomats resisted the penetration of the armed forces on the Chinese mainland and expressed their dissatisfaction with the strategy of befriending the Axis countries.   But its exertions were tempered by an inner sense that the Foreign Ministry could only survive through some measure of co-existence with the military.   The run-up to war may, therefore, be described as a period of Foreign Ministry eclipse, even though it was still able to step in occasionally at moments of crisis. Miyakezaka had triumphed.

This was not merely a confrontation of institutions but also of men with their ambitions in question and their careers at stake.   It is now time to look at some of the important foreign ministers, the men of Kasumigaseki.

Chapter 1

The Iwakura Period
1869-83

In the middle of the nineteenth century the fate of
China was a source of no small concern for Japan.   The
Middle Kingdom with its reputation for great wealth and
vast population became a prey for the commercial
countries of the West.   They wanted trade and, when
they found that it was restricted, they were ready to
resort to warlike means.   When their superiority was
established over China as it was by wars in 1842 and
1858, they concluded Western-style commercial treaties
which secured for them open ports with extra-territorial rights and consular representation and jurisdiction.   These concessions were extended by most-favoured-
nation provisions to all their trading rivals.   These
were involuntary concessions by China because the
strength of the maritime Powers could not be resisted.

If China was unable to resist the inroads of the
foreign merchants and their governments, Japan, a much
smaller country, was doubly at risk.   In mid-century
she was governed by the Tokugawa shogunate which had
ruled by a stern autocratic regime for two and a half
centuries.   In order to consolidate their power, the
rulers had issued regulations which ensured that Japan
continued for two centuries as a 'secluded country'
with only minimal contacts with the West.   By the
1850s this state of seclusion was breaking down.   The
Tokugawa and their feudal rivals, the clans on the
periphery of the Japanese islands, were cultivating
relations with foreigners for the technical know-how
which they obviously possessed and the Japanese badly
wanted.

When Commodore Perry of the United States navy visited
Japan in 1853-4, the shogunate was inclined to drift in
the direction of opening the country.   More or less on
its own responsibility, it concluded that it was too

weak to withhold from the Americans the full commercial
treaty which they sought.   Such was the Treaty of Edo
(Tokyo) of 29 July 1858 which was signed with the
American representative, Townsend Harris - the first of
the so-called 'unequal treaties'.   While this was an
act of wisdom in so far as the shogun's government had
a realistic appreciation of Japan's inability to
resist, it was an act of political desperation within
Japan where its opponents at court who were bitterly
opposed to dealings with foreigners could make political
capital by dwelling on the unpopular foreign treaties.
The 'unequal treaties' were indeed to be used as the
thin end of a wedge which was to be driven into the
already-crumbling Tokugawa administration in the hope
of bringing about its complete collapse.   Thus, from
the very start of the New Japan, issues of foreign
relations were to be sensitive factors in the domestic
politics of the country.

At this time Iwakura Tomomi (1825-83) was an
official of the court of the emperor at Kyoto, which had
throughout the Tokugawa period played no part in government but had performed some formal state functions. (1)
As the Tokugawa regime fell into difficulties, the
court officials were not unaware that they might be
able to organize a coalition which would topple the
shogunate.   It was from a standpoint of opposition that
Iwakura regarded the treaties.   Since he had no hand
in their making, he was ready to see them reversed. (2)
But, when the shogunate pleaded that to end the treaties
would only annoy the foreigner and convince him of
Japan's bad faith, Iwakura was ready to concede the
danger inherent in this: 'the five enemy Powers [pre-
sumably Britain, France, the United States, Prussia and
Russia], crowding in upon our ports, might open hostilities, interfere in our domestic politics, and seize
by aggression such territory as they covet.'   Such was
the fear common to all those in authority: Japan was
growing up in a hostile world and must build up her
military strength before she could beat off the challenge of her 'enemies'.   Iwakura's view was that the
shogunate was too weak to resist the foreigner
effectively and that its weakness could be exploited
by the court in order to secure the restoration of its
authority;   but it would be better to hasten slowly in
order to prevent the outbreak of civil war, which would
only encourage foreign intervention.   If an anti-
foreign atmosphere were to be created, Iwakura thought,
men of violence might well take advantage of the situation by damaging the premises of the five foreign

Powers; and, under the pretext of protecting their
nationals against civil disorder, the foreign Powers
would make common cause and lay claim to territories
along the Japanese coast. Whatever was done should
not give foreigners any justification for raising
their flags on Japanese soil. (3)

Such was the early view of one who, while he had a
political axe to grind, was obsessed with the foreign
danger. While Iwakura was no admirer of the shogunate,
he would not go along with the incautious anti-shogun
forces if they were likely to lay Japan open to the
treatment that the European countries had meted out to
China. This is typical of the balanced and far-
sighted approach which was to characterize Iwakura's
long public career.

After the restoration of the emperor to power in
1868, Iwakura was appointed a member of the imperial
council and acted as foreign minister between July and
November 1871. This might suggest that he had a poor
claim to be regarded as the dominant figure in the early
Foreign Ministry. Yet the claim is tenable. Prince
Iwakura was one of the prime movers in the imperial
restoration and an influential politician in the new
Japan. The fact that he was prepared to accept the
office of foreign minister (gaimu kyo) suggests that
it was the intention of the new leaders that the Foreign
Ministry should be one of the key instruments of the
new government. His reputation in foreign affairs was
enhanced by his statesmanlike mission to the United
States and Europe (1871-3). After his return,
Iwakura, by using the Japanese convention of governing
from behind the scenes, was able to exercise a close
surveillance over the making of external policy for a
decade. After the death of Okubo Toshimichi by
assassination in 1878, Iwakura enjoyed a natural ascendancy at the head of affairs until his death in 1883.

Who was this Iwakura? Unlike the samurai clansmen
who came to prominence in the new Japan, he owed his
status to his being a court noble. In the restive
period of the Bakumatsu, he had been a chamberlain at
the imperial court in Kyoto and appears, at first, to
have advocated an anti-foreign policy. But, when he
was converted to the need for a more moderate approach,
he lost the favour of the Emperor Kōmei (1848-67).
When he was expelled from the imperial capital in 1863,
he sought asylum with the Chōshū clan and through it
built up a political base against the Tokugawa rulers.
The young Emperor Meiji (1867-1912) smiled on Iwakura
when he came to the throne. Hence Iwakura was in a

favourable position to forge a link between the outer
clans and the new imperial government, as a result of
which the Tokugawa shogunate was finally overthrown.

The man himself is more elusive.   Yet he opened
windows to his soul through his 'jikki' [true records].
These are memoranda on policy, of which some were
written by Iwakura himself while others later in his
career were issued in his name but written by Inoue
Kowashi (1844-95), the capable servant of many Meiji
statesmen.   These writings give a good indication of
Iwakura's political ideas, the style of his statesmanship, his tactics and his cautious temperament.
Although they are plentiful enough, they are not easy
to use;   and there are many aspects of his character
and influence which still elude scholars today.

Many Japanese at this period seem to have been drawn
to the study of diplomacy and an awareness of the
primacy of foreign affairs.   As Iwakura wrote pointedly
in April 1869

> We must guard our country's independence.   Foreign
> troops have been stationed in our open ports, and
> even when foreigners who live in our country violate
> our laws, we are forced to stand by while agents of
> their governments exercise jurisdiction over them.
> Our country has never before known such shame and
> disgrace. (4)

As he reiterated time and again, Japan was independent
in name but not independent in practice.   Probably
this was a pessimistic estimate of Japan in the 1870s:
Japan was not as much under foreign tutelage as he
liked to emphasize;   nor were the Western Powers as
anxious to take over Japan as he feared.   But the
threat was grist to his mill: it enabled him to appeal
to his countrymen to increase their wealth and strength
on Western lines.   This was Iwakura's message of
nationalism.

ORIGINS OF THE FOREIGN MINISTRY

The Board of Foreign Affairs of the new imperial government (gaikokukan) addressed the five Powers represented
at the port of Hyogo in January 1868.   It informed them
that domestic and foreign affairs would henceforth come
under the Tennō of Japan and that the word Taikun which
had been used in earlier treaties should be replaced by
'Tennō'.   Officers were appointed to deal with external
relations. (5)   A month later the foreign diplomats and
the members of the Board met and arrangements were made

for the foreign representatives to meet the emperor.
This was a symbolic act to indicate that the Tennō's
government was ready to open up connections with
foreigners.   Doubtless the hope was that in the
struggle which was expected, it should receive if not
the help, at least the benevolent neutrality, of
foreign countries.   By the time that the imperial government through Iwakura Tomomi summoned the foreign
representatives at Yokohama on 3 December, the civil
war was more or less at an end.   By the end of the
year, therefore, the ministers of France, Britain and
the United States (among others) had given up their
earlier neutrality and offered to support him.

When the Dajōkan or imperial government was set up
on 8 July 1869, a Foreign Ministry (6) was provided for
in the official regulations (Shokuinrei) as one of the
six ministries to be instituted.   Sawa Nobuyoshi was
appointed as the first minister (1869-71).   The background to Iwakura's appointment as his successor is not
known.   But, according to Okubo's plan for the new
government structure, the Foreign Ministry was to be a
first-rank ministry.   Hence Iwakura's acceptance of
the appointment can hardly be taken as a surprise.   His
actual tenure of office was remarkably short: on 8
October 1871 Iwakura was appointed minister of the right
and instructed to head the mission of senior statesmen
who were about to proceed overseas.   Since no successor
was named straightaway, he continued with his diplomatic
functions a while longer.   Iwakura was succeeded as
foreign minister by his vice-minister, Soejima Taneomi
of Saga.   He was a Chinese scholar and was to prove a
tough-minded negotiator when he went to China on an
important mission in 1873.   In the absence of Iwakura
and his party, Soejima strongly advocated the need for
a Japanese expedition to Korea.   He must certainly be
judged to have been a protagonist of expansion for
Meiji Japan.   When the members of the Iwakura mission
returned from Europe and succeeded in getting the plans
for a Korean expedition dropped, Soejima was discredited
and resigned.   Iwakura, now on the crest of the wave of
power, was able to appoint as foreign minister the more
moderate and more amenable Terajima Munenori, who held
the post until 1879.   Terajima had returned from two
years' service as minister to Britain.   His overseas
experience stood him in good stead since he had been in
London while the Iwakura mission was carrying out its
investigations there.   As a Satsuma clansman, he was
moreover a useful asset to the new government.

Since the Foreign Ministry was only establishing

itself, one should not expect to find a pattern in its
working.   Those who presided over it in its first
decade differed one from the other.   Some like Iwakura
and Inoue Kaoru were the leading statesmen of the day;
others tended to be subordinates who were responsible
for handling routine affairs and the execution of
policies decided over their heads by their seniors.
The senior whose voice tended to carry most weight in
the 1870s was Iwakura himself.   When he was out of
Japan on his world mission, many of the issues seemed to
be held pending until he returned.

As in so many other fields, Japan proved to be a fast
learner.   Soon after the inauguration of what might be
identified as the Foreign Ministry   in 1869, the
Japanese found themselves adapting well to the complicated patterns of international diplomacy.   The office
was to be located in the new capital of Tokyo at
Kasumigaseki with a branch at Yokohama for dealing with
foreigners. (7)   It soon developed a hierarchy with an
intricate system of ranking and a host of bureaucratic
regulations.   These were not Western importations so
much as something that had passed down from the
Tokugawa period.

Nor was Japan starting from scratch.   Certainly
since Perry Japanese had become aware of the need for
understanding foreign countries and travelling abroad.
They had also turned to the learning of foreign
languages.   One of the first departments set up
within the Ministry had therefore to be a language
school.   While the learning of foreign languages was
not easy for Japanese, they were able to adapt to
social patterns and social conventions with some
expertise.   Indeed, judging from the experiences of
those who went abroad in the nineteenth century, they
were probably happier and better adapters than some of
their successors in the twentieth.

It is one thing to melt chameleon-like into the
foreign scene;   it is another to feel at home with the
paraphernalia and protocol which had grown up over the
centuries to deal with the relations of one Western
state with another.   It is recorded that the first
American minister in 1858 had instructed the Japanese
in the law of nations and that works such as Heaton's
'Elements of International Law' (1836) and Phillimore's
'Commentaries on International Law' (1854-7) were circulating in translation by the late 1860s.   One of the
early tasks of the Ministry was to translate Britain's
most recent treaties in order to achieve some standard
of comparison for those they had concluded since the

coming of Admiral Perry.   There can be little doubt
that Japan learnt fast.

The adaptability of Japan's first representatives
abroad was also beyond question.   They did not suffer
the indignities associated with the earliest Chinese
envoys abroad whose clothes were often regarded as
outlandish and attracted the derisory comments of small
boys.   The Japanese imitated the West in dress and
manners.   Typical in this respect was the aggressively
Westernized Mori Arinori (1847-89), the first envoy to
the United States.   While he was studying in Britain
(1865-7) as one of those selected by his own Satsuma
clan, he was attracted to Thomas Lake Harris, an
American spiritualist, and decided to join him in
America at his community, the Brotherhood of the New
Life.   When he heard the news of the Meiji restoration,
Mori together with Samejima Hisanobu who was later to
serve as Japan's first minister in Paris accepted
Harris's advice to return to Japan.   Mori was appointed
by the new government as representative in Washington
in 1870 at the age of twenty-three and served as acting
minister for two years, during Japan's important mission
there.   In 1879 he became minister to Britain and
stayed there for five years, conducting diplomatic
business but also studying means of modernization,
especially in the educational field.   It was no
surprise, therefore, that on his return to Japan he
should become the first minister for education in 1885
and serve in this capacity until his assassination four
years later. (8)   It would be wrong to submit Mori as
the representative of a group - he was too individualistic for that.   Yet he had an open-mindedness and
readiness to learn which seems to have been shared by
many of his young contemporaries who were adventurous
enough to go overseas.

Mori's career also reminds us of the swift promotion
which was possible in the early Meiji period.   Many of
the young clansmen who entered the new Foreign Ministry
soared in their profession. (9)   While they were thrown
into responsibility at an early age, they were still
held on a tight rein by their elders in Tokyo.   This
is only to be expected when one remembers the circumstances behind the appointments in the early Meiji
period.   Consider again the case of Mori as acting
minister (dairi kōshi) in Washington.   His appointment
was due to his facility in English and to his experience of the country, both of which were considerable.
It was not due to Tokyo's confidence in Mori's judgment.
When Mori's patrons - Iwakura and Okubo - were in the

capital, things went smoothly; but, when they were out
of Japan, there were frequent disagreements between
Mori and Tokyo.   Because the Americanized Mori was
hot-tempered and argumentative rather than submissive,
he often got into hot water with his home authorities.
Because he was despite his youth inclined to be outspoken, he sometimes ran into trouble with the government to which he was accredited.   Thus, the British
government at a later date was to question Japan's
wisdom in appointing callow youths to major diplomatic
assignments.

The early appointments were due to the talent-
spotting of the individual leaders.   They were, therefore, somewhat haphazard.   For example, Mori and his
companion, Samejima, on their return from the United
States, had a fortunate interview with Iwakura, the
new national leader in 1868, and evidently pleased him.
Through his patronage, they received their first posts.
When Mori fell out of favour in 1872, it was left to
Iwakura to administer the necessary rebukes.   It was
again Iwakura who secured his restoration to favour in
the following year.   Mori and his contemporaries owed
their careers to their special relationships with the
great.   They had no idea that they were part of a
secure professional service.   Perhaps they did not yet
look on themselves as diplomats so much as agents for
their country abroad on the broadest plane, cultural,
commercial as well as diplomatic.

In this process the Foreign Ministry had to learn
through its foreign advisers.   The earliest of these
was Erasmus Peshine Smith, an adviser from 1871 until
1880; he was succeeded by Henry W. Denison who served
Japan until his death in 1914.   Of Smith, a graduate
of Columbia and Harvard, who had worked in the State
Department as legal claims adviser, F.V. Dickins, a
British resident of the treaty ports, was to write:

> The salaried prompters of Japanese foreign policy
> were not men of high professional standing or experi-
> ence.   The first of them was an American lawyer of
> some eminence, Mr Peshine Smith, who did his best to
> bring his employers into ridicule by going about in
> a Japanese split jacket and loose trousers with a
> couple of swords in his girdle and declaring in
> public that 'not one foreigner in ten in Japan was
> murdered who ought to have been murdered'. (10)

Dickins for personal reasons was a jaundiced witness.
Evidently Smith, like some foreigners who came to reside
in Japan, responded to his environment in an extreme
way.   He took up a strongly Japanophil position and,

because of his eccentricity, did not win over the
treaty port public and may well have been an embarrassment to his modernizing masters.   Denison appears to
have been a more balanced and popular adviser.   In
his day there were a number of other advisers from
Britain, Germany and France, though these nationalities
were more often recruited in other departments.   There
was, of course, some jealousy that Americans had
secured these key posts but it has to be borne in
mind that there are limits to the influence which
lawyers, expert in diplomatic verbiage, can exert on
policy.

Bear in mind too that the Japanese who were building
from scratch could learn from the foreign diplomats in
Japan.   Indeed, if the truth were to be told, they
were overwhelmed by advice from these quarters.
Iwakura quite often consulted Sir Harry Parkes, the
British minister (1868-83), on higher matters of policy,
despite the fact that Parkes's views cannot have been
popular with Japan's leaders because of his paternalism.

IWAKURA'S POLICY

Japan's foreign policy had to be two-faced.   She had
to look at the continent - and especially China - and
at the Pacific ocean with a sidewards glance, more
remotely, at the other world Powers.   In the first
case, she had to consider the posture of land-based
countries like China or Russia;   in the other, she had
to worry about naval Powers like Britain, the United
States and at times also Russia.   At different times,
one or other has demanded greater attention;   but both
aspects have been in Japan's thoughts at all times in
her modern century.

Throughout the 1870s Iwakura had to deal with both
aspects simultaneously.   The naval Powers were involved
in the problem of treaty revision which the Meiji government regarded as overdue for settlement.   But
Iwakura the pragmatist soon recognized that, with
Japan's existing armed strength and debating position,
she would not find it easy to secure the favourable
review which she sought. (11)   The continental Powers
were another matter.   From the 1840s onwards China
and Japan had stood together in the path of an expansive wave of foreign countries;   if China had caved in,
Japan would have been the next to suffer.   There was a
common interest in mutual defence and protection,
whether China recognized it or not.   At the same time,

the Meiji government was sensitive over areas of dispute
like Korea and, if we may take the celebrated memorandum
by Okubo in 1873 as a guide, (12) had definite fears
over Chinese might and her possible intervention in the
peninsula.   Needless to say, she had even greater
suspicions over Russian intentions there.

The Iwakura mission is an important starting-point
in any account of Japan's foreign policy.   It is
rightly named after Iwakura himself.   There are strong
grounds for believing that the mission in its conception, in its functions and in its composition was much
influenced by its leader.   While there are others who
claim paternity for the mission, like Itō and Okuma,
missionaries such as Guido Verbeck and various diplomats, the idea of a mission of friendship from the
Japanese emperor to the world may be traced in a
detailed memorandum on foreign relations which Iwakura
prepared in February 1869.   In it he recommended that
Japan should send envoys of the emperor to salute the
potentates of other countries and, while confirming
the treaties, should raise the many problems which were
emerging from their operation.   He was, as we have
seen, a believer in the early revision of these unjust
treaties.   From time to time in the following years
this idea was brought back into play with a slight
difference of emphasis.   It was after all a natural
thought on the part of the Japanese that greetings
should be presented to all sovereigns now that their
emperor had been restored and recognized (Document 1).

Iwakura's second contribution was to the debate in
the autumn of 1871 on the scope of the mission.   The
Japanese in their animus against the unequal treaties
had committed themselves to hold conferences for re-
negotiation in 1872.   It began to dawn, however, that
some institutions would have to be reformed before the
treaty Powers would entertain fresh negotiations.   It
was, therefore, debatable whether the mission should
attempt to open negotiations or study the reforms which
foreign governments would deem to be a precondition.
On 28 October Iwakura urged that explicit negotiations
should be avoided and that no date should be mentioned
for negotiations.   Thus, the mission was given a rather
vague and imprecise mandate - to seek knowledge from all
over the world, restore Japan's rights and reform faults
in her institutions.

Iwakura also had the final say over its composition.
The discussion on the size and seniority of the mission
was reserved till late in the day.   The ultimate size
of almost fifty members from Japan was much larger than

had earlier been contemplated.   What was more of an
issue was Iwakura's anxiety over the number of senior
ministers who wished to go, indeed insisted on going.
This raised the question of the government which
would be left to attend to the very difficult financial and commercial problems affecting Japan.   The
fact that Itō, Kido and Okubo, those who had special-
ized in industrial and commercial fields, all joined
the delegation was largely Iwakura's choice.   He,
being slightly above the intrigues of clan loyalties,
decided to make it a delegation of all the talents
which would command respect abroad.   The point may be
made, however, that the existing Japanese diplomats
overseas were young men who carried little weight and
had provoked some complaints from persons like Sir
Harry Parkes that Japan should be represented abroad by
persons of higher calibre.   So Itō, Kido and Okubo
joined the educational Grand Tour, despite Iwakura's
inner doubts that this might destroy his power base
within the ruling elite.   True enough, he secured
undertakings from those that remained that changes of
importance would be deferred until his return.   But it
is hard to see what he could have done if someone in
Tokyo had been determined to defy his authority.   From
Iwakura's standpoint, the gamble was a very risky
one. (13)
     With Iwakura as ambassador plenipotentiary - a title
virtually invented for the purpose in the Foreign
Ministry reforms of 1871 - the mission set sail at the
end of the year from Yokohama.   The mission had a dual
function as a diplomatic embassy and as, in British
terminology, a royal commission of investigation.   Its
report on the second aspect contains a fascinating com-
mentary on America and Europe in 1872 which cannot be
considered in detail here.   Let us, however, remember
the rather special characteristics of Europe at that
time.   Apart from Britain, continental Europe and
America had gone through a period of exceptionally
rapid economic growth.   Countries like France and
Germany had transformed themselves into industrialized
states and societies in the course of three decades.
Italy and Germany had transformed themselves into
nation-states by strong pursuit of nationalist objectives.   This was for Europe unprecedented political
change.   The mission looked wide-eyed at aspects of
Western life but was at the same time selective.   It
knew in advance what it wanted to see and it knew what
it considered to be relevant to Japan. (14)
     On the diplomatic side of the embassy, there were

anomalies implicit in the instructions which were drawn up.   In so far as the members wished to convey a spirit of interest in Westernization, of friendship and of earnestness, they scored a success.   In the United States (March-August), Britain (September-November), France (December-January 1873), Germany (March), Russia (April), they conveyed a sense of high seriousness of purpose and disabused their hosts of the former anti-foreignism which was associated widely in the world with the name of Japan. (15)

Over treaty revision, the embassy must be judged a failure.   The original intention had been for the members to have informal talks with statesmen overseas about the treaties.   In a fundamental sense, the mission was about the treaties.   It was a public affirmation to the foreign powers in their own capitals that the new Meiji government did not intend to cancel the treaties and would endeavour to protect foreign nationals in Japan and keep the country open.   Of course, this had already been known at a diplomatic level and accepted.   In addition there was an under-lying symbolism about the mission: that Japanese states-men were taking the initiative and going out of their way to forge new relationships with foreign countries. As Iwakura said in his speech to President Grant on 4 March 1872:   'We are instructed to consult on all international issues, concentrating on establishing and expanding trade, and to stimulate the cordial friend-ship which already binds together our two peoples.' The mission then was comprehensive and open-minded. Perhaps it gave the initial impression of being more primitive than it was in reality.   On this occasion it appeared in Japanese costume of silk kimono for court wear.   An observer tells

> This was their last appearance, in what to our eyes appeared a grotesque costume, and no doubt did so to the shrewd observation of the Ambassador Iwakura, for not one member of the Embassy ... ever appeared afterwards in public, with what we would call feminine garments made of silks and satins.

Henceforth the delegates wore European costume;   and, as the same observer records, 'the gravity of their dusky visages commanded respect.' (16)

The mission was about the treaties and about inter-national relations in their broadest sense.   The Japanese also had the hope of registering their dis-approval of the treaties.   The Foreign Ministry had presented drafts for their revision which were not well received.   When the mission was decided upon, further

initiatives were assigned to Iwakura who had authority
not to negotiate but to hold conversations with the
statesmen of the treaty Powers.   But the American
secretary of state, Hamilton Fish, urged Iwakura to
begin re-negotiation for which he would require plenipotentiary powers.   Two of the deputy leaders of the
mission, Itō and Okubo, returned to Japan and obtained
the necessary authority.   But on 24 July Iwakura informed Fish that discussions on treaty revision would
be broken off.   A setback, to be sure, but there were
many other facets of the mission which were a success
and more than compensated for the negative answers
received over treaty revision.   In November Iwakura
had three conversations with Lord Granville on the
theme of re-negotiating the treaties; but they were
exploratory and superficial.   There were similar discussions with the statesmen of Europe.   In the end
Iwakura's original cautious approach triumphed: nothing
would be done until the embassy had returned and
examined the issue further.

Members of the overseas delegation returned with
greater understanding but without tangible achievement.
Okubo returned in May; Kido in July.   On 13 September
Iwakura reached Tokyo to find himself in the middle of
a government crisis with the emperor waiting urgently
for his advice.   Assailed by clear evidences of
samurai unrest and agrarian uprisings, the interim government had incautiously agreed, much beyond the terms
of its mandate, to send the prominent expansionist,
Saigō Takamori, to Korea in the full knowledge that it
might provoke a hostile reaction.   Iwakura, a man of
strong will and great firmness, was furious at this
step because he approached the situation no longer from
the parochial view of Japan's national interest.   There
is evidence in the hot-tempered debates that followed
that all the members of the mission had indeed acquired
a cautious approach to foreign affairs and were appalled
at the blatant adventurism which they found in the
Korean policy with which they were confronted on their
return. (17)

KOREAN CRISIS AND ITS AFTERMATH

The foreign issues which faced Iwakura were concerned
with Korea, Taiwan and the Ryūkyūs.   Korea had gravely
offended the new Japan by rejecting out of hand her
overtures for recognition of the new state.   Almost
immediately there were heard voices, calling for a

punitive expedition.   This immediately involved China
which enjoyed a conventional suzerainty over Korea.
In March 1873 Foreign Minister Soejima decided to
visit Peking to discuss the recalcitrant attitude
which the Koreans were showing in the hope that China
would give him freedom of action to send a military
expedition to the peninsula.   In his parleys China
was alleged to have agreed informally not to interfere
in Korea in that event.   (On the side, China did not
object to the natives of the Ryūkyū or Loochoo islands
being called Japanese subjects or to Japan's sending
an expedition against Taiwan.)   Soejima was also
granted an imperial audience, the first diplomat to be
accorded one by the Chinese.   The sanguine Soejima's
report was almost too good to be true: he had received
carte blanche on several points, especially over war
with Korea.   But the Chinese understanding of these
conversations was very different.

Shortly after Soejima's return to Tokyo in July, the
council agreed to make war on Korea.   The prime
minister, Lord Sanjō, gave in to the party, led by
Saigō Takamori, who were calling for an expeditionary
force to be sent.   Since the clans had been abolished
in the reform programme, the lot of the samurai whose
stipends had been abolished had become a difficult one
and they had become a menace to the internal security
of Japan.   A Korean expedition would be one way of
relieving the tension.   But Sanjō, with the emperor's
support, made his approval subject to Iwakura agreeing
on his return from Europe.   When Iwakura returned in
September, the government's plans for invasion were
already well advanced.   Opinion in the council became
sharply divided, those who had been left behind tending
to favour punishment for Korea (Seikanron) and those
returned from abroad being opposed.   At meetings of
the council Iwakura reiterated his old view that Japan's
wealth and strength were not up to world standards,
must be developed without delay and were meanwhile
inadequate for taking a punitive line.   He further
stressed the danger to Japan of Russia's activities in
the north (Document 2).   The longer the debate, the
more evenly the lines of battle were drawn.   In the
height of the crisis, Sanjō withdrew; and Iwakura
threw his weight behind the no-war party, ensuring the
emperor's approval of this course on 23 October.   The
pro-war group resigned; and the charismatic Saigō
retired sullenly to his native Satsuma.   Iwakura, who
had to bear a special weight of responsibility during
this crisis, became the victim of an attempted

assassination in January of the following year by those embittered by his weak policy towards Korea.   But he was fortunate to escape with only a slight wound.   So ended one of the great crises in Iwakura's public career.

The Japanese undertook an expedition to Formosa in 1874 in order to chastise the Formosan barbarians for attacking Japanese subjects in the Ryūkyū (Loochoo) islands.   It was prompted by the lobbying of the disaffected Satsuma clan who claimed that the Ryukyuans were their kinsmen; but it also bore the traces of the council's anxiety that the samurai with their war-thirsty attitude might otherwise take the law into their own hands.   The expedition was ultimately re-called but Japan was able, thanks to mediation by the British minister in Peking, Thomas Wade, to extract from China a sum to defray her expenses and a promise to accept the Ryukyuans as Japanese subjects.   It would appear that the Taiwan affair should not be looked on as an 'abortive colonial venture' but rather as a safety valve for samurai energies. (18)

The other territorial problem involved a great power, Russia.   Japan had tried to argue that she had rights to half of Sakhalin or at least to a joint occu-pation of the island in negotiating with Russia the Shimoda treaty of 1855.   Two embassies were sent in order to clear up Japan's status in 1862 and 1867;   but all schemes for arbitration or purchase of concessions drew a blank from the Russians.   Iwakura came back from his European trip which included a visit to the Russian capital with the conviction that Japan should not dispute with Russia.   He, therefore, sent a depu-tation to St Petersburg which in May 1875 signed an agreement according the Russians the whole of Sakhalin in return for the central and northern Kuriles.   Al-though Iwakura gave up former claims, he retained important mining and fishing privileges.   He was also realistic in that the Japanese were, and would for the future be, inferior in Sakhalin to the Russians in terms of numbers and arms. (19)   For fear of Russia's strength and possible future rivalry, Japan took a conciliatory line towards the Russians.   The govern-ment was understandably severely criticized for its weakness.

Over Korea also, Iwakura adopted a continuously alert stance.   In common with European countries, Japan thought that it would be in her interest if Korea could be brought within the treaty system.   After many threats and provocations, Japan concluded a treaty of

friendship and commerce (1876) which opened Korea's
ports to Japanese trade. (20)   In this, she succeeded
where European powers had earlier failed, in prizing
open the door at Pusan.   But there was unanimity on
the part of Iwakura and his realistic followers that
warlike measures could not be risked against the
Korean peninsula, especially when a disaffected Russia
might well intervene. (21)   It took almost a decade
for Japan's 'unequal treaty' of Kanghwa to be
implemented.

The policy at which Iwakura aimed was a mature and
complex one.   The first priority was domestic: he
must appease the restive elements either by removing
grievances or by absorbing them in government service
(such was the bungled Taiwan expedition); he must aim
at 'fukoku kyōhei' (rich country, strong army) and, in
doing so, must avoid expensive adventures overseas.
There were various priorities within the foreign field:
the first was to resolve differences peacably (this
applied to Russia and, to a lesser degree, China and
Korea); the second was that, if his reform strategy
went well, Japan could in the long run overturn the
unequal treaties.   This is not to say that the members
of the Iwakura mission returned from abroad in an enlightened state and successfully stood up to the old-
style traditionalists like Saigō and Soejima who were
responding to an older tradition in Japan, that of
expansion, which had been suppressed during the
sakoku (closed) period.   The West that the Iwakura
mission saw was expansionist, colonialist and highly
nationalistic.   Iwakura and Ōkubo, when they were met
by calls for expansion into Korea, opposed it on pragmatic grounds rather than 'enlightened' ones.   Each
man had his expansionist moments and his peace-loving
instincts.   But, for the seventies, they felt that,
bearing in mind Japan's national weakness, she must
abjure a policy of conquests in east Asia. (22)

At the same time, it is remarkable how in the
Iwakura period there are so many nationalist signs in
Japan.   The Iwakura mission had enabled them to
measure Japan against the West and also the East.
While there were shortcomings in the first comparison,
there was confidence and strength in the second.
Iwakura returned not a cowed man but a confident one,
aware that Japan had more effectively coped with the
challenge of the West than China.   If she had feelings
of inferiority, her feeling of superiority to China was
doubly confirmed.

It is not so easy to assess how much of early Meiji

policy was authentically Iwakura's.   This is because he
became one of a governing triumvirate.   Since the
power of Kido and Okubo was in origin that of the clans
which had been victorious in the civil war, they had
advantages on which Iwakura could not draw.   On the
other hand, Iwakura had something of an honorific
position, his support coming from the court.   While
he drifted away from Kido, he kept up a working relationship with Okubo.   Despite the attempt on his life
in 1874, Iwakura managed to outlive the others, Kido
dying in 1877 of tuberculosis and Okubo being assassinated by samurai in the following year.   Another
lingering doubt still surrounds the question: how much
that was done in Iwakura's name was his own?   Certainly
Iwakura remained minister of state and continued to be
consulted by the emperor until his death in July 1883;
but he shared power with younger samurai leaders like
Itō Hirobumi, Inoue Kaoru, Matsukata Masayoshi and
Okuma Shigenobu who had experience of clan administration and were eager for governmental duties.   This
meant that Iwakura's position was that of a man among
boys.   It is probably fair to conclude that he had an
influence on the outcome of most issues because of his
seniority and experience.   He remained close to the
centre of political life until his death but his powers
deteriorated because of illness.

   Iwakura was no mere diplomatist; he was a statesman
interested in relations with foreign states.   One cannot fail to be impressed with the quality of his wide-
ranging memoranda on this subject which are never
short-sighted.   Responsive to new ideas from the outside world, he was still determined to control any
foreign ideas adopted.   Although he admired foreign
countries, he was basically scared of them and their
ambitions towards Japan.   Conservative and nationalist,
he was at the same time flexible and a modernizer.   His
contribution to Japan's foreign relations lay not so
much in policies as in attitudes: he led Japan to the
'realistic' policy of cautious and vigilant, even
hesitant, acceptance of the West.

Chapter 2

The Mutsu Period, 1884-96

Mutsu Munemitsu (1844-97) was a diplomat-statesman who became one of Japan's leading foreign ministers. He was in charge of the Foreign Ministry from 1892 to 1896 though even that period was shortened by intervals of ill-health. Yet there is general agreement that he was one of the major Meiji statesmen. He was an exceptional character in his own right - a man of spirit and intellect with wide international interests. Mutsu's other claim to fame is that he left for posterity a contemporary record of the centrepiece of his foreign policy, the war with China (1894-5). 'Kenkenroku' (properly, 'My uphill struggle') was written during a long period of recuperation in the second half of 1895 and supplies an authentic account of the secret diplomacy that led up to the war. It is a prime historical document showing Japan's Realpolitik and Mutsu's reflections on his own policies. (1)

Mutsu entered government service after the Restoration. Though he came from outside the favoured four Western clans, he was appointed governor of various prefectures in 1869 and was able to fit in a visit to London in the following year. After his resignation in 1874, he was nominated as a member of the genroin but he grew dissatisfied with the government dominated by the major clans and joined the conspiracy to overthrow it three years later. He was captured and cast into prison for five years. Mutsu spent the time in writing and, among other things, translating Jeremy Bentham's 'Introduction to the principles of morals and legislation' into Japanese (1883). In the following year he went abroad, staying mainly in London but with journeys to Berlin and Vienna. This was a time of study, mainly in the field of constitutional law.

After his foreign studies Mutsu was a natural choice

for an expanding Foreign Ministry.   At the start of a
new approach to the hoary problem of treaty revision,
he was appointed, due to the friendship of Inoue Kaoru,
to the category of minister in 1886.   Two years later
he was ordered to Washington where he also doubled as
minister to Mexico.   It was he who signed the Mexican
treaty which was a breakthrough in the story of treaty
revision.   In 1889 Mutsu concluded an 'equal' treaty
with the United States which he had earlier negotiated.
At the end of the year he returned home.   It was
clearly a turning-point in his career.   In May 1890 he
was invited to.join the Yamagata Cabinet as minister
for agriculture and commerce and was elected to the
lower house as representative for his native prefecture
of Wakayama.   After two years he joined the Cabinet of
Itō Hirobumi as foreign minister.   He presided over
the first major success in the remaking of the unequal
treaties, the signing of the Anglo-Japanese commercial
treaty in July 1894, and was responsible for the
diplomacy leading to the outbreak of the China war, the
peace-making and the intervention of the three European
Powers.

It is his Washington experiences and his Foreign
Ministry activities which qualify him for special attention in this chapter.   He was not, of course, the
dominant figure in this period;   this title might
arguably be claimed by Itō Hirobumi, Inoue Kaoru or
Yamagata Aritomo.   But he played a key role in the
central crises of Japan's foreign relations after 1868,
and his significance is enhanced by reason of his being
an intellectual with a deep understanding of the West,
though he was an autocrat at heart.

Competent official and bureaucrat though he was,
Mutsu was a great talker, skilled in argument and logic.
But he was too impatient to be a successful politician.
He quickly resigned from the Diet and had little time
for it when he was a hard-pressed minister.   His thin
features and his tall stature remained with him to his
death in 1897.   The distinctive cut of his gaunt face
and the goatee beard suggest the scholar, rather than
the extrovert.   He was indeed known to some in the
1880s as 'the professor'.

MUTSU'S FOREIGN MINISTRY

Mutsu came at the end of an important series of foreign
ministers who presided over the Ministry in a period of
turmoil and change: Inoue Kaoru, an important statesman

whom we have already seen operating under Iwakura (1879-87), Okuma Shigenobu (1888-9), Aoki Shūzō (1889-91) and Enomoto Buyo (1891-2). Their major labour will be considered later; but here we must look at the emerging Ministry. In the first place, a Cabinet system developed by which one minister could consult his colleagues; and the office of foreign minister was defined, the title changing from 'gaimukyo' to 'gaimu daijin'. The ranks within the service were brought into line with those of other countries: ambassador (though this was sparingly used for those on special assignment); minister (the ordinary appointment) and chargé d'affaires.

The formulation of a constitution dominated the thinking of all politicians. Itō had returned from Europe in 1883 with ideas for a modern constitution appropriate to the Japanese state. Political parties, the newspapers and, in a broader sense, public opinion wanted a share in moulding that constitution which was not permitted to them. This had its impact on the foreign policy-making of the period, which was largely concerned with the intricate problem of treaty revision. The bureaucrats would dearly have dealt with this problem without the intrusion of outside influences; but they could not. The parties were determined to make their presence felt. They would not tolerate a solution which was irreconcilable with the proud, new nationalism of the 1880s; and Japanese nationalism had a strong measure of anti-foreignism. (2)   Japanese at large genuinely feared a sell-out by the bureacrats; and politicians saw that here was a stick with which to beat the clan-dominated government.

As a consequence of the state of tension in the Diet, the constitution was slanted against outside political interference in foreign affairs. The leaders ensured that, by the 13th article of the constitution which was handed down by the emperor to the people in 1889 and came into effect with the creation of the Diet in the following year, the power of decision over war and peace and of concluding treaties lay with the throne. Thus, the conduct of diplomatic, as of military, affairs came within the imperial prerogative and was not subject to control by the Diet. Diet resolutions on foreign affairs had to be in the form of petitions to the throne and did not bind the government. The foreign minister might make statements to the Diet but these were made by grace rather than by duty; nor was he required to reply to interpellations. (3)

By the operation of the Cabinet system, the prime

minister was held responsible for the conduct of foreign
business.   Thus, the foreign minister was subordinate
in the exercise of imperial prerogatives.   In practice,
it was necessary for foreign ministers to keep in close
touch with the premier and sometimes with the Cabinet.
But there were the odd occasions when the emperor
charged his foreign minister to transact foreign business without disclosing it to the Cabinet.   Such a
case was that of Inoue who handled the treaty revision
negotiations with the greatest privacy in the hope of
withholding damaging information from the political
opposition.   Generally foreign ministers down to the
turn of the century had greater political influence than
their successors later on.

TREATY REVISION

Let us turn to the unequal treaties, the most popular
issue of the early Meiji era. (4)   Clearly constitutional developments affected the achievement of the new
treaties.   From the government standpoint, there was
some urgency in completing the re-negotiation of the
foreign treaties by hook or by crook during the 1880s
before the inauguration of the Diet which, it was
assumed, would be hostile to the government and would
ventilate the xenophobic political opposition to the
treaties.   From the view point of the politicians
striving to influence the constitution in favour of
popular rights, the tactic was to spin out the revision
of the treaties until 1890 when the Diet came into
being and the popular will could be heard.   Those who
had hitherto been deprived of power by the monopoly
exercised by the oligarchs held out great hopes that
the Diet might become a forum where they could assert
themselves.   By the time that Mutsu became foreign
minister in 1892, it was clear that this was a lost
cause: the constitution had created a Diet which left
authority with the throne and hence with the appointed
government.   Thus, he found that the Diet had to be
tolerated and moulded; but, if it became too incon-
veniently critical, it could always be suspended.   At
the same time, there was a frequent complaint that
successive governments had been 'easy-going towards
foreigners but harsh towards their own nationals'
(gaijū naikō).   As the treaty revision negotiations
dragged on, it was vital for Mutsu to show that Japan
was not being self-effacing towards the demands of
other countries, was not giving too much away.

The other influence was that of foreigners resident
in Japan.   It was extra-territoriality which allowed
foreign settlements to exist.   Within them grew up
communities of treaty port merchants who wished to
maintain their special status.   By the 1880s it was
coming to be grudgingly admitted outside Japan that
foreign settlements were a convenience, but not absolutely
essential, for the expansion of trade and that they were
burdensome to defend adequately.   The treaty port
merchants were losing the exclusive control which they
had once exercised over Japan's foreign trade.   It was
coming to be recognized in European countries that
these same privileges were exciting Japanese opposition
which was reducing their interest in foreign goods.
Be that as it may, foreign governments concluded that,
if these extra-territorial rights were continued in
perpetuity, it might result in a revulsion among the
Japanese which would result in the loss of a large
market.   This revulsion might take many forms.   In the
late 1860s it had been directed against foreigners and
this might at any time happen again.   Moreover, the
Japanese were so overwrought over treaty revision that
it led to much violence against their leaders.   The
most prominent instance was the bomb attack on Foreign
Minister Okuma's carriage on 18 October 1889 by a
member of a right-wing society.   This resulted in the
amputation of one of Okuma's legs and the resignation
of the Cabinet.   Foreign diplomats argued that, if
such measures could be taken against Japanese statesmen, they could easily be directed against foreigners
yet again;   and this argument was frequently used by
the Japanese in treaty revision negotiations.   Foreign
feeling was influenced by these threats to become more
amenable to revision, though the diehards of the treaty
ports would have none of it.

It was possible for Mutsu to draw certain conclusions
from this experience of popular reactions over two
decades.   First, foreign governments were losing confidence in extra-territoriality.   Second, in order to
prevent the debate being caught up in domestic politics
in Japan or leaking out in the treaty ports, it was
better to negotiate secretly overseas.   Since there
was good evidence of commercial competition between
them, it should be possible to divide the jealous
Powers who had hitherto tried to negotiate in Tokyo in
common.   By taking up the problem with them one by one,
Japan could take advantage of jealousies between them
such as the Anglo-German rivalry.

There were also disagreements within the oligarchic

elite as Mutsu learnt from Inoue Kaoru, his friend and
mentor.   Inoue had been immersed in this problem from
1879 to 1887, first as secretary to the Foreign Ministry
and later as minister.   An avowed modernizer, he accepted that the offending foreign treaties would only be
rescinded when Japan's attitudes had been changed, her
law codes Westernized and foreigners had been allowed
open access to the Japanese hinterland.   With the help
of foreign advisers, work was immediately speeded up to
bring the codes up to the standards accepted in the West
in respect of laws, prisons and punishments.   Inoue's
hope was to get the Powers to agree to a self-denying
ordinance without Japan offering anything in return but
a long-term promise of legal reform.   In thirty-six
conferences with foreign diplomats in 1886, Inoue made
considerable progress.   But, when his secret proposal
for mixed courts which foreign governments were understood to be ready to accept was leaked to the Press, it
created a domestic storm.   In July 1887 Viscount
General Tani Kanjō (Tateki) resigned as minister for
agriculture and commerce on this account.   He claimed
that he had stated his opposition to the revised treaties
forcibly on several occasions verbally and in writing
but that he had not been consulted on the present
occasion even though the departments under his control
were so directly affected (Document 3).   Following on
Tani's lead, the anti-government forces objected to the
proposals that Western judges should be appointed to
try cases involving foreigners;   that the import tariff
should continue to be prescribed by treaty;   and that
the whole of Japan should be open for foreign travel.
In reply, Inoue argued that Japan must become 'a civilized state' and adopt more open methods.   But the consensus was against him;   and he had no alternative but
to inform the foreigners that treaty negotiations would
have to be deferred.   Disillusioned and feeling be-
trayed, he resigned in August (Document 3).
   The ground plan for treaty revision had been worked
out;   the tactics for accomplishing it had so far been
unsuccessful.   The granting of the constitution by the
Emperor Meiji on 11 February 1889 made the task at once
easier and more difficult.   On the one hand, it was a
symbol of Japan's willingness to modernize.   Moreover
the new civil and commercial codes were gradually
emerging in a form acceptable to foreign countries.
On the other side of the scales, Inoue's plan to complete the revision before the constitution came into
effect and opened the floodgates of political criticism,
as he saw it, had clearly failed.   Henceforth negotia-

tions would have to be carried on in the face of Diet
debates and questions and in the teeth of resistance
from political parties which were anxious to test their
new wings by exploiting this emotive issue.

When Mutsu became foreign minister in 1892, he was
determined to take the initiative out of the hands of
the party politicians. In his memoirs, he wrote that
Japan had by 1890 adopted a constitution of an occi-
dental kind, achieved substantial modernization and
could no longer accept a system of one-sided treaties
which gave unilateral concessions to foreign nationals.
He set out to devise a treaty which would ensure reciprocal benefits. The Japanese people would never be
satisfied, he thought, by a compromise, short-term
revision. It would have to be a complete settlement
and confer equal rights and obligations on both sides.
His models were taken from the Anglo-Italian treaty
(1883) which had taken the form of a treaty of commerce
and navigation and the Japan-Mexico treaty (1888) which
had been equilateral and Mutsu himself had concluded
while he was acting as minister in Washington. He
readily admitted that negotiations had earlier been
frustrated not because of foreign hostility but in Japan
herself. Instead of negotiating in Japan and exposing
the talks to the opposition of foreign merchants and of
the Japanese, he proposed to conduct them in foreign
capitals, regardless of the additional administrative
difficulties which this would involve. Further, he
would negotiate with the Powers individually and aim at
secrecy wherever possible.

Mutsu obtained the approval of the Cabinet for his
new draft treaty in July 1893. It contained a formula
bringing it into effect after the lapse of some years
during which the legal codes would be revised and fully
introduced; only at the end of that period would
consular jurisdiction and foreign settlements be
abolished. The initial approaches were to be made to
Germany and Britain. The task fell to Aoki Shūzō, the
minister to Germany who, as a former foreign minister
(1889-91), had made an important contribution to the
solution of the treaty revision saga at an earlier
stage. A tentative approach in Berlin showed that
Germany's reaction was far from favourable. Since
Aoki was the only Japanese diplomat in Europe of sufficient calibre to handle the London negotiations, he
was told to visit Britain in September for private
discussions with Hugh Fraser, the British minister to
Japan (1889-94), who was there on furlough. The
Foreign Office was sufficiently sympathetic towards the

talks to agree to Fraser's return to Japan being
deferred.   In November Aoki was appointed as minister
to London.   While he continued to spend some time in
Berlin he took over in London on 27 December, when he
handed over an amended draft.

December saw an outburst of anti-foreign feeling in
Japan.   In the Diet the opposition took up the call
for 'strict enforcement of the existing treaties' in
order to exclude foreigners from the interior of the
country.   The Cabinet opposed this line and suspended
the house for ten days.   When it reopened, the call
for treaty enforcement was renewed; and Mutsu on 29
December made a famous speech declaring that he would
take strong measures against anti-foreign agitation but
concealing the fact that negotiations were being resumed.
On the following day the Diet was once again suspended
for ten days.   Outside the Diet this xenophobia manifested itself against British nationals; and Minister
Fraser had to warn Aoki of the obstacle which this
would put in the way of the negotiations.   At the same
time, London registered the fact that, if it did not
re-negotiate the treaties, the Japanese government might
be forced to denounce them unilaterally under the force
of public opinion.

The formal talks proceeded slowly from April 1894
onwards.   Mutsu was anxious to conclude the treaty with
all haste because of the external crisis: on 8 June she
had sent a mixed brigade to Korea; on 30 June Russia
seemed likely to take a hand in the peninsula.   After
some foot-shuffling, Britain responded; and the treaty
was signed on 16 July.   The agreement consisted of
three documents: the treaty which provided for the
ending of extra-territoriality not earlier than five
years after its signature; an agreed 'ad valorem'
import tariff; and a protocol introducing the new
tariff one month after the exchange of ratifications.
Ratifications were exchanged in Tokyo on 25 August,
after hostilities with China had already begun.

The Anglo-Japanese commercial treaty was the vital
step in resolving the problem of treaty revision.   In
a sense, it was only the first step.   But it set the
pattern for Japan's negotiations with the other Powers.
And it encouraged the others to clinch their own agreements, knowing that Britain with her numerous mercantile
community was ready to contemplate the ending of extra-
territorial jurisdiction.   It was a formidable accomplishment for Mutsu and Aoki after so long a series of
failures (Document 4).   All the more so as these
technical negotiations were accompanied in their last

stages by the most serious crisis which Japan had faced
since the Restoration - the approaching war with
China. (5)

WAR WITH CHINA

What brought China and Japan to declare war on 1 August
1894 was the degenerating situation in Korea. (6)
Korea was a kingdom which had failed to attain stable
government because it was riddled by opposing court
parties, which were supported, some by the Chinese,
some by the Japanese.   China professed to support the
Korean court over which she claimed to have a traditional suzerainty; Japan allied herself to reform
cliques.   With the appointment of Yuan Shih-k'ai as
viceroy in Seoul in 1885, China tried to step up her
control over Korean affairs while Japan too intensified
her efforts to uphold her 'equal rights' as laid down
in the Tientsin treaty of 1885.
    It was more than a simple Sino-Japanese problem.
The powers from outside had interested themselves in
Korea and were active behind the scenes.   Russia was
thought to want a port in south Korea for wintering her
squadron or as a permanent base.   There are disagreements among historians about Russia's true motives but
there can be little doubt that she was assumed by other
interested countries, Britain, the United States and
Japan, to want a port in the sun and to have directed
her glances especially to the coastline at the south of
the Korean peninsula.   Britain resisted any such move.
Thus, when Russia threatened to take Port Lazarev
(Gensan) in 1885, the Royal Navy sent its Far Eastern
squadron to Port Hamilton and occupied it unfruitfully
until 1887.   This was more because of Britain's anti-
Russian policy elsewhere in Asia than because of her
tangible interests in Korea.   The United States was
in a different position, having been the first non-
oriental country to have concluded a treaty with Korea
(1882).   The kingdom had then become an important
American mission field; and the missionaries, like the
diplomats, were not favourable to Russian or Japanese
influence.
    Japan's - and especially Mutsu's - standpoint over
Korea was most complex.   The Japanese of the Meiji
period did not respect Korea or her institutions.   On
the other hand, most of them did not look to Korea as
a fruitful territory for expansion.   Their interest
lay in Korea as a factor in Japanese security.   Mutsu

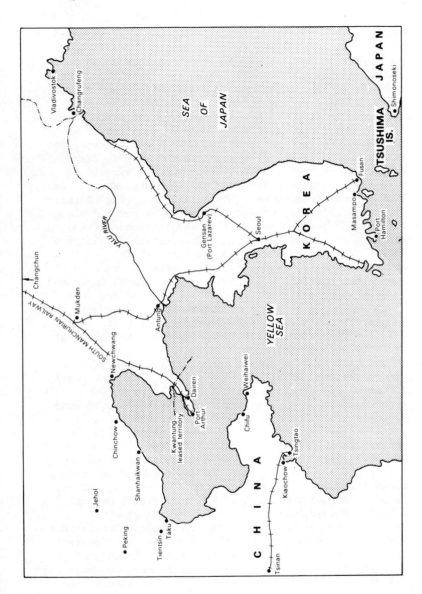

MAP 2   North-East Asia

was to define his views in a classic way when he wrote
that, if another country were to dominate the Korean
peninsula, Japan's safety would be endangered and Japan
could not endure such a situation (Document 5).   For
the present the 'other country' was China; and Mutsu
was vigilant over any attempt by Peking to turn the
situation in Seoul to her advantage.   The party opposition in Japan had grasped the Korean situation as an
instrument to inconvenience the government.   After the
assassination of Kim Ok-kiun on 28 March 1894, they
called on the Tokyo government to send an expedition
with the long-term object of insulating the Korean court
from Chinese influences.   Mutsu and his prime minister,
Itō, were initially determined not to be carried along
on waves of xenophobic hysteria and took no positive
steps.   They must have been sorely tempted to adopt a
course which would have been popular with the people
and the Diet: to send a force to Korea in order to
quench the passions which had been aroused in Japan and
to neutralize political opposition.   Of course, the
cause was not a good one.   But their inaction does seem
to support the thesis of Professor Conroy that 'impro-
visation rather than calculation underlay the moves of
Japanese policy makers' in 1894. (7)

Things came to a crisis early in June when Chinese
troops reached Korea.   Mutsu took the line that 'when
it became clear that China had sent troops to Korea
without offering any justification, we too should send
a considerable force there and provide against unforeseen eventualities and must maintain parity with the
Chinese in the Korean peninsula' (Document 5).
Although there was some doubt about the extent of the
forces which China had sent, it was regarded as unacceptable for China to intervene at all by sending forces.
In Tokyo the deputy chief of the army staff, General
Kawakami Soroku, was known to favour the sending of
Japanese troops and had them at the ready.   In various
meetings in the first week of June, Mutsu and Kawakami
came to the view that Japan was entitled to respond by
sending troops and should send a mixed brigade numbering
7-8,000 men.   They may have conspired to conceal the
true extent of these forces from Prime Minister Itō who
was thought to be against sending such a large force.
While Mutsu had earlier in the year held in check those
who were raring to go, he had gradually become convinced
of the need to send troops to Korea to match the Chinese
forces who had been despatched to the peninsula.   Until
the last moment, Mutsu and his colleagues were very uncertain about the best course to follow as they felt

that the troops sent could not be withdrawn without
having gained something for Japan.   On the basis of
intelligence about the degree of British and Russian
disinterest in Korea, they may have been induced to
come to some decision.   By 15 June Mutsu had convinced
the Cabinet to bring about a Japanese-style solution in
Korea even if it resulted in war with China whose claim
to suzerainty there was the root cause of the trouble
(Document 6).   A plan for a joint approach by China
and Japan to force reforms on Korea was presented to
Peking, the Japanese troops being left in Korea until
the results were known.   The Chinese, of course,
rejected this intrusion into their preserve.   Once
authority had been given by the Cabinet, the Japanese
expedition was sent very fast, thus confirming that
advance preparations had been made on a considerable
scale.   For these steps, a special responsibility lies
with Mutsu and Kawakami. (8)   The European governments
began to move towards preventing any outbreak and urged
moderation.   Itō and Mutsu gave them plentiful assurances that every step would be taken to come to some
understanding with Peking, though they were convinced
that China could hardly accept voluntarily any interference in Korean affairs.   Needless to say, the Korean
court was not responsive to any overtures which Mutsu
made in that quarter.

Although ready to be prodded by public opinion, Mutsu
was hardly ever rash.   One of his considerations in
making war must have been his fear of intervention by
the Powers.   It is probably true that the Powers had
interfered in every serious crisis in east Asia since
1840.   In this instance the Powers did intervene to
try to stop the war but did not carry much weight with
the Japanese.   It is not, as has commonly been assumed,
that Britain overlooked the problem.   She offered
mediation in 1894.   Her minister at Peking suggested
that she should stage a warlike demonstration in the
seas around Japan;   and the suggestion was seriously
considered;   but the decision reached was to keep out.
Japan was regarded in London, as elsewhere in Europe,
as the aggressor and intervention, if it took place,
could only be against her;   but, if Japan were to be
opposed, it would limit her ability to act as a bulwark
against an expanding Russia.   It was, therefore, not
unreasonable for Mutsu to discount an armed incursion
of all the Far Eastern naval Powers which were naturally
divided.   That being the case, it was the first major
crisis in the nineteenth-century Far East in which
foreign influence had proved to have no effect on Japan.

After the war began, there were yet further occasions
- eight in all - when European statesmen discussed how
they could bring it to an end.   With the war going so
much - and perhaps somewhat unexpectedly - in Japan's
favour, these approaches left the Japanese unmoved - but
vigilant.   They knew that mediation could only be rejected at the cost of foreign countries turning from
neutrality to favour China.   Mutsu did, however, offer
those foreign powers who were interested in the continuation of the China trade assurances that no boom would
be erected to impede the Shanghai trade.   In this way,
Mutsu, despite opposition from the armed forces and
public opinion, made minimal concessions to win the early
goodwill of outside Powers while the campaigns swung in
Japan's favour.   But his overall diplomacy during the
war can only be described as unsuccessful. (9)

The direction of the campaign was a preoccupation of
Mutsu as of many European Powers.   The initial campaign
was fought through Korea towards Port Arthur, captured
on 21 November.   The route seemed open to Peking, the
collapse of the Ching dynasty and the partition of
China.   In fact, this could only be accomplished by an
assault on Tientsin and this became difficult after the
freezing up of the river from mid-November onwards.
The Chinese capital was at Japan's mercy when weather
conditions permitted it.   The second route was towards
Shantung.   Following the capture of Port Arthur, the
Japanese decided to attack the Chinese fleet which was
harboured passively at Weihaiwei.   This was an unwieldy
invasion by one and a half divisions which ultimately
captured the forts in mid-February; naval action meanwhile put the Chinese fleet out of action.   A third
route which the Powers, and especially Britain, feared
was an attack on Shanghai or its environs.   From time
to time these countries got wind of Japan's plans for
such an expedition and made their own preparations.
There is no indication, however, that Japan seriously
thought of attacking the Yangtse valley.   A final
route - with its throwback to early Meiji - was an
expedition to Taiwan.   While Japan had ambitions in
this direction, she concentrated on the business in
hand, defeating the Chinese in north China.   It was not
until the Treaty of Shimonoseki had been signed that
military action was taken there in order to attach
Taiwan as a Japanese colony in accordance with the terms
of the peace treaty (May 1895).

Mutsu was aware of Japan's unpopularity in the eyes
of the world.   He had continually to remind military
commanders of the international implications of their

acts.   Fortunately he found both Premier Itō and the
leading general, Yamagata, anxious to respect foreign
rights and to conclude peace as soon as possible.   By
December the Chinese were also ready for peace.   But
Mutsu's main difficulty was 'the Japanese public was
agog with vain ambitions' and would not be satisfied
until the Japanese flag was planted in Peking
(Document 7).

PEACE OVERTURES

A ceasefire took place on 28 March.   At the peace talks
at Shimonoseki Japan presented China on 1 April with her
terms: she demanded the cession of the peninsular part
of Liaotung, Formosa and the Pescadores and the payment
of an indemnity amounting to 200 million taels.   The
Chinese 'leaked' the terms to the world Press and asked
for the intervention of the Powers since Liaotung was
vital to the safety of the Chinese capital.   As a
countermove Japan on 6 April announced her commercial
demands which included the right of all trading nations
to ply up the west river to Wuchow and up the Yangtse
to Chungking.   These were far-reaching terms, even
allowing for the absoluteness of Japan's victory.   They
gave her greater rights than those enjoyed by any other
treaty Power and suggested to the Chinese that Japan
was set on imposing a protectorate over them.   The
treaty of Shimonoseki was signed on 17 April.
     On the initiative of Russia, Germany and France
agreed to join her in offering Japan 'friendly advice'.
They argued that the cession of Liaotung would be a
perpetual obstacle to peace in the area and that if the
peninsula continued in Japanese hands as it had been
since the winter campaign, it would lead to trouble.
While Mutsu had expected some sort of intervention, it
was less of a foregone conclusion than he imagined.
The troika of powers was a temporary marriage of convenience.   Although Russia and France were members of
a European entente, this did not mean that France would
automatically support Russia in all areas of the globe.
On the contrary, she had grave suspicions about Russia's
long-range intentions over Liaotung and would have preferred Japan to keep her hands off Formosa rather than
Liaotung.   But she finally gave in to taking common
action;   as did Germany.   Germany seems at first to
have wanted to stay on the sidelines;   but she had
strong motives in Europe for keeping in alignment with
Russia and France: she wanted to keep them absorbed in

the East.   But there was another consideration.   As
one official explained: 'Do you think that we could
sit by calmly in case Russia and France both tried to
seize some Chinese territory?...   That would be impossible on account of the Kaiser and also German public
opinion.' (10)   This was the diplomacy of imperialism
at its zenith.   Mutsu had certainly aimed high when he
asked for such a large amount of territory or compensation.   But the Powers had stepped in not so much for
hatred of Japan as for their own imperialist urges -
the desire for the territory of China and the perception
that the time of break-up was at hand.   Mutsu had
wrongly gambled that they would be reluctant to become
militarily involved.

It took three weeks of feverish activity before the
outcome was known.   On 23 April the ministers of
Russia, France and Germany presented their notes to
Hayashi Tadasu as foreign vice-minister in Tokyo, while
most of the leaders were in Hiroshima and Mutsu was
confined to bed at Maiko.   The note of the German
minister was longer and sharper in tone.   It therefore
appeared to many Japanese that Germany was the manip-
ulator in this exercise.   On the other hand, the
Foreign Ministry ultimately got the right story.   For
Minister Aoki in Germany who had great hopes of building
up German friendship, recognized that it had been
initiated by Russia and adopted by Germany.   He felt
that the only explanation could be that the kaiser had
moments of madness and was given to excesses of language
in his statements.

Mutsu who had exhausted himself by his endeavours at
Shimonoseki, was recuperating slowly.   He realized
that Japan had not the strength to face new enemies on
her own and that there was no sign of tangible help
coming from Britain, United States or Italy.   But the
various partial concessions offered by Mutsu were not
accepted.   On 1 May Japan agreed to yield the Liaotung
peninsula without giving up Port Arthur.   Russia
obtained the agreement of her partners for a joint
naval demonstration in Korean waters.   The three, who
had held back from more than a diplomatic protest
before this, agreed to a limited operation.   Japan
whose generals and admirals agreed that their forces
could not meet this challenge decided not to call this
bluff.   On 8 May the treaty of Shimonoseki was ratified
by both parties and ratifications were exchanged.   The
objectionable clause over Liaotung still appeared in
the treaty;   but the Japanese Cabinet had agreed to
retrocede the peninsula provided Japan received an

indemnity in its place and her armies held on to
Weihaiwei until China paid the indemnity.   This was in
due course stipulated in an agreement signed on 8
November after China had been successful in fixing up
foreign loans from which to defray the indemnity.

This humiliation could not be hidden from public
opinion.   The Itō 'ministry of all the talents' feared
the parliamentary reaction to this insult from abroad.
In order to safeguard its position, it arranged for the
emperor to announce the retrocession of Liaotung in a
rescript of 10 May in the knowledge that the emperor's
rulings were beyond criticism.   Still there were votes
of no confidence in the Diet against Mutsu and the
Ministry.

Had the decision to go to war in the face of foreign
advice been unwise?   Had Mutsu overplayed his hand
over the peace terms?   Mutsu replied in the negative.
He was right that in both respects public opinion in
Japan which was 'overheated' and jingoist would have
backed actions which were much more extreme than those
which the government took (Document 7).   Mutsu had
been an opportunist throughout the crisis and had
parried advice or suggestions for mediation from outside
Japan.   He had been Machiavellian in fabricating
motives for intervening in Korea and had chanced his
arm that foreign Powers would look on lethargically.
He was to argue that in the comity of nations one Power
which destroyed the balance of power was often pulled
back into line by the others as in the case of the
Treaty of San Stephano where Russia had to disgorge
some of the acquisitions of her war with Turkey. (11)
Perhaps he was injudicious in the demands which he
presented to Li Hung-chang.

The triple intervention, though a blatant example
of Great Power arrogance, was not unhealthy for Japan.
She thought the alliance would continue to menace her
security.   On the contrary, it was an unstable and
erratic partnership which broke up soon afterwards on
financial grounds.   But it forced Japan to change her
policy and be more cautious in future.   With the indemnity which she obtained she was able to increase
the size of her army and navy, while she pursued
moderate objectives.

ASSESSMENT

In June 1895 Mutsu received permission to have temporary
release from the foreign ministership in order to

recuperate from tuberculosis at his country house on the
coast at Oiso.   Mutsu was created count in consequence
of his service as foreign minister during the China war;
and there is no doubt that it was well warranted.   On
the other hand, he had received stinging attacks and
was an embittered man.   Saionji Kimmochi, the education
minister, acted as foreign minister though Mutsu returned to work from time to time.   In his temporary
retirement, he undertook the writing of his memoirs
under the title 'Kenkenroku' which he completed on 31
December.   In the following April he returned to the
Foreign Ministry for two months but resigned in order
to go to Hawaii for further recuperation.   On 24
August 1897 Mutsu died.

    Mutsu left 'Kenkenroku' as his testimony and justi-
fication.   It is a comprehensive record of events down
to the Dreibund crisis and a personal account of his
own thinking.   It is unique among Japan's historical
writing because it cuts out the cant often associated
with Japanese memoirs and ranks among the most revealing
of such writings in the world.   Of course, it is
slanted: it is an answer to the charge that Japan had
won the war but Itō and Mutsu had lost the peace.   As
a defence it is quite convincing.   It gave rise to
problems for the government over whether its publication
should be allowed.   It had been composed on ad hoc
basis with special memoranda on subjects like the Triple
Intervention;   and, when a connected narrative was complete, it was given to the Foreign Ministry.   Since it
contained a large number of state secrets about Cabinet
deliberations and personal views which were controversial, the Ministry tried to prevent publication.   It
appears that it was privately printed in expurgated
versions and that the Foreign Ministry tried to comman-
deer as many copies as it could and forbade further
publication.   It was not wholly available until the
issue of Mutsu's collected papers in 1929.   What
seemed to be most damaging was his criticism of public
opinion (chapter 12) which was likened to the jingoism
of British opinion before the Crimean war. (12)

    Although Mutsu was seriously criticized in his day,
he has claims to be one of the greatest of Japan's
foreign ministers, indeed the founder of Japanese
diplomacy.   Over treaty revision he showed skill and
shrewdness in peacetime.   During the China war, he
showed coolness and objectivity under stress.   In the
Dreibund crisis, he had to cope with a situation which
was quite new for a Japanese minister, the threat of
attack by a combination of foreign Powers.   Mutsu was

not solely responsible either for Japan's successes or
her failures.   He was one of a team.   On the whole,
he worked well with his prime minister, Itō Hirobumi,
who was not content to be excluded from decisions on
foreign affairs, and with Yamagata, who controlled the
army with vigilance.   Yet one has the feeling that
Mutsu was not merely their servant but a very indepen-
dent-minded equal.   He was treated by them as among
the upper ranks of the Meiji leadership, so that in the
crisis of April 1895 they visited him for advice at
Maiko.

     Mutsu was not a member of one of the major clans
and, therefore, had a hard struggle for political power.
His promotion was by talent and not by connections -
which was rare in the years of middle Meiji.   This may
have contributed to that scepticism with which he
approached political and foreign affairs.   It is never
easy to define realism or Realpolitik in foreign
affairs;   but Mutsu (and later Komura) comes close to
living by it.   With his zeal for the ideal of Japan's
natural equality with other nations and his awareness
of her inadequacies compared to the armed might of the
Great Powers, he was applying realism in his policies.
But there are reservations which one would make:
almost inevitably he had to gamble over the reactions
of the Powers to the Sino-Japanese war;   again, while
he strove for his own fatherland's natural rights, he
thought little about those of China and Korea, towards
which he was tough-minded and unsympathetic.   In Mutsu
there was something of Machiavelli and more of Bismarck.
They were all three the representatives of struggling,
ambitious states in a world of jealous competitors.

Chapter 3

The Aoki Period,
1896-1901

Aoki Shūzō (1844-1914) came from an ambitious generation.
Like many of his ambitious contemporaries, he went
abroad at an early age.   Aoki studied Western science
and medicine in Prussia.   After the Restoration, he
took up the diplomatic profession and never was far
from it for the rest of his life.   Going to Berlin as
first secretary in 1873, he became minister plenipotentiary soon after.   Aoki was one of those who advocated
the relevance of Prussian politics and German culture
to Japan and cherished the hope that the new Germany
would stay close to the new Japan. (1)   Returning to
his homeland in 1879, he became consultant on treaty
revision to Inoue Kaoru.   After another varied spell
in Europe, he became vice-minister in 1886 and foreign
minister three years later, when he returned to the
thorny problem of treaty revision.   Deciding to concentrate on the key commercial country, Britain, he
succeeded in achieving a special rapport with the British
minister, Hugh Fraser.   In this way, notable advances
which he made during his early career stood Japan in
good stead for the negotiations which he successfully
carried out in London in 1894.   This chapter is primarily concerned with Aoki's actions when he again
became foreign minister in 1898.   He owed this to the
then prime minister, General Yamagata, who was the
titular leader of the Chōshū clan, to which Aoki
belonged.
　　A confident diplomat, he had no easy passage as a
politician.   Aoki had been overseas for long periods
and had no power base in Japan where he was dependent
on his connections with Yamagata.   His autobiography,
which is an essential source for an understanding of
his unusual personality, shows that he kept up a
regular correspondence with Yamagata, even when he was

abroad.   Aoki was a bold, independent thinker and acquired a reputation for exceeding the authority of his office.   In this way, he fell out with Inoue Kaoru, Itō Hirobumi, Mutsu Munemitsu, Hayashi Tadasu and Saionji Kimmochi and finally strained his relations with his allies, Yamagata and Katsura.

Aoki was probably the most Europeanized among the prominent Meiji diplomats.   In 1877 he had married a wife (Elizabeth) who came from an aristocratic German family;   and he brought up his daughter, Hanna, in European style.   He himself had an excellent grasp of the German language.   Aoki was, therefore, a somewhat rare representative of Meiji Japan.   There is evidence that he was unduly influenced by foreign advice.   Thus, at the time of the three-Power intervention in 1895, he had reported from Berlin that Germany would not join Russia.   Moreover, he was prepared to operate through foreign intermediaries, notably the German, Philipp von Siebold, whom he allowed to call at the Foreign Office in London on his behalf but without specific instructions (Document 4). Needless to say, those in Tokyo tended to look with suspicion on many of his actions and his judgments. He was commonly criticized as being 'high-collared', that is, as aping the dress, and, by extension, the ways, of Europeans.   In retrospect, we may say that he was a useful and talented official, whose views tended to be right-wing.   But his diplomatic experience lacked the breadth of a Mutsu or a Komura.

As one who had spent so much of his time in Berlin, Aoki was gravely suspicious of Russia.   As foreign minister, he had warned his colleagues in a lengthy memorandum of 15 May 1890 against the danger from Russia's inroads into Korea.   These sentiments were shared by his patron, Yamagata, who also alerted his countrymen to the Russian threat in a memorandum of 1890.   Such suspicions were aggravated when Russia set about building the Trans-Siberian railway in 1891. Aoki, like many of the military men, followed the progress of the line with vigilance and distrust. (2)

By a coincidence it was tsarist Russia which interrupted Aoki's first period as foreign minister under Yamagata (1889-91).   In May 1891 when Yamagata resigned, Aoki continued to serve at the Foreign Ministry.   But his time there was shortened by happenings at Otsu.   The Crown Prince Nicholas of Russia, the future tsar, was on a visit to Vladivostok with the object of inaugurating the work of the eastern section of the trans-Siberian railway, which was for many Japanese the symbol of a new wave of Russian encroachment in the Far East.   The Russian party expressed the intention of touring in Japan for the month of May.   On 11 May during a visit to Otsu near Kyoto, Nicholas was assaulted in his rickshaw by a policeman who was guarding the route and who apparently detested Russia and all her ways.   Although wounded, Nicholas was not seriously injured to the point of death.   As he languished in bed in Kyoto, the emperor himself set off from Tokyo to visit him and express Japan's regret.   With the exception of Mutsu (then minister of agriculture), who typically took the line of safeguarding judicial independence, the Cabinet all favoured execution of the policeman on the charge of attempted murder and, needless to say, because of his responsibility for an inconvenient diplomatic imbroglio.   In this, the Cabinet was under strong pressure from the Russian minister who took pains not to overlook the incident.   But the judges, caparisoned in their new constitutional powers, knew that they could not exceed a life sentence for attempted murder and stood out against a vast amount of unfair pressure from the alarmed ministers.   When the crown prince left Japan and the court passed its verdict as a life sentence, Aoki who had gone to Kyoto to appease the Russians offered his resignation as the minister who was responsible for Nicholas's visit. (3)   The expected punishment was avoided: the policeman died from the rigour of the elements in a Hokkaidō prison, unaware of the diplomatic storm he had caused.

AOKI'S ROLE IN TREATY REVISION

The British treaty of 1894 which Aoki had with great skill concluded was intended to be used as the thin end of the wedge.   It was to be the means of extracting similar treaties from other trading countries so that the whole group of new treaties could be brought into force in five years' time when the British treaty would be enforced.   Before this could be done, Japan's laws had to be finally reframed.   The civil code which was to have taken effect in 1893 came into force in July 1898; and the commercial code in June 1899.   This cleared the way for Japan's foreign treaties to be put into operation and for her to join many of the international conventions.   The second necessary step was to negotiate with the more favourable and liberal governments abroad.   Japan's ministers

abroad were to conduct negotiations with governments to
which they were accredited on the basis of the procedure
followed by Mutsu, despite all the delays involved in
this method.   During the war, Japan succeeded in
clinching the American-Japanese commercial treaty (1894).

Aoki had an important role in this process as the
minister charged especially with ending the unequal
treaties with Germany and Belgium.   When he completed
his treaty revision negotiations with Britain, the
Sino-Japanese war was breaking out.   He thought that
it would not be to Japan's advantage for him to leave
London and he stayed on there until the battle of the
Yellow Sea.   Thereafter he returned to Berlin in order
to open discussion on treaty revision with the German
government on 1 September.   But the conversations with
Germany were much more difficult than those with
Britain since, as he himself wrote, the German delegates were academically more highly qualified;   they
'out-doctored' him.   Before negotiations had proceeded
for very long, the triple intervention took place and
Aoki, thinking that the climate for negotiations was
not helpful, broke off the treaty talks. (4)   There
was little scope for negotiation, especially where
Japanese public opinion was so incensed by Germany's
role in the manoeuvre.

When talks were resumed, the progress was slow.
The reasons for this was that the Anglo-Japanese treaty
had conferred results which outstripped.Japan's expectations and were more than Germany had intended.   It
seemed that the Germans did not want to conclude a
treaty which was beneficial to Japan and did not
readily agree to begin talks at all.   They were suspicious of Britain giving away important extra-
territorial rights and could not believe that she had
done so without some ulterior motive.   They complained
about the inadequacy of Japan's laws and about the
tariff proposals.   Aoki therefore prepared a small
pamphlet in defence of Japan's new laws and sent
fifteen copies to the German government which they
evidently read because they passed it on to the Belgian
government which was about to embark on the revision
of its treaties with Japan.   (There was some conspiracy between the European Powers over this question;
it was possible to conclude the Belgian treaty within
two days of concluding the German one.)

The Germans ultimately wavered.   Aoki signed the
commercial treaty on 4 April 1896.   But relations
between Aoki and Tokyo had never been good.   As a
former foreign minister, he was often ready to dispute

his instructions and, in the uncertainty of the telegraph, he was sometimes willing to take the responsibility of going ahead without instructions. He was
ordered home in 1897 for exceeding authority in some
of his statements to Germany over the triple intervention and treaty revision. Unable to reach a
compromise with his superiors, he resigned as minister
in February of the following year. (5)

Fortunately for Aoki, he was able to sail into the
position of foreign minister again in November. This
was because his Chōshū sponsor, General Yamagata, was
manoeuvred into forming a government at this time and,
having earlier formed a good impression of Aoki's
calibre, had no hesitation in offering him the appointment. Yamagata was called to power after a swift
succession of Cabinets between 1895 and 1898 in which
oligarchs had tried to share power with leaders of
the political parties that were becoming so vociferous
in the newly opened Diet. But there was little
harmony within these ministries and they were short-
lived. Yamagata's appointment, it was hoped, would
represent a return to incisiveness in decision-making
and a trend to a firmer line in foreign affairs. Aoki
was known to share many of Yamagata's assumptions; and
they were natural partners in pursuing a strong
foreign policy.

The various treaties which had been so laboriously
extracted from privileged foreign countries came into
force during Aoki's second term of office. They were
all designed to become operative simultaneously and
took effect in August 1899. They were then to
continue in·force for twelve years after which they
could be renounced at one year's notice by either party.
By this group of treaties, extra-territoriality was
removed, the residence of foreigners throughout Japan
and their possession of movable property were authorized, and the most-favoured-nation clauses in the
treaties were made reciprocal and unconditional.
These represented immense gains of substance and of
prestige (Document 8). Japan negotiated a revision
of her tariffs but did not acquire tariff autonomy at
this time. Import duties were fixed by separate
treaties which like the·main treaty would lapse after
twelve years. Though there were differences of rates
between the treaties, uniformity was secured through
the most-favoured-nation clauses.

On 30 June, as the date for operating the new
treaties approached, an imperial rescript was issued
in order to indicate Japan's 'great joy'. In a sense,

the first task to which the diplomacy of the new Meiji
government had set its hand had been achieved after
three decades of effort.   This was due partly to the
great strides which Japan had made and partly to the
growth in her reputation which resulted from her
victory in the war of 1894-5.   But it was only a
partial victory.   The powers had driven a hard
bargain;   and the party politicians were quick to pick
up the shortcomings of the treaties.   The other
problem was the security of foreign nationals, after
the record of anti-foreign violence in the Meiji period.
In the rescript the emperor enjoined his subjects 'to
co-operate in treating foreigners with cordiality'. (6)
      The treaties which took effect in 1899 could be
renounced after twelve years.   In order to secure
revision of them, Japan gave the required one year's
notice in July 1910.   Japan's sense of grievance and
inequality was more concerned with the tariff question
than with anything else.   Japan had been handicapped
in fixing the rate of customs duty chargeable on
imports by the fixed tariffs laid down in annexes to
the original treaties.   She sought to have full discretion to decide on, and apply, such duties as she
herself thought fit.   In a world which was becoming
increasingly protectionist, it was indeed a condition
of full statehood to do so without outside interference.
      In October 1908 the government of the day (in which,
of course, Aoki had no longer a hand) set up a treaty
and tariff committee (Document 13).   This body
had Foreign Minister Komura Jutarō as chairman and
Home Minister Hirata Tosuke and Ambassador Inoue
Katsunosuke as deputy chairmen.   A draft treaty was
approved by the Cabinet in August of the following
year and legislation for revising the customs tariff
was presented.   On 15 April 1910 the revised tariff
law was published and a formula was devised to deal
with perpetual leases in the former treaty ports which
had been the subject of much bitterness on the part of
foreigners throughout the decade.
      From the start it had been decided that the first
approach should be to Britain.   The draft treaty and
tariff proposals were passed to the Whitehall government which felt that, as a free trade country, Britain
was being less favourably treated than countries which
were avowedly protectionist.   London was not prepared
to proceed with negotiations on this basis.   The
Japanese, therefore, deflected their energies to the
United States which was less interested in tariffs

than in the immigration question.   Eventually they
signed the treaty on 21 February 1911, negotiations
having been speeded up in order that it should be
sanctioned by the American senate while the session
lasted.   In return for the tariff concessions, Japan
undertook to continue her policy of restricting emigration to America.   Within six weeks, on 3 April,
the British treaty was signed and the new tariff
agreed.   This secret exercise was then announced and
accepted by the public without the protests with which
the Japanese had greeted earlier formulae for revising
the treaties.

Virtually all countries followed the lead of the
United States and Britain by July 1911.   Japan had to
accept a certain loss of revenue beyond what her
earlier committees had bargained for.   But this was
an inevitable part of the exercise.   She had to give
some quid pro quo in order to persuade foreign
countries to give up the privileges accumulated over
half a century.   At long last, Japan had acquired
tariff autonomy.   There was the fear in the minds of
the Powers that Japan might hasten in the direction
of protectionism and increase the rates steeply to her
own advantage.   In fact, she did not do so and acted
quite responsibly.

By 1911 Japan had won a diplomatic success of an
unprecedented kind.   She had overcome the unwillingness of foreign Powers to make any surrender over the
lives and property of their nationals in Japan.
Statesmen like Inoue, Mutsu and Aoki had achieved this
at some cost: they had found it expedient to change
Japanese institutions by establishing the Diet, reforming the system of justice and introducing new law-
codes based on European principles.   They had,
moreover, overcome the scruples of their own people
that the new treaties would still confer excessive
privileges on foreigners.   On the contrary, Japan
had achieved equal status with the Powers.   She was
unique among developing countries at the time in
opening her country to foreigners without sacrificing
her economy and her resources irretrievably.   And, in
persuading the world's Powers to shed their privileges
in her own territory, Japan was still able to enjoy
privileges under her 'unequal treaties' with China and
Korea (Document 13).

FAR EASTERN CRISIS OF 1898

When Aoki took office as foreign minister in November
1898, he came in at the tail-end of a six-months'
crisis in east Asia.   Since her defeat by Japan,
China had faced the danger of spoliation by the
Powers.   In 1898 she was confronted by the scare of
partition, the so-called 'slicing of the melon'.   In
this crisis Japan could either work alone or alongside
some of the Powers;   she could act like an imperialist
Power and annex territory if China were to be split up
or she could abstain;   she could aim for a role of
leadership or attempt to maintain neutrality.   There
were, of course, vacillations of policy and divergences of view but, by and large, the Itō Cabinet
(January-June 1898) decided to work alone, abstain
from taking territory and avoid a bid for leadership.
Its policy was to pursue her national self-interest
inconspicuously.

In those days Japan's self-interest lay primarily in
ensuring the security of Korea.   Since the war with
China, Japan had been involved in a more or less open
fight with Russia in Korea, in which she had been
coming off second-best.   Now, however, it appeared
that Russia might be bidding for higher stakes by
occupying Port Arthur and calling for a lease of the
adjoining territory.   This was objectionable to Japan
since she had been dispossessed of the area in 1895
but she had no thought of opposing such a move by arms
and wanted instead to capitalize on Russia's new
ambitions by increasing her stake in Korea.   Foreign
Minister Nishi Tokujirō on 19 March handed the Russian
minister, Rosen, a note undertaking that, if affairs
in the peninsula were left to Japan, she would in turn
recognize Russia's new leased territory in south Manchuria as being outside the sphere of Japan's
interests.   Russia was not ready for compromise and
only stated in the Nishi-Rosen note of 25 April that
she would not impede Japan's progress in Korea and
would agree to Japanese advisers being sent there.

The Cabinet also endorsed the navy's view that
Japan should ask the Tsungli Yamen that Fukien province,
which faced the island of Taiwan and the Pescadores,
should be recognized as falling within Japan's sphere
of influence and should not be leased or ceded to any
other power.   On 28 April this request, which was in
line with what European countries were doing elsewhere
in China, was granted;   and Japan secured a sphere
where she would have the first option in case China

needed external aid for the construction of railways.
These negotiations met the demands of the navy through
Admiral Yamamoto and also the army through War Minister
Katsura and the Taiwan authorities.   It also sowed
the seed of future disagreement: should Japan be
directing her energies towards north-east Asia or
towards southern China?

Aoki was one of those who criticized Itō for facing
the 1898 crisis 'with arms folded' (bōkan).   Unjusti-
fiably (as we believe) he blamed Itō for following a
policy of caution which is illustrated by the phleg-
matic account of the Triple Intervention in the Diet
speech of Foreign Minister Okuma (Document 8).   Aoki
looked to the north and was determined to improve his
country's position in Korea.   Encouraged by his old
friend, the German minister in Tokyo, Count Leyden, he
watched fanatically for any sign of Russian infiltration in the peninsula.   Aoki let it be known that he
hoped Russia might promise to give Japan a free hand
in Korea in return for recognizing her position in
Manchuria.   At the same time, he was a believer in
direct action.   In 1899 when Russia was found to be
acquiring land at Masampo, a strategic point on the
southern coast of Korea, it was hard to believe that
Aoki was not involved in foiling the Russian plans, so
fanatical had he become.   Instead Japanese secured the
land and believed that they had prevented the Russians
establishing a dockyard there.   The Masampo incident
lingered on for months and was soon merged into a major
crisis in east Asia in which the so-called 'Boxers'
became active in north China.

BOXER DISTURBANCES

One of the first tests for Aoki after he came to office
was the Boxer uprising which resulted in the siege of
the foreign legations in Peking from 20 June to 14
August 1900.   (7)   Although Japan was not affected in
so far as the Boxer movement was anti-Western and anti-
Christian, she suffered an early casualty when the
chancellor at her Peking legation, Sugiyama Akira, was
killed by the Boxers.   The other factor was that there
was a widespread feeling at the time that the Powers
were treating the disturbances as a moment of opportunity to teach China a lesson and that it might have
serious repercussions for Japan if she too were not on
the scene.

When the allies sent an expedition under Admiral

Seymour which advanced from Taku in order to defend
foreigners in Peking, Aoki induced the Cabinet on 15
June to send a small force.   It did not secure its
objectives.   It was clear that, confronted by the
vast numerical strength of the Boxers, Japan and Russia
were the only countries which could supply troops
speedily.   While Russia was willing, Japan decided
'to await a request for support from the powers'.
Three times Britain asked for Tokyo to send urgent
reinforcements.   Japan asked for an expression of
world opinion.   The response of the powers was less
than enthusiastic: they were jealous and suspicious
of Japan's intentions.   Meanwhile on 25 June the
government, moving towards a decision on its own in
favour of 'a solo performance' regardless of the lack
of unanimity among the Powers, had mobilized one
division.   Later the fifth division was after some
discussion authorized by the Cabinet on 6 July to sail
to north China and about 22,000 troops were added to
the allied expedition which was able to break through
and relieve Peking on 14 August (Document 9).

Although Aoki had ensured that Japan had acted
modestly, she had in the outcome taken a strong,
positive step.   There was a similar uncertainty over
the question of the commander-in-chief of the allied
expedition.   On the one hand, there were those who
called for a Japanese to assume the allied command
since the Japanese had contributed the most numerous
force.   On 7 August when the German emperor cabled
the Japanese emperor asking for his approval to Field-
marshal Waldersee being appointed to the command, the
emperor replied agreeing, as most of the European
monarchs had done.   This matter was, however, handled
by the Imperial Household Ministry and it is not clear
that the emperor's decision reflected the Cabinet's
view or that of Foreign Minister Aoki. (8)

A new test appeared after the legations were
relieved.   The condition of the legations was found
to be less serious than had earlier been feared.   On
25 August the Russians announced that they would withdraw their troops from Peking to Tientsin and hoped
the other Powers would do the same.   Their force was
second only to that of the Japanese; and a voluntary
withdrawal was immediately looked on with intense
suspicion.   To the Russophobe Aoki it seemed clear
that the Russian purpose was merely to enhance the
garrisons which Russia was building up in Manchuria.
In that territory there had been considerable fighting
during the Boxer outbreaks - a sort of 'Russo-Chinese

war' (as one writer has described it). (9) By the
middle of August the Russians had added to their leased
territory of Port Arthur and Dairen by occupying the
Port of Newchwang. The Yamagata Cabinet, faced with
this uncertainty, decided to withdraw the bulk of the
Japanese force, which had been notable for its restrained
behaviour in Peking and its environs, to its base at
Hiroshima in October.

If their actions and statements were moderate and
no more expansionist than those of the other statesmen
of the time, Yamagata and Aoki were vexed by the
problem that faced them in China. It was widely
suspected that the Powers would take the opportunity
afforded by the Boxers to move in on their spheres of
influence in China and the long-awaited 'slicing of
the melon' would take place. What was Japan to do?
Something of the dilemma is shown in Yamagata's memorandum of 20 August to his colleagues. He distinguished between southern and northern projects in
discussing this problem (Nampō keieiron). His broad
conclusion was that Japan should stick in the north
and advance to the south: that is, while adhering to
the status quo in Korea, she should make use of the
disruption to extend her influence in Fukien and
Chekiang, the provinces adjacent to her colony of
Taiwan. (10)

Aoki as the responsible minister admitted that Japan
had faced difficulties through her position in the
south where she had gained a foothold through acquiring
Taiwan as one of the terms of the Shimonoseki treaty.
Her administrators there had been met with massive
obstruction which was thought to be organized by secret
societies operating from Amoy, the leading city of
Fukien. In April 1898, as we have seen, Japan had
unobtrusively, and without objection from any of the
Powers, secured from the Tsungli Yamen an undertaking
not to alienate Fukien province to any other
power. (11) But the various demands for railway
rights in that province which became more and more
threatening were peremptorily turned down by the
Chinese who gained a second wind from the anti-foreign
activities of the Boxers. The aftermath of the Boxer
upheaval represented a great temptation to those
Japanese who wanted firmer measures against Fukien:
the usual rōnin, the Taiwan administration, the army
and the navy. Since there were plenty anti-Japanese
incidents in the neighbourhood of Amoy, this was used
as the pretext for an expedition which was landed on 24
August 1900. But Tokyo soon called off all government

involvement in these manoeuvres on the grounds that it was inopportune at this stage to occupy the Amoy forts. Evidently the 'advance to the south' was deferred.

Consistent with his earlier attitude toward Russia, Yamagata encouraged Aoki to turn the Boxer incident to advantage by approaching Russia for some understanding over Manchuria and Korea. Hence his reference to 'standing still in the north': he did not favour expansion in Korea at this juncture, rather a standstill. On 22 July 1900 Komura, Japan's newly appointed minister to Russia, recommended that, since a Russian occupation of Manchuria was likely to become an accomplished fact, Japan should propose a 'delimitation of spheres of influence': Japan would have a free hand in Korea and Russia in Manchuria while each would guarantee for the other commercial freedom in its sphere of influence. (12) If this overture were to be successful, Japan would have advanced her sphere from south Korea to the whole of the peninsula. Understandably the Russian leaders were in no mood to forego their privileges in Korea; and the overture made no headway. But it is one of the origins of the 'Man-Kan kōkan' proposals which were to assume great significance in the next few years.

There is reason to believe that, while Aoki did not object to Yamagata's approach, he gave it a markedly different slant. There were many groups which felt that Japan had sadly neglected her opportunities in Korea and organized themselves into a lobby, the Kokumin dōmeikai. Aoki was more sensitive to these voices than Yamagata. He recounts that he could not sit idly by as Russia used the crisis to extend gradually into Korea nor did he think that Korea had the national strength to preserve any neutrality. He therefore wanted to see a defensive alliance set up. (13) When the Koreans through their British adviser, (Sir) John McLeavy Brown, asked for a substantial loan, either ¥ 1,000,000 or ¥ 500,000, Aoki went out of his way to assist them through financial circles in Japan, particularly the capitalist Shibusawa Eiichi. Eventually the amount was granted on 29 September as a loan through the Dai-Ichi Bank based on customs revenue at 6 per cent interest.

Aoki also had political schemes on hand for Korea. Perhaps symbolically, Aoki tried to enlist the support for his Korean strategy of the European country with which he was most at home, Germany. He advised the Germans privily that some settlement might be effected in consequence of the Chinese trouble whereby Korea

would be placed under Japan's sphere of influence and
asked whether, if Russia should oppose this, Germany
would observe at least benevolent neutrality.   Germany replied that, her interest in Korea being purely
commercial, she would observe absolute neutrality in
any complication between Japan and any other Power.
This was at least an indication of non-intervention
and a hint that the 1895 Dreibund was no longer
operating.   It gave Aoki the encouragement he needed
to go ahead with his political scheme.   He rather
exceptionally reported his enquiries to the emperor as
commander-in-chief without going through the prime
minister as intermediary.   He urged upon him the
desirability of sending troops to Korea who would be
ready to engage in conflict with the Russians, who
were in the aftermath of the Boxer troubles holding on
to the critical parts of south Manchuria.   In this
appeal, Aoki was reflecting the ambitions of the army
and of nationalist groups like the Kokuryūkai (Amur
River society). (14)

Yamagata was furious over Aoki's action with which
he disagreed.   But he was already weary of power and
offered the resignation of his Cabinet on 26 September.
Whether or not Yamagata resigned because of loss of
face with the emperor, his action was linked to Aoki's
unconstitutional action.   Aoki did not cease to be
minister till 19 October and tried to win over the
succeeding prime minister, Prince Itō, to his views.
Itō, however, refused to be committed to any plan for
sending troops to Korea, to any agreement or alliance
with Korea or to the loan which had been clinched.
While Aoki complained that what he had once accepted
as foreign minister could not be so readily cancelled,
the Cabinet could not support his plans.   On 4
October Aoki had to inform his minister at Seoul that
the agreement envisaged was cancelled.   Moreover,
Aoki was forced, rather sheepishly, to inform Berlin
that the 'political situation here renders it necessary
for me to desire that you will not, under any circumstances, disclose to anyone even in [the] most intimate
relations with you, the matter of my enquiry to Germany
regarding Corea.' (15)   Aoki was bitterly disappointed
that his political strategy had been so firmly rejected.
He had hoped, despite the reluctance of his superiors,
to achieve some arrangement over Korea while attention
was focused on Russia's doings in Manchuria.   Instead
Japan, like the rest of the Powers, gained no territory from the Boxer disturbances.   It was to be
another ten years before the Korean peninsula was
annexed by Japan. (16)

It is rare in Japanese history - though happenings
in 1915 and 1941 prevent it from being unique - for a
foreign minister to bring down a Cabinet.   It is in
a way an indication of Aoki's strong personality and
his capacity for intrigue that things should have
turned out so badly.   In 1901 Aoki was appointed
adviser to the privy council and lost prominence
until 1906 when he was posted as ambassador to Washington.   For one with his roots in European diplomacy,
he was confronted in the immigration problem with an
unfamiliar subject.   It was his instinct to feel
that this was a secondary issue which must be played
down if harmony was to exist between America   and
Japan.   Foreign Minister Hayashi Tadasu with whom
Aoki had a sort of feud, recalled him in 1908 summarily
for exceeding his authority. (17)
Professor Sakane, the editor of his autobiography,
has described Aoki as an important sub-leader of Meiji
times.   He falls short of top-leadership: he is a
distinguished elderly statesmen, not one of Japan's
Elder Statesmen.   His objects as diplomat over twenty-
five years and as foreign minister for six were to
secure equality for Japan with the world Powers and to
expand the Meiji state.   There was nothing exceptional
in this among Meiji bureaucrats; Aoki's distinction
was his desire to achieve it speedily.   He was anti-
Russian and suspicious of Russia's ambitions to overrun
north-east Asia.   For long he had viewed Russia from
Berlin;   and he was encouraged to seek for Japan an
alignment with Russia's world-wide enemies, Germany in
Europe and Britain in Asia.   If Russia was to be
stopped, Japan must take a strong protective role in
Korea, which became almost an obsession with Aoki,
and, if not a protective role, at least a watching
brief in China herself. (18)   In all this he comes
close to the thinking of his patron, Yamagata.   Whereas
Yamagata had a sort of unsoldierly caution and reserve
about him, Aoki was often rash.   In this he was
perhaps expressing the un-Japanese side of his personality - his deep penetration by things German.   He
was inclined to be impulsive and short-tempered.   It
is no accident that on two occasions he had to suffer
the indignity of being recalled from his diplomatic
post abroad for going beyond his instructions.   Another
factor is the extreme to which he would go in order to
get his own way: he had been prepared to act against
his patron, Yamagata, for this purpose in 1900.   Combined with this went his lack of talent for dealing
with the Diet and his contempt for party politicians.

Aoki, despite his desire to please (happō bijin) was
never skilled in politics.   Aoki falls short of being
a first-rank statesman; but he was a rich and unusual
character in Meiji Japan.

Chapter 4

The Komura Period, 1901-11

Komura Jutarō proved to be one of Japan's ablest foreign ministers and influential statesmen. Komura (1955-1911) came from a bushi family in the small Obi clan in Kyushu. After studying with a clan scholarship at what was later to become Tokyo Imperial University, he received government assistance to proceed to Harvard Law School and spent six years (1874-80) in the United States. Recruited into the Foreign Ministry in 1884, he spent a decade in undistinguished work as head of the translation bureau. In 1893 he was plucked from obscurity by Mutsu, who may have felt some fellow-feeling for someone from the lesser clans whose sons had tended to be excluded from major office since the Meiji restoration. But it is unlikely that he was regarded by Mutsu as a diplomat of especial promise. (1)

By good fortune, his appointment to Korea and then to Peking as councillor of legation turned out to be the start of a series of key postings. In Peking he was to play an important part, acting as minister in the run-up to the war of 1894. The war months brought him new tasks: first as civil administrator to the first army in Manchuria where he met Yamagata and Katsura Tarō; then as head of the ministry's political department (seimukyokuchō); and finally, after the disastrous Miura affair, as minister to Korea in days of sharp Russo-Japanese tension. It was in Seoul that he was responsible for the Waeber-Komura agreement. In June 1896 he returned to Tokyo to perform the duties of Vice-minister for the acting foreign minister, Saionji Kimmochi, and two years later he was appointed minister to Washington. Going in 1900 to Russia at the wish of Premier Yamagata, he was responsible (as we saw in the Aoki chapter) for important initiatives during the Boxer emergency. At the

end of the year he was posted back to Peking.   In
these eight years he had been in all the major trouble-
centres of the world.   While such brief postings
might in some cases have suggested dissatisfaction with
his performance, they showed in Komura's case how
swiftly his diplomatic reputation had grown.

On 21 September 1901 Komura became foreign minister
for the first time.   He was to hold office under
General Katsura's ministry until January 1906 throughout the Russo-Japanese war.   For two years he became
ambassador to London, the first person to hold this
office after the status of the legation was raised.
In August 1908 he was again offered appointment as
foreign minister under General Katsura and held office
until the summer of 1911.   He then retired from
public office and died at the comparatively young age
of fifty-seven.   It is reasonable to conclude that
the foreign policy of the 1900s was largely that of
Komura.   Since it covered two of the important events
of Japan's national development - the signature of the
Anglo-Japanese alliance and the outbreak of the Russo-
Japanese war - Komura could well claim to have presided over foreign relations at a vital period. (2)

Komura who came from a family of samurai origins
was, like Aoki and Mutsu who had gone before him, a
believer in a strong foreign policy.   As we shall see,
he was exceptional among foreign ministers who had
been professional diplomats for his contacts among
the military and for the influence which the right
wing had upon his policies.   Like so many in authority
in Japan in the Meiji period, he found it advisable to
be meek towards the West and tough towards Asia.
There is no doubt that the Japanese felt superior to
Asian nations and were, if the need arose, self-confi-
dent enough to take a protective role towards China
and a dominant role in Korea, both of which they discovered to be weak and unstable societies.   The
notion that Japan was submissive towards the West is
perhaps something of a caricature: under Komura,
Japan was not prepared to kowtow to Britain or to
Russia.   She was not yet ready as a nation to challenge
more than one of the European nations at a time but
she was perfectly ready to ignore the advice of
European Powers.   While Komura was expansionist,
aggressive towards weaker Asian countries, it is a mistake to think that he could be spoon-fed by the West.

Part of Komura's tough-mindedness towards Asia
sprang from his association with right-wing groups.
Japan's staggering victory in her China war had brought

to the surface a number of groups with differing
degrees of interest in China.   Among them, the
Genyōsha (Dark Ocean Society) had been founded in
1881 at Fukuoka in Kyushu, relatively soon after the
Korean expedition had been overruled by Iwakura and
his colleagues.   Its members were close to those who
felt disgruntled at the abortive expedition and who
regarded Saigō Takamori as a hero and the symbol of
a departed Japan.   While its avowed intention was to
promote 'kokken' (people's rights), its real interest,
as judged from the record of its activities, was to
agitate for overseas expansion for Japan.   It was the
Genyōsha which had borne responsibility for the attack
on Okuma as foreign minister in 1889.   Its leading
member became Toyama Mitsuru (1855-1944) who was to
be an indefinable force behind the Japanese political
leadership for five decades and had an uncanny ability
to bring his views to the ears of politicians and
officials.

Associated with the Genyōsha was the Kokuryūkai
(Amur River Society) which was founded in 1901.   Its
leader was Uchida Ryōhei, the founder member.   This
group was avowedly anti-Russian and an agency for
encouraging expansion into north-east Asia.   It was
active in Korea and later in Manchuria and China.
With the Genyōsha, it may be said to have controlled,
or boasts in its official history of exercising control over, a group of 'Shina rōnin', supplying them
with funds and acting as a clandestine lobby with
government.   Together they were influential in the
annexation of Korea in 1910 and in moulding Japanese
attitudes towards Manchuria and the Chinese revolution
of 1911-12. (3)

The Foreign Ministry over which Komura presided was
young and ever-changing.   Within the Ministry there
had been an important reform in 1893 which had altered
the structure of departments.   Overseas there were
fourteen legations with a full staff of diplomats and
(at the major postings) military and naval attachés.
At home, the political and commercial affairs bureau
which had hitherto existed as one unit was split into
two departments and continued to function in this way
until greater specialization came to be introduced in
the reforms of 1920.

The most important reform which Komura inherited
was the system of competitive entry to the foreign
service.   This owes its origin to Hara Kei, first a
section head (tsūshō kyokuchō), then vice-minister
under Mutsu, who later became a prominent political

leader and prime minister (1918-21). Hara was the
official largely responsible for drafting the rules
for an examination system which led to recruitment by
examination and the creation of a career service.
Recruits had to pass the special state examination
which was held annually for diplomatic and consular
officers separately. In the 1890s the numbers
appointed from the examinations were very small, from
two to five each year. But the system flourished
and increased vastly after 1905 and again after 1918.
This brought into the service a new type of university
graduate, rather different in character from those
who had gone before. Until then, the diplomats like
Katō Takaaki, Hayashi Gonsuke and Ijūin Hikokichi were
men who, by reason of foreign travel or foreign contacts, had been useful to the government of the day.
Henceforth they would tend to be drawn from Tokyo
Imperial University. This entailed a new system of
preliminary training, partly at Kasumigaseki and
partly at legations abroad. Ironically enough, Hara,
soon after steering through the ordinance, resigned
after fifteen years with the Foreign Ministry. (4)

GENRO AND FOREIGN POLICY

A word should be said about the first Katsura Cabinet
in which Komura became the foreign minister. General
Katsura Tarō (1847-1913) was widely regarded as the
protégé of Genro Yamagata and the Cabinet he formed
on 2 June 1901 came to be described as 'the junior
Yamagata Cabinet'. This was virtually the first
Cabinet which was not presided over by a genro. The
genro were a collection of Elder Statesmen, who,
having been associates of the emperor since the time
of the Restoration, were called on by him for advice
on an ad hoc basis. Down to 1901 it had generally
been possible for the emperor to persuade one of their
number to head a ministry. But two factors had
modified that: one was the emergence of political
parties and the call that the premiership should pass
to party leaders; the other was the advancing age of
the genro. The result was that they no longer had
the ambition or the patience to head the ministries
themselves. While the genro, either individually or
as a body, had no place in the constitution, they had
unquestioned power which derived from the fact that
since 1892 they had advised the emperor on the person
who might be appointed as the next prime minister. By

exploiting this, they gained the privilege of intervening in affairs at moments of emergency and generally
breathing down the necks of incumbents.

Japanese foreign policy-making in the later Meiji
period cannot be understood without reference to the
genro.   Since they included men like Itō, Yamagata,
Inoue and Matsukata, who had a considerable grasp of
foreign affairs, this was one of the spheres in which
they made their influence felt.   For example, over
the British alliance, the negotiations with Russia in
1903 and the Portsmouth peace talks, they were consulted and acted as though they possessed a veto on
policy.   They acted as a review body which was called
on to study major issues before the final decision was
taken.   This injected a 'cooling-down' mechanism into
Japanese policy-making.   But it should not be imagined
that the genro interfered in the minutiae of normal
Foreign Ministry business.   They were, by custom,
shown a selection of telegrams passing between Tokyo
and abroad but only rarely took action on them.

Gradually from 1901 onwards there was a subtle
change in the role of the genro.   They were by this
time operating behind the scenes, but influencing
events through juniors.   They were in the confidence
of the emperor and thus had a power of veto.   There
can be little doubt that their power of intervention
and interference often at a late stage in the policy-
making process was an irritant to members of the
Cabinet, however docile they might be as juniors.
For those, especially at the Foreign Ministry, who
were not docile, genro interference was a distinct
nuisance and an embarrassment in dealings with foreign
governments.   But Komura, on the whole, accepted his
lot of working from within the system and to a remarkable extent got his own way, though even he had his
clashes with the Elder Statesmen.

The existence of the genro also sharpens the
interest of the prime minister in foreign policy.   It
would have been necessary in any case.   But genro
intervention was likely to be directed at him rather
than his junior minister so he was inevitably drawn
in.   The relationship between Prime Minister Katsura
and Komura was a special and enduring one. (5)   In the
China war Katsura had been commander-in-chief of the
third division with which Komura was connected.   In
1896 Katsura became governor-general of Taiwan and
later minister of war under several premiers (1898-
1901).   He disliked party politics though he persevered
with a succession of hostile Diets.   Katsura had no

automatic support from any political party and could
only win their acquiescence by devious tactics during
his three terms as premier (1901-5;   1908-11;   1912-13).

Since prime ministers required to have a strict
oversight of foreign affairs, there were occasions
when divergences arose between the views of the
foreign and prime ministers.   Thus, major disagreements had cropped up between Yamagata and Aoki (1898-
1900) and between their successors, Itō and Katō
(1900-01).   But this was less marked in the long
partnership between Katsura and Komura.   Japanese
Cabinets were still dominated by personalities whether
they were bureaucratic ones like Yamagata's and
Katsura's or political party ones like Itō's and
Saionji's.   The personality of the premier tended to
dwarf that of the foreign minister.   The office of
foreign minister in the later Meiji period almost invariably went to a career diplomat, since the office
came to be treated as a bureaucratic one and, in any
case, Japanese politicians with experience abroad were
comparatively rare.   These career diplomats were
appointed not because they had any political base in
Japan but because they were technically proficient in
the workings of diplomacy.

Despite the superiority of the prime minister's
office, the profession of diplomat did have influence
as well as standing in society.   The fact that the
posts of foreign minister and vice-minister after the
turn of the century went to professional diplomats
meant that in the long term the 'profession' did have
a definite, if indirect, influence on policy.   In
some instances where these officials were content to
be cyphers, their powers were absorbed by others.   In
other cases, like that of Komura, where the minister
was a man of experience and strong opinions, he could
easily influence the course of events.   The officials
at Kasumigaseki were well-informed and of high calibre;
but it is not so easy to judge the effectiveness of
their advice.   Indeed, it is difficult to judge how
far they resorted to the writing of memoranda and
position papers as in Foreign Offices elsewhere.

ANGLO-JAPANESE ALLIANCE

It is conventional to say that there existed in Japan
at the turn of the century a cleavage between two
schools of thought over foreign policy: a pro-Russian
and a pro-British group.   This does not appear to be

a helpful analysis.   It is questionable whether there
was a strong pro-British group in Japan, but it is unlikely that there was a pro-Russian group.   Since
Russia's more active involvement in east Asia with the
building of the trans-Siberian railway and the competition in Korea which followed the Sino-Japanese war,
there were few Japanese who looked to Russia without
rancour and in the spirit of friendship.   There were,
however, some leaders who were sufficiently far-sighted
to see that, if Japan was to remain at peace with
Russia, there would have to be a series of short-term
agreements with her, governing common frontiers and
common interests.

This may be illustrated by disagreements among the
Elder Statesmen.   Although Itō Hirobumi and Yamagata
Aritomo were opponents among the genro, Itō held views
which were on some points complementary to those held
by Yamagata.   General Yamagata, though he was a
military man and deeply suspicious of Russia, had a
very cautious approach to the Powers.   In 1896 he had
used his influence to visit Russia on a special mission
and had there entered into the Yamagata-Lobanov agreement.   His rival, Itō, had tried to go on that mission
but his attempts had been frustrated.   Yamagata continued to play with the idea of a comprehensive
arrangement with the Russians.   In 1900 his minister
in Russia, Komura, had suggested the lines for such a
deal.   In the following year, Yamagata, now out of
office, had come round to favouring a deal with Britain
instead.   This was the time when the sharpest divergence of views occurred.   Itō's conciliatory attitude
is seen when, as prime minister in the spring of 1901,
he tried to hold Japanese opinion in check over
Russian encroachments in Manchuria.   Thus, those who
eventually became identified with the anti-Russian
lobby had earlier been advocates of some rapprochement
with her.

As Komura assumed power in September 1901, there
were differences of view, even if not major ones.   The
Itō group considered that it was in Japan's interest
to recognize Russia's freedom of action in Manchuria
on condition that Russia recognized her supremacy in
Korea.   This was the doctrine of 'exchanging Korea for
Manchuria'.   On the other side were those who may be
described as the Katsura-Komura group who felt that
Russia in Manchuria was inevitably a menace to Korea
and would continue to be so, whatever promises to the
contrary she gave;   and that Manchuria was not unimpor-

tant for Japan's security and she might in the long
term have no alternative but to drive Russia out of
Manchuria.   To this end Japan required the co-operation of powers which shared her interests;   and
Britain was clearly one of these.   Apart from these
groups there were those in Japan who wanted to prevent
the Russian railway systems from running into the
heart of China and to use the Japanese forces which
were in the peak of condition after their various
reorganization schemes had been completed.

   The views of the two main groups were not necessarily contradictory or exclusive.   In some cases the
person espoused one view to the exclusion of the
other;   in others it resolved itself into a question
of priorities.   In any case the Japanese are believers
in consensus and shift their positions continuously;
it is not therefore plausible to think of their
leaders being divided up into rigid pro-Russian or
pro-British groupings. (6)

   The events since the end of the Boxer disturbances
had not helped those who wanted a practical deal with
the Russians.   During the Peking conference (1901)
Russia had acted independently, not wishing to enter
into an international solution of the Boxer problem.
To that end she had tried to conclude with the Chinese
local arrangements for the area where she was most
interested, Manchuria.   This convinced Japan that
Russia was anxious to derive her own special benefit
from the crisis.   There was the suggestion that
Russia, by professions of goodwill toward China and
leniency, would be able to 'feather her own nest'.
It was Japan which stood to lose from Russian acquisitions in north-east Asia.   Not unexpectedly she was
the first to protest openly when Prime Minister Itō
had to make 'diplomatic enquiries' to Russia during
the spring crisis of 1901.   There was no question of
Itō being 'pro-Russian' at that juncture, though he
had also to hold Japanese feelings in check. (7)

   When Komura became foreign minister in September,
he had formed a poor opinion of Russia's conduct in
Manchuria and China.   He had seen her tactics at the
Peking conference and was probably anti-Russian on
that account.   In any case, the options open to Japan
in her foreign relations had unexpectedly been clari-
fied because of London's initiative at the end of
July.   For the first time Japan knew that there was
some possibility of an advantageous agreement being
reached with Britain.   Marquis Itō decided late that
month to go abroad on a convalescent trip which would

take in a personal journey to St Petersburg. Moreover, he had an excuse available to drag a red herring across his trail. In April 1901 Itō Hirobumi as the then prime minister of Japan had been invited, in the company of a large number of world leaders, to receive an honorary degree from Yale University in celebration of its bicentenary. It was not that Itō had any special connection with Yale; it was directed to him because of his office and his status in Japan. Itō replied on 8 April that his official duties prohibited him from being present at the New Haven celebrations. He evidently had second thoughts. On 15 October he was staying at the Hotel Troquois, Buffalo, and wrote that he would not fail to be present for the bicentenary the following week. Thus, the illusion was created that he was travelling for recuperation and academic honours. (8)

Although Komura had not initiated it, he looked sympathetically on the offer of an agreement which came from Britain. The Japanese nation had grown up in the shadow of Europe. In pre-1914 Europe alliances between states were accepted as a matter of course. Although she was 10,000 miles removed from this situation, Japan accepted these premises also. Moreover, by the nature of developments in early Meiji, she was much influenced by happenings in the German empire and especially by the personality of Bismarck. Japanese politicians like Itō Hirobumi, his disciples like Itō Miyoji and diplomats like Aoki Shūzō had fallen under his spell. It was natural for them to feel that Japan was in dangerous isolation and to look for some form of partnership, even if it was as a junior partner. In the 1880s suggestions were discussed in Cabinet for an alliance with France (engaged in war with China), with Britain or with Germany; in some cases feelers were put out to the Powers concerned. As the European Powers were stepping up their expansion in east Asia in the 1890s, the Japanese had even greater feelings of anxiety and many like Aoki favoured a strategy of dividing the colonizing powers by offering to enter into an alliance with one of them. In fact, this did not become a matter of urgency until the vulnerability of European Powers was so strikingly revealed in China during 1900. (9)

One should not date Japan's willingness to enter into alliance with Britain too early. There was much bitter feeling towards London during the Chinese war; and, if London did not join the Dreibund, its advice to Japan to yield did not commend Britain to her.

Mutsu did speculate about the possibilities of a
British alliance but nothing practical was done.
In the five years following, Japan wanted to be
seen and not heard and, if there were evidences of
co-operation, they were limited in scope.

If there were many who thought that Japan should
seek alliances, there was disagreement over who the
ally should be.   The decision in favour of the
British alliance was made in the first week of
December in Tokyo by the inner Cabinet (of which
Komura was a member), by the genrō and by the emperor.
The options open to them were to clinch an agreement
with Britain - the offer on the table - which might
be withdrawn before long; or to delay and negotiate
with Russia on the basis of talks which Itō had been
reporting from St Petersburg.   It was natural to
assume that the bird in the hand was worth two in the
bush.   The emperor overruled Itō's advice and
authorized Komura who had argued strongly in a memorandum for the British agreement to proceed with the
negotiations.   But Japan through Itō also pursued
the bird in the bush a while longer and found it to
be very elusive.   Shortly after the Marquis Itō
appeared in London to set his seal, in a sense, on
the alliance which was signed on 30 January 1902.
In a Japanese sort of way, the two courses had been
reconciled and face had been saved.

Komura was able to claim many practical benefits
for Japan from the alliance.   Russia became more
conciliatory over Manchuria through her agreement on
troop withdrawal (March).   Japan benefited by her
strengthened position in Korea.   Japan's naval
authorities worked out with Britain details of naval
co-operation which enhanced her security in the East.
These gains were by no means one-sidedly favourable
to Britain or to Japan; they were evenly balanced.
At the same time, the signatories entered into the
treaty knowing it to be limited to 'the extreme East'
and wanting it to have little bearing beyond that.
Moreover, there were many points, both of principle
and of detail, especially over the secret naval
clauses, on which the new allies did not see eye to
eye.   It would be a mistake to over-estimate the
impact of the treaty; the world was not thunderstruck;
Japan was proud without being boastful.   Not least
because her leaders had secured from London its
blessing to proceed with talks with Russia on matters
of common interest.   Komura approached these negotiations with a greatly strengthened hand.

PRELUDE TO THE RUSSIAN WAR

The British alliance had in a modest way improved Japan's
standing in Korea.   It guaranteed Korea's independence
and the absence of any aggressive intentions on the part
of the signatories.   Yet Britain recognized Japan's
right to safeguard her interests if threatened by a
disturbance there.   Probably this tilted the balance
in the power struggle which had been going on with
Russia in Korea since 1895.   A British observer reported that the Japanese had 'perceptibly stiffened their
Corean policy which still however proceeds on very
cautious lines where there is any risk of a collision
with Russia'. (10)   It was Japan's immediate object to
consolidate her economic interests rather than push
her political ones.   These lines of development
included: an issue of bank-notes by the Dai-ichi Bank;
extension of branches by the Bank of Japan;   and construction of railway lines, especially the Seoul-Fusan
and Seoul-Uiju lines.   It also entailed the obstruction of Russian enterprises in Korea and undertakings
based on French finance.
   The alliance also had after-effects in Manchuria.
Russia offered China proposals for evacuation of her
troops and the Japanese urged Peking to sign the
Manchurian convention without delay.   On 8 April 1902
an agreement was signed providing for the scaled withdrawal of Russian troops from various sectors of
Manchuria.   Evacuation was to be completed in three
six-month phases;   but the first withdrawal which took
place by 8 October 1902 was the only one to be properly
accomplished. (11)   When March 1903 came and went
without further withdrawals, the Japanese felt fortified
to protest to the Russians.   This represented a coming
of age for Japan which had kept quiet in the past.
   On 21 April 1903 the Murinan conference took place
between Itō and Yamagata, representing the senior
genrō, and Katsura and Komura, representing the Cabinet.
It was agreed that Japan should protest to St Petersburg;   but she should, in order to get Russia's
recognition of her superior rights in Korea, be ready
to recognize Russia's superior rights in Manchuria.
This was the policy which became known as 'Man-Kan
kōkan' which we have already seen to have been advocated
by Komura during his period as minister to St Petersburg in 1900 and was now reiterated by him (Document
10).   The proposals went through the typical procedure
for a major policy step - Cabinet, imperial conference,
Cabinet resignation, restoration of Katsura - and the

note was delivered on 12 August.   When the Russian
reply was received on 5 October, Japan found that
Russia would recognize her position south of the 39th
parallel provided that the area north of it was made
into a neutral zone, while Manchuria was to be regarded
as outside Japan's sphere of interest and the evacuation of Russia's occupying force was not guaranteed.
There followed five conferences in Tokyo before Japan's
reply, declaring the Russian counterproposals to be
unsatisfactory, was transmitted on 30 October.   Japan
agreed to set up a 50-kilometre buffer zone on Korea's
northern frontier where troops would not be sent;
Japan would recognize Russia's commercial rights in
Manchuria providing her own treaty rights were assured.
In her reply on 11 December, Russia would not yield
over her privileged position in Manchuria or Korea.

There was a broad-based enthusiasm for war which
only the genrō seemed anxious to dampen.   The issue of
war and peace was one where the genrō had to be consulted.   Itō and Yamagata, for once united, together
with General Oyama Iwao, chief of the general staff,
wished to continue with negotiations in a conciliatory
spirit.   With Yamagata and Oyama anxious to press
ahead with negotiations and military preparedness
simultaneously, it was difficult for senior officers to
dissent.   But lower down opinion was different;   and
the task of the pro-war faction was to rally support.
This led to the creation of another of the influential
pressure groups, the Kogetsukai, an unholy alliance of
members of the army and navy general staffs and the
Foreign Ministry, which formed itself into a dining
club at the Kogetsu restaurant.   The group aimed at
convincing decision-makers by argument.   It felt that
Japan had taken a weak stance since 1895 and that the
Russian negotiations fell in the same mould and did
not serve Japan's true interest which was speed.   With
the genro and Navy Minister Yamamoto Gombei they
carried no weight.   With Komura who was a member, they
appear to have had some effect: several of his section
chiefs, including Yamaza Enjirō, Ishii Kikujirō and
Honda Kumatarō, were members of the dining club. (12)
Komura - and also Katsura - had little confidence in a
favourable outcome to the negotiations and urged that
Japan should be ready for the fray rather than give in
on her basic demands.   In short, it was the genro who
acted for caution and peace, against the juniors who
were not prepared to be fobbed off and insisted on
Japan's presenting a hard line.

At a genro conference on 16 December, Komura carried

the day with a proposal that Russia should have 'second
thoughts' and discuss Manchuria again.   This was
again the tough line which St Petersburg was unlikely
to accept.   Fresh proposals in the form of an ultimatum were passed to Russia on 21 December.   The genro
still tried to keep a hand in the process but here-
after it was increasingly hard because there had been
so little sign of movement and conciliation on the
part of the Russians.   Professor Okamoto thinks that
there was little prospect of Russia's acceptance and
concludes that the 'decision-makers regarded the
negotiations more as a means to earn time for military
preparations than as serious efforts for a peaceful
solution.' (13)

   It would appear that Komura, though a patient and
diligent negotiator and a professional diplomat in the
normal course, was one of the main promoters of the
hard line.   Had Russia shown any spark of compromise,
Komura's task would have been more difficult.   But
she did not;   and Komura's idée fixe of war with Russia
was achieved.   Komura had, of course, been in the
front line of Russia's intrigues in north-east Asia
for a decade.   He probably accepted, as did many
Japanese, that a day of reckoning, if not of revenge,
would come.   He was probably genuine in his disinterest
in Manchuria at this stage;   but he certainly wanted
to expand Japan's share in Korea.   It was Russia
which was defending the status quo;   and Japan which
was seeking to overturn it.

   Itō and Yamagata reluctantly gave their permission
for war preparations on 24 December.   The weeks that
followed saw all manner of provisional plans for the
war effort.   An imperial conference, convened on 12
January 1904, held that the Russian replies were again
unsatisfactory and not a basis for negotiation.   Yet
it offered a slight restatement of its position 'in a
spirit of conciliation';   it presented what could only
be a second ultimatum.   The Russians withheld their
reply and, despite Japan's many pleas for their
views, it could only be assumed that they, like the
Japanese, were making last-minute preparations for war.
By this time, the reluctant Itō had accepted that war
was inevitable.   Yet all around opinion was deeply
pessimistic that Japan's capacity for war was so
inferior to Russia's, financially, militarily and
navally.   But there was no going back on the negotiations.   As in 1941, the strike could not be delayed;
and it was vital to make the first strike.

THE PORTSMOUTH PEACE

Unquestionably the high point of Komura's career was
as delegate to the peace conference at Portsmouth,
New Hampshire.   On 30 May 1905, after winning the
naval battle of the Japan Sea, the Tokyo Cabinet
asked President Theodore Roosevelt for his good
offices in bringing together the belligerents for
direct discussions while passing off the suggestion
as his own initiative.   The Japanese were clear that
they sought the president's good offices and not his
mediation and Roosevelt seems to have accepted this.
Yet the whole incident suggested that it was Japan's
initiative.

When both powers accepted Roosevelt's good offices,
Japan proceeded to appoint Komura and her minister
to Washington, Takahira, as delegates to the peace
conference to be held at Portsmouth Navy Yard.
They were presented with a brief which was only
agreed after several meetings of the Cabinet and
genro and after receiving the final approval of the
emperor on 5 July.   This classified Japan's demands
roughly as those relating to Korea and Manchuria as
'absolutely essential';   those relating to an indemnity and Sakhalin as 'comparatively essential';   and
several additional demands.   If the 'absolutely
essential' conditions were conceded, Komura was given
the discretion to dispose of the remaining demands
including those dealing with the indemnity and
Sakhalin.   Above all else, Komura was instructed to
make peace.

Some ministers had not complete confidence in
Komura, who was not the first choice for the mission.
The navy minister, Admiral Yamamoto Gombei, asked
that he should be kept under strict control from
Tokyo.   His instructions were, therefore, drafted
so that he should report in detail from time to time
about the progress of the talks.   If they proved to
be unfruitful, he was to cable immediately and to
await a reply from Tokyo before breaking off negotiations.   Evidently the leaders thought that, even
though Komura was experienced enough for the task, he
required to be held in check because of the hard line
he would take, if left to himself.

The first formal meeting of the two delegations was
held at Portsmouth on 10 August.   After a week, deadlock set in when the Russian delegate, Count Witte,
declined to pay any indemnity and was non-committal
over the cession of Sakhalin to Japan.   It will be

observed that Japan's basic demands had by this stage
been met and discussion centred upon demands which
Tokyo had not defined as 'absolutely essential' but
had left to Komura's discretion.   Komura, after the
meeting on 18 August, drew up a compromise plan which
had received the general approval of the home government.   The essence of these proposals was that
Sakhalin should be divided along the 50th parallel;
that Russia should pay Japan ¥ 1,200,000,000 as compensation for the return of the northern part of the
island;   and that, if this was agreed, Japan would
withdraw her demand for reimbursement of war expenses.
Komura sent someone to visit Roosevelt at Oyster Bay
on 21 August to lay this plan before him and obtained
his support.

Imagine the horror of the Japanese when they, like
the Russians, received from the president a letter
calling for caution and restraint.   The essence of
this message was that Japan's 'willingness to retrocede the northern half of Sakhalin gives a chance to
get some money in addition to that which is justly due
for the Russian prisoners, but I do not think that
anything like the amount advanced by Japan as what
she wants - that is six hundred millions [dollars] -
should be asked or could possibly be obtained.'   He
strongly advised Japan not to continue the fight for
a money indemnity.   Komura was asked to cable his
government with all speed and the message reached
Tokyo on 24 August.   Komura was deeply disappointed
with the change in the president's attitude and placed
before him a number of cogent counter-arguments.   But
Roosevelt suggested that it was to Japan's interest
to make peace: 'Remember', he wrote, 'I do not speak
of continuing the war rather than give up Sakhalin,
which I think would be right, but of continuing the
war in order to get a great sum of money from Russia.'
This subtle presidential pressure was transmitted
through Portsmouth to Tokyo.   In doing so, Komura
commented that 'Roosevelt's second letter is only an
enlargement of the first without any new points in
it.   It looks as though he is thinking of our taking
the whole of Sakhalin, while rejecting an indemnity.
I would like you to tell him this differs from Japan's
compromise plan in which he concurred and ask him for
his views on what compensation Japan could receive for
its expenditure on supplies to prisoners'.   Despite
the president's arguments, Komura was still hankering
after some monetary compensation from Russia.
The Imperial Conference agreed that Japan's

compromise plan should be upheld but that she should
be ready to reduce the indemnity. At the secret
session at Portsmouth on 26 August the Russian delegates held out little hope of the compromise being
accepted. Komura reported that the Russians were
intractable and, although he was at odds with his
home government, recommended that Japan should draw
up a declaration which could be made public if the
talks broke down, placing the blame for continuing
the war firmly on Russia and showing that Japan had
been ready to make concessions. He further advised
that he should leave Portsmouth and go to New York
to await developments (Document 11). In Tokyo
Katsura as acting foreign minister replied that
Japan's final decision would take time. There is
an important eye-witness account of the events which
followed. Shidehara Kijurō, acting head of the
telegraphic section at the Foreign Ministry, records
that

> Itō as president of the Privy Council had previously
> invited Prime Minister Katsura, Army Minister
> Terauchi, Navy Minister Yamamoto and Deputy Foreign
> Minister Chinda to his temporary residence Reinan-
> zaka at Akasaka. I attended to act as secretary.
> The conference lasted from 11 p.m. till 2 a.m.
> It was unanimously agreed to withdraw Japan's
> demand for an indemnity and press the demand for
> Sakhalin relentlessly in view of the fact that her
> armies had occupied the island. I drafted a
> telegram to Komura following Itō's directions.
> Itō read it, made a few changes and obtained the
> approval of the others. I immediately returned to
> my ministry with the draft and gave instructions
> for a few fair copies to be made. (14)

Shidehara took the copies to Itō's house at dawn in
preparation for the Imperial Conference meeting and
found that Itō had been up most of the night examining
documents. At a larger meeting of the Cabinet and
genrō, the two demands were both withdrawn. The
Imperial Conference which followed wanted peace quickly
(Document 12). Komura was dismayed to receive these
instructions which were contrary to his own recommendations.

After a brief unofficial meeting, Komura opened the
final session on 29 August by asking whether the
Russians were agreeable to Japan's compromise plan.
Witte handed over a note stating that Russia agreed to
cede to Japan the southern part of Sakhalin on condition that the northern part remained in the possession

of Russia without any monetary compensation.   Komura
then followed his instructions by offering to forego
all reimbursement of war expenses, provided that
Russia accepted as a fait accompli Japan's occupation
of the whole of Sakhalin.   It will be recalled that
the Japanese armies had taken the surrender of the
Russian commander in Sakhalin and his armies.   The
island was in their possession and control as an
accomplished fact.   Witte replied that he could not
go beyond the note presented.   Komura then accepted
the offer of southern Sakhalin provided that the
demarcation line should follow the 50th parallel.
On this basis, the armistice was signed on 1 September
and the peace treaty was concluded four days later.
There is really only a superficial resemblance between
the settlement achieved and that which Komura wanted.
The treaty certainly involved the abandonment by Japan
of an indemnity and to this extent it was much less
than Komura hoped for.   But there was also divergence
between his views and those of Tokyo over Sakhalin.

Clearly Japan's climb-down was made at the Tokyo
end.   Komura and Takahira were men under instructions.
They had been given discretion to decide certain of
the terms but had clear instructions to refer the
final decision to Tokyo.   When they did so, it was
discovered that they were taking a stronger line than
were their superiors.   They were ready to let the
peace talks be broken off rather than concede;   Tokyo
was not.   It may be that the Tokyo authorities
should be blamed for their sheer indecisiveness, a
common feature of late Meiji statesmanship - and for
their delay in stepping in.   But these were largely
due to the idiosyncrasies of the Cabinet system
whereby the genrō stepped in at the last moment to
advise on all major policy decisions.   It was their
intervention which strengthened the hands of those
wanting to conclude peace, even in the face of
Komura's recommendation to end the talks.   Komura
was so convinced of the need for a strong line that he
had by 28 August made preparations for leaving Portsmouth: he had packed his bags and given a substantial
donation to local charities.   But, when he received
Tokyo's final instructions, he accepted them stoically
with the comment: 'I thought it might come to this.'
This was in marked contrast to the sentiments of other
Japanese at Portsmouth who thought they had been let
down by Tokyo.   It only confirmed where the ultimate
power lay.

What evidence is there for Roosevelt's influence on

the Japanese at Portsmouth and Tokyo?   As might be
expected from Komura's attitude, he was not much
under the spell of Roosevelt.   There is no hint in
any of his actions that he was guided by Roosevelt's
advice.   But he fully appreciated the value of the
president's support and genuinely tried to keep him
informed of the Japanese standpoint and to influence
him in favour of Japan.

The leaking of the Portsmouth terms caused a
sensation in Japan.   The information which had been
fed to the public by the Press had shown how successfully the war had gone for Japan.   Public opinion had
concluded that her gains would be proportional to
her victories.   Censorship throughout the war had
left the public unaware of the precarious position
of the Japanese armies in the summer of 1905, which
the generals, the genro and the Cabinet knew well.
(In parenthesis it may be said that Komura in Portsmouth was not well informed of the army's assessment
of the position and made serious miscalculations.)
The disclosure of the terms was met with complete
incredulity and with gasps of humiliation.   This
disillusion led to the Hibiya Park riots of 5 September and to similar movements in other cities in which
a united call was made for the emperor to cancel the
peace treaty and not to ratify it.   The government
was ill-prepared for this expression of a popular
will over foreign policy - a right-wing, nationalistic
voice.   A similar mood had caused trouble for Itō
and Mutsu in 1895; but it had been less violent and
less serious.   In 1905 it was anti-government in
tone though it also had anti-American undercurrents
(as some tried to fasten the blame for the humiliating
peace on President Roosevelt). (15)   The Katsura
Cabinet declared martial law and stability was quickly
restored.   But there was still bamboozlement.

Much of the criticism which poured out in the newspapers was directed personally at Komura.   There was
irony here because Komura was a reluctant agent in
the peace that he had signed.   He had never suspected
that Japan's demands of June in the framing of which
he had played a major part would not be achieved. (16)
He, like many another ill-informed person in Tokyo,
hoped that the Cabinet would call off the negotiations
and return to the battlefield.   Unjust though it was,
he was criticized for his ineptness and lack of
diplomatic skill: why was someone so junior sent for
such a major assignment? asked some.   The answer was
simple enough for those in the know: leaders of

greater seniority foresaw these disappointments for
Japan at the peace conference and the explosive consequences this might have on a volatile public.
Only Komura had been ready to attend.   Others condemned his inaccessibility to the Press.   In fact,
he was remarkably accessible to Japanese and British
newspapermen.   In general, it was not realized that
he was a man acting under instructions and that the
unpopular decision was that of the genro and Cabinet.

Komura slipped back into Japan, disappointed and
in fear of his life.   All publicity regarding his
return was avoided;   and he was given special security
guards attached to his person.   He took up the reins
of office as foreign minister again on 18 October.
The Portsmouth treaty had been ratified by Japan and
published two days earlier.   In order to put the
public in a more favourable spirit, the second Anglo-
Japanese alliance which had been signed in secrecy in
August was published belatedly;   but it was not enough
to restore the Katsura ministry to favour.   It readily
admitted that its days were numbered.   In November
Komura was able to complete the peace treaty by
exchanging ratifications with Russia without any of
the difficulties which he had expected.   He also
embarked on negotiations with China, whose approval
was sought for some of the terms of the Russo-Japanese
treaty bearing on Manchuria.   In January 1906 the
Cabinet finally demitted office in some measure of
disgrace, despite its achievements in leading Japan to
victory in war and concluding a treaty which, if it
can be attacked from Japan's point of view, can also
be stoutly defended because of the benefits it conferred on Japan on the continent of Asia. (17)

SECOND TERM AT KASUMIGASEKI

General Katsura was recalled to form a ministry in
July 1908.   He summoned Komura to act again as his
foreign minister.   Komura had gone to London where
for two years (1906-8) he had been an eminent, but not
very sociable, ambassador.   His personality was
reserved;   and his last year there was dogged by ill-
health.   His continued illnesses lent the end of his
career an air of anti-climax.

His second term at Kasumigaseki lasted three years
and was marred by long absences.   He relied greatly
on his vice-minister, Ishii Kikujirō, to receive
foreign diplomats and conduct other official business.

His biography records that the subjects which he handled
in his second term do not compare in importance with
those of his first. (18)   His earlier period had been
one of great national emergency, in which policies were
vital and leadership was at a premium.   Komura had
supplied that leadership; and it had exhausted him.
From 1908 onwards there were nagging diplomatic
incidents like the accomplishment of tariff autonomy
(already discussed) but the survival of the nation was
not at stake and did not hang on the decisions taken.

There is a sense, too, in which it was a different
country to which he returned.   This point is illustrated by the recollections of a foreign diplomat who
writes of Japan after 1905 that

Japanese public opinion was viewing the nation not
only, and not even primarily, as a power but as an
Asian imperialist in a world dominated by white
nations.   Foreign relations were seen as much more
than diplomatic relations.   The immigration
question then was an inevitable aspect of Japan's
relations with the Western powers. (19)

There is surely justice in the remark that Japan's
victory over Russia had convinced her that she had
become a Pacific power and also a major imperial
country.   She consciously laid claim to the title of
the Empire of Japan and many of her citizens wanted
their country to become the leader of Asia and the
opponent of racialism.

Komura returned to a country which had acquired
status and respect.   Status, because in the aftermath
of the war, the standing of Japan's legations abroad
was increased to that of embassies.   These symbolic
gestures were made in Britain, the United States,
Germany, France, Italy, (20) Austria and finally, in
May 1908, Russia herself.   Japan's victory had, moreover, secured her recognition as a major World Power.
The Portsmouth settlement (while its benefits for
Japan had been grossly underrated by the anti-government party in 1905) did not confer lavish benefits.
But, combined with the renewal of the British alliance
and the conclusion of Taft-Katsura agreement, it helped
towards the creation of permanent peace in the area.
Much depended on the capacity of Russia for revenge;
and Komura inherited a happier relationship with her
than he had earlier left: Russia had entered into an
agreement in 1907, which was to be renewed in 1910 by
Komura.

The largest cloud on the Pacific horizon was American
animosity.   The United States attracted a great deal

of attention because of the immigration issue, the
growth (real or suspected) of naval rivalry, and
American opposition to Japan's continental expansion.
These topics have been discussed in depth in a number
of excellent studies. (21)   It will suffice to set
them in the perspective of Komura's second term.   The
Tokyo government of the day, sitting between the
criticisms of the United States and the propaganda of
their own expansionists, sought to temporize by concluding the Gentlemen's agreement of 1907 but the
Americans soon notified that the formula was unsatisfactory.   When Komura took over in August 1908, he
steered the Cabinet toward a further compromise which
resulted in the Root-Takahira agreement of 30 November.
This was a set of notes laying down practical ways of
restricting the emigration of Japanese labourers
(Document 13).

In the light of this American hostility, Komura
called on the Cabinet to define its position over
Manchuria.   One of the great controversies over the
Russo-Japanese war has been whether Japan made war
because of Manchuria and the commercial opportunities
which she sought there.   A study of the six-months'
negotiations suggests that in 1903-4 Japan was still
preoccupied with Korea and only concerned secondarily
with treaty rights in Manchuria.   In the postwar
period, because of her conquests in south Manchuria,
Japan's perspective had changed.   There were Japanese
leaders, of whom Komura was among the most prominent,
who wanted to promote their country's interests by
consolidation in that area.   But it involved the
supply of funds on a scale which Japan, deprived of an
indemnity, did not possess.

This raised delicate financial problems for the
Cabinet in 1905.   The American financier, Edward H.
Harriman, on a visit to Japan had impressed the
finance minister, Inoue Junnosuke, and Katsura, the
prime minister, with his scheme to purchase from the
Japanese the south Manchurian railway (part of the
Chinese Eastern railway).   It would restore the railway zone by joint Japanese-American control and develop
it as an asset in any conceivable war of revenge waged
by the Russians.   This was seemingly an opportunity
not to be missed.   But Komura, on return from Portsmouth in none too good a mood, himself succeeded in
overturning the provisional agreement which had been
reached on the grounds that it would throw away Japan's
major gain in the Portsmouth settlement and that it
was much too pessimistic to believe that Japan could

not develop the railway with funds which she herself
could raise.   But it does suggest that it was Komura,
rather than Katsura and his colleagues, who had a
real notion of Japan's future role on the continent
and the determination to expand her rights and monopolistic interests there.

Within a month of returning to Tokyo in 1908,
Komura tried to focus the attention of the Cabinet on
Manchuria.   This issue was causing dissension among
Japanese between civilians and the army and abroad
between foreigners advocating the Open Door in Manchuria
and Japanese advocating monopoly there.   He, therefore, drew up a comprehensive statement of Japan's
foreign policy as he saw it and had it endorsed by the
Cabinet at its meeting on 25 September. (22)   The nub
of his argument was that

> while it is inevitable that Japan's foreign trade
> should increasingly compete with that of other
> countries as it develops, Japan should take care
> not to allow trade rivalry to disturb political
> relationships with other countries.   In particular,
> Japan should be scrupulous to use fair trading
> practices and to avoid underhand methods and
> improper tactics (Document 13).

Only in this way could Japan enjoy friendly relations
with China and trading countries like Britain.   But
even more important, it was vital not to antagonize
the United States, with which most of Japan's trade
was conducted, either by her China policy or by provocative immigration incidents.   While this is only a
small fraction of a long and closely argued memorandum,
it illustrates the priority which Komura intended to
observe while he was in office.   Of course, these
Cabinet declarations of policy tended to be anodyne
documents which concealed as much as they revealed.
And there was no guarantee that these guidelines were
communicated to the man on the frontier or observed by
him.   But the nature of the debate and the formal
decision are not without interest.

However friendly Komura professed to be towards
China, the Chinese could hardly be expected to respond
so amiably.   Since they could not rival Japan in arms,
they could only challenge Japan by having recourse to
commercial tactics, that is, by a sort of non-violent
opposition to the (rather creaking) South Manchurian
railway.   In this the Chinese politicians had the
help of a group of American businessmen and financiers.
Over the Hsimintun-Fakumen line there was a strong
American initiative to combine Chinese resources,

American capital and British technical know-how.
Needless to say, it ran into bitter opposition from
Japan which claimed that it was in contravention of
undertakings the Chinese had given Komura in Peking
in December 1905.   The scheme collapsed, but not the
ideas underlying it.   On 6 November 1909 Secretary
of State Knox proposed the neutralization or inter-
nationalization of railways in Manchuria.   The
proposal was made in total disregard of the legitimate
interests of both the powers which considered that
they had spheres of influence in Manchuria - Russia in
the north and Japan in the south.   Once again the
proposal attracted little international support.
Finally, on 18 December the State Department presented
to Japan its plan for securing a railway lease for the
Chinchow-Aigun line in Manchuria, to be confined to
Britain and the United States.   The British government
announced that it would remain a spectator over such a
proposal which was bound to provoke the opposition of
Japan and Russia.   Hence the third American initiative
proved unfruitful.   Indeed, it produced, from the
American standpoint, bitter fruit: consultations
immediately took place between Russia and Japan;   and
a course of common action was mapped out.   On 21
January 1910 the two countries rejected the neutralization scheme and decided to warn China not to proceed
with the Chinchow project.   In the spring the two
countries began to exchange ideas for a closer agreement over Manchuria, which was eventually signed in
July.

Count Komura served till August 1911, renewing the
British alliance yet again in July.   Within three
months of his retirement, he was dead.   For long
Komura was hailed as Japan's most skilful foreign
minister.   He seemed to have provided adeptly for his
country - as Mutsu had done before - in the diplomacy
of a country at war, that is, in the run-up to war, in
the diplomacy of the war years and, despite some disappointments, in the postwar settlement.   This did
not mean that he was universally successful;   over the
Portsmouth settlement, he was criticized by a generation as bitterly as the Germans criticized their
peacemakers at Versailles.   There was a Bismarckian
quality about him: he had cool nerves but was not
slow to resort to war in the last resort. (23)   Under
his administration Japan's diplomacy gained ground, the
country developed and prospered.   Of course, these
judgments have tarnished in the course of time;   and
the tactics of a Komura or a Mutsu are less pleasing to

the present generation.   Like Bismarck he could be
callous and calculating and devious.

  Komura the man is elusive.   Whereas Mutsu took up
the pen and wrote extensive memoirs and other writings,
Komura left no writings and no archives.   This
reflected his character: he was serious-minded and
reticent; he refused to court popular favour by
artificial politeness.   As a bureaucrat he did not
have to be popular and he avoided being so to his
countrymen.   At Portsmouth and elsewhere he did not
cultivate the foreign Press.   Perhaps inadvertently
he gave the impression of being haughty and self-
important; but this may only have been the consequence
of his shyness.   Despite his years at the Harvard Law
School and his American roots, he had, we are told, a
warm regard for England and English institutions.
The two books which he was reading during his last
illness and were found at his bedside after his death
on 26 November 1911 were: Tennyson and the 'Oxford
Book of English Verse'. (24]   They were buried with
him.

Chapter 5

The Katō Period, 1911-15

Katō Takaaki (1860-1926) was already a power in the land
while Komura was foreign minister. (1)   He had been
foreign minister in 1900-1 as the successor to Aoki and
served for an even shorter period of two months in 1906
resigning because he disapproved of the army's policies
in Manchuria.   In retirement he returned to act as
proprietor (shachō) of the 'Nichi-Nichi' newspaper, of
which more anon.   Rather unexpectedly he was appointed
by Komura as his ambassador in London and presided over
the embassy there from August 1908 until December 1912,
including a period of furlough.   He was then recalled
to Tokyo by Katsura with the invitation to become his
foreign minister; but the scheme went wrong for no
sooner had he returned to the capital than the Katsura
ministry had to resign because of trouble in the Diet.
Katō had the opportunity to stay on in Kasumigaseki
but declined.   As in the rest of his career, he never
seems to have wanted office merely for the sake of
power or the fulfilment of his ambitions.   He, therefore, took a period of rest in order to equip himself
for his entry into party politics and to make a visit
to China.   In April 1914 he was recalled to the
Foreign Ministry under the premiership of Okuma
Shigenobu. (2)   He took advantage of the lethargy of
the prime minister to control rigorously Japan's policy
towards the First World War and towards China.   His
decisions at that period left the Japanese a large
legacy which gave a great significance to his years of
office.   It is his last two periods as foreign minister
rather than the earlier two periods which come under
scrutiny here.
    Katō belonged to the pre-examination group of
Japanese career diplomats and had had a varied experience abroad in the Meiji period.   He was too young to

be involved in the Restoration but he had gone overseas
as a journalist and businessman.   As a man of talent
and ambition, he came to be attracted by the prospects
of the foreign service.   In particular, he came to
know that independent spirit, Mutsu.   He therefore
joined the Foreign Ministry and served as secretary to
Okuma during his period as foreign minister (1888-9).
He went to London as minister at a low point in Anglo-
Japanese relations during the war with China and, by
using the Press and cultivating British opinion, he
improved Japan's image greatly.   From this time he
became specially associated with the cause of friendship
with Britain and of the Anglo-Japanese alliance (1902-
23).   He himself claimed to be the originator of the
alliance through his conversations with Joseph
Chamberlain in 1898 and his actions as foreign minister
in 1901. (3)   Be that as it may, he remained to the
end of his days a symbol of Japan's involvement with
the powers and of her search for international status.

Katō's independence of spirit was almost legendary.
As ambassador, he often felt himself to be equal in
stature with those in Tokyo and acted in ways which
were diplomatically indiscreet.   In this he closely
resembled Aoki Shūzō.   He did not hesitate to dispute
his instructions, if he disagreed with them.   His four
years at the London embassy contained many disagreements
between him and the Foreign Ministry.   Katō was later
to become a very opinionated member of a Cabinet and
fought hard for his views to be adopted.   If they were
not, he was quick to resign.   Partly he had independent means and partly he married one of the daughters
of the Iwasaki family which brought him close to the
Mitsubishi fortunes.   Being an independent agent, he
had little concern for time-serving.   As a consequence
he was short-tempered and did not suffer fools gladly.

One factor in Katō's independence of spirit lay in
his newspaper connections.   As a diplomat, Katō had,
like his contemporaries, Aoki and Hayashi Tadasu,
'played' the Press - a not uncommon practice for
bureaucrats in the Meiji period.   This involved feeding
the newspapers with articles, sometimes anonymous, sometimes under pseudonyms, which advocated a certain line
of policy.   In appropriate cases, this was done not
only to Japanese papers but also to foreign papers.
It will be clear from the events of 1895 and 1905 that
the Press, if it moved in an anti-government direction,
could be a dangerous irritant to the Cabinet of the
day.   It was, therefore, necessary for ministers to
placate and influence the Press and its proprietors.

After Katō resigned as foreign minister in 1901, he worked hard to attain the goal of an anti-Russian agreement with Britain and present the public with the case for the alliance.   In October 1904 he became proprietor of the 'Tokyo Nichi-Nichi' newspaper, a leading daily.   From that point on, Katō became more critical of the Katsura-Komura ministry.   People began to talk of 'Komura diplomacy' as being separate and distinct from 'Katō diplomacy'.   Although one was in office and the other had no official function, they came to be regarded as rivals.   This hostility came to the boil with Komura's actions at the Portsmouth conference, even though, as we have shown, he was completely authorized in the last stages to accept a 'second-best' peace treaty.   Here Katō's dilemma was that he had been called in by Premier Katsura and expressed his approval of the government line but that, on the other hand, there was a large outcry of popular annoyance at the terms of the peace, which Katō could not ignore, if he were to sell his newspapers.   In the event, the 'Nichi-Nichi' seemed to side with the popular party and ride on the crest of the anti-government agitation. (4)

The other special characteristic of Katō's power was his party political connections.   Since 1890 the foreign ministers had (with the sole exception of Okuma) been professional diplomats, recalled from their posts to head the ministry.   In many cases they were well qualified to do so because of previous service as vice-minister.   Generally they were subservient to the Cabinet, though in those of Mutsu and Aoki that was far from being the case.   When Katō returned from London in 1913 to become Katsura's foreign minister, he associated himself with the prime minister's newly-formed party, the Dōshikai.   When Prince Katsura died of cancer on 10 October 1913, the presidency of the Dōshikai was offered to Katō who, despite his inexperience of party matters and the compromises which it necessitated, accepted the office.   In this, he followed the path of another ambitious ex-diplomat, Hara Kei.   In accepting, Katō was taking a grave gamble: he might not have the right temperament for the job and might not succeed in attaining the summit of his political ambitions.   But he took the risk and showed courage and tenacity.   When Okuma was forming his Cabinet in April 1914, Katō was invited to bring his party into coalition.   He agreed to do so, providing he was offered the portfolio of foreign affairs.   When this was accepted, he carried some party weight into the

Foreign Ministry, which probably enjoyed more influence in policy-making than under any previous foreign minister.   Katō had other attributes: he was a Westernized Japanese who spoke good English; a clear thinker with a direct manner.   But he was inclined to be gruff.   As one observer summed it up, 'he is very different from his chief, Count Okuma, who never fails to please anybody who comes in touch with him.' (5)

AUTONOMY OF THE FOREIGN MINISTRY

Let it be remembered that the Foreign Ministry was still a developing institution.   It had a comparatively small staff and occupied a small two-storeyed building until it was burnt in the Great Kantō earthquake of 1923.   It still operated on an informal and personal basis. Thus, there is the authenticated story of the prime minister going down from his residence to play a game of billiards with junior officials at the British embassy.   The British ambassador, calling in to speak to Katsura at a crucial point in the Portsmouth talks, was surprised to find that the acting foreign minister produced a large bundle of telegrams, some 150 in number, which were wrapped up in a furoshiki for security.   It was the bundle of telegrams from the delegates at Portsmouth and was produced at 4-5 separate meetings. (6)   The picture of Katsura rummaging through these telegrams reminds us that the Foreign Ministry still had much to learn of Western standards of organ- ization.   Although there was much protocol and form- ality, there was also much rough-and-ready informality.
     It was in these circumstances that genro inter- ference - or control - operated.   It impaired the speedy development of the Gaimushō.   Naturally not everyone in the Cabinets of the time was prepared to accept this outside interference.   Those who had journeyed and studied abroad knew that this was a primitive and unconstitutional arrangement.   Moreover the genro were becoming old and were tending to become more domineering after they had retired from the front of the stage and began to operate behind the scenes. It was, however, dangerous to have a brush with the genro.   They had the power to penalize those who did not conform.   One significant victim was Hayashi Tadasu, the foreign minister (1906-8), who crossed the genro, especially Yamagata, and suffered from this hostility for the rest of his career and was hardly given the financial rewards which he expected. (7)

The establishment figure who most clashed with the genrō was Katō. In the name of Foreign Ministry autonomy, he stood out at various points in his career against the interference in foreign affairs of the genro and the military oligarchy. When he was invited to join the Cabinet in 1900, he accepted on certain conditions which were granted: that senior officials of the ministry should not be changed on each occasion there was a change of foreign minister and that all diplomatic business with officials of foreign states should be conducted through him. (8) Having gained more authority than most of his predecessors, he proceeded to exploit it by withholding papers normally circulated to the genro. He became unpopular with the genro and Yamagata in particular.

A decade later Katō knew that genro power was already on the wane. When he was asked to be foreign minister for the third time in January 1913, Katō insisted on receiving assurances from General Katsura that the practice of two-tier diplomacy (genro and Cabinet) should be abolished and that Katsura would keep the military party in order if it disagreed with Katō's foreign-policy objectives. In short, he sought complete responsibility for the foreign minister and Kasumigaseki. (9) This could only make the genrō suspicious and critical of any of his shortcomings. The result was that Katō was associated with several feuds: the first with the genro and Yamagata, which worsened when Katō took over the leadership of a political party and was to prevent him from becoming prime minister until after Yamagata's death; the second, within the Foreign Ministry, with Komura which was claimed to be a clash of policies but seems to have been much more a clash of personality or philosophy. The existence of these feuds - from which Katō ultimately emerged triumphant in both cases - attests to his strong will. There were few Meiji or Taishō statesmen - even Hara - who were prepared to take on the genro and wage a campaign against them.

At other times in his career, Katō had also come up against another threat to Foreign Ministry autonomy which was still on a minor scale but was gradually to assume greater significance - military interference. In the aftermath of the Russo-Japanese war, the Japanese army of occupation in Manchuria had no wish to be subject to the supervision of the Gaimushō which it regarded as too much under the hostile influence of foreign governments. By devising a body called the Manshū Kyōgikai, the army hoped to continue, if not

perpetuate, military rule in the territory.   The
Kyōgikai was a blatant attempt at cutting out the
Foreign Ministry from the decision-making process.
Katō, finding it impossible to get his way, offered
his resignation in 1906, allegedly over railway
nationalization, which may have been a genuine consideration but was probably secondary. (10)   His
successor, Hayashi, also fought the Kyōgikai which he
claimed to be a challenge to the proper system of
operating through consuls.   Hayashi stuck out for
his convictions, made himself unpopular with the army
and was never forgiven by the genro. (11)   But the
concept of military government was successfully beaten.
The army continued to be powerful in Manchuria; and
the South Manchurian Railway company was a force to
be reckoned with, though its power should not be
exaggerated.   But the Foreign Ministry held out for
the paramountcy of civilian control.   In the climate
of 1906, it was still possible for such a campaign
to be sustained.   It was an important victory which
was not seriously challenged until 1914 and not
effectively reversed until the Manchurian crisis of
1931 itself.   But Katō was unquestionably under
pressure from the army in the 1910s over everything
related to Manchuria and China.

THE CHINESE REVOLUTION

Between his short spell as foreign minister in 1913 and
his longer stint in 1914-15, Katō visited China to make
an on-the-spot survey from April to June 1913.   This
was natural because China was the subject which dominated Japan's Foreign Ministry activities and thinking
from 1910 onwards.   Immigration and trading problems
and international diplomacy could be tricky; but it
was China which increasingly engaged the attention of
diplomats.
    Diplomacy towards China was from the start a most
complex process.   Japan is to China as Britain is to
the continent of Europe.   Just as Britain's diplomacy
towards Europe tends to be more complicated than other
aspects of her diplomacy, so Japan's towards China
tends, by reason of her more frequent contacts, the
greater number of lobbies operating, the activities of
the army and navy, to have been a most complicated
business, sometimes a baffling one.   Since China was
in the period under review a divided country, the process of diplomacy was a confused one.   Throughout the

1910s, the Japanese government boasted of its 'intimate
ties' with all shades of Chinese opinion, though this
was in some cases an illusion since the Chinese were
sometimes more frank to non-Japanese foreigners and
were ready to hoodwink the Japanese.   There is also
an element of 'double-talk' or 'double-think' in discussions of China in Japan, since much of the Japanese
approach to China was said to be aimed at 'improving
Sino-Japanese friendship', which was certainly not a
realistic basis likely to appeal to many Chinese politicians.   This was not uncommon in the age of
imperialism because there was a common illusion that
the imperialist power was indeed striving for the
'friendship' of the lesser country - on its own conditions.   Thus, Katō had told Sir Edward Grey frankly
in 1913 that he saw Japan's role in east Asia as one
of protecting China.

It seems necessary to assess the forces operating
behind foreign policy towards China.   On all problems
of north-east Asia, the officers of the Kwantung army -
not necessarily the commanders but the staff officers -
had a view and had the power to ensure the support of
the general staff.   Then there were the civilian
adventurers (like Kawashima Naniwa in Manchuria, Kita
Ikki in the Yangtse in 1911-12 and the Shina rōnin)
who operated their own strategies among revolutionaries,
local bosses and warlords in Japan's interest as they
conceived it but not always with success.   Then there
were the merchants and industrialists who were anxious
to establish China as a source of much-needed raw
materials.   These groups rarely operated as a co-
ordinated whole;   nor were they under the control of
Tokyo.   In some cases their efforts conflicted one
with the other.   Very often they embarrassed the home
government and were bitterly criticized by the
consuls in their reports.   But sometimes they provided
a convenient device for the government to act through
without commitment.   The fact that China's provinces
acted in the 1910s and 1920s as units independent of
central government naturally encouraged these actions.

It is necessary also to speak of Japan's interests
in the area.   Since the Russo-Japanese war the main
focus of these had been the South Manchurian railway
company.   The line from 'the Japanese frontier' at
Changchun to 'the Russian city' (or so it seemed to
many observers) of Dairen (Dalny) was running well.
But it had to be patrolled by guards and the bridges to
be well watched.   The line from Mukden to Antung was
completed in 1911.   Since Korea had been annexed in

July 1910 and the Korean rail link from Pusan to the
Yalu was in operation, the arterial lines were secure.
But, in fact, the route via Dairen was more popular
than the line through Antung and had been double-
tracked for almost all the distance between Dairen
and Mukden by 1909.   As the situation improved, the
railway company had raised considerable overseas
capital.   It floated four debenture issues, amounting
to £14 millions, in the London money market with full
government guarantee during the period from 1907 to
1911.   Moreover the railway had elaborate plans for
extension which were only hampered by lack of funds.

Katō inherited an ambiguous Japanese policy towards
China.   From the outset of the Chinese revolution in
October 1911, Japan agreed to adopt a policy of neutrality.   In high-level discussions with the Cabinet,
the Elder Statesmen and the general staff agreed to a
policy document which laid down that Japan should try
to maintain the status quo in Manchuria, 'awaiting the
most propitious moment to make a basic settlement of
the position there to our own advantage.   From now on
we must endeavour to establish our influence in China
proper and take steps to get the other powers to
recognize our ascendancy in that area.'   This should
be achieved without alienating China or any of the
interested powers. (12)   But, with the evident appeal
of the revolution to the Chinese people and the return
to Ching service of Yuan Shih-k'ai, it became necessary
for Japan to decide which of these forces she supported.
On 16 November Japan agreed that, if Yuan requested
assistance, she would be prepared to grant him considerable aid.   When Yuan stated that China's unity could
best be secured by setting up a constitutional monarchy,
this certainly accorded with the thinking of most
Japanese leaders, who were not inclined to give tangible support to those revolutionaries who favoured a
republic. (13)   The Hankow armistice of 1 December
and the north-south peace conference at Shanghai forced
the Japanese reluctantly to give up their hopes for a
solution through a constitutional monarchy.   Left to
settle their own destiny, the Chinese declared a
republic and Yuan, having successfully manoeuvred for
the abdication of the Ching monarchy, was himself
appointed interim president on 12 February 1912.   Since
Yuan was no friend of Japan, this development was
viewed by some as a failure of her diplomacy.   In the
Diet, criticisms were heaped on the heads of the unfortunate ministers and diplomats.   However much the
critics complained about the vacillation of the Cabinet,

the fact remains that Japan like other outside countries
was taken unawares by the first revolution.

The southern revolutionaries again rose up against
Yuan in mid-July 1913 in what is generally known as
'the second revolution'.   In a way, this further
north-south confrontation for which outsiders had been
waiting revealed the divergent opinions in Japan better
than the outbreaks of 1911 which had taken them
unawares.   In a note of 9 June, Japan stated her un-
equivocal neutrality in any conflict that arose. (14)
But, when the outbreaks took place, it appears that
many unofficial Japanese assisted the southern party
with arms and money.   The Foreign Ministry issued
orders that consuls should take strict measures against
Japanese joining in the disturbances and supplying
either party with war funds or arms.   The pro-south
party, spear-headed by the Kokuryūkai, was deeply implicated in this traffic.   The revolution collapsed with
the capture of Nanking on 1 September, but the
Kokuryūkai stirred up public criticism of the government for its weak policy over the assaults on Captain
Kawasaki at Yenchow (5 August) and Lieutenant Nishimura
at Hankow (11 August).   Especially vehement was the
opposition over the Nanking incident when General Chang
Hsun's forces had insulted the Japanese flag and killed
three civilians.   The Cabinet decided to make a formal
protest to President Yuan, demanding that General Chang
should be made to apologize.   Yuan bowed before the
wind and reprimanded his general.   Japan indicated
that she desired, but did not insist on, Chang's dis-
missal. (15)   This was ignored.   President Yuan
emerged from the crisis, intact but greatly weakened.
The defeated southern leaders were in the main given
asylum in Japan.

In the aftermath of the revolution there was a flurry
of Japanese commercial activity in China which was
going through a period of turmoil.   Merchant-houses
and industrialists, knowing that Japan was a country
without great natural resources, saw what a valuable
contribution China's raw materials could make to the
Japanese economy.   There was a widespread and deep-
rooted feeling that Japan's interests in the Yangtse
valley were equal, if not superior, to those of Britain
and should be pursued whatever the cost.   There were
also expansionists who thought it politic to abet the
activities of Sun Yat-sen.   Sun had been in Japan in
February and March 1913 and had put out feelers for
loans.   It was not that Japan was unique in this; he
was putting out similar feelers in Britain, France and

the United States at the same time.   What was special
about the Japanese was that they were more ready to
accede to his requests and, in doing so, the bankers
were prepared to take the risk of investing in anti-
cipation of Sun's ultimate triumph in China.   But
this view was by no means universal since Katō, for
one, formed a poor impression of Sun and the southern
party.

It was the object of Japan's diplomacy to ease the
passage of Japanese interests into south China.   She
hoped to enter into commercial bargains to capitalize
on the political goodwill she had acquired by the
support given to the south in the 1913 revolution by
some Japanese.   Although she was a member of the
five-nation consortium, this did not exclude her from
offering industrial - and possibly railway - loans to
China.   (American bankers had left the consortium in
March 1913.)   But she could only enter the south by
encroaching on the Yangtse, the traditional British
sphere of influence.   She was entitled to do this by
appealing to the doctrine of the Open Door but risked
incurring the hostility of Britain.   There were
various options open to the government which ultimately
decided to steer clear of British antagonism and try
to negotiate some deal to obtain Britain's approval for
her activities there.

Meanwhile in the north a coalition of the Kwantung
army, the general staff and the Shina rōnin associated
with them sought to exploit the independence movements
in Manchuria and Mongolia by establishing there a government based on the Ching dynasty.   It was assumed
that the Ching regime, which would have a natural
appeal in Manchuria, would, if restored, be friendly
and subservient to Japan.   The first endeavour, made
in the last months of 1911, collapsed when the scheme
reached the ears of the Saionji Cabinet. (16)   In the
following year General Tanaka Giichi, the vice-chief
of the general staff, visited Manchuria and declared
it was indispensable for Japan's security to obtain
'the management of the continent'.   It was he more
than any other who master-minded the second Manchuria-
Mongolian independence movement in 1915.   But this
ended in failure because of a basic difference of view
over who should be given the leadership of the independence movement.   While there were still those who saw
it as a means to Ching revival, there were others
including Tanaka himself who saw the up-and-coming
Chang Tso-lin as the more efficient and promising
collaborator in Manchuria.   While these movements were

supported by military intrigue, it is hard to trace
the connection between them and the Cabinet or the
Foreign Ministry.   They are evidence that the army,
and especially the Kwantung army, was an active agent
in Japan's policy-making which tended to go its own
way regardless of risks and thrived in the unsettled
atmosphere of China and Manchuria.   Their bold
activities are, moreover, evidence of their subtle
methods.   The Japanese in the main did not seek a
leadership role for themselves; they looked for good
material in Ching circles, ir warlord circles and
among ambitious local politicians and they supported
them by money, arms and ammunition.

FIRST WORLD WAR

On 15 August Japan sent an ultimatum to Germany,
threatening to go to war if it were not complied
with. (17)   This was a critical issue for the Okuma
Cabinet which had come to power in April.   Okuma had
been chosen as prime minister because he was reliable
and likely to be able to keep in order the Seiyūkai
which had by its opposition to the demands of the
army and navy in 1912-13 stimulated the political
crises of these years.   The newly created party, the
Dōshikai, was asked to join Okuma's coalition ministry;
and as its president Katō asked to become foreign
minister.   The circumstances of Okuma's appointment
made him dependent on the Dōshikai and especially on
Katō who therefore enjoyed a good deal of independence
at the Foreign Ministry.
     When war was declared between the powers in Europe,
Japan declared her neutrality.   Within a matter of
days she was approached by Britain for limited help by
the Japanese navy in searching out the German ships in
the north Pacific, though it was recognized that this
would come close to being a belligerent act.   On 8
August, following an emergency Cabinet, a conference
of the genro and ministers was held where it was
decided in principle to enter the war on the allied
side.   In this they accepted the plea of Katō that
Britain was certain to emerge on the winning side and,
even if she did not, Japan had nothing to lose;   to
enter a European war would redound to Japan's credit
internationally and improve her standing in east Asia,
even if she was not required by the terms of the British
alliance to intervene.   Although questions were asked,
the Cabinet and Elder Statesmen did not dissent.

Japan had with the force of an electric shock (as
Katō's biographer describes it) decided informally to
enter the war on Britain's side.   It was a personal
triumph for Katō who was the leading sponsor of this
course.   But it was also a grave risk to take and
the responsibility was largely his. (18)   It was
ultimately decided that the best course would be to
send an ultimatum to Germany and allow a period of
seven days for receipt of the reply;   the essence of
the ultimatum would be that Germany should transfer
her Tsingtao leased territory to Japan, whatever its
ultimate fate (Document 14).   It is important to
observe that Katō told his colleagues not that Japan
had to take part in the war under an obligation imposed
by the alliance but rather that 'obligations of friendship' existed under the alliance.   He did not profess
to take Japan in because of the specific terms of the
alliance but because of the friendly sentiments to
which it gave rise.   He was more concerned to demonstrate the advantages of raising Japan's status through
obliterating German bases from east Asia and to argue
that the practical risks from European quarters whatever the outcome of the war need not cause too much
anxiety.   By his advocacy, he overcame the doubts of
the Elder Statesmen as to whether this was the best
time for Japanese entry. (19)

The Japanese decision, like that of all the belligerents in 1914, was not simple and straightforward.
Many factors played a part.   It would be wrong to
imagine that the Balkan crisis was taken seriously in
Japan.   The Foreign Ministry, to be sure, received a
wide range of reports on developments there after
Serajevo, as befitted a country with a broad diplomatic
representation in Europe.   But this information played
little part in decision-making among the Japanese
leadership. (20)   More important was the perilous
domestic position of the government.   It faced the
opposition of business men to the Business Tax
(Eigyō zei);   and the Diet session in June had been
difficult.   It did not escape the ministers that the
outbreak of war in Europe might lead to boom conditions
in Japanese industry and restore the lesser businessmen
to a quieter frame of mind.   More serious were the
long-standing demands for expansion of the army and
navy which Okuma had inherited along with the bitter
parliamentary opposition of the Seiyūkai.   Okuma set
up a committee of national defence (bōmu kaigi) in June.
The coming of war put this problem in a completely new
perspective.   The committee reported in favour of an

increase of the army by two divisions for Korea and the
completion of the 8-8 programme for the navy.   When
the Diet met late in December, it voted down this proposal and was dissolved.   In the general election in
March 1915 Okuma won a victory which improved his
position in the Diet and the Dōshikai, in particular,
emerged successfully at the expense of the opposition
Seiyūkai.   There were pressing domestic reasons for
wanting Japan to be a belligerent and to be actively
engaged in the war as she was in the successful Tsingtao
campaign from 2 September till 7 November.

Entry was a bureaucratic decision.   Public opinion
and the Press did not fully understand the issues though
the papers reported the European front extensively.
Within the policy-elite there was only limited consultation.   The Elder Statesmen hesitated without applying
a veto.   At the outbreak of war one of them, Inoue
Kaoru, wrote: 'This is the divine aid of the new
Taishō era for the achievement of Japan's destiny.   We
must grasp this opportunity by showing solidarity with
the Powers (Britain, France and Russia) and on this
foundation we must act as the unifier of China.' (21)
This attitude was accepted by the genro who did not
differ from the government on the issue of entering the
war.   They did, however, have doubts about the advis-
ability of such early entry.   On this point, they were
overruled.

It was not that Japan had great animus against
Germany.   There was the old complaint about Germany's
actions in 1895 and about the kaiser's indiscretions
over the Yellow Peril.   But the state of diplomatic
relations was satisfactory. (22)   There was, of
course, the British alliance whose focus had since 1907
moved further away from Russia.   In so far as the
alliance was tending to become in British eyes anti-
German, so it would tend to a lesser extent to become
anti-German in Japanese eyes.   But it could not be
said that the terms of the alliance predisposed Japan
to make war against Germany in 1914. (23)

The person who promoted Japan's immediate entry into
the war was Katō.   He felt that Japan could suffer no
loss from becoming a belligerent, though he himself was
confident that ultimate victory would go to the British
side;   and he told his colleagues that Japan should use
the occasion to build up even more strongly her position
in east Asia.   This implies that Katō thought in terms
of making war on Germany with a view to gains which
Japan could make in the Pacific and in China, especially
in Manchuria.

In these circumstances Japan issued her ultimatum to
Germany on 15 August (Documents 13 and 14) calling for
the handing over of Kiaochow. There is a common
fallacy that this ultimatum was patterned on the
remarks of Freiherr von Gutschmidt, the German minister
in Japan at the time of the Dreibund crisis in 1895.
Certainly his intemperate language on that occasion
had been deeply resented by the Japanese ever since.
But it can be said, from a comparison of the Japanese
and German texts, that there is little warrant for such
an assertion. It is true that in both cases they are
framed in the form of an advice, even a friendly advice,
to hand over territory. Had the ultimatum of 1914 been
a request to Germany to return territory to China, the
resemblance might have been closer. In fact, it was a
demand that the leased territory of Kiaochow, where
China had sovereignty, should be ceded to Japan; and
this differentiates it from the 1895 formula. Both in
1895 and in 1914 the demanding power professed to be
acting for the maintenance of permanent peace in east
Asia; but this is diplomatic jargon and does not amount
to a similarity of substance. In sum, the resemblance
between the two documents in length, in terms and in
language is small. Any deduction that Japan's motive
was purely vengeance for 1895 is over-drawn and
superficial.

Judged by international precedents, Japan's ultimatum
to Germany contained unusual features. It allowed a
time-limit of seven days, which was longer than the 24
or 48 hours which had been allowed by European powers
earlier to Germany. This was necessary because
Ambassador Count Rex was not in direct communication
with his home government so that Japan did not know how
soon after the issue of the ultimatum the Germans would
receive it; it was therefore desirable to allow a
generous interval. But there was also the underlying
object that Germany should be given an opportunity to
settle with Japan direct without any necessity for a
resort to force. Some Japanese ambassadors abroad
asked Tokyo for an explanation of the procedure which
seemed to be more amenable to Germany than other
ultimata. (24)

THE TWENTY-ONE DEMANDS

The text of the ultimatum makes clear that Japan's
interest in the war lay in the German possessions in the
east and especially Tsingtao. Katō had spoken to Grey

in January 1913 of Japan choosing a 'psychological
moment' to sort out her position with the Chinese; and
he probably reckoned that this was the moment.   Down
to 1914 Japan's problem had been to promote her interests
without exciting opposition from competing powers.
Now that war had come, the European powers had lost
their power, if not their interest, in China.   There
is reason to believe that Inoue too, when he used the
extravagant language about the outbreak of war in
Europe being 'an act of divine grace' for the new
Taishō reign, had much the same in mind.   At the same
time, the earlier parts of this chapter have shown that
for Japan to consolidate her position in China at this
juncture was more to follow in the footsteps of her
actions in 1913 than to realize some new brainwave,
dreamt up at the start of the war.   It could have been
a psychological moment for China as well but she was
less adroit and less prepared to take instant action.

Japan's demands took shape slowly but deliberately.
On 20 August a new minister to China, Hioki Eki, was
appointed after the sudden death of Yamaza from excess
of alcohol.   His instructions anticipated just such a
tidying up operation, covering the outstanding bones of
contention with Peking. (25)   Later when the Elder
Statesmen discussed foreign affairs with Premier Okuma
on 24 September, it was agreed inter alia that Japan
should take steps to win over and secure the confidence
of President Yuan, if necessary by force. (26)   The
customary ambiguity!   By this time the military campaign was under way against Germany.   But the attack
on the German lease, avowedly in the name of ridding
China of the German presence, had, if it was to avoid
a direct assault on the leasehold, to cross Chinese
territory.   Under pressure China agreed to declare a
war zone.   Then, after the attack on the leasehold,
the Japanese used the argument that Tsingtao was being
reinforced from Shantung province along the German
Shantung railway and troops proceeded to occupy parts
of it.

After Tsingtao fell to Japanese arms on 7 November,
Katō recalled Hioki to Tokyo.   Hioki had already been
working to prepare some comprehensive settlement with
Yuan Shih-kai and the purpose behind his recall was
that he should dovetail his local knowledge with that
of interested groups in Japan.   By early December a
detailed policy towards China had been worked out and
agreed.   It appears that its real authors were Hioki
and the head of the political affairs section of the
Foreign Ministry with special responsibility for China,

Koike Chōzō, who was thought to have connections with
the military.   But the documentary evidence for its
dependence on the army is slight though there is a
memorandum in November from the war minister, Oka
Ichinosuke, containing 'points for negotiation with
China'.   It is probable that, in the exhilaration of
the Tsingtao victory, many in the army and navy and
financial and private circles supplied ideas which it
was politically undesirable to reject, even though
Katō himself did not rate them highly.   They were compiled into two categories, demands and desires.   Before
Hioki returned to Peking, he was given the approved
document and received instructions on 3 December to
present Japan's demands at an appropriate moment.
Sino-Japanese relations had deteriorated fast since the
Shantung campaign: the Chinese could not look on with
equanimity at the virtual occupation of Shantung province and its capital Tsinan by Japan.

Knowing that Japan would be useful in achieving his
imperial ambitions, President Yuan retaliated in the
only way he could: on 7 January 1915 he withdrew his
original war-zone proclamation, thus indicating that
he expected Japanese troops to be recalled to Germany's
leased territory.   Japan protested;   it was even more
necessary now to regulate the relationship between the
Japanese 'liberating troops' (as they saw it) and the
Chinese.   On 18 January Hioki presented Japan's requirements - 16 demands and 5 'desires' - to Yuan in
person at the presidential palace and swore him to
secrecy. (27)

Foreign Minister Katō envisaged the twenty-one
demands as an attempt at an 'across-the-board' settlement of outstanding problems in exchange for Japan's
promise to return Shantung.   They were divided into
five groups: Group I dealt with Shantung where large
numbers of Japanese troops were stationed and an
administrative arrangement of some sort would have to
be negotiated between Japan and China;   Group II referred to Manchuria where Japan's leases were due to
run out in 1923 and she wanted to obtain an extension
to ninety-nine years.   The other demands covered
industries, arsenals, railways, harbours and dockyards,
the whole spectrum of China's modernization.   Group V
was considered by the Japanese to be different in
character from the rest, containing only 'desirable
items' whose adjustment would be beneficial to both
countries.   It included the 'desire' that China should
employ Japanese political, financial and military
advisers, while, in areas where disputes had arisen

between Japanese and Chinese nationals, policing should
be arranged jointly by the two countries.   These
'desiderata' appear to have been compiled as the result
of representations by sectional interests.   If it was
a bureaucratic triumph to codify them in one document,
it would surely have been better to reserve them until
after the main demands had been negotiated.   In any
event, China - and the rest of the world when the terms
leaked out - did not believe that Group V was in any
way secondary.   To the Chinese, the demands seemed to
portend a serious interference in their domestic
affairs.   To the Japanese, they were a reward for the
Shantung campaign and were not illiberal in so far as
Japan was not demanding territory so much as economic
privileges, especially in the railway and industrial
field.

China was, needless to say, opposed to these overtures.   But, with Japanese forces poised in Shantung
and Manchuria so near to Peking, she was not in a strong
bargaining position.   In the first round, China's
negotiators hoped to temporize by accepting some of the
terms and rejecting others.   But the Japanese insisted
on their being regarded as a package deal which had to
be accepted en bloc.   This meant that China's only
hope of withstanding Japanese pressure was to enlist
support from abroad.   All foreign countries were disturbed over the twenty-one demands and over Japan's
secretiveness in pretending that they did not exist.   185717
But, with the majority being fully stretched in the
European war, they were not anxious to strike a pose of
protest.   The United States, which was not so involved,
initially reacted weakly to the crisis: Secretary of
State Bryan in March issued a message which, while con-
demning some of Japan's demands, conceded that 'propinquity creates special relationships'.   This could
only mean that Japan because of her closeness to China,
especially Shantung and southern Manchuria, could be
expected to have some special relationships there.
Late in April President Wilson became less satisfied
with the earlier line and sent a circular letter to the
Powers, reasserting the Open Door doctrine with a view
to enlisting international support for Chinese resistance to the demands.   Secretary Bryan revealed his
intention to the Japanese who were thoroughly alarmed.
Katō appealed to Britain not to pay attention to the
American overtures.   The Whitehall view was that Washington's move, being at the eleventh hour, was ill-timed
and came far too late in the proceedings.   Hence, the
United States, the only Power which could have assisted

China wanted to avoid acting on her own and failed to
muster any outside support. So more from good luck
than diplomatic skill Katō was able to deal with the
crisis without outside interference.

It was the eleventh hour in the sense that the negotiations between Japan and China had ended on 16 April
and Japan had prepared a statement of modified demands
(still including Group V) ten days later. While some
progress was made in the negotiations, the longer they
lasted the more intractable both sides became on central
issues. In China movements opposing Japan were making
protests: in Shanghai an anti-Japanese association
(dōshikai), organized by students returned from Japan,
was campaigning in favour of boycotting Japanese trade;
some southern groups were even urging Yuan to resist
Japan. But Sun Yat-sen who was in Japan throughout
the crisis was too hostile to Yuan to suspend his
opposition and may even have encouraged the Japanese.
Despite his military weakness and Japan's increased
garrisons, Yuan adopted a harder attitude, clinging to
the forlorn hope that he would finally obtain help from
abroad. At the 25th meeting of delegates on 26 April,
Minister Hioki presented his revised demands; but
these were turned down by China on 1 May. Hioki,
therefore, asked Tokyo for an ultimatum backed by the
threat of force, acting on the assumption that Yuan
with his monarchical ambitions would be ready to yield
if only he could be seen to be capitulating to an
ultimatum.

Katō was in a mess and took his time in deciding
over Hioki's suggested use of strong-arm tactics. The
foreign minister told his advisers that he wanted a
peaceful settlement and did not see the urgency of
sending an ultimatum, while Koike, and with him the
army, thought that there was no alternative to sending
a strong ultimatum. Meanwhile domestic criticism was
mounting among the opposition parties, warming up after
their electoral defeat for the opening of the Diet on
20 May. The Elder Statesmen were also up in arms,
attacking Katō's clumsiness rather than the principle
of the Demands. They had been lobbied by the Japanese
constitutional adviser to Yuan, Ariga Nagao, a former
employee of the Foreign Ministry, who had been sent
over from Peking to present China's case. Elder Statesman Inoue was kept in touch with the intensity of foreign
reactions by his son, the ambassador in London, who
felt Tokyo's handling of the affair to have been so
inept that he offered to resign. (28)

Without necessarily being hostile to the policy of

the Demands, the genro were infuriated that they had
not been adequately consulted by Katō.   Already at
odds with Katō, they were determined to exploit his
embarrassment in order to teach him a lesson.   On
the afternoon of 4 May, the genro, excepting Inoue
who was confined to bed, had a meeting with the
Cabinet, at which Matsukata spoke up against the
duplicity of not passing Group V to foreign countries
and Yamagata expressed his extreme dissatisfaction
with the foreign minister's handling of China.   After
the meeting broke up without agreement, a critical
telegram arrived from Britain and so needled the
Cabinet that it agreed at its meeting later that day
to the more extreme course of sending a threatening
ultimatum while at the same time removing Group V
from it. (29)   It took two more days of mediation
before agreement was reached with the genro on the
terms of the final document (see Documents 15 and 16).

Finding that there was little prospect of foreign
support, China had already taken fright.   Yuan, acting
through Tsao Ju-lin, made it known that he would welcome a reopening of the conference.   Tsao informed
Hioki on 7 May that China was ready to accept Groups I-IV
and was prepared to discuss Group V further.   It was
ironic to find China's attitude so amenable and Hioki
advised Tokyo that better terms could be obtained.   But
the Cabinet, having suffered from the asperity of a genro
intervention, decided that there was no going back on
Group V.   If Japan had abstained from an ultimatum
or had delayed sending it, as Katō had suggested, her
gains from the settlement might have been greater.   By
the same token, Yuan had to concede less than he envisaged under threat of military attack. (30)

Katō passed over the final ultimatum to China on 7
May, giving her forty-eight hours to reply.   Japanese
troops which were estimated at 20,000 in Manchuria and
30,000 in Shantung were placed at the ready.   On 9
May China accepted the revised drafts.   On 25 May
Japan and China signed several treaties which contained
the fruits of these four bitter months of negotiation.
The essence of the settlement was embodied in two
treaties, one relating to Shantung province, the other
to south Manchuria and eastern Inner Mongolia.   By the
first, China promised to accept all matters which Japan
might agree with the German government, pertaining to
German rights, interests and concessions in Shantung
and to give Japanese capitalists first option on loans
for the building of ancillary railway lines in the province.   By the second treaty, which Japan held to be

the most desirable part of the settlement, the Chinese
agreed to extend to ninety-nine years the leases which
Japan held for Port Arthur and Dairen - the so-called
Kwantung Leased Territory - and the terms whereby Japan
operated the south Manchurian railway and the railway
from Mukden to Antung on the border with Korea. These
treaties were ratified on 7 June.

There were also more delicate matters which one
party or the other did not want to crystallize in
treaty form. The most important document exchanged -
and later the most controversial - dealt with the fate
of the former German leased territory of Kiaochow.
Japan stated that 'in the event that the leased territory of Kiaochow is left to the free disposal of Japan
after the war, she will restore it to China under
various conditions', notably that she should be granted
by China a territorial concession in the area for her
exclusive jurisdiction. This implied that, while
ultimate sovereignty would revert to China after the
war, Japan would probably insist on receiving some
compensation such as a lease. It was further agreed
that Group V should be deferred for discussion at a
later date. In this way, the Japanese had received
the endorsement of what they call their 'sixteen
demands'. The notion that Group V çontained 'desiderata' rather than demands was again maintained.
Indeed it is still held by certain Japanese historians
even today. (31)

Japan got her way but her reputation suffered in
China and in the world at large. While Japan had
acquired territories before in 1895, in 1905 and in
Korea in 1910, her reputation had never dipped on these
occasions as they did now. In China she forfeited the
goodwill of many who had been educated in Japan and
looked to her as a safeguard against imperialist
intrusion; now she too came to be branded by them as
an imperialist Power. Yuan Shih-k'ai took some consolation from the outcome, believing that he had
succeeded in modifying Japanese demands by standing
firm. While he had received only the minimum of help
from foreign countries, he had mobilized world opinion
for China in a way that was unprecedented and lingered
on beyond the years of the First World War. In the
world outside Japan there were few people who did not
believe that China had been forced to accept these
demands under duress. It was the comprehensiveness of
Japan's demands which came as the greatest bombshell and
the attempted - and bungled - concealment of Group V
which served to discredit Japanese diplomacy. Japan

had had power enough to enforce her will in the last
resort by going to war.   But she had stopped short of
this, not so much because of the influence of the
foreign Powers as because of the caution of the Elder
Statesmen who stepped in at the eleventh hour and
insisted on Japan's climbing down.   The whole episode
reflects little credit on Foreign Minister Katō, who
was either grasping and scheming himself or unable to
control his officials in their pattern of negotiations.
It likewise confirmed that the Foreign Ministry could
be taken over by a lobby and pushed into a false and
unrepresentative position.

ASSESSMENT

The bulldozer tactics employed to steer through their
Chinese demands are a puzzling feature of the foreign
policy of Katō.   He had had great experience of the
diplomacy of the Powers at the highest level and seemed
to have been much influenced by parliamentary and
other democratic procedures which he had learnt in
London.   On the other hand, he had little experience
of, and less respect for, China.   He was therefore
under the influence of 'China experts' in formulating
his policy.   Instead of controlling the exaggerated
demands which the various experts evolved in what was
an expansionist atmosphere, he seems to have let them
take over policy-making - a feature which seems to be
at odds with his character.   But China policy seems
to have interested him much less than 'haute
politique'. (32)   It is sometimes the case that a
successful ambassador makes a bad aministrator.   Perhaps there was something of this in the enigmatic
Katō.
     Certainly he was inept in handling the political
forces in Japan - and especially the genro.   As we
have seen from the crucial meetings held early in May,
the Elder Statesmen had been disgusted with the prospect of war with China and the way that Katō had
handled the negotiations there.   He had not consulted
them; he had ignored their advice when it was volun-
teered; he had, as they considered, been insensitive
to opinion abroad.   The genro had in any case many
old scores to settle with Katō and were determined to
capitalize on his present failures.   It was Inoue who
was most insistent on getting rid of Katō and came to
Tokyo from his country villa in the middle of June when
the crisis had passed in order to arrange the ouster.

Yet it is hard to judge how successful the demands
were.   Whatever the voice of the elite, the fact
remains that the twenty-one demands were popular in
Japan.   They had given Okuma an electoral victory on
25 March and had boosted the strength of the Dōshikai
party.   As against that, when Okuma's ministry
resigned at the end of July, Katō took the occasion
not to join Okuma's reformed ministry.   The story put
about was that he resigned because the home minister,
Oura, a member of Katō's Dōshikai, was found to have
been involved in the bribery of a number of opposition
members of the Diet.   Even after his resignation,
Katō remained close to the Okuma ministry.   He played
a major part in the appointment of his successor,
Ishii; his Dōshikai continued to support Okuma's government.   When Okuma himself resigned in 1916, he
recommended to the genro the name of Katō as his
successor.   For all these reasons, it cannot simply be
said that he had been dismissed because of the failure
of his much criticized China policy or the damage that
the whole proceedings had done to Japan's reputation
abroad.   To some degree he was recognized as the
scapegoat for a popular policy.

Though it could hardly be justified in the 1970s,
the twenty-one demands can be defended.   From a
Japanese standpoint and within the atmosphere of
imperialism in which they were conceived, a case can
be made for them.   In one of his writings, Katō makes
that case. (33)   His successor, Ishii, who was by no
means committed to the support of Katō, was also ready
to defend them in his better-known writings.   They
were defended before the Japanese Diet.   They did not
result in the collapse of the whole ministry as might
have been expected, had they been widely condemned by
the Japanese people.

Yet Katō's career received a setback because of the
China crisis.   The genro, shortly to lose Inoue from
their number, believed that he was a man of poor judgment.   Yamagata swore that he would never allow Katō
to become prime minister and, until his death in 1922,
Katō and his party were excluded from power.   The
other genro, Saionji and Matsukata, also disliked him
and feared that his reputation for the events of 1915
would detract from Japan's image if he again came to
power.   But Katō succeeded in keeping at the head of
his party and before the public eye (Documents 17 and
18).   Moreover he achieved his ambition by heading a
minority coalition cabinet in 1924 at the age of sixty-
four.   As a reform-minded prime minister, he achieved
substantial successes in the twilight of his career.

Chapter 6

The Ishii Period,
1915-19

Ishii's claim to our attention rests on his many-sided
career during the war years. First, he was ambassador
in Paris (1912-15) and gained a reputation for being
anti-German during the critical early months of war.
Then, he was recalled to Tokyo to act as foreign minister and took up his appointment on 13 October 1915.
After a year in office, he was sent on a special mission
to Washington on 13 August 1917, shortly after the
United States entered the war, and acted as ambassador
there, with breaks, until June 1919. This was a miscellaneous set of appointments but was none the less
typical of Japan's many-sided diplomatic interests
during the second half of the First World War.

In contrast to Katō, Ishii Kikujirō (1866-1945) was
not a politician so much as a distinguished Foreign
Ministry bureaucrat and diplomat. Earlier in his
career, he had played a notable, if junior, role in the
defence of the Peking legations in 1900 and in the
negotiation of the Portsmouth treaty. He had been an
active vice-minister during Komura's second term. To
become ambassador in Paris in 1912 was the culmination
of this part of his career. Indeed, France was probably the place abroad where he was happiest; and he
returned there as ambassador from 1920 to 1927.

Ishii's name is probably better known abroad than
that of any other Japanese diplomat because of his
translated writings. His English writings - 'Diplomatic
Commentaries' and his essay on 'Japan' - have a defensive and conservative slant. (1) Yet his personality
does not shine through clearly. Foreign observers
commented on the limited range of his English and the
bluntness of his speech. British diplomats, in particular, found him rather stiff and difficult to deal
with as foreign minister. (2)

Ishii was probably called home as foreign minister
because of his consistent support from Paris for
Japan's entry into the war. (3)   His task was to
clarify Japan's position now that the campaigns in
China and the Pacific had ended.   By virtue of her
naval exploits, Japan had taken possession of the
south Pacific islands formerly possessed by Germany
and was in the process of educating and 'colonizing'
them.   By virtue of wartime agreements with Britain,
her cruisers and destroyers were operating to good
effect in the Indian ocean.   She was supplying arms
to the allies, especially Russia, and offering them
financial support.

It was natural that Ishii with his Paris background
should be asked to involve his country more in the war
in Europe.   Militarily Japan had refused all proposals to send a force to the Western front and
suggestions that her British alliance be extended to
take in France and Russia.   But Ishii did make changes.
One of his first acts in September 1915 was to agree
to Japan's adhering to the Declaration of London. (4)
The Entente Powers hoped that Japan's promise not to
make peace separately with Germany might lead her to
increase her contribution to the allied cause.   But
any increase was not to be dramatic.   Between March
and May 1916 Japanese diplomats were engaged in certain
devious discussions with German representatives about
a separate peace; and, while there is no evidence
that Ishii or the Japanese government were disloyal to
the London Declaration, it was inevitable that Japan's
allies who were able to intercept many of her overseas
telegrams should regard it as double-dealing.   What
would have happened if the German terms had been more
attractive cannot be known.   But the German Foreign
Ministry was reserved in its offers and the Japanese
passed on the results of their transactions quite
properly to their European allies. (5)

RUSSO-JAPANESE ALLIANCE

Ishii found himself pushed in the extraordinary direction of undertaking negotiations with tsarist Russia,
the old enemy.   The army had not been impressed by
the performance of British units which had fought
alongside its troops in the attack on Tsingtao (1914).
The campaigns in Europe had led it to believe that
Germany was likely to be victorious.   At any rate,
the conviction grew that Japan's adhesion to the British

alliance was narrowing and dangerous.   As early as
February 1915 Genro Yamagata had written in favour
of increasing Japan's options: since the British
alliance was serving its purpose, it might seem that
there was no necessity for forming another alliance;
but reliance on Britain alone was dangerous and it was
the urgent duty of Japan to conclude an alliance with
Russia.   In his view, a Russian alliance should be
regarded not as a substitute for, but as a complement
to, the British alliance (Document 15).   On receipt
of this memorandum, Inoue Kaoru also spoke in favour
of negotiations with Russia.   But, so long as Katō
was foreign minister, this was disregarded in Kasumigaseki.   After his replacement in August by Ishii,
the situation changed.   The genro's ideas may have
been allowed to leak to the Russians by Ambassador
Motono who was himself an enthusiast for closer relationships with them.   The Russians themselves,
especially Foreign Minister Sazonov, favoured this and
saw Japan's adhesion to the London Declaration as the
first step towards such an alliance, which would enable
Russia to move some of her forces from the Far East.
    Those who sought a deepening of the relationship
could take advantage of certain favourable features.
One was that Japan now had a new and favourable wartime trade with Russia along the trans-Siberian line.
Second, the Russo-Japanese agreements of 1907, 1910 and
1912 had prepared the ground.
    In January 1916 Tsar Nicholas II sent his uncle, the
Grand Duke George Michaelovich, on an honorific mission
to the Japanese emperor, which had also a more practical side.   The military and industrial members of the
fifteen-man delegation carried out exhaustive talks
about improving supplies from Japan.   To this end,
the Grand Duke had special discussions with General
Terauchi, the governor-general of Korea and head of the
accompanying delegation, and later with Field-marshal
Yamagata, when he presented him with the order of St
Alexander Nevsky.   The Russian demands for more
munitions went before the military council.   Russia
was informed late in February that it would not be easy
to meet them unless there were some striking proof of
Russian goodwill: could she, in order to make a
favourable impression upon Japanese public opinion,
offer spontaneously to give up to Japan for a reasonable
sum the portion of the Chinese Eastern railway connect-
ing Changchun with Harbin? (6)
    Meanwhile the diplomats were at work.   The Foreign
Ministry representative on the delegation was the head

of its Far Eastern department, Kazakov.   During his
journey to Tokyo and in parleys in the capital, he
put forward the need for some alliance.   On 14 January
he placed before Foreign Minister Ishii the proposals
which he had already mapped out with his own minister,
Sazonov.   Ishii's reply was discouraging.   He
apparently calculated that, since Japan had adhered to
the London Declaration and thus assured herself of a
seat at any peace conference, she had nothing to gain
from a new agreement with Russia.   Moreover, like
his predecessor, Ishii wished to defer any wider proposals for alliance until after the war.   The
Russians, therefore, interceded for the support of the
Elder Statesmen.   On 20 January Ishii had talks in
the palace with three of the genro.   Yamagata was
just as much in favour of negotiations for an alliance
as he had been the previous year.   Like most Japanese
military opinion, he was not satisfied that the Entente
Powers would defeat Germany;   and the British alliance
was something that could no longer be relied on.
Since, however, Japan was heavily committed to the
Entente side, the best course would be to take up the
Russian invitation to open negotiations, not so much
for the direct advantages she would derive as for the
ancillary benefits in Manchuria.   With these arguments
he convinced his fellow-genro;   and the foreign minister
had no choice but to recant.

An emergency Cabinet, held in the Diet building on
14 February, decided to take up negotiations with
Russia.   The proposal was that Japan should supply
arms to the Russians - as she would probably do in any
case - and should in return ask for concessions in
Mongolia and Manchuria, especially the sale of the
Eastern railway south of Harbin.   The decision was
passed on to the Elder Statesmen who were absent from
Tokyo at the time and also to General Terauchi, who
was a strong advocate of a bargain with Russia.

The Russians responded in March that they were
anxious not to make a casus foederis of attempts by
any one Power to dominate China politically;   it would
be prudent for the signatories not to engage in arms
except in cases where they could get the aid of their
other allies, France and Britain.   The new agreement
was therefore to coexist with the British alliance, to
last as long as it lasted and to be amended if it were
amended.   In short, Russia fought shy of offering the
Japanese blanket support for 'the defence of their
territorial rights and their special interests' in
China.

The treaties were finally signed in Petrograd on 3
July.   The open agreement was a simple document,
whereby the two Powers promised each other co-operation
in maintaining their territorial rights and special
interests in the Far East.   The secret agreement
which accompanied it contained the meat of the understanding: it provided that, if one party became
involved in war with a third power, the other party
would, upon demand, come to its aid; and that the two
parties should not make a separate peace without previous consultation. (7)   It was further agreed that
the sale of the railway line between Changchun and
Harbin should be settled by a local commission.   When
the alliance was published five days later, the Japanese
received it with jubilation.   There were lantern
processions by thousands of Tokyo inhabitants, who
were able to obtain a lantern and 25 sen from the
police for taking part. (8)

Why was Japan with her strong bargaining position
content to sign an agreement which imposed great obligations and offered meagre benefits?   Under it she
was committed increasingly to the allied side, and
especially to Russia whose government was unstable,
though this only confirmed her obligations under the
Treaty of London.   On the other hand, she gained so
little: while Russia recognized Japan's position in
Manchuria, she did not acquiesce in her actions in
China, over which she was highly suspicious.   It can
only be concluded that the prospect of purchasing an
extension to her railway lines in Manchuria was an
attractive one, which overcame her reserve.   The rail
talks, as might be imagined, moved at a snail's pace
and fell into abeyance with the revolution in 1917.
Japan did benefit strategically from the withdrawal of
Russian troops from Asia to the European front.   The
alliance was an indication that tsarist Russia was
ready to disinterest herself from east Asia, more
markedly than in 1905.   This suited Japan; and there
was the possibility that, if Germany were to be victorious, there would be a friendly Russia to interpose a
barrier in the path of Germany against Japan.

The case of the Russo-Japanese alliance is an
interesting example in Japan's policy-making.   The
alliance was pushed through by the pressure of Yamagata
and his Chōshū group (including Terauchi) and despite
the better judgment of the Foreign Ministry.   The
group in the ministry to which Katō and later Ishii
belonged was content to rely for Japan's security on
the British alliance and her remoteness.   But it was

not really possible for any Cabinet to overrule the
genro; and the Okuma ministry was no exception.   So
it proceeded with the negotiations.   The puzzle is
that one so shrewd, worldly-wise and cautious as
Yamagata, should advocate alignment with a country as
unstable as Russia where the Petrograd strikes had
taken place in January 1916.   The Russo-Japanese
alliance was overtaken all too soon by revolutions of
cataclysmic magnitude which prevented Japan's advantages from materializing.   In the light of this, it
can only be said that the genro line was wrong, that
the outcome should have been predictable and that the
alliance placed Japan in the false position of being
tied to a crumbling tsarist government which it was
not a Japanese interest to shore up.   It is perhaps a
sign that the Japanese tended to be more sure-footed
in dealing with China than with a European state.
The only defence which can be offered is that those
Japanese who favoured the Russian alignment looked at
it in Far Eastern, and not in European, far less in
Russian domestic, terms.   For them it represented the
possibility of increased power in Manchuria and the
guarantee of Russian support in the Far East against
Germany, possibly in the postwar period.   Japan also
had commercial hopes which were not fulfilled.   From
1916 onwards the eastern section of the trans-Siberian
became a tremendous bottleneck so that the alliance
did not usher in an era of expanded trade as Japan may
have hoped.

It is probable that Foreign Minister Ishii was less
than enthusiastic about the alliance and had been
forced into it against his better judgment.   He did
not have the strong personality of Katō nor his power
base in the political parties.   In his memoirs which
do not have a great reputation for frankness, he
justifies the alliance because of Japan's fear of
Russian treachery towards her wartime allies and her
determination to prevent it.   By this, he seems to
imply that he was aware from the start of his term as
foreign minister of the possibility of Russia's defec-
tion and was afraid that, after making a separate peace,
she might enter into an alliance with the Germans.
This would destroy the security of Japan and harm the
position of the entente of which Japan was a member.
Ishii does not admit that there were disagreements or
that he was under pressure from the genro. (9)   The
public record suggests that Ishii did not have a major
say in the many-sided 'negotiations' which took place
on the occasion of the Russian mission and that, when

he was involved, he tended to place obstacles in the
way of the speedy conclusion of the Russian alliance.
There were those in the foreign service like Ambassador
Motono who thought he was being unnecessarily dilatory.
In any case, Ishii does not reveal the whole truth
about Japan's motives by emphasizing only her fear of
Russian treachery.   A more enlightening statement of
her aspirations is contained in the following note:
    By concluding the alliance with Russia, we have
    established with her a relationship of complete co-
    operation for the final settlement of our policy
    towards Manchuria and Mongolia and have cemented
    our defensive policy towards China.   By using the
    British and Russian alliances conjointly [literally,
    like a two-horse carriage] we can maintain permanent
    peace in the east;   and our great aim of developing
    our power there can be even more strongly rein-
    forced. (10)
The focus here is on national self-interest and on
Japan's opportunity during the war to improve her
position in north-east Asia.

MISSION TO WASHINGTON

Ishii resigned with the Okuma ministry in October 1916
and enjoyed a short spell of retirement.   The prime
ministership passed to General Terauchi whom we have
spoken about as a protagonist of the Russian alliance.
He was nominated by Genro Yamagata in the hope that he
would introduce some new policies which would remedy
the shortcomings of the party policies which had gone
before.   The foreign minister appointed was Motono
Ichirō, who had for many years been ambassador in
Russia.   Motono had a deep knowledge of European
diplomacy and of Russia which was to give him a special
approach to the problems he would face.   But he was
innocent about affairs in the two countries which were
to loom largest for Japan in the second half of the
war, China and the United States.   Over the first,
Terauchi stepped in and took China affairs and especially
the plans for financial aid there out of the hands of
the Foreign Ministry to a great extent.   Over the
second, some of the responsibility passed to Ishii who
was to conduct a special mission to Washington after
the United States entered the war in April 1917.   The
issues which divided Japanese and Americans in the run-
up to the Ishii mission were global.   They related
especially to China and Siberia.   In China the problem

was that the Americans tended to support the Chinese
in their resistance to Japan's gains there earlier in
the war.   It was necessary for Japan to sort out her
position by consultations with the Americans and by
overtures to China which was herself to enter the war
in August 1917.   In Siberia, the problem was created
by the collapse of the tsarist government during 1917.
This posed special difficulties for Japan, who was
Russia's ally and naturally looked to Russia's possessions in Siberia.   But it was clear from the Bolshevik
revolution in November onwards that President Wilson
would not welcome Japanese expansion in Siberia.
These were the problems which Ishii was to encounter
in Washington;   it will not be possible to explore
them here in depth.

But we should turn briefly aside to observe a change
which was made in the process of diplomatic decision-
taking.   In June 1917 Terauchi set up the temporary
council on foreign affairs (Rinji gaikō chōsakai) with
a view to unifying the making of foreign policy and
eliminating party strife over it.   This was thought
to be necessary because of the need for consensus.
Terauchi's was a non-party government: he came to
power with the Kenseikai party ascendant in the Diet
but, after the general election in April 1917, the
Seiyūkai became predominant.   So the idea of achieving
a consensus between the parties on foreign policy was
attractive to Terauchi and his sponsor, Yamagata.
The council consisted of nine members: four from the
Cabinet;   three from the privy council;   and two from
political parties.   (It might have been three but
Katō, now the leader of the Kenseikai, was not wholeheartedly invited and did not agree to join (Document
17).)   Looked at in a non-institutional way, the
council might be said to include representatives for
the army, the navy, the Chōshū and Satsuma clans, the
bureaucrats, conservatives and liberals.   It did not
include the genrō themselves, though they were in
favour of a 'national foreign policy' and had their
own ways of influencing the council. (11)

Over the four years of its 'temporary' existence,
the council greatly affected the position of the
Foreign Ministry.   Hitherto the ministry had been the
originator of a 'bureaucratic' foreign policy which
was in the main adopted uncritically by the Cabinet
and only rarely repudiated by the genro.   It now had
to fight its case first through the Cabinet and then
the new council.   Often the result was that its policy
recommendations were torn to shreds.   The Kasumigaseki

staff complained that they were becoming mere cyphers.
The new body brought to light differences of view on
foreign affairs.   There had been differences in the
past but these had been swept under the carpet.
During the war period Japan had faced new and difficult problems;   and there was diversity of opinion on
the way they should be handled.   Now these diverse
views were debated in the council.   Policy-making
became more difficult;   but the policy, once made,
was more representative.

Perhaps unexpectedly Ishii himself seems to have
favoured the establishment of the Advisory Council
with a view to formulating a foreign policy which
transcended narrow views.   He wrote: 'The failure
[of politicians] to draw a line between national
polity and party politics cannot but be branded as unpatriotic.   Care should be taken to keep questions
of foreign policy apart from domestic issues.' (12)
He seems to imply that opposition over foreign policy
merely to gratify party hostility is unpatriotic and
therefore undesirable.   This tends to confirm the
difference between the bureaucratic and rather conventional approach of Ishii and the more unconventional
and individualistic approach of his predecessors like
Katō, Komura, Aoki and Mutsu.

The existence of the Council created one more hurdle
which stood in the way of the fulfilment of Kasumigaseki
policy.   To some extent, this had advantages.   The
ideas of a political leader like Inukai Tsuyoshi (Ki)
were a breath of fresh air (see his views in Document
18).   Over the three great issues with which it had
to deal in its four-year history, Siberia, the Paris
Peace conference and the Washington conference, it
gave the liberals a voice which they might not otherwise have had.   On the other hand, one cannot import
vocal outsiders into the decision-making process
without running risks.   One can see in the outcome
the result of personal jealousies, haphazard and unpredictable decisions over policy and, of course, delays.
The procedure was bureaucratically inconvenient but
may have had beneficial elements for the long-term
development of the Foreign Ministry.

The Advisory Council was barely in existence when
Ishii was given the assignment which was to become one
of the highpoints of his career.   In April 1917 the
United States entered the war against Germany;   and
thus became involuntarily Japan's ally.   This was
awkward for Japan because Washington had shown itself
to be hostile to her doings in China during the war.

It was not the active defender of China so much as the
force which was most likely to impede Japan's progress
there.   The United States was in a strong position to
make things difficult for Japan which was dependent on
American materials for her war production and rapid
economic growth.   If Washington were to cut off the
export of steel, pig iron etc., on the ground that it
was needed for her own industrial war effort, the
weakness of Japan's wartime industrialization would be
exposed.   Moreover, if the Americans were to embark
on heavy armament programmes and were to tip the
balance in favour of the allies in the war, the world
would be more likely to pay attention to them at a
peace conference than to the exhausted European Powers.
Japan would, therefore, have to change her tactics
towards the United States because of the suspicion and
fear which she now felt. (13)

It was necessary for Japan to improve her relations
with the United States.   Relations between the
Foreign Ministry and the American ambassador in Tokyo,
Roland Morris, were specially cultivated.   Both Motono
and his successor after April 1918, Gotō Shimpei, spoke
to Morris of the fact that their two countries would be
the leading members of the alliance at the end of the
war. (14)   An industrial mission under Baron Megata
crossed the Pacific at the end of 1917 to draw attention to Japan's needs.

A more positive approach than these was tried in
June 1917 when Ishii was selected to head a war mission
to Washington.   Following the example set earlier by
Britain and France, Japan sent a 'mission of solidarity'
to welcome the United States as one of the wartime
allies.   Ishii, now a viscount, thus undertook the
most delicate diplomatic assignment of his career.
Ishii performed well at the propaganda side of the
mission: he had some success in winning over the Press
to a greater understanding of Japan's position; and
he attended many social functions across the country
which assisted the image of Japan.   Another aspect of
his task was to arrange for supplies, especially
American steel.   The embargo which had been placed on
the export of this commodity had seriously affected
the twenty-eight shipbuilding yards which had been
established for the war effort.   On this count, his
mission obtained little.   On another front, the United
States was anxious to work out some arrangement whereby
Japan would assume patrol responsibilities, even in the
eastern Pacific.   The two sides arranged for joint
defensive operations to be conducted throughout the

north Pacific; and Guam, Midway and the Philippines
which were feeling the coldness of isolation were able
to breathe again.

What subsequently assumed a major importance for
the Ishii mission was the secret discussion on China.
This was not a subject which arose out of the war
effort so much as direct American-Japanese relations.
On 13 June Ishii received instructions to make clear
Japan's special relations with China and work for co-
operation between the two countries in the future.
Since the twenty-one demands, the Americans had befriended the Chinese more and more as the European
countries were seen by Chinese eyes to be powerless
giants. It was therefore desirable for Japan to have
the opportunity of discussion with the Wilson administration. European countries advised Washington
strongly against inviting the Japanese for discussion;
but it had naval reasons for its invitation. Ishii's
function was to ask for concessions which the United
States was reluctant to give but could not in the circumstances withhold. Over China the intention was
probably to do a deal in the name of the Open Door,
whereby existing spheres of influence would be disregarded as Wilson was understood to believe necessary
and American and Japanese development funds would co-
operate. These proposals for China proper did not
apply to Manchuria or Inner Mongolia where foreign
governments could do nothing with the Chinese authorities without Tokyo's approval. This was the case
which Ishii was to put forward in Washington in the
turmoil of the early months of America's entry into
the war.

Ishii reached Washington on 22 August and began
negotiations on 8 September. He was overwhelmed by
the warmth of the public welcome he received and was
delighted to hear from President Wilson himself the
statement that he would like to see the abolition of
spheres of influence in China. Considering his own
instructions as vague and regarding Wilson's remark as
an opening which could lead to an American-Japanese
understanding on Japan's role in China, he asked for
fresh instructions from Tokyo. The Foreign Ministry
did not share his enthusiasm for the abolition of
spheres of influence which could hardly be done on a
bilateral basis without consultation with the European
Powers, especially Britain. At the Gaikō chōsakai (15)
on 15 September, the party politicians, Hara, Itō
Miyoji and Inukai were all opposed to Ishii's proposals
and stressed that he did not understand Japan's policy

in China.   Premier Terauchi, however, secured agreement for the proposal that Japan should enquire more
into America's thinking.   As a result Motono on 18
September instructed Ishii simply to get recognition
for Japan's special position in China without becoming
involved over spheres of influence.

Since the reply was so delayed, Ishii entered into
negotiations on his own initiative with Secretary of
State Robert Lansing.   Difficulties soon arose over
Japan's claim to have 'special interests' not to say
'paramount interests' in China.   But eventually a
formula was reached in an exchange of notes on 2
November.   In their notes, Ishii and Lansing affirmed
that 'territorial propinquity creates special relations
between countries, and consequently the Government of
the United States recognizes that Japan has special
interests in China, particularly in the part to which
her possessions are contiguous.'   In a supplementary
understanding which was exchanged but remained unofficial
and unsigned, it was laid down that the two countries
'agree to refrain from taking advantage of the present
state of affairs in order to seek special rights or
privileges which would abridge the rights of subjects
of other nations'.   While Secretary Lansing later told
the Foreign Relations Committee of the Senate that the
terms had no political significance, Japan held that
they had political as well as economic significance,
otherwise there would have been no point in the notes
inasmuch as the Open Door in China was already upheld
in several documents.   Ishii took the line that the
core of Japan's special interests in China was political.
Despite this divergence of view, the Japanese considered
that they had received Washington's moral support for
their claims in China.   On the other hand, they were
limited by their voluntary declaration of self-restraint,
albeit a secret one.   Lansing, who was authorized in
his acts by the president and administration, took some
consolation from this.   But he knew that, though the
United States was not required to take some of the
threats which Ishii used too literally, she was not
playing a strong hand.   He sought, therefore, to be
realistic and to show the Japanese that his country,
while it befriended China, had no intention of disputing
Japan's treaty rights in China. (16)

One is bound to conclude that the Ishii-Lansing notes
are one of those cases where basic disagreements between
the negotiators were concealed in an ambiguous form of
words.   So far as Lansing was concerned, he did not
feel that he was giving away more than had been given

in the Bryan note of 1915.   From Japan's standpoint,
she held that the Open Door did not extend to Manchuria
and further that the 'special interests' mentioned
covered political as well as economic rights.   In
effect, therefore, the negotiators agreed to differ.
Later they pleaded the case for their interpretation of
the notes in their writings.   The result was that
there were no real beneficiaries from the agreement;
both sides claimed to be the moral victor and to have
secured the better of the bargain (Document 19).

There are similar disagreements over the significance
of the notes.   In the American view, they were far
from being the basis for the long overdue relaxation
of tensions with Japan.   They were only a peculiar
offshoot of wartime diplomacy whereby the United States
was hoping to establish the status quo in east Asia
while she diverted her naval forces to the Atlantic.
Whatever else they were, the notes were only temporary
in their consequences.   Secretary Lansing interpreted
them thus before a Senate committee in 1919.   In
Ishii's interpretation they were something of a personal
triumph.   After all, was he not invited at the conclusion of his mission to return to Washington?   When,
in January 1918, the Washington embassy fell vacant,
the government appointed Ishii to that office, deducing
that he had done great things in the previous year.
In accepting, Ishii found himself enmeshed in one of
the first serious fracas with the United States over
the Siberian intervention.   When he presented his cre-
dentials in Washington at the end of April, relations
were in the doldrums and he had to reassure Lansing and
Wilson, who were both suspicious that Japan wanted to
send large forces to Siberia to prevent the spread of
bolshevism there.   It was largely his tact and the
caution of the government leaders in Tokyo which prevented open opposition developing in Washington and
led to the verbal compromises which authorized both
American and Japanese troops to be sent to Siberia.

In later years, the handiwork of Ishii's war mission
rankled in Washington.   Although Japan had been careful to describe the result as the 'American-Japanese
joint declaration' rather than the 'Ishii-Lansing
declaration', the Republican administration which
governed from 1921 had no commitment to it and no liking
for it.   It asked Japan in May 1922 whether it could
be mutually cancelled now that a new set of Washington
treaties for the Far East had been signed.   Needless
to say, it was not Japan's wish that Ishii's declaration
should be reversed;   and the matter occupied the

attention of the gaikō chosakai and the Cabinet for
some time without any compromise solution offering
itself.   Finally Japan accepted the cancellation of
the note in April 1923.   At the same time, she continued to hold that 'special interests', once recognized on the basis of territorial propinquity, could
not be set aside by this cancellation and that they
still held good.   She safeguarded herself by inform-
ing Washington that her readiness to renounce the
Ishii-Lansing declaration did not indicate any change
in Japan's position in China.   Ishii, who was not
consulted over the renunciation, would, one suspects,
have objected strenuously.   He depicts himself and
Lansing as no more than photographers of a real
situation, Japan's established rights in China;   even
if the prints or the negatives are discarded because
they do not suit the Americans, the fact of Japan's
'special interests' remains(17) (Document 19).

This whole episode has to be seen in the context of
Japan's war aims.   She had, as she thought, obtained
the acceptance by Britain, France and Russia, of her
position in China.   She now sought to capitalize on
her war mission by securing America's agreement.   In
view of the Root-Takahira agreement of 1908 and the
Bryan statement of 1915, it was not expected to be
difficult.   Ishii's favourable reception, especially
in New York, led to the ambiguous note signed with
Lansing under the aegis of the Terauchi ministry.
But, even after Terauchi's China policy had become
discredited, there was no intention to depart from
Japan's approach to a China which was suffering from
the dark night of the warlords.

PARIS PEACE CONFERENCE

After the First World War ended in victory for the
allies, the peace conference for which Ishii had been
sedulously preparing the way in the United States,
opened in Paris in January 1919.   Ishii had been
wooing Washington in the knowledge that Japan's relations with the European allies were much closer than
those with the United States, even allowing for the
Ishii-Lansing agreement.   Despite some successes,
Ishii had to concede that the drift of President
Wilson's speeches in 1918 from the Fourteen Points
onwards was favourable to China and held out hopes for
backing in the future, while impressing upon the Chinese
the need to mend their north-south split.   It was not

really good news for him when Wilson announced that
he would personally go to Paris for the conference.
    Japanese representation at Paris was a delicate
matter.   She was represented in the early stages by
her ambassadors in London and Paris, Chinda and Matsui.
At Tokyo Prime Minister Hara was too recently in
office to go overseas, while Foreign Minister Uchida
was not in good health.   Baron Makino was therefore
chosen as delegate and took part in lengthy briefings
before he set off via the United States on 10 December.
He was a politician, a liberal and a former foreign
minister.   He identified himself with the new diplomacy and advocated that Japan should accept the
fourteen points and the concept of a league of nations.
When, however, it was clear that other countries would
appoint plenipotentiaries at the level of prime minister
and president, Japan chose as head of delegation Prince
Saionji Kimmochi, a veteran politician of seventy who
had for five years been inactive in party affairs.
Since he did not reach Paris until 3 March, Saionji
seems to have played largely a titular part.   But he
had been educated in France and claimed to have a long-
standing friendship with Georges Clemenceau.   Following
his lead, the delegation tried to secure their ends by
informal contacts with the leaders rather than by
rhetoric at sessions.
    This was the first multi-nation peace conference at
which Japan had been represented.   Certainly it was
the first at which she enjoyed such high status, being
recognized as one of the five Great Powers.   As long
as decision-making was concentrated in the five, Japan
was well contented; but gradually decisions were concentrated in the Council of Four and Japan was excluded.
    The Japanese delegates were kept on a tight rein by
the Hara government.   This was not only exercised by
the Foreign Ministry and the Cabinet but also - and
most penetratingly - by the Advisory Council on Foreign
Affairs.   In five lengthy sessions in November-
December 1918, the Council had discussed the mandate
to be given to the delegates.   After the negotiations
got under way, it met regularly to debate the instructions to be sent to Paris.   For this reason, the
Japanese delegates probably had less flexibility in
their bargaining position than any other negotiators.
    Japan's demands encountered much opposition from the
start.   Her ambitions in China were harshly attacked
from a quarter which she thought she had won over in
advance - the Chinese.   The Japanese delegates were
unequal to the challenge of Dr Wellington Koo, who

gradually took over the effective leadership of the
Chinese group in Paris.   Makino, who bore the brunt
of presenting the case in various committees, had an
imperfect knowledge of English.   While some writers,
including the secretary-general, Maurice (later Lord)
Hankey, praised him for the lucidity and brevity of
his arguments, his English was not adequate for the
cut-and-thrust of debate at a conference.   It was no
surprise, therefore, that the Japanese tended to
avoid confrontation by absenting themselves from
sessions at which the Chinese were presenting their
case.   On the other hand, the Japanese were not un-
skilled in appealing beyond the delegations to public
opinion by wooing the Press and may have out-smarted
the Chinese in this field where they were active.
The Japanese 'paper warfare' became especially effective after Matsuoka Yōsuke became head of the information section in Paris. (18)

     Ishii's absence from the list of delegates will
immediately be obvious.   By reason of his seniority
and his experience, he would have been a natural
choice.   In view of Wilson's decision to attend the
deliberations in person, it would not have been exceptional for the Washington ambassador to accompany him.
There were two reasons for his exclusion.   First, he
had accepted the post of foreign minister under the
Okuma ministry, which was a ministry composed of
parties opposed to the Seiyūkai, the party that had
come to power in September 1918.   The present prime
minister, Hara, tended not to forgive his political
opponents and gave indications that he did not like
Ishii.   It is probably for this reason that no room
was found for Ishii among the eighty-man delegation
which Japan sent to Paris. (19)

     There is a second reason which may account for
Ishii's rejection.   It is that not all the terms of
the Versailles treaty were completed in the smoke-
filled rooms of Paris.   There is a sense in which the
Versailles treaty was - or seemed likely to be -
influenced by a struggle for world opinion.   In
Japan's case, her struggle was likely to be with the
Chinese and their supporters in the United States.
It was clear that Wellington Koo and the Chinese delegates were anxious to obtain assurances from the
American president in advance of the conference.   In
that context it was valuable to have an experienced
ambassador in Washington in order to bring to bear
what influence was possible on the president and the
State Department.   Before Wilson set off for Europe

and when he returned in mid-conference, Ishii tried to
influence him.   Also in his speeches he sought to
convince American opinion - no easy job - of the
rightness of Japan's demands in Paris. (20)
     The Japanese demands in Paris were mainly two.
The first concerned the Japanese-occupied area of
Kiaochow.   Japan could have asked for permanent
occupation of the territory; but she decided instead
to ask for the transfer of the German lease to herself
and to promise to return the territory to China.   At
the same time she wanted to receive the unconditional
surrender of German rights in Kiaochow and Shantung
and to secure the transfer of railway and other rights
from Germany, according to the Sino-Japanese treaties
of 1915 and 1918.   The second was the transfer of
the German islands in the Pacific north of the equator
which Japanese units had occupied in 1914.   This was
an issue where Japan would have to act in line with
the delegates of the British empire who were hopeful
of acquiring the German islands in the south Pacific
and also the German colonies in Africa.   Apart from
these two overriding demands, it was necessary for
Japan to decide her policy on the proposal for a league
of nations being coupled with the peace settlement.
Japan's leaders, with the notable exception of Makino,
took the view that a league was likely to be restric-
tive and prejudicial to her interests: it might act
unfavourably against a yellow race; it might hinder
Japan's military agreements such as the naval alliance
with Britain.   Japanese opinion had genuine reservations about the proposed institution.   While there
was no real question of Japan not joining any organization which was set up, she had no intention of doing
anything positive to encourage it.   Tokyo's instructions were that, if it came up for discussion, her
delegates should try to defer or delay any resolution
for its practical accomplishment; but, 'if it none
the less came into being, they should seek suitable
guarantees as far as circumstances permit to prevent
damage to Japan which would result from racial considerations'. (21)   On all other matters where Japan's
interests were not affected, it was left to Makino to
adapt to the conference mood.
     It is possible here to deal only with the terms of
the settlement so far as Japan was concerned, not with
the debates as they arose.   The first issue was her
desire to incorporate within the covenant of the League
of Nations words which would remove disadvantages
deriving from racial considerations.   While Wilson was

back in Washington in March, Ishii submitted a note
emphasizing his government's desire for the removal
of discrimination.   In Paris Makino proposed on 11
April that the preamble to the covenant should recognize 'the principle of equality of nations and of just
treatment of their nationals'.   Eleven out of seven-
teen members supported the motion; but President
Wilson, holding that it required a unanimous vote
(being an issue of principle), declared from the chair
that the resolution was lost.   Undaunted, Makino, in
a speech to a plenary session on 28 April, placed on
record that the Japanese government and people regretted their failure to have the racial equality formula
adopted and promised to press the issue through the
League when it came into being.

Japan's failure here may have worked to her advantage over her other demands.   Over the German Pacific
islands, she had a modest success.   These islands
became C-class mandates of the League, which implied
that they could not be fortified.   The Japanese
received the mandate for the islands north of the
equator which they had earlier occupied, while the
British Empire received the mandate for those to the
south.   There was some disappointment in Japan over
this; but she recognized that Japan had not been less
well treated than Britain.   Over Shantung, the
Japanese delegation received instructions that they
were to defer signing the covenant if Japan's demands
were not conceded.   It was generally agreed by other
delegates that the Paris conference was not empowered
to set aside the Sino-Japanese agreement of 1918, whatever view it took of that of 1915.   It was therefore
agreed that Japan might succeed to German rights as
defined in the original Sino-German agreement of 1898
without the accretions which had been added later.
Japan's blackmail about walking out of the conference
had paid dividends.

The peace treaty with Germany was signed at Versailles
on 28 June.   By its terms Germany granted Japan the
unexpired portion of the lease of Kiaochow without compensation, together with such railway and mining rights
as she had held.   In consequence, Japan promised to
hand back the Shantung peninsula in full sovereignty to
China though she set no time limit for this.   Over
racial equality she gained nothing, although she had
put her views on record.   For the German islands in the
Pacific, she obtained a class C mandate from the League
of Nations, rather less than she had hoped.   Her
achievements were less than her aspirations; but this

was true for all the victor powers.   On the other
hand, Japan had much to be thankful for.   As Saionji
admitted in his report, the Japanese 'could not have
accomplished their wishes in total'.   The Advisory
Council on Foreign Affairs was often critical of the
actions of the Japanese delegates who, when they
returned home in August, were given a mixed reception.
The historian must record it as a modest success for
Japan (Document 20).

It was widely said in 1919 that the powers had
favoured Japan rather than China.   It seemed as
though Britain and France had been governed in their
judgment by the 1917 undertakings and Wilson had
renegued on his promises to China.   But these judgments underestimate the conditions on which Kiaochow
had been granted to Japan - the 'small print' as it
were of the Versailles treaty.   It was not that
Wilson, Lloyd George and Clemenceau were unsympathetic
to China but that they found it legally difficult and
politically impossible to resist the Japanese demands.
Had time permitted, it might have been possible to tie
Japan down more.   But, as Secretary-General Hankey
wrote, this Far Eastern imbroglio had been 'an almost
intolerable strain to all concerned coming on top of
the Italian claims and a spate of urgent questions
pouring in about the compilation of the German
Treaty'. (22)   Within the context of the world-wide
problems which they were handling, there was a limit
to the time they could devote to the Far East.
Instead, Britain and the United States reopened the
issue in July as soon as the Versailles treaty was
settled. (23)

Ishii was never at ease in the Washington embassy.
American opinion was hostile to Japan and the Press
never seemed to lose its suspicions of the early war
years.   Ishii had found it impossible to build on the
cordiality which he thought he had created in 1917.
It was the China question which soured relations and
the Sakatani incident which brought the matter to
breaking point.   From the summer of 1918 the Japanese
government wanted to appoint Baron Sakatani Yoshirō
(1863-1941) as Japanese financial adviser to China,
the first such appointment.   Sakatani was eminently
well qualified, having been minister of finance (1906-8)
and Japan's representative to the allied economic
conference in Paris in 1917.   He had, moreover, many
foreign friends.   It was not the man but the post
which annoyed the State Department.   Ishii reported
that he had secured Lansing's approval of the appoint-

ment - or, at least, a statement of his disinterest.
His government, therefore, went ahead with overtures
to China which promptly consulted the American minister
in Peking.   But the Americans denied all knowledge of
their having given advance approval and, when pressed,
stated that the proposals of 1919 for the renewal of
the consortium for China radically changed the situation
and that Japan should not appoint a financial adviser
to that country until the consortium proposals were
worked out.   Since this fundamental disagreement only
emerged after Secretary Lansing and the American establishment had moved to Paris for the peace conference,
it was doubly frustrating for Ishii.   He resigned in
the spring on the ground that he had 'intimate relations' with Sakatani which made it embarrassing for
him to stay on. (24)   But he was clearly bitter over
the administrative sloppiness of the State Department.
Both the United States and Japan asked him to reconsider
his decision.   But Ishii was adamant and was truly
glad to leave - a victim perhaps of the inevitable
American-Japanese tensions.

Ishii was also increasingly depressed and unhappy
over his treatment from Tokyo.   To have been passed
over for the Paris conference had been deeply wounding
to him.   He was annoyed at the anti-American tone of
the Japanese Press.   He was also acutely aware that
Japan, despite all his efforts, was unpopular throughout the United States;   he was conscious of swimming
against the tide of Wilsonian thinking and American
public opinion as shown in a hostile Press.   Specula-
tion about his future abounded from April 1919 onwards.
An American official ruminated:

I do not believe that Ishii is going home because
of the Sakatani incident.   My mind is slowly coming
to the conclusion that our relations are not as good
as they should be and that he sees they are drifting
away and that he does not want to be held personally
or politically responsible for the turn things are
taking. (25)

Be that as it may, he returned to Japan in July.

Although Ishii left Washington and wartime diplomacy
with a sense of failure, it would be wrong to suggest
that his later years were not full of honour and distinction as a diplomat and public servant.   In October
1920 he became his country's ambassador in Paris and
delegate to the League of Nations (1920-27).   As
president of the League of Nations Association (Japan),
he was a frequent representative at international conferences, notably at the world economic conference in

1933.   But his speeches and remarks suggest that his
thinking was moving to the right;   he had, as his publications in the 1930s indicate, become an apologist
for his country.   The atmosphere of fear and the
prospect of poverty for officials on the point of
retirement drove men in this direction.   But Ishii
went far by any standards.

Chapter 7

The Shidehara Period, 1920-7

The twenties are the age of Shidehara in Japanese
diplomacy. As ambassador in Washington and foreign
minister at critical periods, he set the tone of his
country's foreign policy with its reputation for
internationalism, commercialism and pacifism. While
we shall have occasion to question some of the des-
criptions commonly applied to his policies, there is
little doubt that they were popularly regarded as the
hallmark of Shidehara diplomacy. (1)
    Shidehara Kijūrō (1872-1951) was born in Osaka and
educated in the law faculty of Tokyo Imperial University. He passed the entrance examination for the
Foreign Ministry in 1896, the fourth year that it
operated. After a wide variety of postings and two
long sojourns in the ministry, the first from 1904 to
1911 and the second as vice-minister from 1915 to
1919, he was sent to the key post of ambassador in
Washington from 1919 to 1922. His period there coincided with the Washington conference where he served
as one of Japan's plenipotentiaries. Returning to
Tokyo on account of illness in 1922, he was appointed
by Katō Takaaki as foreign minister in his three-party
coalition Cabinet formed in June 1924 and served
through to 1927. It is this period of his career
which will be discussed in this chapter, except for
his China policy which will be deferred to the next
chapter. Shidehara returned as foreign minister from
1929 to 1931 and thus held office for five out of the
seven years from 1924 to 1931.
    Shidehara was by no means an elementary character.
He was a loner and did not suffer fools gladly. These,
it has to be confessed, are rare attributes in a diplomat. He was not a completely popular figure with
his colleagues. As an ambassador he did not provide

for his favourite subordinates as the old-style Japanese
diplomats had done (2) and as Japanese in his position
were expected to do.   As foreign minister, he is frequently criticized for his inability to decentralize
and for the unnecessarily long hours which he worked on
his documents.   But to foreigners he appeared to be
friendly, even jolly;   and to friends communicative
and frank.

Shidehara had great independence of judgment.
Partly this sprang from his strong Kansai character.
Partly it came doubtless from his financial independence.   In 1903 he had married Iwasaki Masako, the
youngest child of the family of the Mitsubishi
zaibatsu.   (This made him incidentally a brother-in-
law of Katō Takaaki.)   It is difficult to assess how
much practical difference this made to his career and
to his policies.   But it gave him the independence to
give up the diplomatic career if he disliked the way
that the Foreign Ministry was shaping.   Thus, when he
had to resign with the ministry in December 1931, he
was able to accept an inactive retirement with nominal
membership of the House of Peers.   He was not, however,
prepared to enter seriously into party politics which
he probably despised;   he often stressed that his
foreign policy was non-partisan and this was in his
philosophy the ideal state.

Shidehara was the most successful of the early
entrants to the Foreign Ministry by examination.   He
was from a young age picked out for his special
capacity.   His greatest quality was his excellent
knowledge of English and especially of the written
language.   He was the one official of whom Henry W.
Denison, the American-born adviser to the Japanese
Foreign Ministry, boasted.   Shidehara for his part
was a great admirer of Denison who had guided his early
steps and shared many common interests with him.
Quite apart from this, he was widely regarded as being
cut out for high office.   His knowledge of English
stood him in good stead for this was a period when
this was an essential asset to a Japanese diplomat.

Shidehara was the first product of the examination
system to become foreign minister.   His appointment
marked the start of the professional service in Japan
and indicated that the reforms of the Foreign Ministry
in the 1890s had worked through the system.   On
balance, this was an advantage for the creation of a
Kasumigaseki spirit.   The new generation of foreign
ministers and top diplomats were men of high intelligence, diplomatic skill and world experience.   At the

same time, it has to be said that the older generation
had thrown up men of strong character like Komura, men
of political influence like Katō and men of great competence in foreign languages like Aoki and Hayashi
Tadasu.

Shidehara's long stint as vice-minister extended
into the postwar period.   It was important that one
who had done so much behind the scenes to lay the
foundations of Japan's peace terms should stay on
after the armistice.   In September 1918 a new party
Cabinet came in under Hara Kei, who was an active
member of the Gaikō Chōsakai and as a former diplomat
had well-formed views on most aspects of external
relations.   Like Shidehara, Hara regarded it as
essential for Japan to keep on the best possible
terms with the United States.   Despite the mutual suspicions of the war years which had come to a head over
the Siberian intervention, Hara with his energetic
and out-reaching personality was determined to
cultivate American goodwill.   In this he recognized
Vice-minister Shidehara as an ally and, after retaining him in Tokyo until September 1919, appointed him
as ambassador to Washington.

Hara had to convince others to his way of thinking.
Even in those days of 'Taishō democracy', consultation
with the Diet was a comparatively minor matter.   It
was largely confined to formal ministerial speeches at
irregular intervals; and, although interpellations
could be awkward, they had little effect on policy-
making and ministers were generally able to avoid
giving away too much information.   Japan still operated
under the canons of secret diplomacy.   The Cabinet
was, of course, consulted regularly.   There was also
inter-party consultation in the Gaikō Chōsakai, but
this was a less influential instrument after the war
in view of Hara's large parliamentary majority.   It
had been intended to abolish this emergency committee
after the peace conference.   But this was not done;
and it continued to be a forum where opposition leaders
could be consulted down to 1922, thereby limiting the
powers of the executive and slowing down the pace of
its actions.

Hara also had to consult the Elder Statesmen.   The
time had passed when the genro held meetings to stage
dramatic interventions into foreign affairs.   But it
was necessary for the premier to consult individual
genro and keep them abreast of ministerial decisions.
Yamagata (1838-1922), the most important of the remaining genro, was suspicious of political parties but was

content to work with Hara, provided he was kept informed.
Thus, detailed conversations took place, on an average
about twice a month, with Hara visiting Yamagata's home
at Odawara or the trim figure of Yamagata with his straw
hat calling on the prime minister in Tokyo.   It
required someone of the unrivalled stamina of Hara to
fulfil this remarkable unwritten obligation.   His
reward was to secure Yamagata's broad collaboration,
though relations were always delicate.   Yamagata was
an indispensable ally during the Siberian intervention
when the General Staff and the War Ministry claimed
special prerogatives.   In this situation, it was
essential for Hara through Yamagata to win over his
Chōshū protégé, the war minister, General Tanaka, if
the civilian government was to have a say, or even to
exercise control, in winding up the Siberian expedition.
By contrast, it was a much smaller problem to keep in
touch with the other senior genro, Matsukata (1837-1924)
who was not especially active or Prince Saionji (1849-
1940) who had left politics in the 1910s and slipped all
unnoticed into the ranks of the Elder Statesmen.

   Because Japan's position was being challenged, Hara
was a prime minister much exercised by foreign policy.
In 1919 Japan was in occupation of parts of Shantung
and the German Pacific islands (by virtue of the
Versailles treaty);   in possession of substantial
interests in Manchuria and China (by her treaties of
1915 and 1918);   and in military occupation of parts
of the Russian Far East (by her actions since the
Siberian intervention).   These were in a sense the
fruits of her war effort;   and the United States and
Britain were broadly anxious to establish the status quo
that had existed before the war.   So long as the peace
conference was still in being, their priority was to
conclude the treaty with Germany, even if it meant
rough justice for some.   After that they approached
Japan in a more combative spirit and urged her to change
her continental policy radically.   In this the foreign
governments had their own public opinion behind them. (3)

   In a strange way Hara sympathized with this point of
view and was prepared to meet it halfway.   One of the
forms which the dispute took from 1919 onwards was the
battle over the conclusion of a new international loan
consortium for China.   It will be recalled that the prewar consortium had consisted of Britain, France, Germany,
Russia and Japan, the United States having left it in
1913 under President Wilson.   Germany's membership was
deemed to have automatically lapsed during the war.   In
1916 Britain had put out feelers for the reconstitution

of the consortium with American membership but Japan in
a communication of 20 July would not agree to America
rejoining either through an old group of bankers or a
new group.   There was no alternative to the matter
being held in abeyance until the end of the war when
the omens would be brighter.   Indeed they seemed to
be brighter.   In October 1918 Premier Hara gave
instructions that Japan should not enter into any more
loans on the lines of the Nishihara ones.

This led to an important new initiative by the
Americans.   During the Paris peace conference repre-
sentatives of the banking groups had met and laid the
foundations for a new four-Power consortium from which
Germany would be excluded.   The Japanese bankers
asked for the exclusion from the consortium of south
Manchuria and eastern Inner Mongolia.   But this was
to stick out for spheres of influence which the other
Powers were anxious to eliminate from the postwar Far
East.   Japan was urged to withdraw her reservations
over these provinces but, after frequent meetings, her
Cabinet refused.   By March 1920 the Americans, while
still opposing the Japanese demands, promised that the
consortium would avoid 'any operation inimical to the
vital interests of Japan'.   This formula being acceptable to Japan, she agreed to join the new consortium on
11 May.   The consortium bankers held conferences in
New York which led to the signing of an agreement on
15 October.   This contained no reference to the exclusion from the consortium of any 'special sphere'
and Japan accepted instead the private assurance that
her vital interests would be upheld.   Underlying all
this banking diplomacy there were some traces of an
Anglo-American common front over Chinese finances.
Aware of this, Hara still thought that there was no
point in holding out for Japan's reservations, as many
of his colleagues wanted;   and Shidehara for his part
thought so even more strongly.

The compromise left each side to interpret the new
consortium as its own interests dictated.   But in
practice loan negotiations under the new consortium
were few so that its significance in history comes more
from the acrimonious bargaining which took place in
the months before its formation.   The consortium
talks were for Japan a symbol of the Anglo-American
common front which she faced and of the dilemma it
posed: should she liberalize her attitudes in China or
cling to her wartime gains?

WASHINGTON YEARS, 1919-22

In November 1919 Shidehara returned to the scene where
he had earlier been councillor.   In Japanese eyes, it
had become a 'hot seat' from which Ambassador Ishii
had been happy to escape.   There were disputes right
across the board.   It is perhaps understandable that
Washington's estimate of the new ambassador was not
wholly favourable: at the State Department he seemed
occasionally to be regarded rather unfavourably as a
man who promised more than he could achieve.   Over
Siberia which was the main bone of contention, he
claimed that Japan only wanted an Open Door policy for
her commerce and had no thought of holding on to
territory.   Such remarks seemed to bear little relation to the situation on the ground and were heard by
American officials with incredulity.

Shidehara's early endeavours were specially concerned with the problem of Japanese emigration to the
United States.   We have dealt with this earlier as
far as the first interim solution, the Gentlemen's
Agreement of 1907-8.   Shidehara had devoted much time
when he was in America   during 1913-14, to the related
problem of landholding by Japanese.   In 1913 the
Californian legislature considered a land bill, the
effect of which was to prohibit Japanese from owning
land.   Despite efforts on the part of Japan and the
federal government, the bill was enacted.   Three notes
of protest were addressed to Washington against the
legislation on the ground that it violated the principle
and spirit of the Japanese-American treaty.   Needless
to say, Japanese opinion was exceedingly aroused;   and
the foreign minister was closely questioned in the Diet
in January 1914.   While he condemned the American
action as unsatisfactory, he refrained from publishing
the protests and the replies received.   Very much
worried at the prospect of public opinion getting out
of hand, the Cabinet avoided whipping up racial feeling
which must be directed at the United States since the
British colonies had resolved the issue with some
success. (4)

In 1920 the Californian legislature amended their
land law in such a way as to exclude Japanese from even
leasing land there.   It was an example of the fierce
exclusionist postwar mood.   Ambassador Shidehara with
his mandate to improve American-Japanese relations had
to address himself to this problem.   His method was
to enter into a series of conversations with Roland
Morris, the American ambassador in Tokyo who was in

Washington on leave.   Their purpose was to reach some
sort of executive agreement which would undercut the
Californian moves and remove the tension between
Washington and Tokyo.   But 1920 was a difficult year
for this in view of the coming presidential election.
The two ambassadors were authorized to meet in informal conferences: 'Their conclusions would not be
binding on their two governments; but they were none
the less to explore possible means for the removal or
prevention of discriminatory measures against Japan
and possible amendments for the existing [sic] Gentlemen's Agreement.'   The conferences ran from 15
September 1920 to the twenty-third and final meeting
on 24 January 1921.   After a number of clarifications
of existing legislation going back to 1894, Shidehara
on 26 October presented the terms of an acceptable
immigration treaty.   This, however, failed to meet
the requirements of the State Department.   Morris, who
was in the later stages accompanied by J.V.A. McMurray
from the Far Eastern section in order to give the
talks an air of authority in view of the change from a
Democratic to a Republican administration, in turn
presented his own draft.   Finally, on 24 January 1921,
Morris stated his intention to close the conferences
and prepare his report for the secretary of state.
The meeting of minds and the atmosphere of 'give and
take' had been considerable.   What is less easy to
define is how far the arrangements conceived were reflected in subsequent Washington attitudes.

When the election brought President Harding to the
White House, a new Republican approach towards east
Asia took shape.   Secretary of State Charles Evans
Hughes, untied to the presuppositions of the Versailles
settlement, was virtually able to examine the issues
from scratch.   But it was still the approach of a
United States predominantly hostile and antipathetic
towards Japan.   The Republicans with the backing of a
strong Press campaign seriously suspected Japan's long-
term plans about naval expansion and her intentions in
China.

Tokyo was discussing in February the possibility
that some of this anti-Japanese bias could be overcome
by the crown prince visiting the United States in the
course of the world tour on which he was about to
embark.   It would have been possible to extend his
cruise to Britain and the various European countries
in order to take in America if this was likely to
improve the political climate.   He could then have
returned to Japan via Panama.   But for reasons which
are not yet clear, the proposal was not pursued. (5)

Out of the maelstrom of events in 1921 emerged the
proposal for a Far Eastern Conference and a Pacific
Naval Conference. The Washington administration, who
eventually became convenors of a single conference to
consider these issues, had in mind many different
aspects which were in need of settlement. But
American-Japanese relations were central to the conference. The kernel of the Far Eastern Conference
was Japan's ambitions in China, while the centrepoint
of the naval problem was Japan's announced shipbuilding
programme. It was to tax Shidehara's skill to the
uttermost to negotiate the preparations of this
conference.

THE WASHINGTON CONFERENCE OF 1921-2

Shidehara's greatest achievement as ambassador was at
the Washington conference which opened in November 1921.
His first task was to make arrangements for Japan's
participation, which was fraught with trouble. Responding to the first feelers about the conference,
Japan, while agreeing to be present, expressed the hope
that 'reserved subjects' - which were deemed to cover
the problems of Shantung and the Anglo-Japanese
alliance - should not be discussed. Secretary Hughes
was reluctant to give undertakings along these lines
but ultimately assured Shidehara that he would not
raise embarrassing subjects at the conference. Thus,
when the official invitations went out on 13 August,
Japan accepted with hesitation. In the long run,
Shidehara was successful in his negotiations, because
Hughes raised the 'reserved subjects' not at conference
sessions, but at separate talks.
Behind the scenes Shidehara had to placate Washington
and Tokyo. He was perfectly sincere in telling Hughes
that it was important that the conference should be held
in as friendly an atmosphere as possible in order that
it should be a success. By this means, he was able to
convince Hughes that it was important not to alienate
the Japanese government and public opinion. An even
greater problem was to dispel the doubts in Japan. It
was commonly believed there that the forthcoming conference was a ruse by which Japan would be arraigned
before an international tribunal of the Anglo-Saxon
powers for her doings in China over the previous decade.
Even when the Americans tabled their draft of items to
be raised, the Japanese Cabinet took the view that the
so-called Pacific items were virtually related to China

and only served to excite her hopes in a way prejudicial
to Japan. (6)   Those like Shidehara himself and
Hayashi Gonsuke, the ambassador in London, suggested
that Japan should turn the meeting to her advantage by
making a revision of her policies, especially improving
her relations with the United States and correcting her
past errors towards China.   But they were in a minority.

Turning to the question of representation, the
Americans had suggested, unofficially but none the less
strongly, that the chief delegates should all be civilians.   This posed special problems for the Japanese
leaders who considered that they could hardly be represented at a naval disarmament conference exclusively
by civilians, in view of the privileged position enjoyed
by the armed services.   So on 27 September Prime
Minister Hara announced as his country's delegates:
Admiral Katō Tomosaburō, the navy minister, Ambassador
Shidehara and Prince Tokugawa.   The presence of two
civilians placated the Americans.

What role did Shidehara play at the conference?
Clearly he could not claim seniority: Katō was a member
of the Cabinet, while Tokugawa was president of the
House of Peers.   Then again, Shidehara was ill for
three weeks after the start of the conference;   and
Hanihara Masanao had to be added as a supernumerary
plenipotentiary.   This might seem to detract from
Shidehara's role.   But this would be a false conclusion.
In title Tokugawa was the chief delegate;   in practice
his role was nominal.   Katō had to deputize for both
Tokugawa and Shidehara on political matters.   But in
several instances Shidehara's was the most powerful
influence.   Thus, in the chaos which prevailed before
the conference got under way, Shidehara had an important mediatory role with his home government and with
Hughes;   and even when he was confined to bed after the
start of the conference, he still attended to business.
Since it took much longer to clinch the treaties than
optimists had originally predicted (many had expected
all to be concluded by Christmas), Shidehara was able,
after his recovery, to have a hand in practically all
aspects of the settlement, including the naval treaty. (7)

It is now necessary to turn to the three crucial
results of the conference: the ending of the British
alliance, the settlement of Shantung and capital ship
limitation.   The first two matters were technically
resolved at meetings held outside the purview of the
conference.   The last was the work of the disarmament
committee which was one of the two divisions into which
the conference was split.   Shidehara's prime responsi-

bility was to deal with the Pacific and Far Eastern committee.

The future of the Anglo-Japanese alliance was an essential subject for discussion because it had been one of the central threads in Anglo-American and Japanese-American tensions in the preceding years. It was debated between the heads of delegation for much of November in desultory fashion. But there was no breakthrough in negotiations until Shidehara, confined to bed, obtained a copy of Britain's rough draft of a successor treaty and, thinking it to be unacceptable to American political opinion, prepared a counter-draft on the lines of a consultative pact: disputes occurring in the Pacific area were to be referred to a conference of the major interested powers (Document 21). This draft commended itself to the American and British delegates; but was it more than the personal composition of Shidehara himself, as the Japanese presented it? Evidently Shidehara did pen it without more than the approval of the other Japanese plenipotentiaries. But it fell within the mandate given by Tokyo to the delegates. From 26 November the talks moved faster. The Japanese Cabinet approved the experimental Shidehara draft on 6 December; and at a meeting held at Hughes's house two days later the final terms were worked out in the presence of a delegate from France. In this way the four-Power treaty was signed on 13 December between Japan, Britain, the United States and France. After the ratifications of all the Washington treaties had been exchanged, the Anglo-Japanese alliance came to an end on 17 August 1923. (8)

SHANTUNG

The other matter which was settled outside the Washington conference was the complex and emotional issue of Shantung province, where the former German lease had been transferred to Japan by the Versailles treaty. Since the Paris conference, the Shantung issue had been snarled up. On 16 January 1920 Japan had tried to open negotiations through Minister Obata in Peking 'with the intention of withdrawing Japanese troops from the Shantung railway zone'. China made no reply till 22 May when she declined to negotiate directly with the Japanese. Since the Chinese were looking to the support of Washington and the Japanese were not anxious to contribute to a deterioration of relations with the

United States, Japan let the matter ride a while,
saying that she would welcome at any time a proposal
for negotiations which was considered suitable to
the Chinese authorities.

On 7 September 1921, after the Washington conference had been called, Japan again took the initiative.
She announced to the Chinese a new set of terms.
Basically, it set out that Japan would restore to
China the leasehold of Kiaochow (Tsingtao) provided
that China opened that territory as an Open Door port;
that the former German Kiaochow-Tsinanfu railway and
mines associated with it should be operated as a joint
Sino-Japanese enterprise; and that Japan would recall
her troops from the railway zone as soon as China organized a police force to take over protection of the
railway. The Japanese had re-thought their position
in the light of their difficult financial position in
1921 and their international unpopularity. Doubtless
the Chinese were suspicious about the generosity of
the terms offered. But, even if discussions did not
get under way before the conference, this statement of
Japanese terms cleared the path for direct parleys at
Washington.

The Japanese initiative of September was not purely
an attempt to steal a march on the international conference. It was not unnatural for Japan to endeavour
again to sort out the position with the Peking government, which was likely to be more amenable to her than
the Chinese conference delegates. It appears that
Charles Evans Hughes, in an endeavour to trim the
formidable agenda of the conference in advance, had
been putting out feelers on this subject. On 11
August he explored the ground with China by urging her
to negotiate on Shantung directly with Japan before the
conference on the ground that the conference could not
be relied on for results. Despite China's request,
he declined to mediate between the parties.

By a surprising about-face, the secretary of state
on 18 August offered his good offices to Japan over
Shantung, doubtless realizing that it was better to
take preliminary soundings. It was therefore natural
for the Japanese Cabinet on 2 September to give the go-
ahead on an approach to China over Shantung. On 7
September Minister Obata presented Japan's compromise
plan to China. China replied that, if this was her
final offer, it fell short of solving the question.
It was to Japan's advantage to have her concessions on
record.

When the conference opened, it was the hope of the

Chinese delegates that the Shantung question would be
raised in open session, though Professor Ichihashi
states that they positively avoided raising the subject. (9)   Japan's prior undertaking from Hughes
prevented the United States from acceding to this
wish.   The Chinese delegates were aware of the folly
of expecting the good offices of Britain and the
United States to be exercised in open session.   So,
when Admiral Katō under Anglo-American persuasion
agreed to the subject of Shantung being raised in
direct private talks late in November, the Chinese
delegates, despite the known opposition of the Peking
government and of Chinese public opinion, allowed the
talks to proceed.

The mandate to Japan's delegates on this point was
'to maintain control of the Tsingtao-Tsinan railway
as an instrument of "conquest by rail"'.   Discussions
began on 1 December in the presence of foreign observers.   Three weeks later the conversations which had
appeared to be nearing a settlement were interrupted
by the Japanese on the ground that instructions from
Tokyo were required.   The Japanese government, more
uncompromising than its delegates, decided to take the
matter in hand itself.   It asked Obata Torikichi, its
minister in Peking (1918-23), to obtain the answer of
the Peking government to the offer of a Japanese railway loan, predicated on the appointment of a Japanese
chief traffic manager.   This message also carried the
threat that, if the reply were unfavourable, Japan
would call off the Washington conversations.   Liang
Shih-yi, the new prime minister who had a reputation
for leaning to Japan, told Obata on 29 December that he
agreed to a long-term loan.   He later denied this
statement and said that his agreement required the
approval of the delegates in Washington.   So the
thorny Shantung issue became twisted yet further by the
complexities of Chinese politics.

It was late in January that Hughes took the initiative in enlisting the support of Balfour for direct
intervention in the mediation.   The nub of the dispute
was over the future of the Shantung railway: Japan
would originally take nothing less than joint partnership with the Chinese.   She then agreed that China
might purchase the railway and accepted Chinese
Treasury notes maturing in fifteen years and redeemable
in five, subject to her having Japanese nationals
appointed as Traffic Manager and Chief Accountant until
redemption.   China would not agree to these Japanese
officials.   Hughes and Balfour stepped in to remind

the two parties about the discredit which would fall on
them if their obstinacy on what seemed to be small
issues threatened to wreck the solution of greater conference issues.   Shidehara's plea to Tokyo on 24
January eventually broke the deadlock.   But Japan may
not have been unwilling to pull out because her seven
years' occupation of Shantung had not been a commercial
and political success.

It is probable that China and Japan would not have
reached a settlement without the good offices of foreign
observers.   The Chinese delegates were in a difficult
position and Alfred Sze, especially, could be grossly
provocative during the talks.   Even the Americans who
took a broad-minded view of the Chinese case begged
them to behave in a more responsible fashion.   By contrast Shidehara and the Japanese delegates impressed
Americans and British alike by their seriousness of
purpose and enlightenment.   It was no small tribute
to Japan's decision to be represented by diplomats
rather than politicians over Chinese issues.

Even if Japan's negotiators enhanced their reputations, it was China which had earlier sunk so low that
mounted high at Washington at the expense of Japan.
By signing the nine-Power treaty Japan seemed to have
joined other Powers in renouncing the policy of obtaining concessions which she had been following since 1914
by subscribing to the Open Door, abjuring spheres of
influence for the future and promising to uphold
China's territorial integrity.   Possibly Japan made
mental reservations over her position in Manchuria,
where she had so recently won a battle over the international banking consortium. (10)   In these respects
Japan left the general impression upon foreigners of
'mending her ways' on the continent of Asia and
appears to have driven home the message in a way she
failed to do at Paris.   Much of this depended on
Shidehara who was personally convincing in his declaration that Japan would pull out of Siberia and Shantung
and that Japan had no objection to the ending of the
Ishii-Lansing agreement.   It was still an open question
how far Shidehara's assurances would be sustained by
the government and other authorities in Tokyo.

WASHINGTON NAVAL TREATY

By 1921 Japan was already one of the world's leading
naval powers.   The postwar battleships, 'Nagato' and
'Mutsu', were super-dreadnoughts among the very biggest

in the world.   The 1920 building programme of eight
battleships and eight cruisers to be completed by 1928
was a formidable and expensive one.   It was formidable
and dangerous in the sense that it had serious political implications.   In Japan's naval thinking, the
United States had been identified as the Power most
likely to be hostile to Japan.   If Japan were to
build to these limits, she must expect the Americans
with their ambition to create a 'navy second to none'
to respond.   The programme was also expensive and
probably beyond the level which the political parties
in the Diet would support after the full consequences
of the postwar slump were known.

The Hara Cabinet was in the process of re-thinking
its naval position.   The navy minister (1914-23),
Admiral Katō, who had been largely responsible for the
various navy expansion plans, had on several occasions
admitted that

> Japan was unable, for financial and technical
> reasons, to equal the achievements of the leading
> maritime Powers.   She was contented with fewer
> vessels, but aimed at the ideal that her capital
> ships should equal ship for ship those of the other
> Powers, hence the construction of the largest type
> of battleships.

When Hughes revealed to Shidehara in March 1921 his
idea of convening a naval conference, the ambassador
responded quite favourably.

The mandate for the naval talks allowed the delegates some discretion.   It read:

> Although we take the 8-8 fleet as the target for
> naval strength, we are not bound to persist with it
> as originally planned.   We ought to comply with
> any limitation treaty proposed within the context
> of the 8-8 fleet provided it includes a ratio of
> strength in line with that of Britain and the United
> States. (Document 22)

Using this discretion, Admiral Katō was able to
announce on 15 December that Japan accepted the 5.5.3
ratio for battleship tonnage provided that the other
powers agreed to maintain the status quo in fortifications and bases in the Pacific area and also permitted
Japan to dispose of the older 'Settsu' instead of the
newly-launched 'Mutsu'.   While the American and
British delegates were with reservations ready to
observe the status quo, they only reluctantly agreed
to Japan retaining the two post-Jutland ships, 'Nagato'
and 'Mutsu'.   Eventually a formula for the 'Mutsu' was
devised and the announcement on fortifications was

published: 'there shall be no increase in these fortifications and naval bases, except that this restriction
shall not apply to the Hawaiian islands, Australia, New
Zealand and the islands composing Japan proper.' The
Japanese were suspicious about the vagueness of this.
They did not want to be ordered in this way not to
fortify two islands which they held to be covered by
the phrase 'Japan proper', namely Amami-Oshima and
Ogasawara (Bonin islands). (11)

Shidehara's role over the disarmament issue was a
subtle one. His knowledge of naval matters was
limited and it might be assumed that he left this issue
to Admiral Katō. This would be untrue. Because of
Katō's diplomatic inexperience, Shidehara's advice was
often needed. Because of the sharp rift in the
Japanese naval delegation, many of whose members blamed
their leader for not consulting them enough, Katō
relied on Shidehara and Tokugawa for reassurance.
Again, the disarmament issue trailed off into a series
of drafts and counter-drafts; and it appears that the
critical clause of the four-Power naval treaty was
drafted by Shidehara (12) (Document 22).

Tokyo, where, in the absence of strong government,
some weight was carried by the Advisory Council, wanted
to be specific over the fortification issue. At a
meeting with heads of delegation on 10 January 1922,
Katō asked for a separate document to cover Oshima and
the Bonins. The other leaders were opposed; and
Katō urged his home government that Japan should swallow
her pride since she would gain greatly from the American undertaking not to fortify Guam and the Philippines.
But the government resisted this on the ground that,
though it was ready to maintain the status quo in
Oshima and the Bonins, it did not want to be forced
into this by international agreement.

At such a moment of disagreement, collaboration
within the Japanese delegation was essential. Admiral
Katō, feeling that Tokyo was ready to wreck the conference because of amour propre, offered to resign on
18 January rather than comply with Tokyo's orders.
Shidehara maintained solidarity with him. The Cabinet
was in a quandary because it had already received the
resignations of leading members of the Gaikō chōsakai.
Finally, thanks to Shidehara's drafting, a fresh formula
was presented whereby Japan named the islands that she
would not fortify further: the Ryukyus, Bonins, Amami
Oshima, Formosa and the Pescadores. The Advisory
Council relented, insisting only on the inclusion of
the Aleutians by the United States in return for the

Kuriles by Japan.   This was circulated to the other
Powers and incorporated in the five-Power naval
agreement which was signed on 6 February.

The naval treaty seems to have been a fair bargain.
Japan accepted a tonnage ratio inferior to Britain's
and America's in return for the assurance that the
Philippines and Guam would not be fortified by the
Americans and in the knowledge that she would not be
involved in a building race with the United States
with all the outlay which that would entail.   Katō
and Shidehara were believers in 'Tai-Bei hisenron',
in avoiding war with America at all costs.   They
greeted the whole package of Washington treaties with
enthusiasm.

WASHINGTON AFTERMATH

It is the China settlement which gives rise to the
phrases, the 'Washington structure' or 'Washington
system', which are commonly used in American or
Japanese monographs.   This is the notion that the
various aspects of the China and Pacific settlement
were cleverly interlocked to give a 'system'.   I do
not find this terminology used at all in British or
French sources.   It reflects a perception of the
Washington conference which seems to have been influenced by the retrospective writings of American
officials.   But it has to be admitted that each
participant had a different perception of the results
of the conference.   Thus, British and Americans
generally regarded it as an overwhelming success;
Japanese regarded it as at least a partial failure. (13)
While Chinese delegates also thought that their gains
had not come up to expectations on many points,
Wellington Koo returned to a hero's welcome because
of the Shantung agreement.

The use of the term 'system' ('taisei' in Japanese)
is strange.   It is doubtful whether in the hasty,
secret preparation of the conference there was enough
time, or indeed organization, to set the hopes of the
participants as high as the achievement of a 'system'.
Nor was there in the proceedings of the conference
much awareness that they were devising a carefully
balanced structure.   As in most conferences, there was
a good deal of give and take, of bending to the wind.
There were compromises introduced late in the proceedings of which the non-fortification agreement is the
supreme example.   There was no sign of a master plan.

Nor do any of the participants appear to have had a
clear plan.   They knew so little of the shape the
conference would take before their delegations reached
Washington that they could hardly do so.

The Washington Conference had the beneficial result
of relieving some of the acute tension which had prevailed between Japan and the United States.
There was an awareness among Japanese that America
had disliked many of Japan's past actions and had
been suspicious of her future intentions.   Japanese
negotiators were ready to make limited concessions,
recognizing that they had to toe the American line.
Japan had to avoid all-out naval building competition
with the Americans;   she had to avoid the greater
excesses of commercial competition;   she had to make
sure of American supplies of materials, remembering
the steel problem of the war years.   But the Japanese
were not prepared to make large-scale concessions
which did not suit Japan economically or strategically.
So there was a close-fought diplomatic battle.   From
such a conflict it is a fluke if any party emerges
unscathed;   and certainly Japan was less successful
than at the earlier Paris conference.

While those in Washington and London cheered because
the Washington treaties enshrined some degree of Anglo-
American co-operation, the Japanese were reticent and
afraid of a new isolation. Japan was concerned over her
evident defeat.   In the course of 1922 her troops were
withdrawn from Shantung and the Soviet Far East.
There were good political and financial grounds for
this but it has to be said that the popular reaction
was one of failure.   The British ambassador felt
impelled to report 'the growth of feeling that at and
since the Washington Conference Japan had yielded
everything and gained nothing'.   Much of the blame
was attached to Count Uchida, who as foreign minister
since 1918 was much criticized: 'he must have some
qualities which render him valuable but they are not
appreciated outside a very small circle.' (14)   He
eventually gave up in September 1923.

Shidehara to whom some of the 'blame' was also
attached, returned to Tokyo in April 1922 on sick leave.
While he hoped to return to Washington, his ill health
was such that this plan was scrapped in November and he
was placed on temporary Foreign Ministry duty.   His
years at Washington and his conference experiences had
deeply impressed Shidehara and influenced his thinking.
He developed as a man of Republican Washington rather
than of Versailles.

On the whole, little time was lost in Tokyo, where
reaction was less marked than in 1905, in debating
the various Washington treaties.   Their ratification
took place in August 1922.   Britain too had taken
steps for ratification for herself and for the
Empire.   France and Italy, piqued by the naval
formulae, were slower to ratify;   and President Harding
held out until their response was clearer.   But the
exchange of ratifications eventually took place in
Washington on 17 August 1923.   The elaborate package
covering naval disarmament and the Pacific, China and
Shantung, the ending of the alliance and the four-Power
treaty was in being.

Japan, like other signatories, had to operate in the
twenties consistently with the Washington agreements.
But, as with virtually all treaties, the signatories
interpreted them as suited their own interests.   Those
groups in Japan which opposed the naval settlement
adopted counter-measures in order to by-pass the
restrictions imposed on naval building programmes.
Similarly, there were those in Japan who were suspicious
of the nine-Power treaty on China which carried with it
the approval of the signatories for Open Door doctrine
there and their promise to respect the territorial and
administrative integrity of China.   But the delegates
to Washington, who had shown themselves to be sensitive
to world opinion, were given the reins of power -
Admiral Katō as prime minister (1922-3) - and tried to
implement the findings of the conference with good
faith and some measure of popular support.

Since the Hara Cabinet had collapsed with the assassination of its leader in November 1921, ministries
had been short-lived.   But the Cabinets of Takahashi,
Admiral Katō Tomosaburō, Admiral Yamamoto and Kiyoura
had all been broad supporters of the Washington settlement, pioneered by Shidehara.   Much of their attention
was inevitably devoted to the economic consequences of
the great Kantō earthquake of 1 September 1923.   In
June of the following year an unsteady coalition government was formed under Katō Takaaki, whose rapid rise
and equally sudden fall we have already studied.   He
invited Shidehara to become foreign minister, even
though he was not a party member so much as an experienced professional diplomat.   Shidehara, who had left
Washington in the spring of 1922 a sick man, had rested
for eighteen months and was recalled to Kasumigaseki
to deal with growing American tensions.   Now greatly
recovered, he was a natural choice as foreign minister.

In his initial Diet speech on 1 July 1924, Shidehara

made clear that he wanted to give an economic orientation to Japanese policy.   He hoped to focus on Japan's
economic interests rather than her political ambitions
which had given her such a bad image in the world
since 1915.   He was to use the Foreign Ministry establishment to give positive encouragement to trade of
new kinds and in new directions.   He came to power in
the midst of a crisis over American immigration legislation which he sought to keep cool.   A selective
immigration bill which had been introduced into
Congress contained an exclusion clause which particularly affected the Japanese.   Japan had protested
from various points of view which seemed to draw a
sympathetic response from the Washington administration.
Despite this the law was finally enacted on 26 May
1924. (15)   In disappointment Japan protested that
'neither the representations of the Japanese Government
nor the recommendations of the President and Secretary
of State were heeded by Congress' (Document 23).

Almost the earliest problem which Shidehara was to
face when he became foreign minister in June was to
draft a memorial of protest against the forthcoming
immigration restrictions.   On 1 July, the day of his
first policy speech to the Diet, the United States
announced her quota immigration legislation, which
entailed the repeal of the Gentlemen's Agreement of
1908.   The provision that Japanese should be included
with other Asiatics as 'undesirable aliens' was a great
affront for they had always considered themselves as
superior to other Asiatics.   Immediately the Japanese
lower house passed a resolution of regret over the
legislation; and the government made a number of protests to President Coolidge.   But it was a symbol of
a genuine anti-Japanese sentiment which prevailed in
the States; and it was too late to do anything constructive about it.

A wave of anti-American feeling spread in Japan.
It resulted in hostile demonstrations such as that
against the Stars and Stripes flag which was stolen
from the embassy flagpole in Tokyo.   Foreign Minister
Shidehara made appropriate apologies to the Americans
and later gave an especially sympathetic account of
the American position to the Diet.   But the sense of
outrage continued; and protests went on into 1925.
It was deeply ironic - not to say, tragic - that
Shidehara, whose main policy objective was to improve
relations with the Americans, should have had to face
this hostile legislation from Washington.   He received
little help from the United States in trying to readjust

the deteriorating relationship.   The result was that
the anti-American climate in Japanese political opinion
made it difficult for him to make approaches which
had any chance of success.

But this account of emigration problems has taken
us beyond the issues which absorbed Shidehara's Washington years and we must return to consider the head-
aches which he faced on becoming foreign minister.

RELATIONS WITH THE SOVIETS

Another problem which Shidehara inherited was the unhappy state of relations with Soviet Russia.   By his
diplomacy of conciliation, he was able to make a
breakthrough by his treaty of January 1925.   But, in
order to overcome Russia's intense hostility towards
Japan left over after the Siberian intervention, substantial allowances had to be made to the Russians.

Shidehara's connection with the Siberian issue went
back to his days as deputy minister.   He had then
found himself in the strange position that both his
superiors, Motono Ichirō (1916-18) and Gotō Shimpei
(1918) favoured intervention against the Bolsheviks
in Siberia and the Maritime provinces.   In this they
had the support of some section chiefs in the ministry.
But the majority 'Shidehara clique' at Kasumigaseki
opposed the intervention because of its implicit
dangers and also because of the strong opposition
initially shown by the United States towards Japan's
involvement.   In this Shidehara had the support of
Baron Makino, who kept up a rearguard action in the
Gaikō chōsakai against the intervention. (16)   Inter-
estingly enough, despite his disagreement with his
superiors, Shidehara does not appear to have wanted
to resign.   The compromise over the intervention
which Japan reached with the United States in August
1918 enabled him to stay on without qualms of conscience.   But he was sufficiently identified with
the anti-Siberian group to be persona grata with the
United States and to be acceptable as ambassador there.

By December 1919 the White Russian government at
Omsk had collapsed and the British, Americans and
Czechs were on the point of withdrawal.   What were
the Japanese to do?   An allied conference in London
concluded that the arguments pointed to the desirability of Japan staying on.   When Ambassador Chinda
advocated that Japan should maintain the status quo
even if it involved sending 5-6,000 extra troops to

strengthen weak points on the front, the other Powers
raised no objection.   It is important to view Japan's
actions not in terms of American attitudes so much as
allied ones.   Both the American government and
American opinion were deeply hostile to the full
extent of Japan's intervention.   But, when the
Americans announced the pulling out of their troops
in January 1920, they did not object to Japan increasing her contingent.   The Japanese accordingly
sent an extra half division. (17)

On 31 March 1920 Japan published a new policy for
Siberia.   This had been hammered out in the Gaikō
Chōsakai and the Cabinet with a considerable measure
of disagreement, especially between War Minister
General Tanaka and Finance Minister Takahashi.   The
broad conclusion was that the bolsheviks would take
Vladivostok, move into north Manchuria and menace
Korea - matters that Japan could not ignore - and
that Japanese armies would have to be pulled back
from Trans-Baikal and directed at Vladivostok and the
Chinese Eastern railway.   This was a major change in
conception, a movement to the Maritime Provinces from
Baikalia.   It was in effect a gesture of moderation
in deference to hostile American opinion, though it
is unclear how far this was the conscious intention.
At any rate, the effect of this policy was perverted
by the occurrence of the Nikolaievsk incident.

Nikolaievsk was a major town at the mouth of the
Amur river which, because of Japan's fishery activity,
had a relatively large population of Japanese and a
consulate.   Japanese who lived there were very vul-
nerable and during the winter months there was little
hope of speedy reinforcements.   In February 1920 a
force of partisans, about 1,500 Russians, 200 Koreans,
and 300 Chinese, surrounded the town and forced it to
surrender and sign peace terms.   But the Japanese
army planned the re-capture of the town and, breaking
the treaty, attacked partisan headquarters on 12
March.   After a week of fighting the outnumbered
Japanese force had to admit defeat.   On 25 May, just
as the partisans were about to withdraw in fear of a
further Japanese summer attack, they killed off over
700 Japanese prisoners. (18)   This tragedy was a
great shock to the Japanese.   On 3 July the Japanese
government announced that, as guarantee for settlement
of the incident, it would undertake the occupation of
northern Sakhalin, thus completing its possession of
the island.   The Russian commander, being apprehended
by the revolutionary authorities in July, was tried

and executed because of his responsibility for the
outrage.   Triaptsin was condemned as half-mad;   but
it was another matter for the soviets to make a
public declaration, admitting responsibility.

It is possible to argue that the various incidents
of 1920 were not the real cause of action at Sakhalin.
Certainly the Japanese had been quietly taking action
there since April, long before the announcement of
what was a fait accompli.   On the other hand, a
Japanese attack up the Amur was not feasible and the
tactic of securing compensation in Sakhalin was a
natural idea for any commander. (19)

In May 1921, the Far Eastern Republic of Siberia
(Kyokutō kyōwakoku) which was based on Chita and
claimed to represent an anti-communist form of administration, sought negotiations with the Japanese,
the sole remaining occupying power.   The Japanese
Cabinet at its meeting on 13 May was interested in
approaching the republic unofficially, in the hope
of obtaining trade benefits in return for the withdrawal of its troops.   Japan wanted to limit her
continental commitments, partly because of the heavy
expenditure entailed in maintaining her army overseas
and partly because of the criticisms she was receiving
in newspapers for her continued presence in Siberia.
Even the army was not opposed to talks since it could
not readily see any favourable outcome to its endeavours.   A conference was accordingly held at Dairen
on 26 August but negotiations dragged on fruitlessly.

On 23 January 1922 Ambassador Shidehara tried to
clarify Japan's position for the benefit of the Far
East Commission at the Washington conference.   His
ambiguous assurance was that her troops would be withdrawn from eastern Siberia when she received safeguards
about the security of her interests.   But her troops
would be 'detained' pending the satisfactory conclusion
of the Dairen negotiations, and she would occupy key
points in Sakhalin until she could obtain due satis-
faction for the Nikolaievsk massacre.   In making this
statement which many hailed as an important breakthrough, Shidehara was speaking with the full authority
of his government and in line with statements which
Japanese diplomats had been making throughout 1921.
The Dairen conference broke down.   But, by an announcement of 24 June, Japan promised to evacuate her troops
by the end of October.   The recall of units began
immediately and the promised withdrawal was completed
by the target date, except for the division which was
left in Sakhalin.   This was followed, ironically, by

the Far Eastern Republic being admitted to the Soviet
Union. (20)

Because of the Foreign Ministry's indignation over
the previous failures with the Soviet Union, the next
initiative rested with an individual, Viscount Gotō
Shimpei.   Gotō, a former foreign minister (1918), had
become mayor of Tokyo city and chairman of the Soviet-
Japan society.   A doctor by profession, Gotō invited
Joffe, the Soviet representative in China, who had
been seriously ill, to visit Tokyo for treatment.
Joffe, who had taken part in the abortive Changchun
talks, was ready to take part in political discussions.
It appears that Gotō at first failed to convince the
foreign minister who agreed with his officials that
it was too soon and too risky and then went over his
head and successfully persuaded Admiral Katō, the
prime minister.   Katō may have been influenced by
the navy's desire to get some settlement over
Sakhalin's oil resources on which it was coming increasingly to depend and its readiness to recognize
the USSR in order to do this.   From his arrival in
February, Joffe took part in informal conversations
with Gotō.   On 20 April the Cabinet agreed that there
was no objection in principle to opening a third round
of professional discussions with the Soviet Union.

Joffe opened his talks on 28 June with Kawakami
Toshihiko, one of the Foreign Ministry's Russian lin-
guists and one of the few diplomats who favoured
recognition of the Soviet Union.   Joffe explained
the terms on which Soviet Russia would reopen negotiations.   After a month of abortive discussion, he
asked for the preliminary unofficial negotiations to
be ended, insisting on the withdrawal of Japan's
forces from northern Sakhalin.   Joffe, whose treatment
had not really succeeded, left Japan for home on 11
August and was replaced as Far Eastern representative
by Karakhan.   It was he who, by exploiting the
fisheries issue and insinuating that it would be undesirable for Japan to follow too far behind the
European Powers in recognizing the Soviet Union,
engineered the reopening of official talks, this time
on Chinese soil.

A month before Shidehara took office, Karakhan
opened discussions with Yoshizawa Kenkichi, the
minister in Peking, on 15 May 1924.   Almost immediately after the Cabinet change in Tokyo, Shidehara
recalled Yoshizawa from Peking for consultations on
dealing with Soviet Russia.   They decided to continue
with the negotiation in Peking but to 'adjust the

demands previously made of Russia'.   This was because
the items insisted on up till then had been an accumu-
lation made up from all manner of interest groups and
these were in many cases not important issues.   So
Premier Katō and Shidehara laid down that 'it was better
not to put forward demands which anyone would regard as
unreasonable;   one must respect the views of the other
party and remember the circumstances.'   Yoshizawa was
sent back to Peking with instructions to present the
important demands from the national standpoint and
struggle to get them accepted. (21)   The delegate returned to Peking and re-started discussions.

It is well to pause and reflect on the new mandate
that Shidehara had drawn up.   First, it reflected
the pragmatism of the minister and of Premier Katō,
which served to carry it through against the reservations of some members of the Cabinet.   There was no
purpose in making outrageous demands from a near
neighbour with whom one wanted trade and tranquillity.
Second, time was no longer on the side of Japan.
Soviet Russia had already been recognized by Germany
in the treaty of Rapallo (1922), by Britain and Italy
in February 1924.   Moreover there were suspicions of
the deal which was being hatched between the soviet
representatives and one of the parties in China;   and
there was a distinct fear that the Sino-Soviet treaty
of 30 May 1924 might turn out to be a treaty aimed at
Japan.   There were strong arguments, therefore, for
avoiding delay and extracting some of the poison from
existing relations.   Third, there were commercial
grounds for a settlement - fisheries and oil, to name
only two. (22)

Yoshizawa passed over the Japanese plan on 4 August.
From that point to the signature of the basic treaty
on 20 January 1925, there were seventy-seven preparatory committee meetings and sixty-one formal conferences.   It is not necessary to follow the tough,
protracted negotiations which led to the signing of
six treaties, two protocols and other documents.   The
underlying principles were that Japan should recognize
the Soviet Union and restore diplomatic and consular
relations with her;   and that Russia should apologize
for the Nikolaievsk affair.   This was a formal structure for co-existence.   The other agreement related
to Sakhalin.   Japanese forces were to be withdrawn
from northern Sakhalin - this was duly done by 15 May
1925, though there were many Japanese voices raised in
objection.   In return concession contracts were signed,
giving Japan concessions in Sakhalin oil and coal

fields.   The amounts allotted were considerably
smaller than Japan wanted.   The extent of this
commercial gain was more debatable and depended on
the ease with which business could in future be done
with the soviets.   The concession contracts were
duly signed in December of that year, while the
fisheries convention was signed in January 1928 after
more protracted negotiations. (23)

The concession made by Shidehara in these long,
hard negotiations had been considerable and the
advantages which he gained for his realistic, economic foreign policy were extremely uncertain.   But,
as the Wang-Karakhan understanding had shown, there
was every likelihood that a treaty between Peking
and Moscow would injure Japanese interests.   Beyond
that, there were hopes of profit from establishing
friendly relations.   It would be ludicrous to speak
of friendship developing: the years of Japanese
activity in Siberia were not forgotten and there
was really little Russian repentance for Nikolaievsk.
Yet the Bolshevik regime some seven years after it
was set up was recognized by the Japanese who had
earlier considered it to be sinister for their
interests in Korea, Manchuria and their homeland.

The Wakatsuki ministry collapsed in 1927 (Wakatsuki had succeeded Katō on his death in 1926).
Although Shidehara resigned, his career was by no
means at an end.   Indeed, he was in mid-career.
This would normally not be the stage at which to
attempt an assessment of Shidehara's first stint as
foreign minister, all the more so because we shall
consider his China policy in the next chapter and to
judge Shidehara without considering his approach to
China would be like considering Hamlet without the
Prince of Denmark.   Yet there are elements in his
first period which differentiate it from the second
one and make it desirable to assess it separately.
In the first place, Kasumigaseki probably occupied a
more prestigious position in Japan and in the world
at large in the years before 1927 than it did afterwards.   This was the peak of Kasumigaseki diplomacy.
Shidehara appears to have been genuinely pro-American,
a sincere believer in carrying out the Washington
treaties.   Despite initial scepticism about the
League of Nations, he kept Japan firmly within it.
He also favoured disarmament and unreservedly subscribed to the peace resolution of October 1924. (24)
In this sense he was internationalist.   But he was
not necessarily or invariably co-operative with other

Powers (as the next chapter on his China policy will try to show). His tendency was to co-operate with the United States rather than Britain (or so Britain thought). Moreover, even when his policy was most amenable politically, it contained the element of trade rivalry which was at its highest point during his years. One cannot, however, realistically judge a foreign minister by the criterion of his popularity abroad. In Japan herself, the Shidehara years were, on the whole, good for Japan but they did not necessarily command universal popularity.

Chapter 8

The Tanaka Period,
1927-31

General Tanaka Giichi came to power as the head of a
Seiyūkai ministry on 20 April 1927.   He became his
own foreign minister and also took on the newly-
created office of colonial minister.   His ministry
only lasted two years and was to end in disaster.
Because of the personal humiliation which he suffered,
he was to die prematurely in September 1929.   Yet
Tanaka's followers had established themselves so
successfully in the army and government that his
shadow fell across the Mukden incident and the catastrophic events that followed it.   This chapter will
deal with the China policy which Tanaka inherited
from Shidehara, with Tanaka's own China policy and
with Shidehara's policies after his return to power
(1929-31) and will end with an assessment of the two
'rivals'. (1)
      Born in the heartland of the Chōshū clan in 1863,
Tanaka entered the army.   After service in the China
war, he went as attaché to Russia for four years.
Returning to join the general staff, he played a large
part in military mobilization for the Russo-Japanese
war and the political machinations which pushed the
genro into declaring war.   From this point onwards
his career was that of an ambitious political soldier.
For a while he acted as a conscientious brigade commander but by the time the crisis developed over
increasing the size of the army in 1912 he was back
in the general staff as a hard-liner.   In 1915 he
became a lieutenant-general and three years later he
joined Hara's Cabinet as war minister, resigning in
June 1921.   He was already recognized as a top
leader and, when Yamagata died in 1922, he had a
strong claim to be regarded as the heir of the
'Chōshū clan'.   On 13 May 1925 Tanaka, who had

hitherto looked askance at the activities of politicians, was chosen as chairman of the deeply divided
Seiyū party and vowed his opposition to every Kenseikai
policy, especially those of Shidehara. (2)

Tanaka was something of a conundrum.   Though he
had kept close to party politicians, he had little
respect for them and the military did not respect
him for such links.   Yet he was every inch a political soldier;   and his policies were in most cases
army policies, such as the Siberian intervention.
His position as foreign minister was even more
anomalous.   He had been influenced by his sojourn
in Russia but largely in the sense that his Japanese
nationalism had been accentuated by his experiences
there.   His other associations were his army ones
with Germany.   Tanaka had travelled abroad.   He
could hardly be regarded as an internationalist but
he was not totally lacking in experience of America.
In his attitudes, he was essentially a homespun
Japanese cloth with a distinctive Japanese way of
doing things and using men.   Tanaka's premiership is
reminiscent of that of General Terauchi (1916-18);
he was to be a forerunner of the political generals
of the thirties such as Hayashi and Tōjō.   He was
essentially a successful military bureaucrat who
differed from the others only in owing his support to
his party affiliation.

In the Foreign Ministry it was scarcely likely
that he would involve himself with much detail.
Part of his mantle was assumed by Mori Kaku (1882-
1933), parliamentary vice-minister, who had served in
China as a clerk and was thought to have aspirations
as a Japanese Cecil Rhodes.   He had sought political
office in order to direct Japan's management of the
continent.   He rose rapidly within the Seiyūkai by
clever political manoeuvring and personal connections
and was head councillor of the party when Tanaka
became prime minister. (3)   Understandably Mori had
a sense of Japan's historic mission for the peoples
of Asia which he was to trumpet openly until his
death in 1933;   he was to sketch plans for what later
became the Greater East Asia Co-prosperity sphere.
There can be no doubt that he was influential with
Tanaka, though the latter was essentially cautious
and conscious of his responsibilities as foreign
minister.

Tanaka undertook the duties of the office with the
assistance also of his appointed vice-ministers, first
Debuchi Katsuji whom he inherited from Shidehara;   and

then Yoshida Shigeru (July 1928-December 1930),
formerly consul-general at Mukden.   Debuchi was
sent to Washington in 1928 as part of a general
switch of embassies.   Yoshida had first come to
notice through his activities in Mukden, a post
which was diplomatic rather than consular.   He had
been recalled to Tokyo for the Eastern Conference
in May 1927 as a result of which he was given an
important mandate.   He was, therefore, a natural
choice as vice-minister though it was naturally unusual to be promoted from consul-general to high
office. (4)
     Tanaka had no deep-rooted political principles.
He had an inclination towards 'positive action' as
against 'weak-kneed action' which he associated with
Shidehara.   His experience with Siberia and with
the situation in Japan in the 1920s made him anti-
bolshevik and anti-revolutionary (Document 24).   In
so far as China policy was his main worry, his problem
was to find a strong Chinese with anti-communist
leanings on whom Japan could rely for keeping order.
For long the most promising among the Chinese leaders
was Chang Tso-lin of Manchuria who seemed to be
willing to accept Sino-Japanese co-operation as the
basis for China's unification.   His supporters included military officers who had received training in
Japan's military academies and officials who had
experience of a modern bureaucracy.   But Chang
tested the patience of the Japanese and did not prove
to be their ideal pupil; and Tanaka had perforce to
take a strong line towards him.   While his central
concern was China, Tanaka wanted to enhance Japan's
position in the world at large and was widely regarded
as being reasonable to deal with.   It is in this way
that we must regard Japan's signing of the anti-war
treaty at Paris on August 1928 which was largely the
work of American and French initiatives, though
Tanaka shared the British cynicism about such an act.
He was also ready to adopt inconspicuous tactics at
the Geneva naval conference in 1927.

SHIDEHARA'S CHINA POLICY, 1924-7

Tanaka inherited the policies towards China of his
predecessor, Shidehara.   In common with so many
liberal politicians of his time, Shidehara was influenced by Japan's tricky economic position.   Thus,
Japan's leading banker who had served as finance

minister in 1923-4, Inoue Junnosuke, had argued in
1926 that he believed Japan's problems to be population and foodstuffs;   and that if she was to avoid
a warlike solution which was in the nature of Japan's
state, she must find a means of peaceful expansion,
such as developing her mercantile marine. (5)
Shidehara, elaborating on this theme, wrote in 1924

> In our restricted islands we suffer from a popu-
> lation increase of 700,000-800,000 annually.
> There is, therefore, no alternative but to proceed
> with our industrialization.   It follows from this
> that it is essential to secure overseas markets
> and this can only be done by adopting an economic
> diplomacy.   If we try to cure our economic prob-
> lems by territorial expansion, we will merely
> destroy international cooperation....   Japan,
> being closest to China, has an advantage by way of
> transport costs and she has also the greatest com-
> petitive power because of her wages.   It must
> therefore be a priority for Japan to maintain the
> great market of China. (6)

This was Shidehara's philosophy in a nutshell.   He
elaborated it in countless memoranda and it was the
common belief of many thinking Japanese.   Japan was
now more than ever dependent on imports of foodstuffs
for her expanding population and raw materials for
her expanding industries;   hence she must cultivate
all markets but particularly those close to her.
Shidehara shared with many Japanese the notion of the
inexhaustible China market and the importance of
Japanese enterprise there;   but Japan's goals in
central China were solely economic and she was vul-
nerable to China's economic weapon, the boycott.
This had been used with great effect over Shantung in
the aftermath of the Paris peace conference.   Later,
when the anti-foreign trouble was aimed at the British
and confined largely to southern China, Japan escaped
without too much interruption of her enterprises.
It was only when the threat affected Shanghai and the
Yangtse area that Japan began to suffer heavily.
Shidehara was therefore doubly cautious to avoid
arousing hostile opinion in central China by adopting
policies of restraint where possible.

These were policies which suited Japan commercially.
She was only one of many trading nations operating in
China and competing energetically.   There was a sense
in which Japan stood to suffer more from boycott than
the European countries.   Her imports to China amounted
on average to about 25 per cent of her total trade;   if

they were to be cut off, it would create great problems
of redistribution.   The offtake of European countries
in China was a much smaller proportion (5 per cent of
British exports) and the difficulty of diverting it
elsewhere was less formidable.   This made Shidehara -
and Tanaka too - slow to accept the many suggestions
which he received that Japan should join the other
Powers in common action in China.   It did not suit
her national interests to do so.   To this extent,
Shidehara appeared to foreign diplomats of his own
generation as being far from an international-minded
statesman: he gave no indication of seeing any 'international interest' in solving the China problem.
Towards Manchuria, he held strong convictions about
Japan's special rights as did most Japanese of his
time.   For China, he advocated restraint.   Thus, on
grounds of political philosophy, and not simply because
of the trading aspirations of the zaibatsu with which
he had marriage connections, he was determined to aim
at an understanding and conciliatory policy towards
China.

On 1 July 1924 Shidehara made his first testing
speech to the new Diet on foreign affairs and enunciated
the principle that Japan should follow a policy of
absolute non-interference in the internal affairs of
China.   The genuineness of this avowal was soon
challenged in the outbreak of the second Fengtien-
Chihli war between Chang Tso-lin and Wu Pei-fu.
Japan had traditionally given moderate support to
Chang; and there were voices within the Cabinet in
favour of this again.   But Shidehara reaffirmed on
22 September his intention not to intervene.   A month
later, the danger of Chang becoming submerged forced
the Cabinet to examine its policy afresh; Shidehara
was in a minority and offered his resignation; but
Katō agreed to continue the existing line and declined
to accept his resignation.   Wu's defeat followed
almost immediately; but not without this interesting
example of Shidehara's strong-minded, even obstinate,
refusal to allow Japan to be embroiled in the warlord
coalitions of the day.   A conciliatory policy still
found its backers among Press and politicians, but
already there were rumblings of hostility among the
army who condemned it as weakness towards China and
lack of resolution toward the other Powers.   It was
not without contradictions.   Thus, in the 30 May Movement of 1925, the nationalist-revolutionary ardour of
the urban Chinese was directed against overseas
countries with the largest stake in Chinese industry,

Japan and Britain.   Despite strong pressure from
Japanese industrialists and from Britain, Shidehara
would take no steps and may thereby have diverted the
animus away from Japan.

In October and November when a further rising took
place against Chang Tso-lin, Japan on her own sent a
force to Mukden to ensure the safety of Japanese lives
and property.   The rebellion of Kuo Sung-ling, the
representative of a modernizing group in north China,
seriously tested the standing of Chang's warlord
regime.   The Japanese, though disillusioned with
many of Chang's acts, saw in him the only source of
peace and stability in Manchuria which was essential
to the development of their industrial sphere there.
When the conflict broke out, Shidehara speedily
offered mediation.   When this failed, the commander-
in-chief of the Kwantung army warned both parties
against violating Japanese rights and approaching the
south Manchurian railway zone.   On 15 December the
Tokyo Cabinet decided to send to Manchuria 1,000
troops from Korea and 2,500 from Japan.   Although
this was explicitly for the security of Japanese
nationals and their railway rights, it had the effect
of weighting the conflict in favour of Chang Tso-lin.
By the end of the year Chang's armies won.   But it
was not a popular victory and soon afterwards an anti-
Japanese movement sprang up.   The mere fact that
Kuo's forces were not permitted to use the Japanese-
controlled railway limited their mobility and their
chances of success. (7)

When the northern expedition began in 1926, non-
interference was not scrupulously observed if it
seriously violated Japan's interests.   It is difficult to establish how far this was the work of the
civil government and how far of the high command.
Foreigners assumed that Japan's interference in China
was the work of both.   But Shidehara came under
attack from the opposition Seiyūkai in the Diet
because of it;   and within the Cabinet, the war
minister, Ugaki Kazushige (Issei), complained that
there would have to be amendments to Shidehara's
China policy.   They criticized its weakness and its
refusal to collaborate with the Powers.   It would
seem, therefore, that, though Shidehara was a party to
the Cabinet decision to send troops, he wanted to
limit their role to the minimum. (8)   He also confined himself to protests over the Hankow and Nanking
incidents early in 1927.

TANAKA'S CHINA POLICY, 1927-9

In May 1927 the Kuomintang armies were ready to continue their advance northward towards Peking and
Tientsin.   Those countries with nationals in that
area enquired what the new Tanaka government proposed
to do.   Though he had taken over the premiership in
a financial crisis, Tanaka announced that he had no
intention of evacuating the Peking-Tientsin area as
Shidehara had earlier proposed and would despatch a
force of 2,000 from Manchuria to Tsingtao, thus leaving troops available for service further north if
required.   The force was sent; and on 1 June the
three governments operating in China sent their protests against this 'invasion'.   Tanaka then sought
the advice of the Eastern Conference (Tōhō kaigi) - a
series of conferences which met between 27 June and 7
July to discuss Far Eastern policy in the presence of
representatives of the Foreign, Navy and Army Ministries and the various general staff officers. (9)
After their deliberations, Tanaka made a policy statement warning China that, if Japanese lives and property
were at risk, even by boycott, Japan could not fail to
take decisive measures in self-defence.   Accordingly
he despatched a further 2,200 men to Shantung.   Needless to say, this action of a government which had come
to power to resolve a financial crisis, was open to
widespread criticism in the Press and among politicians.
From the Chinese side, it led to the outbreak of anti-
Japanese demonstrations and the boycott of Japanese
goods throughout China.   But the Kuomintang offensive
collapsed, and the troops were returned from Shantung
to Japan early in September.   In the north the situation improved for Chang Tso-lin.   As the season for
serious fighting ended, the danger to foreign nationals
also was lessened.   But the garrisons kept in the area
under treaty rights had during the crisis been increased
to eight companies of infantry and one section of field
artillery. (10)
    Tanaka boasted of his 'positive policy' (sekkyoku
seisaku).   By comparison with Shidehara, he was avowedly interventionist and a hard-liner.   It will be
observed that his expeditions had hitherto led to no
tangible result, unless his object was merely to 'fire
a warning shot across the Kuomintang bows'.   Knowing
Japan's financial weakness, Tanaka had been forced to
call back his forces.   Meanwhile his action had had a
deleterious effect on trade in central China which was
henceforth to be severely crippled.   The anti-foreign

animus among the Chinese was switched from Britain to
Japan - and this did not please the merchant houses
and banks.

While this was proceeding, Tanaka had sent his
minister to China, Yoshizawa Kenkichi, to Nanking to
meet Chiang Kai-shek.   It was after this gesture in
August that Chiang left the Nanking government and
retired for a vacation in Japan.   On 5 November he
called on Tanaka who offered him his strong general
support.   Tanaka wanted to avoid giving any guarantees
about the northern expedition - the real object of
Chiang's enquiries - and was merely encouraging Chiang
as the only politician likely to be able to keep the
Kuomintang detached from Russian communism.   Tanaka
had called on Chiang to work for anti-communist consolidation 'in the south' - central China.   There
was hardly a meeting of minds; but Chiang, when he
returned to power in December, may have been more
confident in dealing with Tanaka's shuffling diplomacy.

In April 1928 the Seiyūkai, returned to power after
a closely fought election, was again confronted by
news of Chiang's columns moving north.   If Chiang
was under the impression that he had received a wink
from Tanaka for the northern expedition, he was to be
sadly disabused.   On 18 April Tanaka ordered the
despatch of 5,000 troops from Kumamoto and three
companies from the Japanese contingent at Tientsin.
By 3 May the expedition had penetrated to the provincial capital of Tsinan and there encountered the
Kuomintang.   This may not have been contrived by
Tanaka so much as the commander, General Fukuda Hikosuke.
The clash did not end with a truce until 5 May and,
because Chiang refused to accept Japan's insistence on
the disarming of the Chinese forces, fighting was
renewed from 8 May.   On the following day another
15,000 Japanese troops were ordered to Shantung.
Within three days Chiang's troops were dislodged from
Tsinan with heavy casualties and the action was over.

The consequences were on the same lines as in the
previous year but on a greater scale.   For a year
Japanese troops remained in occupation of Tsingtao and
Tsinan; they controlled the railway zone of the
Kiao-Tsi (Kiaochow-Tsinan) railway and prevented
access to Chinese troops.   On the deficit side, the
anti-Japanese boycott of which Tanaka had complained
in 1927 was renewed with greater fury; and Japanese
trade suffered great losses.   The governments of
Peking and Nanking appealed to the League of Nations
without result.   Of course, there was world-wide

suspicion about Japan's ultimate object: was the focus
of her interest on Shantung or the Peking-Tientsin
area or Manchuria?   Tanaka spoke ambiguously as usual
and mainly of the future: if the disturbances spread
to Manchuria, Japan might be forced to take effective
steps to maintain law and order there. (11)   It would
have been possible for Tanaka to increase Japan's
stake in Manchuria at this time; and some speculated
that he lost his nerve because of world opinion and
was diverted from his true object.   There is no evidence for this.   His object seems to have been to
prevent Nationalist armies coming within striking
distance of Manchuria and, as a corollary, to create
a cordon sanitaire around Peking and Tientsin.   This
implied that he regarded Japan as having 'special
rights' in Manchuria and Mongolia.   His statement
made clear that Japan intended to assume a protecting
role in Manchuria for the future.

If the consequences of the Tanaka line were great,
its results were doubtful.   Tanaka failed to deal
with any of her outstanding disputes with China: the
Nanking incident of March 1927 and the tariff question, which all the other Powers had settled for
themselves by negotiation, became even more deadlocked.
If Japan continued with her policy of armed intervention, she risked an all-out struggle with a China
which was united if only by the bond of common detestation of Japan and all her works.   The much-vaunted
'positive policy' had proved to be a failure.

The result was that Tanaka revised his policies
early in 1929.   The trade returns showed him that a
more accommodating attitude towards the China problem
was indispensable in the precarious state of world
trade.   Japan, finding her isolated position unten-
able among the powers, changed to a policy of adaptation and compromise (chōsei).   This made possible
the settlement of some questions concerning the Tsinan
incident, tariffs and recognition.

MANCHURIAN DEVELOPMENTS

There were differences of emphasis in Japanese visions
of the China problem.   After consulting his experts
at the Eastern Conference, Tanaka had in a statement
drawn a clear distinction between Manchuria-Mongolia
in which Japan had 'special rights' and China proper
where Japan was largely concerned with stability.
Over Manchuria, her 'outer enclosure', Japan had a

responsibility to increase prosperity and ensure that
her special position was not injured.   His policy
was one of Manchuria-first, in contrast to Shidehara
who said that he placed considerations of Japan's
trade with China before Manchuria.   This was the
line Tanaka took with Britain and the United States
(Document 25).

Tanaka was influenced by the views of other men.
Two months before taking office, he had in his capacity
as Seiyūkai chairman sent Mori Kaku, Yamamoto Jōtarō
and Matsuoka Yōsuke on a fact-finding mission to China.
Mori later became his vice-minister, while Yamamoto
was appointed general manager of the south Manchurian
railway, with Matsuoka as his deputy (July 1927).
Yamamoto's assignment was to settle outstanding disputes with Chang Tso-lin and obtain leases for the
building of seven more railway lines.   What emerged
was a private understanding between the two - which
was not ratified by Chang's council - for the building
of five of the lines.   The lack of consultation with
the minister at Peking and with the Foreign Ministry
aroused a great deal of ill-feeling and protest.
Minister Yoshizawa was ordered, despite his pique, to
sign the understanding with Chang.   It was, as he
wrote in his memoirs, a bitter moment in his diplomatic career (12) for it showed that Tanaka had no
intention to act through the established channels.
He assumed that Chang Tso-lin was becoming more and
more dependent on Japan as the northern expedition was
threatened and that Japan could charge her price for
services.

In his role as self-appointed policeman, Tanaka
intended to keep the forces of Chiang and Chang apart.
He was ready to allow Chang to govern Manchuria and
would promise to insulate him against any attack by
the Kuomintang and their allies beyond Shanhaikwan.
Tanaka took the view that Japan was observing a civil
war which she would take all steps to prevent spreading to Manchuria;   she had made the Three Eastern
Provinces an area of prosperity and would not see her
investment ruined.   In May 1928 as the crisis increased, Minister Yoshizawa repeatedly asked Chang to
retire to Manchuria.   Chang, as a military man, was
inclined to resist the Kuomintang armies and refuse
Japan until the enemy was at the gate.   He had after
all a nominal half a million men under his command.
But he was finally prevailed upon and left on 3 June
by train for Mukden.   Chang died in an explosion on
his train, perpetrated by Colonel Kōmoto Daisaku at

the outskirts of Mukden.   Tanaka was not an accessory
to this incident and expressed his sorrow.   Indeed,
it spoilt all his plans for there was no strong candidate to take Chang's place and the situation changed
to Japan's disadvantage.

Chang Hsueh-liang, son of the Old Marshal, took
the reins of power but he was in a weak position and
could only survive by a policy of 'divide and rule'.
By playing on the fervour of the anti-Japanese movement in south Manchuria at the time, he hoped to
withstand Japanese pressure.   He was aware that the
Kuomintang armies had entered Peking and symbolically
completed the unification of China.   Clearly he was
strongly tempted to throw in his lot with the
Nationalists.   Tanaka offered all sorts of threats
to dissuade him from this course.   While Chang agreed
to defer his decision, he finally threw caution to the
winds and on 29 December declared his loyalty to the
Kuomintang government.   In a disastrous way, Tanaka's
desire to insulate Manchuria from China proper - the
goal of many Japanese for a decade - had for the
present failed.   The ill-judged military conspiracy
of Kōmoto had gravely embarrassed Tokyo and thwarted
his objectives.

Although his policy had failed, Tanaka determined to
live with the new situation.   There was really no more
than a nominal union between Mukden and Nanking, a
union of convenience in which Chang Hsueh-liang would
shelter beneath a higher authority while he developed
his personal power.   It was, however, a god-given
opportunity for Chang's officials to fob off the
Japanese who had countless complaints by saying that
they must be referred to the Kuomintang authorities.
Tanaka merely restated Japan's treaty rights and
threatened serious consequences if order was disrupted
in Manchuria.

In the new year Tanaka decided to revise his
policies fundamentally.   They came to be widely described as a complete volte face and a reversion to the
former Shidehara policy of non-interference in China
while maintaining the claim to recognition of Japan's
special position in Manchuria.   Tanaka's aim was to
seek understandings on all major points of dispute
between Tokyo and Nanking.   On the tariff problem,
Japan had fallen behind the other powers.   Tanaka now
authorized   detailed discussions which resulted in a
complex arrangement whereby Japan consented to China's
new tariff schedule, while the Chinese undertook to
set up a debt consolidation fund and to abolish likin

duties within two years.   The revised tariffs came
into force two days later on 1 February 1929.   Next,
Tanaka tackled the vexed question of Tsinan and the
withdrawal of Japanese troops.   It required someone
of Tanaka's standing within the army to overrule the
wish of the military to stay on in Shantung awhile;
and Tanaka, accepting the diplomatic considerations
put before him by Minister Yoshizawa and the financial considerations of which he was reminded by
Seiyūkai party members, rejected this idea.   By both
declaring their regret over the Tsinan incident,
China and Japan got over the awkward issue of who
should apologize the more for the clash, and Japan
agreed to withdraw her troops within two months.   The
delicate disagreements involved were overcome by the
setting up of a Sino-Japanese committee of investigation and this face-saving device enabled the treaty
to be signed on 28 March.   The Nanking and Hankow
incidents, which had remained unresolved since 1927,
were satisfactorily settled in accordance with this
new spirit of live-and-let-live.   After the other
outstanding grievance about formal commercial relations
had been disposed of, Japan recognized the Kuomintang
government at Nanking on 3 June.   It was not that
these various agreements were watertight but they
indicated a new atmosphere between the two countries.

How can Tanaka's volte face be explained?   Certainly it cannot have been a comfortable position for
Japan to be so isolated in China, finding that all the
other powers were settling down to a new relationship
with the Kuomintang while Japan was still suffering
boycotts.   Tanaka's Seiyūkai backers from the commercial and banking communities were not slow to blame
Japan's troubles on the failure of the 'positive policy'
- though it was less 'positive' than Tanaka professed -
and insisted on a more accommodating attitude being
taken towards Nanking.   Perhaps the main factor was
a change in Tanaka's attitude towards the army.   The
assassination of Chang Tso-lin had wrecked his policies;
and he was ready to try the culprits.   The newspapers
were anxious to get to the bottom of the plot and
were supported by many in public life, including the
emperor.   The army refused to allow the officers to
be court-martialled and took the offensive by trying
to persuade Seiyūkai members to its standpoint.   In
view of his clash with the army, it was easier for
Tanaka to disavow the military policies towards China
which he had tended to support early in his ministry
over Manchuria, Tsinan, etc.   There was, therefore,

some symbolic significance in Mori Kaku with his close
links with middle officer groups, tendering his resignation on 25 April from his post as supplementary vice-
minister (seimu jikan) in the Foreign Ministry. He
was clearly dissatisfied that Tanaka was switching
his policy to one of 'adaptation' towards the exploits
of Chinese nationalism instead of the strong line
which he had successfully advocated for the previous
eighteen months.

Because of the mounting discontent with his government, Tanaka resigned on 2 July. After his lengthy
dispute with the army over the punishment of Chang
Tso-lin's assassins, he had extracted a statement from
the war ministry the previous day imposing suspension
on General Muraoka and Colonel Kōmoto. Yet over
China (excluding Manchuria) he had made his peace with
the Nanking government. He died some months later, a
disappointed man.

As a legacy Tanaka left behind him a strong feeling
of hostility towards Japan in China. The all-China
anti-Japanese movement held its regular rallies.
Japan had become the focus of Chinese xenophobia. It
was in this context that there appeared another of
Tanaka's legacies, 'the Tanaka memorial' (Tanaka
Jōsōbun). This document was circulating in China
from 1929 and professed to be a report from Tanaka to
the emperor setting out a draft programme for Japan's
strategy towards China. Since no such memorial is
thought to have existed, it was presumably a compilation by Chinese who may perhaps have had access to
the findings of the Eastern Conference of 1927. It
was a most successful piece of propaganda, since it
came to circulate quite widely in the world in 1931
and seemed to acquire the stamp of plausibility from
the fact that Japan's actions in the Mukden incident
bore out some of Tanaka's programme. In the present
state of our knowledge, one can only conclude that
the memorial was a fraud. (13)

Looking back on Tanaka's policy, it was an erratic
one. Tanaka was given to making contradictory statements, which reflected the views of those with whom he
was currently in contact. By reason of devolving
responsibility where he could, he found himself confronted by policies emanating from three quarters:
the army with its spokesman in Mori Kaku; the south
Manchurian railway; and the Foreign Ministry. In
these circumstances, Tanaka had his ear only partially
cocked to pick up the advice of the Kasumigaseki
officials. Like Terauchi before him, he was inclined

to transact his business in China through non-profes-
sionals (e.g. Suzuki Teiichi) and outside professional
channels (as in the case of the Yamamoto-Chang talks).

BACK TO SHIDEHARA

With the formation of the Minseitō Cabinet on 2 July
1929 under Hamaguchi Osachi (Yūkō), Shidehara returned
to the Foreign Ministry.   He had been critical of
Tanaka's policy in 1928 (Document 26).   We shall
deal only briefly with his second period of directing
China policy because Tanaka had in his closing months
in power wiped the slate clean by disposing of some
of the major differences and Shidehara on return to
office did not make any obvious departure from Tanaka
policy.   Like Tanaka, Shidehara hoped for an overall
diplomatic settlement.   Through his minister to
China, Saburi Sadao, he made some headway;   but
Saburi lost his life in mysterious circumstances at
Hakone during a period of furlough in November.   Negotiations were disrupted because China declined to
issue an agrément, accepting the successor nominated
by the Japanese. (14)   In the new year chargé
d'affaires Shigemitsu was   able to claim some progress
in talks with Nanking officials.   Negotiations for a
tariff treaty were settled by a compromise in March
1930 whereby Japan recognized China's tariff autonomy
while China undertook to apply a schedule of duties
based on the levels operating in the previous year.
Thus, Japan had been able to catch up with the other
Powers in her dealings with the Nanking government.
In line with them, she was able to take up the question
of extra-territorial rights in China from the discussion of which she had earlier been excluded.   While
Britain was inclined to impose conditions for the
surrender of treaty rights by her nationals and the
United States was ready to be more lenient, Japan had
the difficult problem of her rights in Manchuria.   In
any case, China which was in the grip of another North-
South confrontation in the summer of 1930 did not
offer a climate propitious for negotiations.   But
Kasumigaseki officials showed readiness to yield on
most of Japan's concessions in China proper if only it
would lead to the return of stability in China. (15)
   Shidehara diplomacy in this period differed from
that of his earlier period in at least three respects.
In the first place, he carried on Tanaka's attempts
to work out Japan's destiny in China in line with the

other Powers and showed no sign of wanting to go it
alone there.   Second, when the chance of common
action arose in July 1930, Shidehara approved of
Japanese, American and British gunboats at Changsha
responding to the request of Hunan authorities for a
bombardment against communist forces who had captured
the city.   This was a use of force which Shidehara
would probably not have sanctioned in 1925; but the
fact that it was in defence of the recognized Chinese
government rather than of specifically foreign
interests presumably altered his thinking.   He was,
of course, anti-communist as Tanaka had been; and,
now that the Kuomintang government had been recogn-
nized, communist military activity was a menace to
stability, as the Japanese defined it.   Third, China
was an important party issue: both Shidehara's
earlier policy and Tanaka's policy had been subjected
to devastating attacks.   The most serious of these
criticisms of Shidehara came from the army.   In Japan
military voices were being raised against the weak-
kneed (nanjaku) stand of Shidehara, who was regarded
as too indulgent to China, and against the shortcomings
of the Chinese who were not over-zealous in dealing
with Japanese grievances which had been dragging on
for years.   Shidehara, in reply, was ready to admit
that peace and order had not existed in China for some
time (Document 27).

Yet there was still plenty evidence of Shidehara's
former moderation.   Witness the assessment of the
British minister in Peking that

Japan during 1930 had almost developed ... a policy
of self-effacement....   Neither in Manchuria nor
in China proper has she allowed herself to come to
the fore with any salient move, and on the contrary,
where matters of common interest were concerned,
[she] has shown a tendency to keep in shelter
behind the other Powers.   This access of retiring-
ness is no doubt the result of extreme financial
and industrial depression. (6)

LONDON NAVAL CONFERENCE, 1930

China was not the only forum where Japan ran into
trouble with foreign governments.   Another was the
forum of the Pacific which had since 1914 been a
Japanese lake.   This was a topic which gave rise to
controversy within Japan between the navy on the one
hand and the government, Foreign Ministry and parties

on the other.   Because the Pacific question impinged
so much on other Powers' interests, it had an even
greater international impact than the problems of
China.

The Washington naval treaty had left considerable
loopholes.   Japan set about compensating herself for
the restrictions on her battleship building by
announcing increases in her cruiser, destroyer and
submarine strength.   Since she proposed to build
10,000 ton cruisers with 8-inch guns, there developed
a cruiser-building 'race' in which the interests of
the naval powers were disparate and mutually irreconcilable.   This was quite out of line with the desire
for retrenchment which these governments were expressing.
It was, therefore, natural that President Coolidge
should invite the naval Powers to assemble in Geneva
in 1927 to extend some form of restriction to the
category of auxiliary vessels and especially cruisers.

Midway through this conference the British and
Japanese delegations reached a compromise agreement
whereby Britain and the United States would be limited
in their building of cruisers to 500,000 tons and
Japan to 325,000 tons, while the ratio of cruisers of
10,000 tons would be 12:12:8.   This formula was rejected by the Americans;   and the conference petered
out in August in a flood of mutual recrimination which
the world Press reported in elaborate and embarrassing
detail.

Since there was some fear of building re-starting
in 1930, the first soundings for a new conference took
place as soon as the second Labour government came to
office in Britain in June 1929.   So far as Japan was
concerned, this brought the matter for consideration
before the Tanaka Cabinet on 28 June, shortly before
its resignation.   In endorsing two memoranda on disarmament, it laid down that in auxiliary craft Japan
needed 70 per cent of the world's largest fleet.
Such was the legacy of Tanaka to Hamaguchi when he
became prime minister at the head of the Minseitō
ministry on 2 July.   It was part of his programme to
work for disarmament;   but he too upheld Japan's insistence on a ratio of 70 per cent.   On 19 July he sent
instructions to Ambassador Matsudaira Tsuneo in London
to present Japan's case to the American Ambassador
Charles Dawes and the British prime minister, Ramsay
MacDonald. (17)

There was a widely held view that the Geneva parleys
had broken down because the parties did not know each
other's standpoint until they sat down at the conference

table.   That was to some extent resolved by MacDonald's
preliminary talks with President Hoover at Rapidan in
October.   The Japanese who accepted the invitation to
the conference on 16 October looked on vigilantly but
without resentment.   They themselves had advance parleys with the Americans when their delegation left
Tokyo on 30 November via the United States where it
was able to talk over its fundamental demand that a
70 per cent ratio vis-à-vis the United States was the
absolute minimum needed for Japan's national defence.

The Japanese delegation to London consisted of a
civilian head, Wakatsuki Reijirō, who had been passed
over as party head in 1928 but had been chief minister
(1926-7). (18)   He was accompanied by Admiral Takarabe,
the navy minister, who was regarded by the party men as
reliable.   His absence from Tokyo left the Navy
Ministry in the charge of Admiral Yamanashi Katsunoshin,
who was described as mild-mannered and moderate and
held office as vice-minister.   These men were the inheritors of the treaty group which was associated with
Katō Tomosaburō's name. (19)   In Takarabe's absence,
the post of acting minister was assumed by Prime
Minister Hamaguchi himself.   This practice was not
without precedent since Hara Kei in 1921 had filled
the top post in the Navy Ministry during Katō's absence
in Washington on the ground that the Cabinet had the
right to control the military services.   Just as
Hara's act had been resented, so Hamaguchi's was
exposed to widespread criticism.   In addition to
these were Admirals Sakonji and Yamamoto Isoroku with
Admiral Abo, the naval attaché in London, as adviser.
To balance this, there were two diplomats, Matsudaira
who knew both the American and British delegations
well and Nagai Matsuzō from Belgium.   So vital was
the conference that Saitō Hiroshi was sent from Washington to act as Wakatsuki's interpreter since
Wakatsuki himself spoke little English. (20)

The proceedings opened on 21 January 1930.   Japan
put forward her demands: a 70 per cent ratio vis-à-vis
America in tonnage of auxiliary vessels overall; a
70 per cent ratio vis-à-vis America in heavy cruisers;
70,000 tons in submarines, to maintain the amount
currently held.   The American delegates did not wish
to see Japan with more than the Washington ratio of
60 per cent overall; and the conference seemed to be
on the verge of an impasse.   But on 13 March a formula
was reached after several sittings between one of the
American plenipotentiaries, Senator David A. Reed, and
the Japanese plenipotentiary, Matsudaira, assisted by

Saitō Hiroshi.   This laid down that Japan should have
69.75 per cent vis-à-vis America in overall tonnage;
that in large cruisers she should have a ratio of
60.02 per cent vis-à-vis America which could be raised
to an actual 70 per cent by the next conference in
1935;   and that each country should have equality in
submarines at 52,700 tons.   Wakatsuki asked Tokyo to
accept this compromise plan since it would be difficult
to ask the United States for concessions beyond this
and Japan must avoid being held responsible for the
breakdown of the conference.

This suggested compromise created dissension in
Japanese naval ranks.   The British reported that
'Wakatsuki and Matsudaira have not been able to win
over their naval colleagues in the delegation.' (21)
Admiral Takarabe who had not been able to gain acceptance for the three principles with which he had set
off from Tokyo, sent a separate telegram (though he
had seemed to associate himself fully with Wakatsuki's
telegram), hinting that Matsudaira had not pressed
hard enough and that there was more scope for further
negotiation, since it was too early yet to conclude
that there was no hope of concessions from Britain and
the United States. (22)   When Navy Minister Hamaguchi
sent the compromise for comment to the Navy General
Staff, it generated great opposition.   The chief of
the general staff, Admiral Katō Kanji, and his deputy,
Admiral Suetsugu, had all along been opposed to the
secretive way in which the Satsuma leadership had
accepted the treaty limitation of the Japanese fleet.
Now they claimed that the delegation in London had
violated its mandate and that on so vital a matter for
the navy the general staff must have the final say.
In this the hard-liners were supported by Prince
Fushimi and the veteran Admiral Tōgō.   On the other
hand, there was other naval opinion like Admiral
Yamamoto Gombei and Admiral Saitō, the chief delegate
at Geneva, who did not offer the hard-liners their
approval.

At a Cabinet on 1 April it was decided to adopt the
draft reply prepared by Shidehara and reject that
proposed by the navy.   In effect it accepted the compromise and authorized the delegates to sign the naval
limitation treaty forthwith in case Japan should be
made the scapegoat for the breakdown of the conference.
Hamaguchi thereby adopted Wakatsuki's recommendation
of 25 March and doubtless assumed that, after his
landslide victory in the general election of 20
February, he would have no difficulty in obtaining

support in the Diet.   On the other hand, Admiral Katō
Kanji, using his right of direct access to the emperor,
presented the throne on 2 April with his opinion that
the American-Japanese compromise was unsatisfactory to
the Japanese navy and would be a great hindrance to its
naval strategy.   In fact, Hamaguchi had neutralized
Katō's moves in advance with some political skill: he
had taken the precaution of obtaining the formal sanction of the Supreme War Council on 25 March; and he
had delayed Katō's audience with the emperor until
after instructions had gone off to London.   While,
therefore, he tried to obtain a consensus with the
serving officers, he ended up by out-manoeuvring them.
These tactics could only result in a further confrontation in the future.

On 2 April Wakatsuki conveyed to his American and
British colleagues the news that the Tokyo government
accepted the American-Japanese compromise.   His message
was couched in the language of reluctance and he predicted that much anxiety would be felt in Japan because
the treaty would decrease her relative naval strength.
But there was no doubt that Tokyo's agreement eased
the task of Wakatsuki and Matsudaira immensely.   The
technical advisers set about drawing up the final
terms.   A plenary session was held on 14 April which
laid down that there should be parity between Britain
and the United States and that the principle of 10:10:7
should be incorporated in practice but not in principle.
Wakatsuki let it be known that the Japanese accepted
the treaty on the understanding that it bound them
only until 1936.   The London treaty for the control
and limitation of naval armaments was duly signed by
the delegates at a plenary session of the conference
on 22 April.

This left the problem of ratification which was
another headache for the Japanese ministers.   Before
the agreement was signed, much had depended on the
fact that Hamaguchi was acting as navy minister and
was prepared to overrule the views of the general
staff.   Had that post been held as was usual by a
naval officer, he would probably have resigned because
of his divided loyalties and the Cabinet might have
faced a crisis which would have led to its downfall.
Hamaguchi's insistence and strong will deprived the
general staff of the final say.   On 21 April Katō
Kanji gave notice that the battle was to be rejoined by
sending a statement of general staff policy to the
privy council which was considering whether to ratify:
'The naval general staff cannot accept the London naval

treaty, because of the inadequacy in the tonnage of
auxiliary vessels permitted to us by the treaty when
compared with the minimum necessary for imperial
defence.' (23)   The privy council was confronted
with the problem not only of the merits of the naval
treaty but also of the constitutional issue of the
'tōsuiken' (the right of supreme command).   Because
Shidehara had many enemies in the council, especially
the veteran Itō Miyoji, the discussion on ratification
in the Investigation Committee in August was long and
hard.   But Hamaguchi and Takarabe stuck to Shidehara
and presented an unyielding front. (24)   The result
was that on 1 October the treaty passed the council
and was placed before the emperor for ratification.
Ratification was completed on 27 November.

By this time, Katō Kanji and his allies in the
Seiyūkai party had stirred up opposition throughout
the country.   He had resigned after delivering a
broadside on 10 June and placed the government in an
awkward position.   There were tricky parliamentary
questions.   On 14 November there was an assassination
attempt on Hamaguchi at Tokyo station from which he
ultimately died.   The emperor too was under pressure
from the navy.   In the end, however, after an episode
intriguing to the constitutional historian of Japan
but less relevant perhaps to the diplomatic historian,
the treaty was published on New Year's day, 1931.
Shidehara (by now acting premier) was able to announce
in the Diet on 3 February that ratification by the
emperor was complete and expressed the view that the
acceptance of the London naval treaty would not ad-
versely affect national security. (25)

The powers looked on at the outcome of the constitutional struggle with embarrassment.   Japan had
shown the strength of her institutions and the prev-
alence of civilian control - but only by a hair's
breadth.   An extension of the naval holiday had been
secured for five years;   the ratios had been applied
to most categories of warships.   But it was doubtful
whether the same formulae could be applied again.
The blood-letting of the summer of 1930 made that
unlikely.

Naval formulae agreed at international level can be
academic if the governments concerned will not build
up to their treaty limits.   Even though the naval
leaders had been worsted over the acceptance of the
treaty terms, they had underscored the shortcomings
which they expected to find in Japan's naval defence
under the new formula.   The Hamaguchi government had

apparently yielded to the navy that budgetary provision
would be made in order to enable it to build up to the
new treaty limits.   After the privy council had recommended ratification, the navy minister reverted to this
undertaking early in October, asking for a supplementary
budget to this end.   The Finance Ministry tried to
obstruct the proposal because of the parlous economic
position of the country but the Cabinet, faced with a
threat that the navy would bring it down, finally
supported its additional building programme to cover
the period 1931-6. (26)   The coming of the Manchurian
and Shanghai crises in 1931-2 gave the navy further
grounds for building up to its limits in view of the
obvious hostility of other naval Powers.

The London naval conference and the problems it
generated for the Hamaguchi government were a landmark
for Japan.   It had brought to the surface an extreme
group within the navy whose members in the testing-
time of 1930 showed their strength, even if they could
be outmanoeuvred in the short term.   Two years
earlier, with the assassination of Chang Tso-lin, the
middle-ranking officers of the Manchurian army had
gone their own way and emerged unscathed.   For the
future both services were therefore inclined to challenge budgetary restraints which they had reluctantly
accepted in the first half of the 1920s.   Nor would
they be ready to accept without question the foreign
policy dictates of a civilian administration.

TANAKA AND SHIDEHARA - SOME CONCLUDING THOUGHTS

Shidehara continued as foreign minister until December
1931 with a high domestic and international reputation.
He it was who had taken the mantle of Prime Minister
Hamaguchi when it looked as though his retirement
might be short; but he did not have the basic support
in party terms to keep the appointment permanently,
when Hamaguchi died.   His second term had been less
memorable than the first.   Barring the London naval
treaty, which was in Japan a victory for internationalism and for confidence in the advantages of co-
operation with the Western world, but may have been a
pyrrhic victory because of the dissension it created,
it was not very successful.   His China policy failed
to get the positive response which had been hoped for
from the nationalist government.   Certainly the phrase
'Shidehara diplomacy' tends to describe his policies
during his first term, because the circumstances of

the second were less propitious for the professional
diplomat.   Since the actions of Tanaka, the emergence of the military and the right wing was a factor
which could not be ignored.   The revival of Shidehara
diplomacy was not likely to be easy. (27)

There has developed a Shidehara-Tanaka debate
among historians.   It would be foolish to deny that
there were not vast differences between the two in
terms of personality and principles.   Shidehara was
bureaucratic, meek and withdrawn;   Tanaka was open,
possibly incautious and ready to work through subordinates.   Shidehara had principles and ideals
that underpinned his policies.   For China, his vision
was that stable government should be established, if
possible favourable to Japan and without interference
from her;   and that Sino-Japanese economic co-operation should be pursued.   These were mercantile
objectives and certainly Shidehara saw his object as
being to promote Japan's economic expansion on the
continent.   Tanaka was not a 'man of principle';   he
might not have dissented too much from these objectives but he did not formulate any for himself.

Tanaka was a pragmatist who reacted to situations.
Since he came after Shidehara, he seems to have
adopted many aspects of his policy in central China
and Manchuria.   But, with the second stage of Chiang's
northern expedition, he was confronted by a new situation.   Even Shidehara had found it necessary to
depart from non-interference at times towards the end
of his first term.   Indeed, Tanaka did try to 'create
a new order of Sino-Japanese relations based on a
workable compromise between Chinese nationalism and
Japanese interests'. (28)   But for the difficulty of
finding some solution for Manchuria, Tanaka might
have achieved some modus vivendi with Chiang.   When
it failed, Tanaka responded to Chiang's northward
march by his successive expeditions to Shantung.
These were counter-productive because of the boycotts
they provoked;   but they left with the weak and
fumbling Nanking government the indelible threat that
Japan could - and in an emergency would - take care
of her own interests by force.

When Shidehara returned to Kasumigaseki in 1929, it
was his methods rather than his policies that differed
from Tanaka's. He would not authorize the use of force
because he detested the army, which was his major
critic.   But the activities of the Kwantung army were
a constant reminder to the Chinese negotiators that
the threat of force always existed.   The Nationalist

government was a disappointment for Shidehara; and
his dreams of negotiated settlements for all outstanding problems were never fulfilled. Even if
his methods were those of the velvet glove, Shidehara
was second to none in upholding Japan's rights in
Manchuria and Inner Mongolia. (29)

The personal test for Shidehara came in 1930 when
he was manhandled in the Diet by opposition politicians over the London naval treaty. He survived this
ordeal as acting prime minister. But he resigned
with the Wakatsuki ministry in December 1931. He
played no part in politics or policy-making for
fourteen years; he was admitted to the House of
Peers but he hardly spoke. Shidehara despised party
politics and found it too late for him at the age of
sixty to become fully involved in them.

Within a closed circle of diplomats who retired
voluntarily from the service or were forced to resign,
Shidehara's views were well known. Men like Minister
Tokugawa from Ottawa and Ambassador Yoshida after his
return from London met with him and heard his criticisms. He even approached Konoe on occasion. But
his views carried little weight. In 1935 he wrote
ironically that in the formulation of Japan's China
policy

Kasumigaseki and the prime minister's office at
Nagata-chō are being superseded by the military.
There seems to have been surprise at army headquarters at Miyakezaka that the anxiety this has
generated at home and abroad should be so great.
It persists in explaining that this was based on a
decision between the 'three ministries' but, when
one looks further into it, one finds that Kasumigaseki was not among those consulted'. (30)

On his own role, Shidehara confessed to a friend in
1938 that, having lost one battle with the right wing,
he had to be ultra-cautious in talking of politics. (31)
His only serious brush with authority after retirement
was over the Imperial Rule Assistance association
(Taisei Yokusankai). As a member of the House of
Peers, Shidehara was expected in the charged atmosphere of 1940 to declare his solidarity by joining it;
but he refused, despite threats of imprisonment and
denunciation as a traitor.

His refusal to collaborate with the governments of
the 1930s stood him in good stead. On 9 October 1945
Shidehara became prime minister and remained so for
six months, when he retired to become for five years an
honoured Elder Statesman.

Chapter 9

The Uchida Period, 1931-3

The Manchurian crisis was 'presided over' - this phrase is surely more appropriate than 'steered' - by three Cabinets and three foreign ministers. It began in September 1931 under the Minseitō Cabinet of Wakatsuki and Foreign Minister Shidehara which had earlier gained great goodwill abroad. Within three months power passed to the opposition leader, Inukai Tsuyoshi, who recalled Yoshizawa Kenkichi to the Foreign Ministry since he had had intimate experience both of Peking and of Geneva's reactions to early developments in the Manchurian crisis. But the Seiyūkai ministry collapsed after Inukai's assassination in May. The genro then chose Admiral Saitō Makoto to head the Cabinet while Uchida Yasuya (1865-1936) was selected as foreign minister to preside over the final phase of the crisis. (1)

The appointment of Uchida was a perfectly sensible one. Uchida had first been foreign minister as far back as 1911-12. After a period as ambassador to tsarist Russia (1916-17), he had again acted at Kasumi-gaseki from 1918 to 1923, a long haul at an especially crucial time. He had been responsible for the Washington treaties and must therefore be judged a liberal, though not a very popular one. Having married the daughter of a millionaire and being a man of independent means, he did not revert to his career as a professional diplomat but became adviser to the privy council. It was in this capacity that he visited Europe and the United States for high-level discussions in 1928. Uchida, therefore, had the expertise for his new task and a wealth of experience. He was moreover described by foreign diplomats as suave and 'socially agreeable'. (2) Among Japanese he had a reputation for good looks and for frequent sampling of the good life of Akasaka.

Yet he did not have the reputation for strong leadership.   Hence it may seem odd to place the Manchurian
crisis under the umbrella of 'the Uchida period'.
Uchida Yasuya, after all, only became foreign minister
on 6 July 1932 when the crisis was already ten months
under way.   But he did make a perceptible, if not a
dramatic, change in the policies which he found on
assuming office.   There is, of course, a sense in
which he as president of the south Manchurian Railway
had influenced the crisis from its early days.   He
was, moreover, one of the civilians with whom the
military leaders were prepared to work and who was
prepared to work with them.   In fact, those crucial
decisions of the Manchurian crisis which were made at
the Tokyo end - the recognition of Manchukuo, the
departure from the League and the conclusion of a
ceasefire with China - were steered through by Uchida
and were civilian rather than military decisions.   He
seems to have become by 1932 a hard-liner and the
accomplice - even if only the occasional accomplice -
of the army which had escaped from the rigours of
civilian control in the wartime atmosphere which prevailed at the time.
     There is an advantage in approaching from an un-
accustomed angle what was in Japanese domestic terms
and in international affairs a central crisis in the
inter-war period.   It is usual - and creditable to
Japan from an international standpoint - to approach
the Manchurian problem by giving an account of the
actions of Foreign Minister Shidehara, of Ambassador
Debuchi in Washington, of Ambassador Matsudaira in
London and the various Japanese officials at the League
of Nations.   But their line - the line of the diplomats - did not necessarily reflect the mood of the
country at the time.   They were in a worthy way trying
to prevent, or at least to restrain, the military from
faits accomplis in China.   But this was a minority
line because voices which urge restraint out of consideration for international opinion are hardly ever
popular at a time when national aspirations are seen
to be fulfilled before the eyes of the people.

MUKDEN INCIDENT

The Manchurian crisis was a major crisis in Japan and
in the world at large.   For the world the problem was
the failure of collective security;   for Britain and
France the inability of the League of Nations to cope

with the emergency;   for the United States the inadequacy
of the Washington treaties and the pact of Paris.   In
Japan the problem for some was how to secure her ends
in Manchuria without international interference and for
others how to do it by peaceful means.   Space does not
permit us to examine the international aspect of the
emergency or to do justice to the complexities of the
domestic situation in Japan or China.

The aspect which concerns us is the line that the
Foreign Ministry took throughout the crisis.   It will
be our argument that the Ministry had little to do with
the making of the Mukden incident;   indeed, that the
incident was manufactured because the diplomats were
in measurable distance of resolving the China problem -
or were thought to be so.   But, after the incident
took place and the League became involved, the Foreign
Ministry tried to bring the army to order but took up
a defensive and apologetic posture.   As the Cabinet
changed in December and again in May 1932, the Foreign
Ministry tended slowly to move towards the standpoint
of the military because of the isolation in which
Japan stood.   Perhaps for the first time in modern
Japan, the Ministry had conspicuously lost its autonomous control over the making of policy and become a
subordinate partner in framing national policy.   This
was the result of what Mrs Ogata has called 'Defiance
in Manchuria', defiance, that is, against the civilian
government, but especially defiance directed at the
conciliatory approach which Shidehara had been trying
to adopt towards China since 1929.   It seems to be
established that there was a cross-section of Japanese
leaders - mainly military - who favoured both the Manchurian plan and plots from the start.   Just as there
were some within the military who did not approve of
the tactics of the Kwantung army, so there were some
in the Foreign Ministry secretariat who justified the
military arguments.

On 18 September 1931 there took place an explosion
on the Japanese-owned south Manchurian railway which
led to Japanese troops overrunning the area.   Why did
this Mukden incident take place when it did?   Probably
it should be seen in terms of Chinese politics at the
time.   Since Chang Hsueh-liang had hoisted the Kuomintang flag in 1928, relations had not been good and
there had been jealousies between him and Chiang Kai-
shek.   The latter's position was weakened in 1931 by
the catastrophic floods and by a serious dispute with
his nearest rivals, Hu Han-min and Wang Ching-wei, over
the need for constitutional government.   Hu was

arrested and only released when the Japanese began to
take military action. He then sided with Wang until
the latter was in December elected president of the
Executive Yuan when he packed administrative positions
with his own followers and began to offer a real
challenge to Chiang's power. China's political
leadership was clearly split.

The Japanese with their treaty rights in the leased
territory of Kwantung and the railway zones and with
responsibilities for Koreans living in Manchuria found
Chang Hsueh-liang hard to deal with. He tended to
refer disputes to Nanking, despite the fact that the
Kuomintang's writ did not in practice run in the Three
Provinces. The army officers who were the main
agents of Japanese policy in Manchuria were exasperated by the number of unresolved disputes. They were
turning over three schemes: to extort concessions
from Chang; to replace Chang by a government more
favourable to Japan; or to occupy Manchuria militarily. In short, they did not recognize Nanking as
being a party to the balance of power in Manchuria.
Meanwhile Shidehara was working along quite a different
tack with his minister, Shigemitsu (1931-2), and his
consuls in Manchuria. This was, without kowtowing to
China's revolutionary diplomacy, to negotiate with the
Nanking government for a settlement of the more
serious disputes. Shigemitsu and T.V. Soong visited
Manchuria to that end. While Soong tried to persuade
Chang in Peking to adopt a less pugnacious line,
Shigemitsu similarly held discussions with Japanese
authorities in Dairen. A further visit by Soong and
Shigemitsu to implement the resolution of disputes was
planned for 20 September. (3)

As soon as she found south Manchuria overrun by
Japanese forces, China raised the matter at the council
of the League on 19 September. The unhappy Japanese
delegate, Yoshizawa Kenkichi, replied that Japan 'had
taken all measures possible to prevent this local incident from leading to undesirable complications'. He
later expressed the rash hope that Japanese troops had
already been withdrawn in the main to the railway zone
and only a few remained outside it and did not consti-
tute a military occupation; these would be withdrawn
'as the situation improved'. Faced by hostile world
reaction and the determination that the League would
interfere, the Japanese government, deeply divided
after 18 September, closed its ranks and decided to
settle with the Chinese direct. The League council
welcomed Japan's assurance that it had no territorial

designs in Manchuria but could not go further than to
invite both parties 'to hasten the restoration of
normal relations between them.'

By the time the League council met in mid-October,
the situation had worsened or was worsening. So far
from withdrawing, the Kwantung army had fanned out
far and wide. It had, moreover, bombed Chinchow on
the Peking-Mukden railway fifty miles from the Japanese
railway zone. On 17 October Tokyo was shocked by
the disclosure that ten officers had been arrested in
connection with a plot to kill Premier Wakatsuki,
Foreign Minister Shidehara and Count Makino, the
keeper of the Privy Seal, all of them statesmen recognized as being opposed to the ideas of the military
who were now riding high. Moreover, the League had
succeeded in enlisting the United States' moral
support. Secretary of State Stimson saw the problem
as being to 'help Shidehara who is on the right side
and not play into the hands of any nationalist agita-
tors'.

On 24 October the council called on Japan to proceed
progressively with the withdrawal of her troops into
her railway zone by 16 November, the date fixed for
the next meeting of council. But Japan argued successfully that unanimity was required and that, in view of
her veto, the resolution was null and void. Briand,
the council chairman, argued that it still had moral
force. By the time the council met in November, the
Kwantung army had fought at Nonni Bridge in the north.
This was in blatant disregard of the views of the
Wakatsuki-Shidehara group who were now convinced that
the Japanese army overseas had engineered the Mukden
incident. Wakatsuki had told the war minister who
had asked for increased troops in Manchuria that the
Kwantung army must stop to the south of the Chinese
Eastern railway;

> so far I have made every effort to maintain our
> country's face by offering to the League explanations
> regarding the Kwantung army's action which, though
> at times rather flimsy, still had some semblance of
> truth. But, if the army should ever advance beyond
> the Chinese Eastern railway and attack Tsitsihar, I
> can no longer assume responsibility for its actions.

The army, using as its pretext the banditry in the
area and exercising its right of self-defence, attacked
Tsitsihar on 18 November and occupied it. Wakatsuki
did not resign, doubtless in the knowledge that there
was no hope of his being succeeded by a group more
moderate than himself and more able to restrain the
military. (4)

Wakatsuki's motives may well have included the consideration that there would have to be a last-ditch stand.   This was to focus on the city of Chinchow, the administrative capital of that part of Manchuria just to the north of the Great Wall, and well away from Japan's railway zone which had already been bombed in October.   At the end of November the Japanese general entrained his troops for an attack on the city.   Shidehara received an assurance from the chief of the general staff, General Kanaya, that he would forbid the attack on Chinchow; and, not a little to the surprise of the Chinese, the troops were recalled to the east of the Liao river.   This victory of the civilians was secured by enlisting the support of the emperor who called in General Kanaya and insisted on an order being issued for the withdrawal of troops.   It was an act of personal courage on the part of Kanaya, who was shortly after replaced by Prince Kanin.   It was an attempt of the Cabinet to assert its strength, not only to avoid foreign criticisms but also to limit army indiscipline.   As the Cabinet was divided, Wakatsuki resigned on 10 December and was replaced by a candidate from the rival Seiyūkai party, the veteran Inukai.

Inukai's appointment was not intended by the Elder Statesmen as a blatant pandering to the military, although in the outcome it tended to weaken the opposition to them.   Inukai was commissioned to regulate the dabbling of the army in domestic and foreign policy; he was also known to be anxious to negotiate some settlement direct with China through his long-standing contacts there.   But the selection of people for his Cabinet tended to pull it in the other direction.   In order to placate and 'discipline' the army, he appointed as war minister General Araki Sadao, sometimes described as the 'darling of the younger officers', who tended to advocate extreme courses.   He also placed in the key position of Cabinet secretary, Mori Kaku, a civilian who was close to the Kwantung army.   Although there was little doubt about Inukai's good intentions, there was considerable doubt about his strength to exercise control over his colleagues.   Not only did his personal ambitions for a peaceful solution with Nanking come to nothing, but the civilian triumph of November was soon thrown away.

Under pressure the Chinese evacuated their troops from Chinchow on 29 December and within a week the Japanese were in occupation of it.   A city well out-

side the railway zone had been taken and all sign of
Kuomintang administration disappeared from Manchuria.
It might be said that, but for mopping up, the Japanese
campaign was at an end; and the Kwantung army had to
look for political remedies.   But Chinchow was a
symbol in international opinion which was roused by
the new deterioration of the situation and considered
it to be a grave violation of assurances earlier given
by Japanese diplomats.
   Thus far Japan had encountered little or no trouble
from abroad.   The military in Manchuria had chosen
their time well so that they need not fear intervention by the Great Powers.   The Cabinet and Foreign
Ministry were sensitive to world opinion and to the
deliberations of the League of Nations.   Indeed
Wakatsuki and Shidehara had traded their good reputations in the chanceries of the world in the quest for
a compromise solution and created the impression that
they would be able to discipline the army and reassert
civilian superiority through party strength.   In
retrospect it seems to have been a slim chance.   For
their part, the Powers were not ready for armed intervention.   But some statesmen, relying on an untested
illusion, spoke of using sanctions.   In retrospect,
this was hardly feasible in the state of the various
national economies and the circumstances in the Far
East.   But the Japanese civilians viewed this threat
seriously and took pains to follow a conciliatory
diplomacy.   It did not, however, deter the military
from expansion 'for self-protection' in Manchuria.
And, of course, the threat of sanctions was wearing
rather thin by 1932.   For their own purposes the
Powers chose initially to treat the incident as a
domestic affair, allowing time for the liberals to
re-establish control and abstaining from vain protest
which might make Japanese public opinion turn against
the ministry in favour of the army.
   With the downfall of Shidehara and the taking of
Chinchow, these cosy illusions among the Powers had to
be abandoned.   On 7 January Stimson declared that his
government did 'not intend to recognize any treaty or
agreement' between China and Japan which impaired her
treaty rights 'including those which related to the
territorial and administrative integrity' of China.
This bombshell was treated rather contemptuously in
Tokyo.   But the government was still hopeful of a
conciliatory settlement.   When the League met again
on 25 January, the Japanese delegate repeated with
emphasis Yoshizawa's statement to the Diet four days

before: 'Japan harbours no territorial designs on
Manchuria and she will uphold the principles of the
"open door" and equal opportunity, as well as all
existing treaties relating to that territory.'
Naturally an anodyne statement of this kind did not
create much confidence abroad.   Stimson, so far from
reversing his earlier stand which had placed the
United States out on an anti-Japanese limb, endorsed
it in his note of 25 February to Senator Borah.   The
League Assembly, after an agonizing delay, passed a
resolution which closely resembled Stimson's January
statement on 11 March.

Meanwhile the attitude of the Powers had been much
influenced by the outbreak of hostilities at Shanghai
where Japan had landed a force of marines in the
International Settlement.   Under pressure from the
local Japanese community at Shanghai, the Tokyo government sent reinforcements which encountered unexpectedly strong opposition from the 19th Route army
but also tried to avoid further involvement by
inviting foreign governments to 'let her off the hook'.
Matsuoka Yōsuke was sent to the spot, claiming that
the Japanese had no desire to extend operations to
any parts of China and that 'the sooner they were
through with it and pulled out the better the Japanese
people would be pleased.' (5)   Foreign countries
could not fail to take a serious view of these
developments.   As in Manchuria previously, the
actions of the Japanese troops seemed to belie the
professions of the Japanese diplomats.   The 9th
division reached Woosung on 13 February.   By its
decision on 23rd, the Cabinet sent the 11th and 14th
divisions as reinforcements.   In the face of this
great strength, the Chinese armies had little alternative but to retire.   Critical discussions were held
on board the British flagship at Shanghai, the 'Kent',
between Admiral Nomura Kichisaburō and Admiral Howard
Kelly.   Conferences were then opened between Chinese
and Japanese, Matsuoka and Shigemitsu representing
Japan, and eventually led to an armistice being
declared just before the League assembly met on 4
March.   The Shanghai incident was initially an error
of judgment on the part of the local naval commander
who may have regarded it as an opportunity for the
navy to outshine the army.   The strong, positive
support of Tokyo was due to the pleas of the Japanese
community in Shanghai, which came in just as the
general election was under way.

Inukai's position was both strong and weak.   In the

general election on 20 February, his Seiyūkai party,
benefiting from the war feeling and the unpopularity
of the Minseitō, was able to secure 304 seats over
its opponents' 147.   But his strength was illusory.
The wave of assassinations continued: the former
finance minister, Inoue Junnosuke, and later Baron
Dan were assassinated by the Ketsumeidan.   In any
case parliamentary backing carried little weight in
Inukai's conflict with the Kwantung army, which had
occupied Harbin and was treating the incident as
though it was over.   It was moving towards the
creation of an independent state in Manchuria;   and
the former emperor, Pu Yi, was already waiting in
the wings in a hotel in Dairen for his call to act
the part of the new ruler.   Inukai and his foreign
minister, Yoshizawa, who had taken over from Inukai
on 14 January, recognized that this course would be
anathema to the interested foreign Powers and endeav-
oured to avoid it by negotiating with Nanking for
self-government for Manchuria within the context of
overall Chinese sovereignty.   But these feelers came
to nought.   On 1 March the setting up of an independent Manchukuo was announced in Mukden.

The new Manchukuo administration asked for recognition by the Powers and the Japanese Cabinet considered its position on 12 March.   Its decision was
equivocal: it encouraged the independence of Manchuria
and Mongolia (as though it were something in which it
had had no hand) but it also withheld recognition of
the new state.   In part, this was intended as a means
of overcoming accusations from abroad and especially
from the League Assembly then in session;   in part,
it was hoped that non-recognition would give the
ministry time for negotiations with Nanking;   in part,
it was a civilian protest against the fait accompli
of the military in Manchuria.   Understandably it was
regarded in the outside world as a complicated
charade.   At the assembly in Geneva on 11 March a
resolution was passed, calling on members not to
recognize any situation which might be brought about
by means contrary to the covenant of the League or the
pact of Paris.

UCHIDA AS FOREIGN MINISTER

On 15 May Premier Inukai was assassinated;   and his
administration was replaced by a 'whole nation' Cabinet
presided over by Admiral Saitō who sought the services

of Uchida Yasuya as foreign minister.   On behalf of
the Kasumigaseki secretariat, Arita Hachirō, the
vice-minister, asked Uchida to accept the offer.   It
is worth examining what qualities Uchida was thought
to possess.   Uchida had been appointed president of
the south Manchurian Railway on 11 June 1931 by
Shidehara and initially declined on the grounds that
he was unsuitable.   He was to some extent opposed by
the army.   His initial thoughts on taking up the
appointment were unexceptionable and unrevealing.
His transfer was swiftly followed by the Mukden
incident to which he was not a party.   Uchida soon
found himself as the party in the middle between the
Kwantung army who wanted a free hand to conquer the
country for Japan and the Foreign Ministry officials
in Manchuria who were trying to implement the government's non-escalation policy. (6)

But his neutral position seems to have changed.
He decided to return to the capital and visited Mukden
for prior discussions with all Japanese officials on
8 October. (7)   They agreed that it was necessary
for someone on the spot to report their case to the
Cabinet and the court.   But the army still felt that
Uchida might be seduced by Wakatsuki and Shidehara
and should be closely watched.   After calling on
Saionji in Kyoto and meeting the prime minister,
Uchida spoke to the foreign minister who, on hearing
his exposition in favour of a strong policy, offered
him his own position.   Uchida received the approval
for this of both the army in Kwantung and Tokyo for
they both were bitterly anti-Shidehara.   Instead, he
returned to Dairen after three weeks of politicking
in Tokyo on 7 November.(8)   He was evidently thought
to possess a capacity for reconciliation which commended him to the genro, the Cabinet and even the army.

From the new year Uchida was in the good books of
the army.   He received encouragement from Cabinet
members like Settlement Minister General Hata and War
Minister General Araki and, on the other side, from
Genrō Saionji.   In April took place an interesting
incident of which there is no account in his biography.
It was then that the government under pressure from
the army wanted rid of the cautious vice-president of
the railway, Eguchi, a particular friend of Uchida,
who insisted on offering his own resignation.   The
War Ministry, however, knowing that the Lytton Commission was already taking evidence in Manchuria did not
want to lose the experienced hand of Uchida.   They
insisted on the prime minister appealing to Uchida to

remain at his post.   Uchida accordingly withdrew his resignation. (9)

It was in May that Uchida penned a number of memoranda on the Manchurian problem.   These took a line very favourable to the newly created Manchukuo and to Japan's recognition of that country: the Manchurian crisis was over, barring the inevitable recognition. (10)   There could be no doubt that he was now acknowledged among Japanese as a hard-liner and was distrusted in sections of the Foreign Ministry among whom his views were well known through his frequent visits to Tokyo.

On 26 May the incoming prime minister, Admiral Saitō, asked Uchida to become foreign minister.   At first Uchida prevaricated, saying that he would visit Tokyo at the end of June.   Prevailed upon by Kwantung spokesmen, however, he returned to Japan earlier on 12 June.   He claimed that he was quite content to solve the Manchuria-Mongolian problem from Dairen; and that, if he were to give up the railway presidency, there would be a difficulty over a suitable successor. But, after hearing the views of the Cabinet, he acceded to Saitō's insistence.   On 24 June he returned to Dairen to attend to outstanding matters;   but he had by this time given his consent. (11)

The first test which Uchida faced on taking up office was to meet for the second time the members of the Lytton commission who were visiting Tokyo again for discussions with the new government.   When they arrived on 4 July, the situation had deteriorated: in June the Manchukuo authorities had insisted on retaining for their own use the maritime customs revenue collected at Manchurian ports instead of remitting it to the Chinese customs headquarters at Shanghai;   the Diet had unanimously passed a resolution, calling for recognition of Manchukuo.   On 25 June Foreign Vice-Minister Arita had given an undertaking to the British ambassador that Japan would not recognize Manchukuo before the League commission left the East;   but, when this leaked out in Japan, it raised a storm of protest. (12)   There was an increasing firmness on Japan's part when Uchida finally opened discussions with Lytton on 12 July and told him categorically that Japan would shortly deal with the recognition issue on her own, thus implying that he would not consult signatories of the nine-Power pact.   He is reported to have added that the existence of Manchukuo was an established fact and could not be ignored.   At a final interview two days later, Uchida

informed the commission that the government was intending to ignore the League entirely. It remains doubtful to this day how far this was the task for which
Uchida had been appointed and how far it merely
appeared to him to be the inevitable course after he
assumed office. Certainly his mind had been moving
in the direction of recognition, despite all its international implications, before he took up office.

At any rate, it was as much the manner of Uchida's
announcement as the substance of the policy which
caused offence abroad. At their meetings Lytton and
his colleagues had indulged in some 'extremely straight
talking' and encountered a 'marked brusqueness and
stubbornness in Uchida's replies'; Lytton had said
that Japan was guilty of violating the nine-Power pact
and, unless she gave up her present course of action,
she would incur the censure of the whole world, while
Uchida had replied that the nine-Power pact was outside the purview of the League and should not be
raised. While Uchida was doubtless speaking with the
sanction of the Cabinet, the intonation was distinctly
his own. (13)

The Lytton commission left Japan on 15 July. Japan
had asked its members to stay longer since she felt
that it would be better if their report were drafted
in Tokyo rather than in Peking. Indeed, they were
prepared to write sections of their report in Japan
and would have stayed on if Japan's reactions had not
been so hostile to the League. Uchida had kept the
commission waiting in Tokyo for a week before he saw
them for substantive discussions. They had called on
him on 7 July to offer congratulations on his new
appointment; but Uchida did not agree to discuss
matters until 12 July. In the commission's eyes,
there was no reason for this; in Japan's eyes, the
commission had chosen a most inconvenient time to pay
its second visit. It was not that Uchida was unaware
of his line of approach: he had penned his views
while he was on the journey home from Dairen on the
'Ussuri Maru'. He held to the opinion expressed to
the commission in Manchuria that there was no way for
Japan out of the problem but recognition of Manchukuo:
'there is no need to change that view in the slightest
even today.' He added:

when Manchukuo was in turmoil because Japan had
deferred recognizing it, Japan would have to decide
on recognition on grounds of self-defence since
peace is a matter of life and death. We cannot
promise to wait for the completion of the League

report.   If we could hear the commission's conclusions, there might perhaps be grounds for
reconsideration. (14)
But it was not to be.   Uchida's colleagues backed his
findings; he conveyed them to Lytton and his commis-
sioners; and other ministers, notably War Minister
Araki, communicated them even more strongly.   Lytton
considered that the delay and general treatment of the
mission was detrimental to the prestige of the League
and that the hostile Press did not provide an atmosphere for negotiations.   Hence the commission which
had come to Tokyo a second time in a conciliatory
spirit left in the huff.   This was Uchida's responsibility.

These conversations were critical for the League
and for Japan.   On 7 August General Honjō, the
commander-in-chief, concluded a treaty with the Manchukuo authorities safeguarding Japan's commercial
interests there.   On the following day General Mutō
Nobuyoshi was sent out as a special envoy to negotiate
a Japan-Manchukuo defence agreement.   Pu Yi proved
to be a hard bargainer but eventually gave in on the
understanding that it was Japan's ultimate intention
to make him emperor of Manchukuo.   On 25 August
Premier Saitō told the Diet that the government had
decided to recognize Manchukuo and Uchida had earlier
affirmed in answer to an interpellation from Mori Kaku
that it would be done in the face of hostile world
opinion, even if it meant turning the country to
'scorched earth'. (15)   Within a fortnight the
necessary treaties were signed and approved, offering
Manchukuo the protection of Japanese forces provided
they were given the right to remain in Manchuria and
to have the final say in all matters of security.
Once these preliminaries had been completed, Japan
granted recognition to Manchukuo on 15 September (see
Uchida's views in Document 28).

Uchida's notorious remarks about 'scorched earth'
were a great turning-point.   The Japanese knew that
they were flying in the face of world opinion.   They
predicted the drift of the Lytton report in advance
from the July visit.   They considered that it was
the lesser of two evils to recognize the new state
before the report was published rather than wait for
the publication and then take the step of recognition,
which would only be doubly offensive in the light of
the report.   In fact, the commission finished its
report on 4 September in Peking and it was carried
quickly to Geneva and published there on 2 October.

LEAGUE OF NATIONS IMBROGLIO

The Japanese asked the League for a deferment of six weeks in which they could translate, study and prepare their rejoinder to the report. The official Foreign Ministry translation gave rise to some dissatisfaction in Japan because it clearly carried an implication of the commission's hostility to her case. The Japanese League of Nations Association accordingly proceeded to make its own translation in co-operation with (Sir) George Sansom, the notable Japanese scholar on the staff of the British embassy in Tokyo. (16)

In order to present its case to the League Assembly, the government appointed Matsuoka Yōsuke on 11 October as special plenipotentiary. Matsuoka had originally served with the Foreign Ministry (1904-21) and later joined the staff of the south Manchurian railway (1921-9). He then became a Seiyūkai member of the Diet and was enlisted in the Shanghai crisis early in 1932 to use his good offices to achieve a settlement. He was well fitted for his new task by the superior knowledge of English which he had acquired during his education in Oregon; but his experience had been largely American rather than European. Matsuoka was initially hesitant about accepting and suggested other names. When he was finally prevailed upon to go to Geneva with an imperial mandate, he seems genuinely to have hoped that he would be able to accomplish a negotiated settlement and that there was still room for negotiation. Matsuoka had qualities to offer - fluency and eloquence - which none of Japan's earlier 'ambassadorial' representatives at the League could rival; and he had the advantage of direct consulta- tion with the ministers about their intentions. Against that, he took a harder line than most of the ambassadors at Geneva and was convinced that Japan's recognition of Manchukuo was irrevocable. (17)

It is impossible to deal in detail with the Lytton report here except to say that it was intended to be conciliatory to Japan. It did not blame the Japanese military outright for the Mukden incident of 18 Septem- ber 1931; it did castigate the Kuomintang government for the unrest, insecurity and boycotts in China and especially in Manchuria. The commission was, however, adamant that the Manchukuo government was not 'called into existence by a genuine and spontaneous indepen- dence movement' so much as by 'the activities of Japanese officials, both civil and military'. More- over, there was 'no general Chinese support for the

Manchukuo Government which is regarded by local Chinese
as an instrument of the Japanese'.   In its recommendations the commission stated that any solution which
failed to recognize the rights and interests of Japan
in Manchuria would not be satisfactory and new Sino-
Japanese treaties would be necessary if friction was
to be avoided: government in Manchuria should be
modified in such a way as to secure, consistently with
the sovereignty and administrative integrity of China,
a large measure of autonomy.   These were sane and
realistic recommendations and should have been acceptable to moderate groups in both countries.   It can
only be said that the Japanese politicians reacted to
the report from a prejudged position.   Some writers
blame Shiratori Toshio, head of the Foreign Ministry's
Information Office, for misleading the public on its
contents.

   The League commission's findings were out of line
with the Saitō Cabinet's thinking (Document 29).
Matsuoka made clear the nature of his instructions
when the council of the League met on 21 November to
consider the report.   He was immediately involved in
altercations with his equally fluent and outspoken
opposite number, Wellington Koo, on three main points:
Japan was completely opposed to the League accepting
the basis of the Lytton report; to the United States
and Soviet Union joining the committee of nineteen
charged with examining it; and to the cancellation of
recognition of the rights of Manchukuo.   Almost
inevitably Japan failed to get her way on these points.
Yet Matsuoka was able to make capital at home by his
strong speeches, especially his emotional plea on
'Japan crucified' on 8 December.   The council was in
any case required to remit the issue to a plenary
meeting of the League which opened on 6 December.
Rather out of line with the findings of the Lytton
report, the representatives of the smaller Powers
came out strongly and almost unanimously against
Japan.   The Great Powers who were aware that
Matsuoka's threat to take Japan out of the League was
no idle one, were more circumspect.   After a great
deal of heart-searching, the representatives of France
and Britain (Briand and Simon) reminded delegates that
the report had criticized both parties to the dispute.
But this attempt to create a climate suitable for conciliation signally failed.   Matsuoka claimed that
Simon had said what he (Matsuoka) in his poor English
had been trying to say for some time.   When the task
of conciliation was passed to the Committee of

Nineteen, Matsuoka opposed the inclusion of the United
States, not a member of the League, on the commission.
When he failed to get his way, he showed himself to be
intransigent.   On 4 January Britain appealed over his
head in Tokyo for some Japanese concessions.   This
may have prompted a last-minute initiative for conciliation.   On 14 January the secretary-general of the
League, Sir Eric Drummond drew up with Sugimura Yōtaro,
the Japanese member of the League secretariat, an
amended resolution which represented the minimum terms
that the Japanese would accept.   This was a doubtful
endeavour because Uchida had already taken a rigid
position of no compromise: if the League were to con-
demn Japan, his government would not hesitate to
withdraw since China was patently the aggressor and
Japan was the only stable country in East Asia.

In declarations in the world Press, Japan made it
clear that she would not alter her policy over Manchukuo and that she would not accept China's sovereignty
in that territory.   The Committee of Nineteen, confronted with this and with the advance of the Japanese
troops into Jehol, drew up a report insisting on the
withdrawal of Japanese troops into the railway zone
and the recognition of China's sovereignty in Manchuria.
The Tokyo Cabinet decided that, if the full assembly
adopted the offending report, they would oppose it;
and Matsuoka notified the League accordingly.   On 24
February the League, admitting that conciliation proceedings were impossible and that the best that could
be done was to give publicity to their findings and
leave the matter for direct negotiation between the
parties with such help from the League as they
required, passed the report of the Committee of Nineteen by forty-two votes to one.   Matsuoka then rose
to read a statement and, followed by the Japanese
delegation in solemn procession, dramatically left the
chamber.   This was a fully authorized act and not the
act of the delegate himself.   But it was not immediately clear what it implied; and many of the
officials were reluctant to follow their instructions. (18)

It was left to the authorities in Tokyo to decide
on the next step.   There does not appear to have been
any serious attempt to prevent Japan from leaving the
League.   So exhausted had the League Powers become
in mediation, when the matter was before the Committee
of Nineteen, that they left Japan to her own devices.
The Cabinet agreed to the Foreign Ministry draft statement on withdrawal, but the emperor who was to issue

it as a rescript insisted on including two amendments:
one that some expression of regret should be included;
the other that there should be an injunction that
public officials should observe orders and maintain
discipline.   On 27 March the rescript was issued and
a communication sent to the League giving two years
notice of the intention of Japan to resign (Document
30).

There was something symbolic about the emperor's
insisting upon some mention of official indiscipline
being made - rather oddly - in the rescript.   In the
realm of foreign policy, there is the feeling that
Japan's actions during the Manchurian crisis reflected
the voice of a rebellious military party more than any
other.   With the coming of Uchida and Matsuoka, this
was perhaps more obvious.

The evidence on Japan's attitude towards leaving
the League is admittedly confusing.   It had, of
course, been spoken of as an ultimate possibility
since the start of the Manchurian incident, especially
in military circles.   It was an ideal threat for
Japan to keep under her cloak.   Uchida had been men-
tioning it in his position papers throughout 1932.
But, when the threat came close to being a reality,
the more cautious statesmen appear to have shown
reluctance to implement the bluff.   We have it on
good authority that Prime Minister Saitō, Foreign
Minister Uchida and even Matsuoka at Geneva who urged
the acceptance of the Drummond-Sugimura formula recognized that withdrawal was not the best possible
policy. (19)   Even on 19 February Premier Saitō told
Elder Statesman Saionji at Okitsu that the government's
attitude had not been decided, though there was not
always much candour shown to Saionji.   Those who
favoured the course of going it alone were middle-
grade officers in the army, the right-wing organiza-
tions who convened mass meetings, part of the Renovationist clique among the Foreign Ministry officials
(like Shiratori Toshio) and some party politicians.
At an emergency meeting on 20 February, the Cabinet
reached its final decision;   and the premier and
foreign minister presented the draft instructions for
Matsuoka to the emperor.   After obtaining his consent,
they sent off the message to Geneva and announced it
to newspapermen in Tokyo. (20)

A willingness to leave the League seems to have
been the natural outcome of Uchida's policy from the
start of his tenure at the Foreign Ministry.   It may
have been hinted at previously but it never became

such a serious threat until Uchida came to Kasumigaseki.
In this major aspect of his policy, he was, as on so
many other aspects, at one with the military.   Yet it
has to be said that both Uchida and Matsuoka felt that,
while it was a perfectly logical position, it was a
course which was forced on Japan rather than desirable
in itself.

The final break with the international body, which
took effect in 1935, has to be seen in perspective.
On the one hand, it did not mean that Japan was automatically isolated;   many countries got along quite
well without being members of the League.   Nor did
it prevent her from having cordial relations with
foreign Powers.   On the other, it was bound to lead
her to hope for a free hand in a wider field.   It
was, therefore, on the cards that she would try to
gain release from the multi-Power agreements of the
postwar period to which she had subscribed.   It was
likely that she would denounce naval disarmament
restrictions to which she was a party.   In so far as
the story of Japan's foreign policy in this period is
the struggle for ascendancy between those who were
calling for, or sensitive to, international co-operation and those calling for national self-sufficiency,
this decision could not fail to tip the scales in
favour of the second group.   It was not so much that
Japan in the Manchurian incident had shown outright
opposition to international opinion but that, knowing
that there was no likelihood of international intervention, she had gone her own way.   Those Japanese
who wanted Japan to go her own way in future could at
least reason from the lack of effective interest shown
by the Powers in the eighteen months of crisis in
Manchuria.

Uchida's tenure came to an end in September 1933.
His role had been important for he had like Arita, his
vice-minister, tried to compromise with a dominant
military.   His predecessors, Shidehara and Yoshizawa,
had shown ambivalence.   The first had been seen by
the army leaders as an obstacle to their autonomy;
the second, less assertive and with less political
acumen, sat firmly on the fence.   Uchida, whom we
have pictured earlier as Hara's liberal assistant,
became after the Mukden incident more and more an
intellectual convert to the ideas of the Kwantung army
leaders.   Perhaps he was influenced in this by the
financial needs of the south Manchurian railway whose
existence as a vast commercial-industrial complex was
greatly eased by what the Japanese forces had done.

But the fact remains that the courses which he adopted
had the effect of encouraging continental expansion
through the agency of an army which was not greatly
under the influence of the Cabinet, far less the
Foreign Ministry.   Thus, in the history of the
Ministry, he must be looked upon as a minister who
allowed its prestige to sink and its privileges to
lapse.   The whole Manchurian issue had an unfortunate
divisive effect on the Ministry itself.   A serious
dispute developed between Shiratori and Vice-minister
Arita, who wanted to defend the ascendancy of the
office in foreign-policy matters.   This meant that
one of Uchida's last duties was to give overseas
postings to his vice-minister, to Shiratori who was
sent to Sweden and to his ally, Tani, the head of the
Asia Affairs Bureau. (21)   It was therefore with a
sense of failure that Uchida finally resigned after
recurrent and serious ill-health.   He admitted that a
grave responsibility rested with him for the shape
which the Manchurian solution ultimately took. (22)

AFTERMATH OF MANCHUKUO

While the negotiations before the League were at their
most sensitive stage in January and February 1933, the
Kwantung army was engaged in campaigns to the south
and west.   The first action was a collision with the
Chinese army at Shanhaikwan on New Year's day and the
occupation of the city, which was strategically located
at the point where the Great Wall of China came down
to the sea.   Japan called for its demilitarization.
This was an intrusion into China proper or at least an
attempt to command the corridor by which forces could
be moved in or out of Manchuria.   China protested and
appealed to the League, but there was little that it
could now effectively do in east Asia.
    On 17 February the Cabinet had before it an army
proposal to move into, and pacify, the province of
Jehol.   Jehol was a province of China beyond the wall
and was populated by people of Mongol origin.   Jehol
was included in the declaration of independence from
China which was made by Manchukuo in March 1932.   It
was nominally under the rule of Chang Hsueh-liang.
There were various complaints that could be made
against that rule: that the country was a hotbed of
bandits who made raids against Manchuria; that it
was a source of opium whose revenues went into the
coffers of Chang; and that the population had appealed

to the League against Chinese tyranny.   Finally a
twenty-four-hour ultimatum for the withdrawal of
Chinese troops was issued; and after a brief
campaign the city of Jehol was occupied on 4 March
and the whole province was brought under control
without serious opposition being met.   The timing
of these operations may be regarded as odd, if Japan
had not already decided to act regardless of the
League.   In a sense, however, the timing was dictated by military exigencies: the action had to be
taken after the winter but before the melting of the
snows.

True enough, Foreign Vice-minister Arita gave the
diplomatic body an assurance that Japan would not
proceed into Chinese territory unless there were
provocation by China.   But, contrary to this, the
army went its own way.   On 23 May the new minister
to China, Ariyoshi, reported to Uchida his doubts
about the actions of the Kwantung army in north China
and about the non-recognition of the Kuomintang.
Negotiations for a ceasefire began almost immediately
and resulted in the so-called Tangku truce of 31 May.
A demilitarized zone some thirty miles wide to the
south of the Great Wall was prescribed; the Chinese
were to move south of this and the Japanese north.
But the Japanese were entitled to observe the demilitarization by the use of reconnaissance aircraft.
It was a unilateral settlement which was signed by
generals in the field and never ratified.   It suited
the Nanking government which was preoccupied with its
struggle with the communists.   It gave Japan a strong
position in north China from which she could later
assert her dominance.   But would it lead to a warlord-
type war as in Manchuria or a people's war as at
Shanghai?   For the present it gave Japan a respite
from which she could observe the activity - or
inactivity - of the other Powers. (23)

The situation to the north was equally delicate.
The Kwantung army had during the crisis taken
Tsitsihar and Harbin, key points in the Soviet sphere
of influence in north Manchuria.   By this time it
was threatening the Chinese Eastern railway which
was like a strip of dry land washed by the sea on
both sides.   The Soviet Union which was losing
interest in this railway took no steps to resist
Japan on Chinese territory; and this induced some
Japanese officers to discuss a madcap scheme for a
'preventive war' against the Soviet Union.   While
this was not taken up seriously, the Foreign Ministry

was following a different tack by discussing with
Moscow the possibility of a non-aggression pact.   It
was no new proposal; it had been raised in a practical
way by Yoshizawa when he was returning in December 1931
from Geneva to become foreign minister in the Inukai
ministry.   Litvinov, the foreign affairs commissar,
had responded cordially and welcomed the prospect of a
pact with Japan which would fit into a series of non-
aggression treaties his country had been concluding in
the West.   On Uchida's orders, the matter was pursued
by Ambassador Hirota in 1932 and was encouraged by
Matsuoka on his way to Geneva for the League meetings.
Then suddenly in January 1933 the nature of the negotiations was divulged and the talks were allowed to
lapse on the Japanese side. (24)

None the less the Russians still persisted.   When
the League passed on their recommendation that Manchukuo
should not be recognized by any World Power, the Soviet
Union reserved her right of independent action and did
not undertake to follow suit.   On 2 May Litvinov
announced that he was prepared to sell the Chinese
Eastern railway either to Japan or to Manchukuo, even
if this implied Soviet recognition for Manchukuo.
Negotiations opened immediately in Tokyo but, despite
sessions in June and July, Uchida ran into acute legal
problems, the railway being jointly Chinese and
Russian, and the talks were indefinitely suspended.
Rumours flew around that Japan would wrest the railway
by armed force; and the Soviet Union seems to have
increased her armies in Siberia.   But this mood
passed.   In September 1934 Hirota, a former ambassador
in Moscow and now foreign minister, reopened discussions
over the railway with Yureniev, the Soviet ambassador
in Tokyo.   Agreement was reached in the following
January and the final instruments were signed on 23
March. (25)

By this act which had been in the making since
Uchida's day, the Soviet rulers recognized the new
state of Manchukuo.   This was apparently a matter of
indifference to them.   Their motive was to acquire
the money for one of their major assets; to cut their
losses on an asset which was engulfed in someone else's
territory and was hardly capable of defence; and to
relieve tension in an area of peculiar difficulty.
For the Japanese the triumph was considerable for they
were in the process of lobbying for recognition of
Manchukuo by the major Powers.   But this was their
first and most unexpected victory, unless one includes
the recognition of Manchukuo by the state of Salvador
in the summer of 1934.

It was important for Japan to broaden the basis of
recognition.   The rest of the World Powers were
differently placed in so far as the League had given
a definite injunction against Manchukuo being recognized.   It was an important aspect of Japan's
diplomacy to tempt some of the Great Powers to recognize the new state, especially after 1 March 1934,
when Pu Yi ascended the imperial Manchu throne.   To
this end, Matsuoka had already made plain that 'for
those who recognized Manchukuo the door would be open'
no small inducement at a time when trading conditions
were so depressed.   Towards the end of 1933 Ambassador
Dirksen of Germany was invited to take part in an unofficial, sightseeing trip to the area, but his
foreign minister instructed him not to accept, doubtless because of the military relations which Germany
was cementing with the Kuomintang. (26)   It was not
until 20 February 1938 that Germany, shortly after
Ribbentrop had become foreign minister, accorded
recognition in a speech by Hitler to the Reichstag.
Rather earlier on 18 November 1936, Italy had appointed
a consul-general to Mukden and a year later official
recognition was announced.   Since Germany and Italy
were no longer members of the League, this was not a
direct challenge to its ruling.   Indeed, it was a
natural outcome of the anti-comintern pact.   Mercantile opinion in Britain was divided: those involved
in stimulating exports overseas viewed Japan and
Manchukuo favourably, regardless of the League resolution.   It was much the same in the United States,
where recognition could be used as a political bargaining counter as it was in Britain.   In both cases
lobbies in favour of the ploy were vocal; but the
governments were immovable and recognition was never
accorded. (27)   As the thirties progressed, the
nature of the Manchurian problem changed; but the
vast majority of Japanese were determined to see the
Manchukuo experiment prosper.

Chapter 10

The Hirota Period, 1933-7

When Uchida resigned because of ill-health and disillusion in September 1933, Hirota Kōki (1878-1948) was chosen as foreign minister. He was in Tokyo on leave from Moscow where he had been ambassador (1930-2). Hirota was a career diplomat who had served in Washington and several European capitals. Appointed by Admiral Saitō, he continued to serve under Admiral Okada. After the military mutiny of February 1936, he was chosen to head the new ministry which lasted for one year. After a period out of office, he returned to his former post as foreign minister (1937-8). While Hirota did not hold major office thereafter, he was at the Foreign Ministry in 1937 at the time of the Nanking atrocities and was adjudged by the International Military Tribunal for the Far East to be one of those responsible for that great human tragedy. He was found guilty and condemned to death in 1946. (1)

By the very nature of his years at the top, Hirota was bound to have a great influence on foreign policy-making. This was 'the Hirota period'. Yet Hirota was not a strong character; and his influence should not be exaggerated. Essentially pragmatic and vacillating, Hirota imparted a certain consistency to policy-making without dominating its course. His relation to right-wing forces is ambiguous. There is hardly an account of him which does not dwell on his early connections with the Genyōsha (the Dark Ocean society) as a disciple of Tōyama Mitsuru and his continuing closeness with the army. While these facts have been authenticated, it is less easy to see how they affected his actions in this period of high office. Perhaps the Genyōsha connection was unduly played up because it was a good credential for survival in the dangerous atmosphere of assassination

in the early 1930s.   But foreign observers found it
hard to pinpoint instances where his ultranationalist
tendencies had affected his attitude to them.   R.L.
Craigie saw Hirota go 'with genuine regret' when
Konoe dismissed him in 1938. (2)

Let us look at a character sketch of the new
minister given by Shigemitsu Mamoru who was his vice-
minister from 1933 to 1936. He believed that Hirota,
though well qualified for the Foreign Ministry, was
ill at ease at its head and did not approve the
policies of the army, with which he could not wholeheartedly co-operate, though from the way he talked
one might have assumed that he was advocating military
policies:

What he really meant was that those who held the
authority to discharge the functions of government
should openly reflect the people as a whole.   If
they could not prevent the machinations of those
working behind the scenes, government would never
be clear-cut; it would lack a sense of responsibility; it would ever be the prey of the
schemers. (3)

By this interpretation Hirota was preoccupied with
preventive policies rather than with acting boldly
and constructively; he tended to respond to initiatives by others.   It is probably true that his policy
at the Foreign Ministry was not militaristic or
dominated by the military. He tried hard to keep on
good terms with the Powers and to restore relationships after the Manchurian crisis. Yet his record
shows that he was weak; and it will always remain a
puzzle why it was he that the genro and his advisers
thought would be the most suitable statesman to lead
Japan out of the slough of the 1936 crisis.   Perhaps
Hirota was among the most ready of the Foreign Ministry
professionals to compromise with the army though it can
be argued that he was only keeping its leaders alive
to world opinion. (4)

It is necessary to write of the influence on Hirota
of his vice-minister, Shigemitsu. Shigemitsu had been
minister to China when he was recalled by Uchida to
replace Arita as vice-minister after his banishment
(May 1933). He was in short inherited by Hirota.
It is said by some scholars that Hirota inherited from
Uchida the failure of 'Foreign Ministry diplomacy'
[Gaimushō no gaikō] and its replacement by a new form
of 'individual (free for all) diplomacy' [Dokuji no
gaikō] which Uchida had pursued. The break from
Japan's foreign policy of the twenties took place under

Uchida rather than Hirota. (5)   Since Hirota was not
a man of great originality of ideas, it is probable
that he adopted much of Shigemitsu's philosophy as the
centrepiece of his foreign policy, at least in the
period before he became premier himself in 1936.   It
has to be remembered that Shigemitsu was only four
years junior to Hirota in the service and his career
pattern (Paris conference, London, Shanghai, Peking)
was perhaps more relevant to Japan's political problems in the mid-1930s than Hirota's.   The foreign
minister was specially indebted to Shigemitsu for his
China policy, for the so-called East Asian Monroe
doctrine, for the ideas underlying the Amō (Amau)
statement and for his attitude over foreign garrisons
in China. (6)   Basically both were content to let
various aspects of the China problem be settled by
military means where Japan was unquestionably superior
rather than diplomatic means where China had infinite
capacity for confusing the issue.

CHANGES IN KASUMIGASEKI'S ROLE

So long as Japan remained within the League, she was
treated with a cordiality which was artificial.   As
soon as she took herself out of the world body, she
was exposed to an avalanche of hostility and suspicion:
over China; over trade; over naval matters.   Confronted by this new spirit, diplomacy did not cease
but it did not have its former stature.   There was a
willingness to patch up things but Japan was no longer
cowed by international opinion nor restrained by the
fear of foreign intervention which the Manchurian
crisis had proved to be an insubstantial threat.   Un-
restrained, she was able to pursue self-interested
policies.   By and large, the Japanese were happy with
their new-found independence.   They were no longer
responding to the actions of others but initiating
policies for themselves.   They were proud that at
long last they were not hanging on to the coat-tails
of the world but considering their national self-
interest and casting only a sideways glance at foreign
views.
     In the clash between the military and civilians
which dominated the thirties, the Japanese Foreign
Ministry was pushed into a secondary position.
Hitherto it had been the standard-bearer of Japanese
internationalism and liberalism.   In the 1930s it was
still so but it was becoming increasingly a divided

house.   The ministers had to make their peace with
more militant spirits in the Cabinets or at most act
as a minor corrective, if they were to succeed professionally.   But at the same time they made the
right noises on the advice of their secretariat: for
a decade they called for peace and the removal of
tensions and victimization.   Consistently with this,
their representatives at the major diplomatic posts
abroad tried sedulously to promote goodwill, notably
Matsudaira Tsuneo in London.   And this despite the
fact that the Foreign Ministry had to bear the responsibility in international circles for actions which
were not of its contrivance.   The Ministry had the
new role of apologist for others whose views it often
did not share.   Meanwhile, behind the scenes it chose
to restrain the military expansionists rather than
stage an outright confrontation with them.

Among the divisions which existed within the
Foreign Ministry was a group identified vaguely as the
Ei-Bei-ha (Anglo-American group).   This was a group
of moderate, international-minded diplomats who had
spent time in Britain and America at formative stages
in their careers.   It implied more broadly the demo-
cratic faction; and some scholars have called it the
'Europe-American faction', so taking in those like
Satō Naotake, the ambassador in Paris (1933-6) who had
been more strongly influenced by French traditions.
Among foreign ministers, it seems to have been supported by Shidehara Kijurō (F.M. 1924-7;   1929-31),
General Ugaki Issei (Kazushige) (1938) and Admiral
Nomura Kichisaburō (1939-40).   From the Manchurian
crisis onwards, this faction lost ground within the
Foreign Ministry to the 'China faction', associated
with the names of Arita Hachirō (F.M. 1937-7;   1938-9;
1940) and Shigemitsu Mamoru (F.M. 1943;   1945).   This
group is sometimes given the title of 'the renovationist faction' because of its connection with the
scheme for the renovation of the Foreign Ministry
which was launched by Arita.   Linked with this
was the 'axis faction', led by Shiratori Toshio who
never became foreign minister but was influential both
as ambassador and as adviser to the Ministry and
carried weight with a kindred spirit in Matsuoka
Yōsuke (F.M. 1940-1).   It was the last two factions
which held sway in the Foreign Ministry bureaucracy in
the later thirties, which was a time of much chopping
and changing.   Yet in the interplay of cliques which
went to the making of a consensus in Japan's foreign
policy the Ei-Bei-ha still had some residual influence,

partly thanks to the favour of Genrō Saionji and palace
circles which it enjoyed. (7)

The difficulty of foreign ministers was that they
were bureaucrats who returned from overseas postings
to find a complicated web of court-party-military
intrigue. They had no political power or, if one
excepts Matsudaira Tsuneo, influence at court.
Unless they had had China postings they would have
limited experience of the military and no standing with
them. They were increasingly becoming executants
rather than policy-makers. These 'men from the profession' were prepared to accept continuity without
pursuing completely individual policies. And assassination lurked in the wings though no one from the
Foreign Ministry fell victim in the 1930s.

The main limitation on the foreign ministers and
Foreign Ministry bureaucrats was imposed by the army.
Because the military had exercised much independence
after the Mukden incident, 'Japan's foreign policy
initiatives during the 1930's became limited to
choices between the various perceptions the Japanese
military had of the nation's external interests and
strategic problems.' (8) In China and north-east
Asia, the army had sources of information not inferior
to those available to civilians. No diplomat was
strong enough to impede the army from undertaking
Chinese adventures. So foreign policy was executed in
effect within guidelines laid down by the army. Since
there were disagreements within the army, there were a
number of policy options, but they were restricted in
practice. The diplomats were limping behind the army
and navy, unhappily aware of international hostility to
which the military was insensitive.

The army naturally took the offensive in this
struggle. The Manchurian Affairs bureau of the Cabinet
was set up in 1934 and accepted by Hirota without
demur. (9) It sought to extend the process by
depriving the Foreign Ministry of responsibility for
China. The army took the battle into diplomatic
postings overseas. Let us illustrate this by two
examples. The army with its long connections with
Germany was anxious to have a major say in dealings at
axis capitals. The British Foreign Office got a
report that:

> In February 1937 Ambassador Sugimura went from Rome
> to Berlin for ten days. Japan's ambassador there
> (Mushakōji) was on his way to Tokyo and Kasumigaseki
> felt that the reports he would bring might not be
> trustworthy so it had asked Sugimura for an inde-
> pendent assessment. (10)

This was a typical case of the consequences of dual
diplomacy with one party spying on the judgments of
the other.   It was also a Foreign Ministry move
against the army and the anti-comintern pact in which
Sugimura Yōtarō was not a believer.   He had been
chief Japanese secretary on the staff of the League
of Nations and had many friends in axis countries,
though he was firmly anti-fascist.   The second
instance comes from the experience of Sir Frederick
Leith Ross, a British Treasury official, who visited
Japan in 1935 and 1936.   While he had discussions
with ministers, officials, bankers, his key discussion
which related to the financial problems of China was
held with Major-general Isogai Rensuke, a staff
officer of the occupying army in China.   It was
Isogai who stated the Japanese position finally and
without compromise.   Leith Ross was in no doubt on
this point. (11)   Despite this, there was an undoub-
ted rapport which developed between the two.

Why was there so little opposition to this attempted
military takeover of the Foreign Ministry?   First, as
in the Sugimura case above, there was opposition but
it was small-scale and devious rather than a frontal
attack on the military from which the top political
leaders drew back.   Second, some from whom leadership
might have been expected chose to go into premature
retirement.   Many diplomats such as Shidehara and
Debuchi were old enough to be on the verge of retirement and were happy to sink into oblivion.   Others
like Yoshida Shigeru and Tokugawa Iemasa had private
means which saved them compromising themselves and
gave them an independence of view which attracted the
attentions of the Kempeitai.

Many were not in this happy position.   They had
entered upon a prestigious career which they could not
throw up in midstream.   As we have seen, there were
those who saw Japan's destiny in the same terms as
did the army.   On the other hand, there were those
who claimed later that they had stayed on - and
accepted high office - in order to control the army
or the right-wing forces.   It is hardly possible any
longer to sustain the argument that the debate - or
the struggle - was one purely between the military
on the one hand and the civilians on the other.   Japan
was deeply torn;   and there were both military and
civilians on both sides of the laceration.   This was
as true of the 26 February affair as it was of most
foreign policy decisions. (12)

Assuming that there were these coalitions, it has

to be said that the moderate civilians did not effectively resist the military in the long term for the
control of foreign policy.   To be sure, there were
short-term successes.   But the liberal civilians had
neither the strength nor the popular backing to stem
the tide of expansion or adventure.   Since the Diet
was so weak there was no strength there on which they
could depend; since public opinion had been whipped
up in favour of the army during the Manchurian successes,
there was little hope of popular revulsion at the
doings of the army.

Hirota and his colleagues were the prototypes of
those important bureaucrats who found it desirable to
co-operate with the system.   They were not bad,
adventurous, irresponsible men.   They were essentially
trimmers.   The result was that the only policy that
was really unacceptable to the army was that of
Shidehara.   After him Foreign Ministry officials
strove for compromise and consensus with the army and
by and large worked out an acceptable policy.
Professor Usui presents the dilemma of Hirota in the
words of one of his senior officials, Morishima Gorō,

> His task was not to oppose openly the actions of the
> militarists, for this could in no way serve the
> objective of controlling them.   Had he opposed them
> openly, he either would have been obliged to resign
> or, at worst, would have been assassinated.   Hirota
> was the kind of man who would have accepted either
> alternative, but where would this have led?...   The
> 'difficult task' that confronted Hirota was, there-
> fore, to remain in his position, irrespective of the
> cost to himself, and, while making some concessions,
> attempt to restrain and guide the military. (13)

These are the best grounds for the defence of Hirota.
Against it, it has to be said that he failed to restrain
or guide the military in the long run and, further,
that, when he was in acute disagreement with the military - and his apologists say that this happened often -
he had not the courage to resign and risk his position
for the sake of his beliefs.

NAVAL DISARMAMENT

Japan had looked with suspicion at the proceedings of
the Disarmament Conference at Geneva which was in
session from 1932 to 1934, although she had been represented at it.   In a way this suspicion reflected
the divide within ruling circles in Japan.   On the

one hand, there were the prime minister, finance
minister and Hirota as foreign minister who wanted
to maintain an international posture and for political
reasons to economize all the while.   On the other,
there were the Army and Navy Ministries which were
opposed to disarmament, either qualitatively or quan-
titatively, except on their own terms.   Each ministry
was divided against itself; but the majorities in
both were urging the government to overcome Japan's
lack of 'military preparedness'.   There was a war
psychology abroad and a call for increased military
budgets.

The issue of Japan's defence was discussed in the
light of the Manchukuo situation at a critical meeting
of the five ministers in October 1933.   The foreign,
war, navy and finance ministers agreed by consensus
that some crisis or confrontation would arise for
Japan about 1936.   While War Minister Araki Sadao
spoke with accustomed loquacity of the likely war
being with the Soviet Union, the burden of the discussion was on naval disarmament and on the proposals
which Admiral Osumi Mineo, the navy minister, was
shortly to table on this subject in preparation for
the international naval limitation conference.
Osumi was the spokesman of the fleet faction which
had long been dominant in the naval general staff and
was making a bid for power in the Navy Ministry also.
Its old rival, the treaty faction, had lost much of
its influence in policy-making, though it still
commanded the support of a distinguished coterie of
admirals.   In any event, it was no longer able to
sustain the Japanese support for naval treaties which
were coming up for review. (14)

The position was that the existing naval treaties
were on a different legal footing.   The Washington
treaty of 1922, though it ran on automatically, could
be terminated at the end of 1936 on two years' notice
being given in 1934.   The London treaty was to lose
its validity on the last day of December 1936 so the
contracting countries were required to hold a conference in order to prepare a successor treaty.   Before
this could be convened, a preliminary conference was
necessary.   It was held in London in June 1934 with
Ambassador Matsudaira as Japan's representative.
Since the topics discussed proved to be more than pro-
cedural, it had to be adjourned.   When the meeting
was again called for October, the delegates were given
fresh orders in which Japan's policy was described as
follows:

Japan's basic view is that all countries possess
equally the right of having the armaments necessary
for their national security and it is necessary to
establish the principles that the security of all
countries shall not be destroyed and that force and
aggression shall not be resorted to.   That being
so, it is our aim as a method of achieving disarmament among the major naval Powers to lay down the
maximum levels of strength which each country can
possess.   It must be the principle of any treaty
to keep these levels low in order to demonstrate
the spirit of disarmament, while cutting offensive
strength down to the bone and providing only for
defensive strength; while there should be no
anxiety about countries defending themselves, we
should make it difficult for countries to attack. (15)
From this, the Japanese delegates were to propose, if
the talks went satisfactorily, the abolition of capital
ships and aircraft carriers.   Although the discussions
were carried on in cordial mood when the preparatory
conference reopened, there were many fundamental
differences between the various delegations (Document
31).

The Japanese view was that differential ratios were
no longer in keeping with national prestige and were
unacceptable.   If ratio restrictions were to be
abolished, then all Powers must have equal rights to
build, though this did not necessarily mean complete
parity.   In their contention for 'equality without
parity', there was a substantial consensus.   That is,
even Admiral Yamamoto Isoroku, who might claim to be
one of the inheritors of Admiral Katō Tomosaburō among
serving officers, wanted release for Japan from ratio
restrictions. (16)   Where the consensus broke down
was over the navy's demand that the treaties should be
speedily denounced.   At the five-minister conference
on 24 July, Premier Okada, an admiral of the orthodox
school who was also one of the protégés of Katō
Tomosaburō, and Hirota argued that the treaties should
not be abandoned until more talking had taken place,
because they feared Japan's bankruptcy and an Anglo-
American common front.   The navy minister wanted to
avoid delay in bringing Japan's defences up to the
mark and used the threat of the unruliness of the
younger officers, of which there had been examples in
the assassinations of the past few years.   On 7
September the Cabinet agreed that it would before the
end of 1934 give the two years' notice required for
withdrawal from the Washington naval treaty.   Naturally

this tied the hands of Admiral Yamamoto who was chosen
to represent Japan and set off on 20 September for
London.   Less well-known than later events were to
make him, Yamamoto was familiar with many American
officers from his days at Harvard (1919-20) and as
naval attaché at the Washington embassy and with
British officers through his pioneering efforts in
naval flying.   He had moreover attended the limitation talks in London in 1930 with Matsudaira, who was
to act as the civilian delegate. (17)

Anxious to salvage something from the preparatory
conference, Britain proposed that discussions should
go ahead on the basis of her own draft.   This
accepted the ratio differentials which had been such
a hard-fought issue at earlier conferences and rejected the Japanese basis from which we quoted before.
Hirota approved this procedure but the navy minister
would not agree.   America's proposal for 20 per cent
reduction and Britain's for automatic communication of
naval strengths were not acceptable.   The pattern of
preliminary parleys being clear, Japan asked France
and Italy who were opposed unreservedly to naval
ratios, whether they would join her in a combined
withdrawal but the European Powers would not associate
with this.   The Americans adhered resolutely to their
20 per cent reduction formula.   On 20 December
Britain proposed the adjournment of the discussions.
Before the end of the year Japan notified the Powers
of her intention to withdraw from the treaties. (18)

The adjournment proved to be a permanent postpone-
ment.   The preparatory talks were never restarted.
Despite the navy-civilian confrontation in Tokyo,
there was much cordiality among the delegates in
London;   and the Japanese, feeling that they were
making some progress, regretted the adjournment.
Witness the views of Admiral Enomoto who was a member
of the delegation:

This [postponement of the conference] was a matter
of a thousand regrets.   It was an excellent opportunity for co-operation between Matsudaira, who was
experienced in disarmament questions and a genuine
lover of peace, and Yamamoto, a distinguished and
knowledgeable sailor with wide sympathies.   If the
talks could have been continued a little longer,
they could have yielded important results and I
feel that it might have prevented the situation in
Japan and the world at large turning in a new
direction. (19)

At the formal naval conference in London which

assembled on 9 December 1935, Japan was represented by
Admiral Nagano Osami and Ambassador Nagai Matsuzō.
Nagano was among the extreme members of the fleet
school, while Nagai, a former ambassador in Germany, was
appointed in place of Ambassador Matsudaira, then on
long leave in Japan.   The impression given is that
they were kept on a tight leash by instructions from
Tokyo.   After the plenary the conference business was
transacted through the First Committee, which held ten
meetings down to 15 January 1936. (20)

   The Japanese position had hardened since the earlier
parleys and changed very little.   They still sought a
common upper limit for battleships which should be kept
at the lowest possible level;   they wanted to minimize
combatant units and maximize defensive units such as
submarines;   each Power was to give undertakings not to
commit aggression or to threaten.   The committee gave
an attentive hearing to the Japanese common upper limit
proposals which did not appeal to any other delegation.
If the Japanese had been uncompromising, they could
easily have acted on their instructions and withdrawn
if their proposed 'ceiling' did not command wide
support.   Instead they agreed to the adjournment of
discussion on their proposal, which permitted the conference to proceed with the British proposal for
'qualitative limitation'.   It was early in January
that they reminded the meeting that their sole instruc-
tion was to promote the 'ceiling' and, if this failed,
they would have to withdraw.   After the tenth
Committee on 15 January Japan announced her official
departure from the conference.   Thus, when the conference ended on 25 March with the conclusion of a
treaty for the limitation of naval armament, Japan was
not bound by it.   She ceased to be bound by the
apparatus of naval treaties at the end of 1936, as her
navy had desired and lobbied for.

   It might seem to be a complete victory for the
Japanese navy.   The more extreme and uncompromising
group in the navy had got its way over the more
moderate wing which had still had influence at the
preparatory conference, over the civilians and over
the foreigners.   Foreign naval Powers regarded the
Japanese proposal for a 'ceiling' as a purely wrecking
one, as R.L. Craigie, the British official most closely
connected with the conference, described it. (21)   In
particular, the United States was resolved not to
accept either Japan's desire for parity or a major
relaxation of ratios in favour of Japan.   Britain
took a less extreme position and, as sponsor of the

conference, did try to move the Japanese from their
initial position.   But she had no success;   and Japan
was released from naval limitation.

But the navy's victory was less complete than
appeared on the surface.   The Foreign Ministry, which
had a much smaller say than in 1921 or 1930, was not
completely outpointed.   Hirota was able to boast that
his plea that Japanese should continue to attend as
'observers' which had at first been rejected by the
navy, had been sustained.   They continued to attend
sessions of the First Committee until the plenary in
March.   Japan was not bound by the final provisions
but she did accept the rules governing submarine warfare which emerged.   She signed them together with
the other naval Powers on 6 November.

Hirota's second ploy was to propose in December 1935
some political understanding between Britain and Japan.
His proposal on the lines of a non-aggression pact or
an understanding on China was based on the notion that
no general naval agreement would result from the deliberations.   It was made first to Britain who, it was
hoped, would act as the bridge to the hostile United
States.   Britain, for her part, was gratified by the
proposal which reflected a desire which she had had
since 1934.   The Americans were not interested in a
non-aggression pact.   While Britain tried to get the
Japanese to be more specific about their proposal, her
final answer was delivered on 27 January:

If a political pact would have helped us to achieve
an acceptable Naval Treaty, Mr Hirota's idea might
well have been worth pursuing.   The situation has,
however, been entirely changed by the action of the
Japanese, since ... we could not consider the
possibility of concluding a political pact with the
United States and Japan as a substitute for a Naval
Treaty.   Indeed it is difficult to see what benefit
in the present circumstances such a pact could be to
us. (22)

Hirota was still anxious for some diplomatic result to
emerge from the conference which had been conducted in
a cordial atmosphere.   On 24 February, therefore, he
proposed that Article 19 of the Washington naval treaty,
that dealing with non-fortification, should form the
basis of a new agreement.   But Britain replied that it
had originally been agreed to in return for Japanese
acceptance of the 5-5-3 ratio and, now that the ratios
were to be dishonoured by Japan, it was doubtful
whether renewal of the clause was in her interests or
those of the United States who were privately

consulted. (23)   Hirota was unsuccessful in forging
any new political relationship with the Powers, with
whom the naval relationship had broken down.   Thus,
the Foreign Ministry emerged from the second London
Naval Conference with the international reputation of
being weak: the ministry and the whole Cabinet had
not restrained the navy in its demands.   But Hirota
was still willing to negotiate whenever possible.

CHINA, 1933-7

Over China Hirota faced internal dissension and
external suspicion.   China was one but also many.
She had a seeming unity under the Nanking government
of the Kuomintang.   There was a strong army and a
sense of revolutionary nationalism.   But, on the
whole, the grasp of Nanking was restricted and the
Kuomintang was riddled by faction and counter-faction.
The foreign Powers in the main were relieved to see
this semblance of unity and the successes of the New
Life movement and ready to encourage it by offers of
reform and treaty revision.   In this, Japan was a
notable exception.   Her China policy was largely the
product of the army where mainstream opinion proved
to be strangely insensitive to the claims of Chinese
nationalism and to be obsessed with the call for law
and order which had earlier been its rallying cry in
the Manchurian crisis.
     Japan had limited interests in China to the south
of the Yangtse river which enjoyed comparative
stability.   Japan with her industrial investment was
content to operate through her treaty rights and to
improve her position (say) in Shanghai Municipality
wherever possible at the expense of other Powers.
She dodged direct confrontation with Nanking or with
the Powers whose business interests straddled that
area.
     Japanese expansion was directed mainly to the north
of the Yangtse.   Manchukuo and Shantung were old
stories.   But gradually the army became active from
the Great Wall to Peking and Tientsin and from Manchukuo against their recognized enemy, Soviet Russia,
by striking at Inner Mongolia, a convenient buffer-
state.   These were not intended as strategic moves
purely and involved economic calculations by the army.
The army officers who were to the fore in this thrust
were confronted also with the political problems of
setting up and encouraging autonomous regional govern-

ments through disaffected Chinese.   They built up in
this way an expertise - often unsavoury - which those
of the Foreign Ministry could not match.   While
Japanese statesmen wanted to settle the various China
questions, too much practical power to obstruct and
complicate rested at the local level.

After the Tangku truce, there was a period of lull.
Hirota, who had joined the Saitō Cabinet in September
1933, was deeply distressed and in a quandary.   Meetings like the five ministers' conference devised a
plan for foreign relations, approved by the Cabinet
on 21 October.   Someone within the Foreign Ministry
like Shiratori Toshio who held the key post of head
of the information services, was quite open in his
defence of the military position. (24)   These uncer-
tainties expressed themselves at the time of the so-
called Amau declaration, a statement made on 17 April
1934 by Amau Eiji, whom Hirota had known in Moscow and
now chose as Shiratori's successor.   It asserted that
Japan had the sole responsibility for the preservation
of peace in east Asia and that she opposed any efforts
on the part of China to seek foreign assistance in
order to resist Japan, and any technical, financial or
military assistance by a third party or parties to
China.   Although efforts were made to explain away
the abruptness of this statement, it merely reaffirmed
that Japan would not tolerate military aid and foreign
loans to China, both of which were likely to be anti-
Japanese in their effects.   It was a warning simultaneously to China and the Powers.   It was not the
ideal first move in Hirota's supposedly conciliatory
policy over China.   It therefore leaves the impression
of Hirota as an indecisive, inconsistent and spineless
figure, anxious outwardly for a diplomatic settlement
but in the last resort swayed by those more extreme.
There can be little doubt about Hirota's personal responsibility in this affair because the Amau statement
was apparently copied quite properly from one of
Hirota's instructions to Peking of 18 March with their
intense opposition to any British loan to China.
Moreover, these views were in line with the recommendations which were reaching Tokyo from Minister Ariyoshi
in Peking.   Hence there was an influential consensus
over the nature of China policy. (25)

After the years of relative tranquillity in 1933-4,
there was a fresh burst of activity in north China.
While the Tokyo government seems to have been genuinely
trying to achieve a settlement of the disputes with
China, the army in Manchuria and Tientsin were planning

to subvert these attempts as they had done with success
in 1931.   This is not to say that Foreign Minister
Hirota would necessarily have had enough vision to
achieve a formula acceptable to the nationalist
Chinese, although the will seems to have been there.
In the meantime the army pursued Manchukuo tactics in
north China, seeking to promote an independence movement or an autonomy movement there.   General Ishiwara
Kanji had foretold in 1933 that Japan, in establishing
(as he hoped) an East Asian League, would encounter
opposition from China as well as the United States,
Britain and Russia and must, therefore

> establish control over China proper as speedily and
> skilfully as possible, create a self-sufficient
> economic bloc encompassing Japan, China and Man-
> chukuo, protect our position in the East Asian League
> by force against the land force of the Soviet Union
> and the naval forces of the United States and
> Britain. (26)

Chiang Kai-shek indeed seemed to the Japanese to be
like a ripe persimmon.   He was confronted by splits
within his Kuomintang party and among the generals.
He was, moreover, especially absorbed with his anti-
communist campaigns which ended with qualified success
by forcing the communists to leave their base in Kiangsi
province and undertake their Long March in 1934.
Thereafter it was Chiang's hope to exterminate the
communists at Yenan by using the warlord army from
Manchuria.   While the communists acted boldly to
declare war on Japan, Nanking gave the impression of
taking rather ignominious rearguard action against
Japan.

The Japanese operated by a mixture of military and
civil action.   Major-General Umezu Yoshijirō, the
commander-in-chief of the occupying forces in China,
conducted a campaign in Chahar to the north of Peking
for the first half of 1935.   The Kuomintang began
'local negotiations' with him over Hopei and consented
by the Umezu-Ho agreement to the withdrawal of its
forces from the Tientsin-Peking region.   Also in June
after the occupation of east Chahar, Major-General
Doihara Kenji secured from the local warlord, Marshal
Chin, undertakings that the region north of the Yellow
river would be demilitarized;   that KMT influence would
be excluded from it;   and that Chinese officials who
resisted Japan were to be replaced.   Though these
arrangements were spoken of as 'local', there can be
little doubt that they committed Nanking.   In the
view of the Japanese army, these moves were the first

steps in the creation of an economic bloc between north
China, Manchukuo and Japan. (27)

Foreign Minister Hirota approached things in a
negotiating spirit.   In a gesture of sympathy for the
Kuomintang, he agreed to the exchange of ambassadors
in May despite the opposition of the military whose
view was that Chiang Kai-shek was only one warlord
among many and should not be singled out for special
favours.   Hirota then put forward his so-called three
principles on China.   Ariyoshi, who had become the
first ambassador, raised these in a meeting with Chiang
Kai-shek on 20 November.   The generalissimo showed his
agreement in principle but asked that the scheme for
independence in north China should be stopped.   In
January 1936 the principles were finally published:
cessation of all unfriendly acts by China towards
Japan; recognition by China of Manchukuo; Sino-
Japanese co-operation for the eradication of communism.
These represented a sort of highest common factor in
the desires of the various Japanese groups who shared
in the evolution of China policy.   The terms were
marginally milder than those of the army negotiations
but were still very far-reaching.

The army's objects vis-à-vis the KMT and Soviet
Russia were best served by encouraging the separatist
tendencies in north China.   The essence of its ideas
was to create a buffer zone against Russian exploits
under Japanese influence by separating the five northern
provinces (Hopei, Chahar, Suiyuan, Shansi and Shantung)
from KMT control.   In this it notched up some
successes.   In November 1935 the eastern Hopei Autonomous Council declared its independence of Nanking
and set up a government under a Japanese protégé, Yin
Ju-ken.   In December was set up the Hopei-Chahar
council which virtually meant that the KMT accepted
the independence of Peking and Tientsin.   The proposal
for an autonomous region remained on the table between
Tokyo and Nanking throughout 1936 but Chiang, perhaps
hoping for foreign support, stalled on the issue.

All this progress was dearly bought.   It had the
natural effect of bringing together rival groups in
China, notably the student protest movements who
rallied against the Japanese.   Moreover, the boycott
of Japanese goods was taking its toll.   There was
fear in Japan of Russia's attitude and the measures
which other Powers might take.   As a result, the
strength of the Japanese army in China was increased.
It continued to assist those Mongol rulers who sought
to establish an independent regime based on Chahar but

claiming the right to govern over the neighbouring
provinces of Suiyuan and Ningsia.   Taking it one
step further, Japan inspired the Mongol autonomy
council in June 1936, which took the name of Mangkukuo.
But in October a combined Japanese-Manchukuo attack
on Suiyuan was repulsed by China and gave her leaders
new heart.

Japan's activities left the sympathies of the world
much on the Chinese side.   But the Powers were slow
and reluctant to act.   The only real international
showdown - and that a minor one - arose out of
Britain's decision to send to China in 1935 Sir
Frederick Leith Ross, chief economic adviser and an
eminent international financial authority.   His prime
role was to investigate and advise but, underlying
this, was the desire to organize an international
effort to rehabilitate the Chinese economy.   Since
the United States, France and Japan declined to send
parallel missions, the British mission stood on its
own as an attempt to build up the Chinese economy and
the Kuomintang and, by implication, to prevent the
expansion of Japanese monopolistic practices there. (28)

The leading Japanese expert has recently described
the mission as 'the climax of a battle between Britain
and Japan for the control of China's economy'. (29)
What stuck in the Japanese throat was that the mission
had been sent in blatant disregard of the Amau declaration, although it is arguable that Hirota had in
assurances withdrawn the more excessive aspects of
that doctrine.   The attempt to induce Japan to share
in the enterprise or to send a parallel mission seemed
to them to be a smokescreen.   The majority of army
leaders - and the politicians who went with them -
were of the opinion that Britain was the main impediment to their country's ascendancy in China and that
Japan's growth there could not be sustained without
the exclusion of foreign interests there.   In this
context Leith Ross's mission was anathema and the
Japanese could not co-operate with it.

When Leith Ross reached Tokyo in September, he found
the Japanese unwilling to join the British in the
economic rehabilitation of China.   Japan's officials
concluded that the British were about to become competitors there.   Leith Ross probably did not advise
the Chinese on their currency reform schemes which were
published in November; but it is likely that some
tacit endorsement by him was essential to any success
it had. (30)

Towards the end of May Leith Ross re-visited Tokyo

and found his conversations with officials more cordial
than previously.   But the government was in his view
unable or unwilling to modify the policy of the military
in China in relation to finance or trade.   He left
some criticisms of Japanese policy with General Isogai,
chief of the military affairs bureau of the War
Ministry and until recently GOC of Japan's forces in
China.   It was naturally unusual to hold major discussions with a military man.   In return he received
a statement of military-cum-diplomatic policy which is
unique in its way:

> Japan was not antagonistic towards the Nanking gov-
> ernment but was sceptical over its real attitude
> towards the suppression of communism.   It was the
> monetary policy of the Nanking government which had
> given impetus to the autonomous movement in north
> China of which [Leith Ross] complained and he dis-
> claimed Japanese involvement.   While the Nanking
> government's attitude with regard to the special
> relations between Japan, Manchukuo and north China,
> to the control of anti-Japanese activities and the
> suppression of communism remained unsatisfactory,
> the Japanese government could not remain in-
> different. (31)

This was as uncompromising a statement of Japan's
position as had ever been made.   In fact, it was
modified in August in the light of Leith Ross's visit.
The Hirota Cabinet which had been in office since March
undertook an overall review of national policy and
foreign relations and re-examined the measures to be
taken in north China - a sort of second instalment
(Document 32).

In the Japanese view, one of the props of KMT
strength and survival was the Soviet Union.   It was
Japan's fear that Russia which was increasing her
forces in east Asia, would intervene to assist Chiang
Kai-shek.   This induced her to try to neutralize
Russian activities and to negotiate with Germany from
September 1936 onwards.   The anti-comintern pact was
signed between Ribbentrop and Ambassador Mushakōji in
Berlin in November.   After the navy had given its
belated approval, the Cabinet gave its authorization.
Although vague in its terms, the pact had wide-ranging
global implications and even greater symbolic importance.   Perhaps the secret notes exchanged at the same
time as the pact were more significant than the treaty
itself.   In Tokyo's eyes, it was an attempt to neutralize Soviet influence in east Asia and convince the
Chinese that there was not much practical assistance

that they could expect from Moscow.   Japan was too
optimistic by half in expecting such favourable
results from the pact.   At all events, the pact
fitted neatly in with the 'Fundamental Principles of
National Policy', a document which had been drawn up
in February and was kept regularly under review
during the year.

The Japanese had some reason for believing that
the political climate in China was moving against them.
Throughout 1936 the communist party had stressed the
need for a nation-wide anti-Japanese front and shown
a willingness to sacrifice some of its principles in
order to reach an accommodation with the KMT Government.   A consensus was emerging for the view that it
was more sensible for Chinese to fight Japanese rather
than each other.   There was general agreement that,
if China was to cement her unity, she needed a cause
and that the cause could best be found by concentrating on foreign issues.   In December Chiang Kai-shek
dramatically visited Chang Hsueh-liang in Sian allegedly in order to arrange with him as the commander of
the north-west bandit suppression corps how to conduct
one of his campaigns.   The world - most of all Japan -
was horrified when it heard that Chiang was being held
captive by the supposedly loyal Chang.   When it first
became known, it was understood that the generalissimo
had been killed.   Later, when he emerged alive, it was
assumed that he had only been released on giving
assurances that the Kuomintang would henceforth collaborate with the communist party in making common
cause against the Japanese.   There is, of course, much
that is still not clear about the Sian incident and
the formula which brought it to an end.   But the
Japanese, judging from the tougher attitude which the
Chinese were later to show in negotiations, had to
conclude that the sapping conflict between the Kuomintang and the Chinese communists was suspended, at
least temporarily, and had to devise their operations
on the assumption that there was a united anti-Japanese
front in China and that it could rely on the outside
support of Soviet Russia.

In February 1937 Hirota resigned as prime minister.
He was to return to positions of high authority when
he became foreign minister to the Konoe Cabinet.   But
'the Hirota period' had ended.   At the time, Japanese
scholars described Hirota's as a 'policy of co-operation and conciliation much as Baron Shidehara had done
during the preceding decade'. (32)   Yet the evidence
in this chapter suggests a very different conclusion.

Quite apart from Japanese trade expansion which was
making Japan unpopular in the world, Hirota had not
assisted an international solution of the China problem
or an international solution of the naval armament
problem.   It is perhaps true that he prevented ugly
scenes and took avoiding action which prevented a
major conflagration over China; but he was less
skilful in steering towards an acceptable international
solution in the naval disarmament conferences.   It
has been our argument that Hirota was outpointed by
the army and the navy on these issues and that the
Foreign Ministry began to play a less significant
role under his leadership.   Yet Hirota was much more
a man of the middle course than Uchida in 1933 and
many of his successors.   He was therefore to some
extent a victim of his circumstances.   He left behind
golden reputations with Joseph Grew, Robert Craigie
and many another foreign observer.   But there was a
vagueness and ambiguity in his observations which
enabled him to be both the author of assurances to
Washington and London and the ultimate authority for
the Amau declaration.   It is in our view difficult
to argue (with Professor Akagi) that 'Hirota diplomacy
is the modified revival of the Shidehara policy,
modified to meet the new situation in east Asia,
namely, the emergence of Manchoukuo.' (33)   Shidehara
was above all blunt and frank while Hirota obfuscated
the issue out of a desire to secure an artificial
meeting of minds.

These views were reflected also in the Foreign
Ministry.   In February 1937 when the Hirota ministry
was replaced by that of General Hayashi Senjurō,
Arita was replaced as foreign minister by Satō Naotake,
who having been for long in Europe brought a new
orientation to foreign policy.   At a four-ministers
conference in April it was agreed not to interfere in
north China and to seek new alignment with the powers.
In his statement in the Diet on 12 March, Satō had
earlier reflected:

> Whether Japan gets involved in crises, that is, in
> serious crises in the sense of leading to the out-
> break of war, depends on the thinking of Japan her-
> self.   If the people themselves want crises of
> this sort, the crises will always come.   If, on
> the other hand, Japanese do not want crises and
> there is a conviction that crises must be avoided,
> Japan can ensure that they are avoided. (34)

Unquestionably Japan was in control of her destiny in
China and could not blame her problems on China, the

Soviet Union or foreign countries.   This might be the
obituary of 'the Hirota period' with its self-centred
pursuit of Japanese objectives without any instinct
for compromise and with a readiness for brinkmanship.
So superior was Japan's power that she need have no
fear of provoking military crises.   A low valuation
was accorded to diplomacy, the art of compromise and
of composing conflict without resort to fighting.
Though Japan might well be cock-a-whoop with her
achievements over the past six years, the record tells
that Satō's remarks were received in the Diet with
applause.

Hirota's retirement did not remove him from the
scene as in the case of Shidehara and Uchida.   From
1939 onwards more and more use was made of a body
called the Jūshin which was in effect a gathering of
former prime ministers.   Since they were consulted on
a wide variety of issues of a diplomatic kind, Hirota's
advice was sought as a matter of course.   At the
crucial meeting on 29 November 1941, Hirota spoke with
the ambiguity of the Delphic oracle.   In 1944 Prime
Minister Tōjō asked Hirota to join his Cabinet in the
capacity of minister without portfolio in order to
assemble a Cabinet of national unity in which the
presence of ex-premiers would give the people greater
confidence.   But Hirota, who was sixty-six at the
time, refused to serve and the Tōjō Cabinet fell.
After the war he stood trial as one of those responsible
for the atrocities associated with the taking of
Nanking at the end of 1937.   Hirota, who had been
foreign minister at the time, was condemned to death
as a Class A war criminal in 1946.   Despite an appeal
to the United States supreme court, he was executed by
hanging in December 1948.

For the historian Hirota presents something of a
puzzle.   He seems to have been all things to all men.
Both Craigie and Grew regarded him as an internationalist statesman who was relatively well disposed to
their countries.   The Japanese tend to label him
differently.   Professor Usui believes that Hirota
took an ambiguous position in the factional strife
within the Foreign Ministry but cannot see any serious
division between his policy towards China and that of
the military. (35)   Hirota, therefore, favoured a
special role for Japan in east Asia and was ready to
take strong measures against China.   Perhaps it is
true that his early experience as a student of Tokyo
Imperial University when he was specially chosen to go
on a conducted tour of Korea and Manchuria in 1903 may
have cast a shadow over his adult years.

Chapter 11

The Konoe Period,
1937-40

Konoe Fumimaro was prime minister from 1937 to 1939
and, after a brief entracte, from July 1940 to October
1941.   His first spell as prime minister will be
dealt with in this chapter. (1)   Since it was the
critical period of the China war, we are entitled to
call it 'the Konoe period'.   The equally critical
period of 1940-1 will be examined in the next chapter
under the name of his foreign minister, Matsuoka.

Although he never was foreign minister, Konoe was
increasingly drawn into the field of top-level diplomacy.   Like most prime ministers of his time, he
found himself playing a large role in foreign affairs.
Even during the 'Matsuoka period', when he was confronted by a strong and confident foreign minister,
he had inevitably to involve himself.   It was, indeed,
widely understood that Konoe had a forte for dealing
with overseas problems: he had had some experience of
them as a member of the Saionji-Makino delegation at
the Paris peace conference of 1919.   He was appointed
prime minister in order to solve the China problem in
1937; he was assumed to have the skill to negotiate
with F.D. Roosevelt in 1941; and it was hoped that he
could solve the problem of peace-making by paying a
visit to Moscow in 1944.   In all these quests he
failed; yet men trusted in his capacity to make the
attempts.   Among the many enigmas surrounding Konoe
is the discrepancy between the expectation of him and
his poor fulfilment.   Even at his death in 1945 he
enjoyed a residual popularity.

In retrospect one has to say that Konoe was not a
collossus who dominated his generation.   He was not a
charismatic leader; nor did he want to be.   He was
an important political figure who was to some extent
carried along by forces which were beyond his compre-

hension.   Photographed on the stairs up to his residence in 1937, he stands two steps below his Cabinet
colleagues because he was so much taller.   Yet, with
his shoulders hunched, he gives the impression of a
shy, sensitive and retiring man.   He is dressed in
the wing-collar and the Victorian frockcoat which go
to confirm his patrician origins.   Yet his support
came not wholly from an aristocratic, court party.
Konoe was initially a political neutral, having been
president of the House of Peers since 1933.   He
derived much support from the middle-class, intellectual circles.   As a student he had imbibed much left-
wing doctrine at Kyoto university which was regarded
at the time as a leftist institution.   Perhaps
because of this, the intellectuals welcomed his
appointment with over-optimism.   He was liked by all.
He responded by making use of intellectuals in his
brains trust, the Showa kenkyūkai. (2)   They, in
turn, believed that he was the only force remaining
to contain the power of the military in Japan and to
limit the China war.   This explains something of the
good Press which he had for so much of his career.
While he was flexible and open-minded, he was to
prove weak and indecisive.   Moreover, he showed
little evidence of socialist thinking and became more
and more towards the end of the 1930s the nominal
leader of fascist forces.   On these two counts Konoe
fell short of his supporters' hopes.   Konoe indeed
was a man caught up in a cascade of events and ensnared
in a complicated political scene which he could pre-
scribe for but which he could hardly control.   He
leaves a shadow rather than a sharp imprint on the
manuscript of history.   Konoe enjoyed the elusive
popularity of the aristocrat who appears to be reluctant for power but yet responds to a call to duty. (3)
He was the figure of reconciliation who could bring
together bureaucrats, military men and party
politicians.
     When Prince Saionji, as the remaining Elder States-
man, recommended Konoe as premier, he did so because
of their association which went back to the Paris
peace conference in 1919.   He respected Konoe's family
connections and his youthfulness.   Konoe seemed to
combine two rare qualities: as the son of Konoe
Atsumarō, a nationalist politician who had founded the
right-wing Kokumin Dōmeikai in the late Meiji period,
he had rightist connections; as the author of the
pamphlet 'Rejecting the Anglo-American peace', the
fruits of his Paris experiences, he was a radical

thinker in international affairs. (4)   Perhaps
Saionji was more subtly relying on him to act as a
brake on the armed services who were badly in need
of discipline.   Konoe tackled this problem by
indirect and devious means, e.g. by placing mili-
tarists in positions where they might be manipulated.
But such tactics can be dangerous and counter-productive.   Especially in the circumstances of the China
war when the military was assuming ever larger
privileges, it was all too easy for the military to
turn the tables and manipulate rather than being
themselves manipulated.   Saionji's confidence in
Konoe was in many respects misplaced, and in some
positively frustrated.

Konoe's Cabinets were wartime Cabinets where diplomacy had to take second place to military considerations.   This fact may be observed in the various
bodies who took the key decisions.   Konoe, trying to
avoid formalized meetings of the Cabinet, progressively
relied on an inner Cabinet, the so-called four or five-
minister conferences.   The membership varied according
to the topic but the war and navy ministers were always
there.   More often than not the foreign minister also
attended so he had not by any means forfeited power.
By 1941 it was the liaison conference which had become
the principal decision-making body in foreign affairs,
leaving the Cabinet to deal with domestic affairs.
These were meetings of the inner Cabinet with members
of the general staffs.   From this body recommendations
were passed to the imperial conference, where again
military representatives had their say. (5)

More important perhaps than the agencies of consultation were the failures of consultation.   The chiefs
of staff had considerable independent power under the
right of supreme command (tōsuiken) system.   After
1937 this led to real anxiety when the failure of the
military to co-operate placed the civilian government
in an ambiguous position.   This is well illustrated
in the writings of Konoe himself where he describes
the crisis of the American-Japanese negotiations of the
summer of 1941 in these words:

While my government was negotiating with all its
energy, the military were pursuing war preparations
to meet the eventuality that negotiations might
fail.   It was impossible for us who knew nothing
about these preparations to align our diplomacy
with them.   Washington got to know that our ships
were being switched about and became very sceptical
of our sincerity. (6)

Later General Tōjō refused to disclose military plans
to the civilian leaders.   The result of this could
only be for inconsistencies to develop between foreign
policy and military foreign policy.   Even the military holders of high office failed to get the forces
to disclose vital information.

The major sufferer in all this was the Foreign
Ministry.   There was an inevitable trend towards the
prime minister having a larger say in policy-making.
The paramountcy of the foreign minister, which may
have existed in part under Shidehara, had passed.
Foreign ministers in this period were of mixed
quality and changed frequently.   Some had strong
personalities such as General Ugaki while others such
as Arita were weak.   By and large, however, they were
not long enough in power to overturn Konoe's fence-
sitting posture. (7)

The professional service itself was subject to new
difficulties.   The ministry was declining: Manchuria
and then China had been taken from its control though
consuls continued to serve there.   The creation of
the Tai-Man Jimukyoku, the Kō-A-in and later the Dai-
Tō-A-shō ate into its prerogatives.   The old high
standards were deteriorating.   When the military
became increasingly political, especially after the
revolt of 26 February 1936, they posted at all the
vital capitals attachés who rapidly became involved in
politicking.   This had inevitable effects on the
diplomatic process, when reports on events reached
Tokyo from the attachés before they came through
diplomatic channels.   Though this might have advantages, it was an inconvenience that foreign governments
should come to learn through the attachés things which
the diplomats did not disclose.   When men with military backgrounds became ambassadors, they were subject
to influences other than the Foreign Ministry and
their reporting was less adept. (8)   This is particularly
notable in the case of General Oshima Hiroshi, ambassador in Berlin (1938-9 and 1941-5) and Admiral Nomura
Kichisaburō, ambassador in Washington (1940-2).   Of
course, it is conventional to say that Japan was
following a dual diplomacy - military and civil.   This
is true; but quite a number of countries were following more than one policy in the crises of the 1930s.
The contradictions implicit in Japan's policy and the
deep disagreements within the policy-making elite were on
a vast scale and caused widespread suspicion abroad. (9)
They far exceeded the powers of any co-ordinating
agency.

While the Foreign Ministry tended to favour courses
which were cautious, vigilant and opposed to expansion,
these courses did not appeal to public opinion.
Public opinion was ill-informed on foreign policy and,
being led by political activists, continuously demanded
a tough line.   With notable exceptions like 'Tōyō
Keizai Shimpō', the Press fed Japan's deteriorated
leadership of the 1930s with what it wanted to hear.
Of course, had public opinion come out in favour of
more moderate courses, it is still possible that it
would have been ignored.   There is much truth in what
Konoe was later to write: 'Domestic and foreign
policies were determined, changed and abandoned at the
whim of the military which was able to act regardless
of public opinion.' (10)

THE CHINA ULCER

There is a rich irony in Konoe, who was appointed
because of his supposed capacity to deal with the China
question, being confronted only one month after this
with the outbreak of the China incident.   On 7 July
1937 the Marco Polo bridge incident took place south
of Peking just when Japan seemed to be in the process
of retreat from China and Chiang's government was
expecting to extend its authority to the north.   Konoe
was taken unawares by the outbreak.   On 11 July a
ceasefire was locally arranged.   While the chiefs of
staff were opposed to any extension, there was a pro-
war faction in Japan which, since there had been no
strategic planning for it, thought otherwise.   Konoe
had a particularly difficult task, holding together a
coalition of people with widely differing objects.
He seems to have been initially opposed to sending
troops to the area but later conceded the request of
the war minister, provided that the conflict was
localized.   But the war enthusiasm grew and the expeditionary forces predictably took the law into their
hands.   The war minister asked Konoe for a strong
statement of government objectives to be issued and,
since no one spoke up against it in Cabinet, the prime
minister gave in against his better judgment.   It was
to be an early example of what Professor Oka Yoshitake
calls 'government by acquiescence'.   Examples are to
be found in plenty in Konoe's later years.
The sending of an expeditionary force was confirmed
by the five-ministers' conference and put into effect
during August.   Meanwhile the two armies clashed at

Shanghai on 13 August and Konoe concurred in the navy's
request that a reinforcement of two divisions should be
sent there.   Japan represented her actions as being
'defensive' but at a Cabinet on 17 August it was
decided to reverse the policy of non-extension:
communiqués began to speak not of 'the north China
incident' but of 'the China incident'.   In effect a
war was in being, though the word was not used in Tokyo
because of American neutrality legislation.

The Chinese who had no qualms about speaking of
'war' referred the matter to the League of Nations
which recommended a 'prompt suspension of hostilities'.
The assembly on 28 September unanimously resolved
against the bombing of Chinese cities and later on 6
October branded Japan's actions as a violation of the
Washington nine-Power treaty and the anti-war treaty.
Largely at Britain's instance, a nine-Power conference
opened in Brussels on 3 November without Japan being
represented.   But Japan was not obliged to accept its
findings; and the participants were not prepared to
over-extend themselves by individual or joint action
against Japan. (11)   The Powers passed a resolution
calling on themselves to avoid taking action which
might have the effect of weakening China's resistance.
Japan had dissociated herself from the League's doings,
insisting that the problems must be sorted out between
China and Japan; refusing to co-operate in the League's
political functions; and resenting the League's unfriendly resolutions towards her.   She now rejected
the findings of the conference which adjourned on 24
November without achievement.

Meanwhile mediation was being undertaken by Germany,
the quasi-ally of Japan and China.   Germany was in the
unusual position of being close to the Japanese general
staff where a majority still wanted to avoid escalation
and being close to the Kuomintang and to the army of
the Nanking government to which they had for some years
supplied advisory teams.   The basis of their mediation
was that a full-scale war would destroy the unity of
China and give a fillip to the Chinese communists and
that this would give a boost to the Soviet Union and
thus injure the objects of the anti-Comintern treaty.
Negotiations involving her minister in China, Oskar P.
Trautmann, and ambassador in Tokyo, Dirksen, seemed to
be making headway with Chiang Kai-shek in December
when the Japanese stepped up their terms and thus
destroyed all hope of effective outside mediation. (12)

In settling with China, Japan was left to her own
devices and disagreements.   Anxious not to be caught

as Tokyo had been in 1932 by the army overseas, the
Konoe Cabinet on 1 October 1937 forbade the setting
up of an independent regime in north China.   But
would the army accept?   A provisional government was
set up in Peking under Wang Ko-min, a banker-politi-
cian who had been trained in Japan.   The army commanders seem to have had the major hand in this, desperate
as they were to build up a regime favourable to Japan
and Manchukuo.   The Konoe Cabinet, though it had been
guarded in its statements and critical of Chiang Kai-
shek, does not seem to have taken the initiative.
But it clearly hoped to use the Peking government
as a lever with the KMT.
     The occupation of Nanking with its accompanying
brutality did nothing to get Japan a settlement with
Chiang.   He was able to retire upriver to Chungking
and take on a new lease of life as a national, anti-
Japanese leader.   In the early part of January 1938,
military and civil leaders debated in Tokyo at
committees, liaison conferences, and even an imperial
conference (15 January).   The anti-expansionists -
inheritors of Ishiwara's mantle in the army - wanted
to leave the way open for negotiation from a position
of strength with Chiang.   The others, Konoe himself,
War Minister Sugiyama and Foreign Minister Hirota, were
indignant at the intransigence of the Chinese and in
any case rejected the bolshevik scare which underlay
so much of army thinking.   On 16 January Konoe
announced that Japan would 'stop dealing with the
Kuomintang government and await the establishment of
a new Chinese administration, with which she would co-
operate wholeheartedly in adjusting Sino-Japanese relations and building a New China'.   This was the famous
'Aite ni sezu' declaration which marked a distinct
deterioration of relations with the Kuomintang and
made the job of peace-making more difficult.   The
statement was no mere slip of the tongue but a closely
debated, compromise formula.   Konoe justified it on
the ground that it cleared his government of the
accusation that it had sat on the fence too long (13)
(Document 33).   It was no coincidence that a new
session of the Diet was due to open in four days' time;
and Konoe thought it desirable to present some announcement in order to catch the mood of the people which was
not too squeamish about expansion in China.   But the
statement was tantamount to the identification of the
civil government with the military view of the China
problem.
     By May Konoe was dissatisfied with the political

failures which had accompanied the military successes
in China.   True, the 'Reformed Government of the
Republic of China' had been set up in Nanking in
March.   Following the Manchukuo pattern, the Japanese
general for the area, General Harada Kumakichi, became
senior adviser and a string of Japanese officers held
the other key posts.   But the arrangement was unlikely
to lead to peace.   Konoe was anxious to backslide
from his 'Aite ni sezu' announcement.   Rightly or
wrongly he blamed Hirota and the Foreign Ministry for
its offensiveness.   In a Cabinet reshuffle he dropped
Hirota and appointed in his place General Ugaki
Kazushige (Issei) with the specific task of changing
policy towards China.   Ugaki set out to make peace
with the Nationalists and made it a condition of his
entry to the Cabinet that the policy of 'no truck with
the Kuomintang' should be reversed.   He embarked upon
indirect negotiations through Hongkong but they broke
down, over Japan's insistence that Chiang Kai-shek
should step down.

Ugaki's case is important in any history of the
Foreign Ministry.   He had been a Cabinet adviser for
some months in advance of his appointment and was well
known to Konoe.   But he had no diplomatic experience
and was virtually the first non-professional foreign
minister in Japan since the turn of the century. (14)
That did not mean that Ugaki was the nominee of the
military or in any sense their candidate.   Quite the
contrary, they had little confidence in him and had
previously excluded him from being war minister (he
was a general in the army reserve) and premier by withholding their support.   His value to Konoe was that
he had great experience of China and was well connected
in Kuomintang quarters.   He had acquired a reputation
as a believer in improving Japan-Kuomintang relations,
which led him to negotiate straight away.   Try as he
might, Ugaki could neither limit the war nor undo the
'aite ni sezu' policy.   Finding it difficult to
achieve his aims by direct means, he tried to obtain
the mediation of foreign Powers, even the unpopular
Britain.   To this end he was prepared to compromise
with Britain over China; but Japanese opinion did not
allow him to gain his objectives. (15)   The East Asia
bureau chief, Ishii Itarō, produced a blueprint for
solving problems with China but this was also discarded.

As a tough-minded and principled man, General Ugaki
found himself unwilling to take lying down the proposal
for a China board (Kō-A-in) which the army was pushing.
Its effect would have been to detach China from the

control of the Foreign Ministry.   This was in his
personal view a nonsense.   He had been appointed by
Konoe with the express mandate to solve the China
incident and now his ministry was about to be
deprived of its right to negotiate with the Chinese.
Ugaki was opposed by the service ministers in a five
ministers' conference and, failing to get his way in
September, he offered his resignation.   With his
departure one phase in the endeavour to limit the
China incident had ended.

After the Japanese armies had occupied Canton and
Hankow in October, Japan made another of her unilateral
attempts to remedy the political situation.   Under
the persuasion of the army the policy of befriending
Wang Ching-wei, the deputy president of KMT, was
pursued.   On 3 November as the first step Konoe published his proposals for a New Order in east Asia
(cf. Document 34).   On 20 November secret arrangements
were made between the army and Wang's associates for
him to co-operate with Japan in a peace move where
Japan would support Wang and co-operate with New China.
Ten days later at an imperial conference they adopted
a policy for adjusting relations with China put up by
the army, which would not discard the KMT provided it
rejected its past policies and restructured itself.
On 16 December the Kō-A-in was founded to consider
Japan's political and economic policies towards China.
It was to be under the wing of the premier and was
thus to by-pass the Foreign Ministry.   Six days later
Konoe announced his basic policy for adjusting relations between Japan and China.   On 30 December Wang,
from the safety of Hanoi where he had gone from Chungking, called on Chiang to negotiate for peace and save
the country from communism.   Wang failed to secure
the expected support in south China and had no option
but to set up government in Japanese occupied areas.
Even there he would be required to recognize the Provisional and Reformed governments to which the Japanese
were bound.   Much of the idealism of Wang over the
new order had been dispersed by its practical
realities. (16)   But, in the words of one of the
Western experts on this subject, 'No matter how affec-
tionately Tokyo paraded its fiancee in public, it
remained privately sceptical about the marriage with
the Wang regime.   For all the vilification Chiang Kai-
shek received in Tokyo, he remained the more alluring
partner.' (17)   Wang was uncomfortable with Japan's
collaboration, while Chiang in Chungking maintained a
dignified unresponsiveness which left Konoe exasperated.

Within two years of the Marco Polo bridge incident
Japan had developed a stranglehold over the economy of
China.   This was exercised through the army, national
policy companies, banking and currency and tariff
arrangements.   The vital coastal and riverine ports
had been occupied and customs revenue had fallen into
Japanese hands.   Having penetrated the Yangtse river
as far as the Ichang rapids, the army called on the
Nationalist government, now in exile at Chungking, to
capitulate.   When it refused, the army was not ready
to extend its lines of communication and had to content
itself with the status quo.   The situation had become
a military embarrassment and a political dilemma.

Konoe, who lacked the resilience of the professional
politician, resigned on 4 January 1939.   His writings
tell us that he was frustrated at his inability to
solve the China conundrum, faced with failures on all
aspects of foreign relations and disgruntled over the
lack of enthusiasm for his New Order (Document 33).
He was content to bow out and steer the succession in
the direction of the rightist, Hiranuma Kiichirō.   As
premier he had to take the blame for the desolate state
of foreign relations. (18)

ENTRACTE IN SEVERAL SHORT MOVEMENTS

Konoe's ministry was followed by three short-lived ones.
The prince's tenure had been taken up with the China
war which had evoked a great deal of public criticism
and led to his resigning in some disarray.   Yet Konoe
was not destroyed and was able to stage a comeback
some eighteen months later.   In the meantime the
ministries were led by Baron Hiranuma, who had been
home minister under Konoe, by General Abe and Admiral
Yonai.   These Cabinets held office during a period of
great uncertainty and exhibited caution and shrewdness
in their international dealings.

We shall place the focus arbitrarily on one aspect
of Japan's foreign policy in this period - her relations
with the axis countries.   These had for five years been
manipulated by a pressure group whose power rested
mainly, but not exclusively, with the army.   Its most
prominent member was General Oshima Hiroshi, military
attaché in Berlin (1934-8) and later ambassador there
(1938-9).   But there was also a civilian ingredient
of some strength in the Foreign Ministry, where the
central figure was Shiratori Toshio, who had acquired
some prominence as head of its information bureau

during the Manchurian crisis for issuing a number of
extreme statements.   With its natural desire to get
rid of troublemakers, the ministry had posted Shiratori as minister to Sweden (1933-6).   When the post
of foreign minister fell vacant after the resignation
of Ugaki, petitions in favour of Shiratori's candida-
ture were received but passed over.   He was instead
posted to Rome as ambassador and became automatically
the collaborator of Oshima in Berlin.   On at least
one occasion they issued statements on their own
authority which the emperor held to be an infringement
of the imperial prerogative.   Both were recalled from
Europe around the outbreak of war there; and Shiratori
again became a candidate for the foreign ministership.
Again his sponsors were out-manoeuvred without being
defeated. (19)

The most significant piece of Japanese diplomacy
after her decision to leave the League of Nations was
the series of steps taken to establish links with the
axis Powers.   Partly Japan after the 1936 revolt had
developed some political affinity with Germany and
Italy through her increasing steps towards authoritarian
solutions.   On an economic plane, too, there were many
resemblances between Japanese capitalism and German
national socialism.   These did not make the partnership inevitable but it did give those who were dissatisfied with democratic institutions an alternative
which they could exploit.

The first step towards an axis alliance was the
anti-comintern pact signed on 25 November 1936.   Oshima,
who was thought to have known Hitler from his early
Munich days and was appointed military attaché in
Berlin in March 1934, took with him a mandate from the
army general staff to hold discussions to cover the
eventuality of a war with the Soviet Union.   It was
he who opened up talks with Ribbentrop in 1935.   The
themes were a closely guarded secret until the coming
of the Hirota Cabinet when talks were transferred to
the two foreign ministries.   In any case the premier
and Foreign Minister Arita were understood to favour
such a solution and steered it through the five minister
conferences in August (Document 32.I.3).   Finally
Ambassador Mushakōji returned from leave in Tokyo and
was required to sign the instrument in the negotiation
of which he had played a negligible part.   There were
a number of instruments exchanged at the time of the
treaty which are not without significance.   While the
pact was anodyne and was communicated to the Russians
two days before its publication, the secret note whose

existence was strongly denied by Germany and Japan, was more forthright.   It stated that 'should one of the parties be unprovokedly attacked or threatened by the Soviet Union, the other party agrees not to carry out any measures which would relieve the position of the Soviet Union but will immediately consult on measures to preserve their common interests.'

There was, of course, an important Chinese context in Japanese thinking on the anti-comintern pact.   Not only did she want to prevent the spread of the communist international's activities in Manchuria and Korea but also in China.   After the Sian incident a common front seemed to have been established.   On 21 August 1937 Nanking entered into a pact of non-aggression with the Soviet Union.   Before this Japan had hoped to find common ground with the anti-communist factions of the Kuomintang.   When this failed, Japan sought partners where she could.   Shortly after the Marco Polo bridge incident, Japan, which had earlier opposed doing so, agreed to Italy's accession to the anti-comintern pact.   This took place on 6 November and later that month Italy as a token of good faith recognized Manchukuo.

Those who opposed the anti-comintern pact had many grounds for objection.   Many Japanese diplomats - including most of the ambassadors like Yoshida in London, Satō Naotake in Paris, and Shigemitsu in Moscow - were not slow to register their opposition. It was not professionally negotiated.   Apart from being vague and out of line with Japan's treaties in the past, the anti-comintern pact seemed to be patently one-sided.   As Sugimura Yōtarō, ambassador in Italy, told the Germans in 1937, they stood to gain because they would, regardless of the pact, continue many of their friendly arrangements with the Soviet Union, such as the treaty of Rapallo had envisaged.   The agreement was reluctantly accepted by the Foreign Ministry with considerable mental reservations.   In the view of many diplomats - and Satō in particular because he became foreign minister and was especially quizzed on this point - the German-Japanese pact was dead soon after it was signed.   Perhaps this comes close to being the view of the mainstream of Kasumigaseki opinion, though there was an element of wishful thinking in it.

Shortly after the China campaign seemed to get immersed in a quagmire in spring 1938, there was talk of strengthening the pact with the axis Powers.   On the Japanese side the decision was taken at the five-ministers conference on 26 August 1938.   It was

supported by Foreign Minister Arita (he had a second
term between 1938 and September 1939) who eventually
sent a special emissary from the Foreign Ministry, Itō
Nobufumi, to Europe in order to explain the amendments
which Japan required.   The ambassadors in Berlin and
Rome, Oshima and Shiratori, with the support of War
Minister Itagaki did not favour these or think them
likely of acceptance by Germany.   During the negotiations the issue turned on whether Britain and France
should be specified in the revised pact as possible
enemies [taizō].   While the Japanese were prepared
to recognize in principle that Britain and France
should be included among the 'taizō', they did not
want such phrases actually included in the terms; and
Germany would not accept this.   It will be clear that
such an extension of the pact would be more valuable
to Germany than to Japan.   It would be no longer anti-
comintern in conception but concerned with Germany's
European enemies.

There were those in Japan who were anti-British and
French.   These blamed Britain on the whole for the
failure of the China campaign and for bolstering up
Chiang's resistance.   But the Navy Ministry rejected
an all-out alliance with Germany and Italy because of
the great obligations it would impose on Japan in
Europe and because of its fear of an Anglo-American
coalition.   Many held that this last was unlikely to
come about because isolationist feeling was so strong
in the United States.   This disagreement developed
into an army-navy wrangle and at innumerable meetings
of the five-minister conference in the spring of 1939
the matter was discussed.   The more moderate element
in the navy staved off the required concessions to
Germany, though many on the naval general staff were
now turning in favour of a southern thrust and were
thus becoming more responsive to Germany's approaches.

The Japanese told Germany that they must have a
specific understanding that they need only fight
against the Soviet Union as they had no wish for
commitments with other European Powers.   Hiranuma
told Arita that 'he was opposed to strengthening the
anti-comintern pact to the extent of waging war against
Britain and France' and threatened to resign if the
army insisted on such a course.   While Japan modified
her position in March, she refused to accept the obligation of military action unconditionally.   When Japan
held out for freedom of action, Ribbentrop became
thoroughly frustrated with the delays and decided to
proceed with Italy alone.   On 22 May 1939, therefore,

Italy and Germany signed 'the pact of steel', though
it was intended that Japan should be invited to join
at a later stage.   The Hiranuma Cabinet, and especially
the navy which was dependent on American goodwill and
supplies, never said 'no'; but the question does not
seem to have been raised again from Berlin or Tokyo
for the time being.   Japan refused to commit herself
to the axis over Europe and still considered herself as
a suitable party to offer mediation, either by herself
or with the United States, in order to prevent the
outbreak of war in Europe.

Shortly before war did break out, the scheme for a
tripartite alliance, including Japan, was effectively
blocked by the German-Soviet non-aggression pact of 23
August 1939.   Although Japan's consent was required
by the terms of the anti-comintern pact, Germany only
notified Japan of the forthcoming event two days in
advance of signing and without asking for approval.
This conduct she excused with the argument that Germany
had only resorted to a Soviet treaty because of Japan's
earlier dilatoriness in coming to a decision over her
relations with the axis.   While this was a plausible
view, it was probably not the prime motive for Germany's
action.

It is not possible to exaggerate the ill effects of
the Nazi-Soviet pact on Japan.   It created immense
anti-German resentment among Japanese at the blatant
violation of their anti-comintern pact.   It destroyed
for a while the image of Germany who, it was felt, had
humiliated Japan by accepting her overtures while con-
templating something different.   It brought down the
Hiranuma ministry and replaced it by one of a different
stamp: the new ministry under Premier Abe with Admiral
Nomura as foreign minister was, by and large, pro-
Western and anti-German.   Finally it again set back
the proposals for a tri-partite pact after a great
deal of wasted negotiation.   This was a double tragedy
from Japan's point of view because, after the start of
the European war in September, she might have benefited from Germany's reassurance in putting the screws
on Britain in China.   As it was, the whole episode
only confirmed the scepticism of those Japanese diplomats - probably in a majority - who had opposed the
anti-comintern pact and now regretted the consequences
which sprang from it.

The German debacle was particularly ill-timed
because of Japan's clashes with the Russian forces in
north-east Asia.   For some years these clashes had
been happening with a certain regularity: in 1937 on

the Amur river; in 1938 at Changkufeng, some seventy
miles south of Vladivostok.   In May-June 1939 the
most serious of these clashes took place at Nomonhan
between Mongolia and Manchukuo.   The Soviet forces
under the (then) little-known General Zhukov quickly
gained the upper hand by the skilled use of tanks and
aircraft; and the Japanese commander sued for peace.
For the first time in a decade, perhaps even in forty
years, Japan had suffered a major defeat and sustained
heavy casualties.   On this occasion it was the crack
Kwantung army which had been humbled.   In September
a ceasefire was reached.   Thereafter these frontier
incidents, which were always savage affairs, were
noticeably reduced.   Some attempt was made to impose
stricter discipline on the Kwantung army. (20)   Needless to say, this campaign generated in the army and
among the people at large - even though much was concealed from them - intense anti-soviet feeling.   The
fact that the Soviet Union was to enter into a pact
with Germany added fuel to the flames.   Japan declared
her neutrality towards the European war.   It was an
inescapable act because of the diplomatic reverses
which she had just suffered.

The disparity of objectives between the army and
the navy was particularly obvious in 1939.   The army,
prompted by the perennial frontier incidents, had its
sights set on the north.   It is estimated that it kept
about twenty divisions in Manchukuo facing the soviet
frontier with another twenty divisions in north China.
By contrast the navy was gradually becoming committed,
at the instance of its general staff, to a southward
strategy.   If the navy were to pursue its notion of
advancing south, it needed to pursue bases in the south
China seas.   It was instrumental in pushing the China
campaigns to south China and was already drawing up
plans for the occupation of Hainan.

An essential point of difference between them was
over the recurring proposals for a stronger axis military alliance.   The army had through Oshima sponsored
this idea from the start.   The navy had traditionally
opposed it.   By 1940 some support for it was growing
among the naval general staff.   But it was opposed by
older, more liberal officers like Admirals Yonai and
Yamamoto Isoroku who were afraid of the reaction of
the Western Powers and the adverse effect this would
have on the Japanese navy.   As navy minister and later
as prime minister, Yonai countered all talk of a German-
Italian-Japanese military alliance, which would be
aimed jointly at Britain and the Soviet Union, with the

argument that it would only persuade the United States
to throw in her lot with Britain, something which the
Japanese were trying to avoid.   This was not because
of any special sentiment towards Britain but because
of fear of the United States and the navy's dependence
on supplies from that quarter.

The Abe Cabinet encountered unexpected opposition
from the Foreign Ministry.   It set about establishing
a Ministry of Trade (Bōeki-shō) who would take over
the bulk of the duties of the Commercial section of
the Foreign Ministry.   This demand originated in the
army and also in sections of the bureaucracy which
were hostile to the Foreign Ministry bureaucracy.
The officials rallied round and over one hundred
offered their resignations to Foreign Minister Nomura
on the ground that commercial relations were an essential part of foreign relations - a central tenet of
Shidehara's thinking and of Kasumigaseki orthodoxy.
Confronted by this bureaucratic mutiny of the Foreign
Ministry, the Cabinet had no alternative but to withdraw its proposals.   Yet the lack of dexterity in
pushing through this disruptive proposal was one factor
in bringing about the unpopularity of the Abe Cabinet
and its premature downfall after only a little over
four months. (21)

This is a symbolic story.   It shows that the
Foreign Ministry still had a residual strength and
esprit de corps in 1939 despite the humiliations it
had suffered in the previous decade.   It was conscious
of its rights and was aware of the need to defend them
stoutly, as it did over the Kō-A-in proposals.   Moreover the divisions within the ministry on which we
have dwelt did not affect the solidarity of the
opposition which it offered to any proposals which
were intended to break its traditional position in
Japan's policy-making.   There were internal forces
which were trying to rock the boat of Japanese foreign
policy in 1939-40, yet even they did not want to see
the Bōeki-shō set up independently.

In January 1940 General Abe was succeeded by Admiral
Yonai with Arita as foreign minister.   The new voices
were remarkably subdued, considering the strength of
Japan's position.   After many months of talks the
dispute over Britain's concession at Tientsin was
resolved.   The catalogue of Germany's victories
lengthened - Poland, Denmark, Belgium, Norway, Holland,
Luxemburg and, after the disaster of Dunkirk, the
surrender of France on 22 June.   Not unnaturally this
last led the Japanese to thoughts of pressure on French

Indochina.   But the army was dissatisfied with the
puny efforts of the Cabinet over possible southern
expansion and became increasingly assertive towards
Foreign Minister Arita and his officials.   Partly
because of the weakness of this moderate ministry,
Britain contemplated offering concessions on the
Yonai ministry's two basic demands that she close
Hongkong and the Burma road in order to cut off
supplies travelling to Chungking.   Nothing was done
over Hongkong but Britain agreed on 15 July to the
temporary closure of the Burma road for three months.
It was a feather in the cap of the ministry.   Yet
within a week Prince Konoe took over again as
premier.

   We shall defer to the next chapter the consideration of Konoe's new ministry and confine ourselves
here to Konoe's first three years in high politics.
After his resignation he had become president of the
privy council and in his leisure had spent much time
busying himself over the New Order.   Since the spring
of 1940 he had been preparing the way for the Imperial
Rule Assistance association (Taisei Yokusankai) as a
means of overcoming party differences and uniting the
nation.   In spite of eloquent claims, this was to
prove a failure in practice.   But it confirmed the
tendencies of Konoe's first period: Japan was a
nation mobilized for war and prone to expansion in
association with the fascist countries of Europe.
The anti-comintern pact was perhaps only a symbol.
But the fact remains that Japan was slowly moving to a
closer association with Germany and Italy.

Chapter 12

The Matsuoka Period, 1940-1

After his return to power in July 1940, Konoe was a changed man. He had lent his name to the founding of the Imperial Rule Preservation Association (Taisei Yokusankai) which was ultimately set up in October. This was intended to ensure that political parties would all be merged into one with a view to the eventual creation of a unified national structure. Loyal to the imperial institution, Konoe managed to work with the army; but how far this was to check the extremists within the army is still a matter of debate among Japanese scholars. The Elder Statesman, Saionji, ailing and shortly to depart from the distressing scene, looked on Konoe with sympathetic distaste, saying: he is skilful at formulating doctrines but less so with actual policies; it would be better if he were more decisive. (1)

It was perhaps no coincidence that the flexible Konoe should in this personal dilemma resort to the appointment of Matsuoka Yōsuke (1880-1946) as foreign minister. (2) The two had known each other since 1919 at Paris where, as younger members of the delegation, they had found themselves distrustful of Anglo-American imperialism. Matsuoka had then left the diplomatic service where he had served from 1904 until 1921. He then joined the south Manchurian railway, rising to vice-president (1927-9). (3) Becoming a politician, he came to the fore in 1932-3 as Japan's chief representative at the League of Nations at the tail-end of the Manchurian crisis. Coming back as something of a national hero, he resigned his Diet seat and identified himself with the political party liquidation movement, the moves towards the axis and greater involvement in China. He thereafter became president of the south Manchurian railway (1935-9). By 1940 he

was a man of known reputation.   When it was mooted
abroad that Premier Konoe was thinking of appointing
him as foreign minister, his chauvinism told against
him; and the proposal was opposed by Kido as Lord
Privy Seal and Konoe's entourage.   Even the
emperor urged the premier to have second thoughts.
But Konoe was stubborn.   He evidently liked Matsuoka
as a man and admired his directness, impulsiveness
and unwillingness to sit on the fence.   Underlying
all this may have been Konoe's hope that Matsuoka's
friends in the army would help him control the
activities of the military.   Matsuoka, possessing
'the Manchurian mind', might help in ending the
China war. (4)

Konoe reaped the whirlwind.   Matsuoka proved to
be of unstable personality and made many irrational
judgments in the foreign field.   Although he was
probably more dynamic and strong-willed than any of
his predecessors for twenty-five years, he was self-
centred and determined to become the dominant figure
in the Cabinet.   He was therefore unwilling to brook
interference by his colleagues.   Though Konoe may
have had a sneaking regard for Matsuoka's self-
confident judgments, he came to be embarrassed by his
foreign minister's other qualities.   It was no longer
a question of using him to stop the impulsive military
but of stopping the impulsive Matsuoka himself. (5)

Even before the formation of his Cabinet on 22
July, Konoe had private discussions with his major
ministers about the nature of the policies required
to meet the national emergency.   The Outline of a
Basic National Policy which was drawn up was announced
as an historic turning-point.   It dwelt on the need
to escape from Japan's dependence on foreign countries
and devoted more attention than in previous policy
statements to the southern problem.   The new phrase,
the Great East Asia Co-prosperity Sphere, was now
coined by Matsuoka and used to include French Indochina and the Dutch Indies where Japan would have to
avoid alienating Washington.   Japan was clearly set
on controlling south-east Asia in a way which might
not appeal to the Germans.   But Matsuoka belonged to
those who favoured a German alliance and now was his
opportunity.

TRIPARTITE PACT

Konoe laid down a new basic policy which dwelt much on solving the southern problem while at the same time maintaining closer relations with Germany.   On 22 September after much procrastination by Vichy and Saigon, a military convention was signed for Indochina between the local Japanese and French generals.   This did not prevent Japanese forces sending an expedition from south China into northern Indochina three days later which defeated the French armies before it was withdrawn on orders from Tokyo.   These manoeuvres were not unrelated to Germany, who, the Japanese suspected, might have ambitions in Indochina because of her strong position in Vichy and might in that event menace Japan's ascendancy there.   Quite apart from other reasons for re-opening the negotiations with Germany broken off in 1939, it was desirable from the point of view of southern strategy that some understanding be reached.   Matsuoka had discussions with the German ambassador in Tokyo, Eugen Ott, whom Ribbentrop did not completely trust, and Germany announced on 23 August that she proposed to send Heinrich Stahmer to Tokyo in order to negotiate a new treaty and establish Japan's true intentions.   At a four-minister meeting on 6 September, it was agreed to embark on talks for the strengthening of ties with Germany and Italy.

Even then the traditional hostility of the navy to Germany was only overcome with reservations.   The navy minister, Admiral Yoshida Zengō, resigned with heart trouble, exacerbated, it was thought, by the pro-German element among younger officers in the navy who could no longer be held in check.   His successor, Admiral Oikawa, finally told the liaison conference on 14 September that the navy withdrew its objections to an axis alliance, provided that Japan retained the right to determine the circumstances in which she would have to offer military assistance to her allies. The navy was clearly moving closer to the army though it was still anxious to reverse the prior claim to funds which the army had enjoyed since the China war broke out. (6)

It was perhaps not unreasonable for the navy ultimately to come round to support for the German entanglement.   Germany seemed to be clearly winning and to be likely to stage an invasion of Britain in the autumn.   The battle of Britain had not yet forced Hitler to re-consider his priorities.   It made

good sense therefore for Japan to clinch negotiations.
In Berlin on 27 September, Germany, Italy and Japan
signed the tripartite alliance.   It was technically
not a full military alliance though it did pledge the
parties to 'assist one another with all political,
economic and military means if one of the three contracting Powers is attacked by a Power at present not
involved in the current struggles'.   This offered
redress in practice only in the eventuality of an
attack on any of the three by the United States or
the Soviet Union.   It therefore showed Germany's
lack of confidence in the effectiveness of her non-
aggression pact and caused Russia to protest vehemently
to Germany.

Since the negotiations were carried on largely by
Matsuoka on the Japanese side, the treaty bore his
authentic stamp and seemed to serve his own purposes.
It achieved a certain consistency with the nationalist wave which was sweeping Japan at the time with
the 'new political structure' and the Imperial Rule
Assistance Association due to be founded in October.
Externally it accorded well with the New Order and the
Great East Asia Co-prosperity Sphere.   At a diplomatic
level Japan's purposes seem to have been two: to
encourage co-operation with the Soviet Union and to
keep the United States out of the war.   In these
objectives there was substantial accord with Germany,
especially in so far as persuading the Americans to
keep out of the European war was concerned.   In the
short term, these objects were unsuccessful: the
United States was already taking a larger share in
Asian affairs and it was not impossible that further
Japanese expansion would result in American intervention; and the Soviet Union was far from wanting to
cement relations with Japan through the good offices
of Germany, though her view was later to be modified.
In a way when the popular image of the tripartite
alliance differed from the motives of the signatories.

There were many doubts and dismays in Japan.
Konoe himself was later to write in his memoirs that,
just as Admiral Saitō had been a party to leaving the
League in 1933 against his better judgment, so he had
been a party to the tripartite pact as a result of
force majeure.   But there was no evidence that the
decision was in any sense a rushed one (Document 33).
It has to be borne in mind that the final achievement
of a triple alliance came at the end of a period of
agonized reappraisal over long years.   Those who had
opposed all along were still in doubt.   All the more

so as it had been concluded by the new government in
extreme terms. The emperor was full of anxieties
over its effects on the United States. So too was
Saionji. Within the Foreign Ministry, it led to the
recall of the ambassador in Rome, Amau Eiji, who told
the Italians that it was too far-reaching to be in
Japan's national interest. It led also to some
switches within the diplomatic establishment by which
members of the renovationist group benefited. Most
significantly Oshima who had with Shiratori been very
busy in Japan doing propaganda for the new alliance,
was reluctantly persuaded to go back to Berlin. He
finally replaced Kurusu in February 1941. (7) Another
anti-Kasumigaseki figure had been posted as ambassador. Clearly Matsuoka was giving precedence to
officials of his own stamp.

It was all part of what Matsuoka was to speak of
later to Stalin as his 'revolutionary tactics' in
foreign affairs. What he did not say to Stalin - but
Stalin must surely have known - was that it replaced
the professional diplomats by those who were prepared
to accept his German strategy as the bedrock of the
country's foreign policy.

The tripartite pact did not help Japan to deal with
China and to ensure supplies of raw materials there.
It is arguable that Matsuoka was appointed because of
his knowledge and experience of the China scene. Yet
it was here that he made insignificant progress:
Japanese armies were still bogged down in China;
Japan, which had occupied much of coastal and riverine
China, was still trying to plug systematically all
access routes for supplies to the nationalist capital
of Chungking. The Burma road had been closed, even
if temporarily. Yet this did not destroy the will of
Chungking whose self-image grew with the years.
Japan's propaganda might claim that Chungking was
only a poor provincial regime in command of its
neighbouring areas but in receipt of massive foreign
support. But resistance gave Chiang Kai-shek a
popular following and increased his will to impede the
Japanese who were in any case not in full control of
the areas they occupied. There was much to make the
Japanese convinced that they had failed militarily and
politically.

While he cemented the arrangements with Wang Ching-
wei by signing a defence treaty with his new government
in Nanking in November, Matsuoka still treated the
Chungking government with respect. He seems to have
realized that a long-term settlement could be achieved

only through parleys with Chiang himself.   The
corollary of this was that a reconciliation with Wang
could never establish an equilibrium.   He hardly
offered Wang the concessions that he might have
offered Chungking.   Wang was often used as a lever
for overtures to Chiang.   This only increased the
inclination of Washington and London to identify
themselves with Chungking.   Matsuoka set out to
close the access routes: first Canton, then the
Hanoi route, then the Thai route.   There was, in
short, a Chinese backdrop for all the more spectacular
aspects of Matsuoka's world diplomacy.   Yet he, as a
'China expert', had no greater success there than his
predecessors.

JAPANESE-SOVIET RELATIONS

The Nomonhan crisis had a shattering psychological
effect on the army which had hitherto been the spear-
head of the anti-soviet front in Japan.   The leaders
wanted above all a settlement with the Soviet Union
rather than an outright victory over it.   To this
end, they tried to use their friend, Germany, whose
links with the Soviets they probably over-estimated.
Germany, of course, had her own self-interest to serve
in bringing the two together, namely that it would
free Japan from the huge expense of maintaining troops
on the Soviet-Mongolian frontier and enable her to
strike south.   To this end, an agreement had been
reached on 9 June 1940 between Manchukuo and Mongolia
which defined the frontier and, of course, implicated
the Japanese.
    In July Ambassador Tōgō had presented Moscow with a
proposal for a neutrality pact and met with a favourable response.   This was swiftly followed by his
recall and replacement by one of Matsuoka's 'revolutionary postings', that of General Tatekawa Yoshitsugu,
a leader of the military party since the time of the
Manchurian incident.   While his reputation was well-
known in Moscow and might have made him ill-qualified
for his new task, Tatekawa was really only the manifestation of the new army policy.   He soon revealed
that Japan had misjudged the strength of Soviet
forces before Nomonhan and that he himself was an
enthusiast for detente.   Matsuoka too reminded the
Soviet ambassador of his longstanding desire for
Soviet-Japanese rapprochement, going back to his early
days in the foreign service.   In Matsuoka's view,

the tripartite pact strengthened the moral obligation
on Germany's part to foster an understanding between
Tokyo and Moscow.   On the whole, Ott, Stahmer and
Ribbentrop seem to have left the Japanese with a false
impression that they supported the overture.

On 30 October Tatekawa, reversing the thrust of
Tōgō's overture, presented the Soviet leaders with the
draft of a non-aggression pact.   This was considerably
stronger than the earlier draft and was received with
great suspicion.   Japan also asked for outstanding
matters (fisheries, Sakhalin, Japanese oil and coal
concessions) to be taken up after the basic treaty was
agreed.   Suspicious ever, Foreign Commissar Molotov,
who felt that he was in a strong bargaining position,
asked that the miscellaneous issues should be resolved
beforehand and duly insisted that a neutrality pact
was the most that was acceptable to Russia for the
present.

At a critical meeting of the liaison conference on
3 February 1941, Matsuoka set out his plans for negotiations with Germany, Italy and Soviet Russia.   The
meeting fully approved the commencement of negotiations
with Moscow with a view to 'adjusting' Japanese-Soviet
relations and authorized Matsuoka to go on his European
trip.   Arriving in Moscow on 23 March, he met Molotov
and Stalin and discussed his 'revolutionary new diplomatic offensive'.   He left with Molotov a statement
(in English) of Japan's case.   Matsuoka proceeded to
Berlin (26-29 March), Rome (1 April) and Berlin again
(4 April).   There seems to be little doubt that
Foreign Minister Ribbentrop (as well as urging Japan
to attack Singapore) mentioned the massing of German
troops on the east Prussian border; and that Matsuoka
mentioned Japan's desire for an understanding with
the Soviet Union.   The Germans discounted the latter
as self-confidently as Matsuoka discounted the implications of the former.   To be sure, he was genuinely
worried and puzzled. (9)   There was a lack of candour
on both sides but it was basically a case of misjudg-
ment by those who had an exaggerated confidence in
their own perceptiveness.   Back in Moscow on 7 April,
Matsuoka had the first of several encounters with
Molotov where his proposal for a non-aggression pact
was again turned down.   On 12 April he finally saw
Stalin who sympathetically discussed with him the
neutrality pact which Russia had all along sought and
obtained Matsuoka's agreement in principle.   It was
signed the following day.

The neutrality pact laid down that, if one of the

parties were to be attacked by one or more Powers, the other would observe neutrality.   It would run for five years;   and the problem of the Sakhalin concessions which had bedeviled the earlier talks were, according to a Japanese undertaking, to be resolved separately within a few months.   How much did the pact mean to Russia?   Stalin did not yet awhile remove his forces from eastern Siberia, thereby suggesting that he was still suspicious of Japan seizing the opportunity of staging an invasion.   It was only when he had clear proof that Japanese units in Manchuria were being withdrawn that he too did so.   Yet it did remove some of the tensions felt after Matsuoka's visit to Berlin. What did it mean to Japan?   Here too there were sus- picions: did not the Soviet Union enter into a mutual assistance pact with Mongolia?   But it did not dis- please those who saw the only outcome as negotiations with the United States for it seemed to enhance Japan's bargaining position.   It was not immediately apparent that it would impose restrictions on Japanese action when Germany later launched her offensive.   For the present it could be hailed publicly as a triumph of Matsuoka's diplomatic skill.

There is much controversy associated with this pact. There are those like Kutakov who say that Matsuoka merely bought time until the outbreak of war between Germany and USSR could provide the opportunity for a Japanese attack on the latter. (10)   There is a double accusation here: against his judgment and his duplic- ity.   But most of the evidence now suggests that Matsuoka did not believe that war would break out between Germany and USSR.   This is averred by Nishi Haruhiko who was his minister in Moscow.   And Matsuoka told the liaison conference on 25 June with the dis- arming frankness which he displayed on occasion that:

> I concluded a Neutrality Pact because I thought
> that Germany and Soviet Russia would not go to war.
> If I had known that they would go to war, I would
> have preferred to take a more friendly position
> towards Germany, and I would not have concluded the
> Neutrality Pact. (11)

Thus, Matsuoka acted as though he valued the triple alliance more than the Soviet pact;   and it seems that Moscow viewed it that way too.

If we accept that statement as evidence, Matsuoka's direct agreement with Stalin was an arrangement between two parties who did not foresee what ultimately took place.   Matsuoka had not been specifically told of this possibility while he was in Berlin because of the

German mistrust of him; Stalin would not accept the
intelligence that a summer offensive was likely when
Britain passed it on to him.   Nor did the results
of the Soviet-Japanese pact prove to be world-
shattering.   Stalin may at a Kremlin reception have
offered rather a tipsy toast to Japan and her advance
to the south; he may have hugged Matsuoka at the
Trans-Siberian rail terminal; but he had little
trust in him.   Stalin held his armies in Siberia,
even after the German attack on the theory that Japan
would attack Russia despite the existence of the
neutrality pact.   In the Russian view, their pact
would be treated as subordinate to the triple alliance.
It appears to have been only when the spy Sorge
informed his masters in October that Japanese armies
were looking to the south that Stalin moved these
crack divisions towards his own desperate battle-lines.
For his part, Matsuoka was opportunistic enough to
advocate to his colleagues when Germany did attack
Russia on 22 June 1941 that Japan should take the
opportunity to attack the Soviet Union in the rear -
a course which the Konoe Cabinet did not adopt for
fear of American reactions. (12)

There is something pathetic about these wartime
diplomatic instruments which seem to have conferred
little benefit and were little more than symbols of
temporary cordiality.   In the last resort, the
national interests of the Powers concerned ultimately
asserted themselves and affirmed they had little in
common.

THE AMERICAN DILEMMA

On 21 April Matsuoka returned from Moscow to find
that talks with the United States had already advanced
to a critical point.   Admiral Nomura, the former
foreign minister, whom he had appointed to Washington
as part of his purge of professionals in November had
made substantial efforts towards some sort of understanding.   He had earlier spent three years as naval
attaché in the US and had known F.D. Roosevelt in his
Navy department days (1913-20).   Matsuoka found that
there was unalloyed optimism about the prospects of
the Nomura talks, which he did not share.   He was,
moreover, under great pressure from the Germans who
had had their worst suspicions confirmed by the Moscow
parleys that they must be consulted before any talks
took place with the Americans.   While he was not

opposed to talks, Matsuoka professed to be in need of
a pause for reflection.   From this point must be
dated the progressive alienation of Matsuoka from his
colleagues.   Moreover, on another tack, he was
clearly identified by Secretary of State Cordell Hull
as the major impediment to constructive negotiations
in a note of 21 June.

The watershed was the decision reached at the
imperial conference on 2 July that Japan should proceed
with the invasion of Indochina even if it meant going
to war with Britain and the United States.   At the
preceding liaison conferences, the service chiefs had
been advocating the acceleration of the southern
policy while Matsuoka had been urging against the
occupation of bases in southern Indochina and in
favour of action on the northern front.   Following
the German attack on Soviet frontiers on 22 June,
Matsuoka argued in favour of agreeing to attack the
Russian Far East as the Germans were asking.   But
Konoe took sides with the military chiefs against the
foreign minister and favoured ignoring the north and
concentrating on the south.   Thereafter Matsuoka
interposed objections to many of the drafts intended
for Washington and behaved in an insubordinate way.
He was evidently offended by Hull's personal criticisms
of him and went so far as to propose that negotiations
be broken off, which was clearly a minority view.
Matsuoka was boasting that Japan could bargain with
the Americans from a position of strength.   Contrary
to his predictions, however, his tough-minded diplomacy
only ruffled American feelings.   Matsuoka thought
nothing of revealing the nature of the American
exchanges to German representatives and even sent
instructions overruling his colleagues in an objectionable way.   He openly attacked Konoe in a public
speech at Hibiya.   There may have been in Matsuoka's
mind the thought that he might succeed Konoe as prime
minister, an ambition which he had long cherished and
in which he would not have been without support. (13)

Although Konoe was impatient for progress with the
American negotiations, he hesitated to get rid of his
foreign minister.   Consulted about Konoe's dilemma,
the emperor is understood to have suggested the
natural course of dismissing the troublemaker.
Eventually on 10 July Konoe met privately with the
army, navy and home ministers who all supported the
need for further negotiations with Washington; they
took the view that, because of Matsuoka's influential
backing, it would be better for the whole Cabinet to

resign.   This would avoid any recriminations that the
Japanese Cabinet was merely in Washington's pocket.
The Cabinet duly resigned.   Konoe then received an
imperial summons to form a new ministry and did so
with Admiral Toyoda in place of Matsuoka on 18 July. (14)

After his enforced retirement Matsuoka cut a tragic
figure.   Shigemitsu who met him on return from London
late in July heard him say that Japan would face
trouble both north and south and that she could not
come to her senses without first falling to the depths
of hell. (15)   Although there are those who would
apologize for Matsuoka on the grounds that he was
desperately striving for peace, he was too much the
apostle of brinkmanship for this to be wholly convincing.

The Japanese elite was divided in its attitude to
foreign powers.   There were two main streams flowing
simultaneously: the American and the Axis.   Admiral
Toyoda publicly announced that he would continue with
the policies of his predecessor, though this was
probably untrue and, in any case, a tactical mistake.
On 21 July America announced the freezing of Japanese
funds, the last of a number of swingeing economic
measures.   While the Nomura talks were broken off by
the Americans, the new Tokyo government was enthusiastic that they should be reopened.   From early August
formula after formula was presented.   Konoe proposed
a summit meeting with Roosevelt.   Hull and Roosevelt
were sceptical and unresponsive about Konoe's capacity
to carry through any negotiated terms.   Konoe said
that he would be accompanied by representative military and naval leaders.   But the offer was eventually
declined.   It is hard to see that Konoe carried
enough weight to push through the sort of settlement
to which Washington was likely to agree.   In the
critical first half of October, with all other members
of Cabinet vacillating, the war minister, General
Tōjō, took the view that the United States was unyielding while Japan was making concession after
concession; with no diplomatic outlet, Japan had
better prepare for war since her supply position was
daily deteriorating.

Prince Konoe resigned on 16 October and the succession was passed reluctantly to War Minister Tōjō.
Pragmatic and realistic, Tōjō was a representative of
the hard-line group within the Cabinet.   From this
point the Washington negotiations, though not devoid
of good faith, had to be viewed against a cascade of
war preparations.   The mainstream of diplomacy flowed
towards Germany which had since Matsuoka's departure
been deprived of inside information from Kasumigaseki.

TŌJŌ AND THE SUPREME GAMBLE

The tougher Tōjō Cabinet was far from convinced that
Russian resistance had been broken or that it would
be worth Japan's while to stage an attack on the
Soviet Far East as Germany was urging.   On the other
hand, the Japanese needed German co-operation.   They
wanted to establish whether, if they took the initiative in attacking the United States, Germany would
declare war on that country since it was only provided
in the tripartite pact that Germany would come to
their assistance if they were themselves attacked.
Since they proposed to go to war if their two formulae
were not accepted by the White House by 25 November,
it was a matter of urgency to obtain German assurances.
On 21 November Ribbentrop gave an assurance that
Germany would come in - a great relief to Japan.
Four days later Japan joined Germany and Italy in
signing in Berlin a memorandum extending the anti-
comintern pact of 1936 by another five years.   This
was celebrated with jubilation at a mass rally at which
General Tōjō made an intemperate, bellicose speech.
How this action was deemed to be consistent with
Matsuoka's earlier Soviet-Japanese neutrality pact is
hard to imagine.   On 30 November Foreign Minister
Tōgō cabled ambassadors in Berlin and Rome with drafts
of a 'no separate peace' agreement.   Considering how
urgent the assignment was, it ran into two obstacles:
first, General Oshima in Berlin was on a visit to
Vienna for a music festival;   and Hitler, without
whose sanction this could not have been approved, was
on a visit to the collapsing eastern front and could
not be contacted.   For her part, Italy was very much
divided but agreed to Japan's proposals.   On 3
December Ribbentrop told Oshima that Germany too
accepted the draft treaty.   Japan responded with
assurances of confidence in the German offensive
against Moscow.   She could well be extravagant in
her praise when she had cast-iron guarantees of support
in advance of her military action.   First, at 2 a.m.
on 8 December (Tokyo time), Japanese armies landed at
Khota Bahru in Malaya;   at 3.20 a.m. the attack on
Pearl Harbor took place.   On 11 December Germany and
Italy, under Japanese prompting, declared war on the
United States and entered into fresh undertakings
about conducting the war in common and not entering
into a separate peace.   The Germans, for their part,
were anxious to show complete axis solidarity in their
desire to build a new world order all the more so as

allied troops were withdrawn from the north African
desert to supply the Malayan sector.   In order to
regain their aplomb after their catastrophic reverses
in Russia, they needed a propaganda weapon.   It
appears that they were especially anxious to prevent
Mussolini stealing the limelight.   Needless to say,
the Japanese foreign minister, who wanted assurances
rather than demonstrations of unity, disliked the
rhetorical extravagances of this period.

The tripartite alliance was assuming a changed form.
Japan pressed hard for a new military agreement.
Eventually, on 18 January 1942, the representatives
on the tripartite military commission, which had been
set up in Berlin, signed an agreement defining their
spheres of operation.   The Japanese sphere was to be
the waters eastward from about 70° east longitude to
the west coast of the American continent, covering the
continent and islands.   It was further laid down
that, if the American and British navies were to
devote their main efforts to the Atlantic theatre of
operations - as, of course, they did - Japan would
send her navy there while Germany and Italy would send
equivalent assistance if enemy naval concentration
were primarily in the Pacific. (16)   These terms were
to be studiously ignored.   It was easy to draw up
documents dividing the world between them.   But it
was more difficult to extract more than the most
limited co-operation.   Germany and Japan fought
separate wars and generally preferred it that way. (17)

Such was the positive side of Japan's diplomacy in
the second half of 1941.   Less familiar, and arguably
less important, than the American-Japanese negotiations
which led ultimately to the blind, unthinking plunge
of Pearl Harbor.   Yet, despite its positiveness, the
relationship with Germany was never popular.   In
personal terms Ambassador Ott, the reluctant Nazi
accomplice, was withdrawn from Japan as a result of
the Sorge trial; (18)   and his successor, Stahmer,
who should have reaped a harvest of goodwill for his
exploits over the tripartite pact was not really
treated with the warmth of an ally.   Japan fought shy
of German economic assistance and little resulted.
Oddly, considering the long-standing co-operation which
had existed between the armies on both sides and their
mutual respect, there was little co-ordination of
effort.   Japan and Germany fought separate wars which
had no real point of effective contact: there was
little scope for military or economic aid.

The reasons are myriad.   They were divided over the

bone which lay between them: the Soviet Union.
Hitler's pursuit of the disastrous eastern front had
nothing in common with Japan's pursuit of Soviet
neutrality.   The Japanese attempts at mediation
between Germany and Russia were out of touch with
Hitler's real spirit. (19)   Because the Japanese
military kept their Foreign Ministry ill-informed
about their dealings with Germany, there was much
political ineptness.   There were personal inconsistencies.   The German path had always been a controversial path which had been opposed by influential
men.   The events of 1940-2 in no way lessened their
detestation.   When the news of German failures
arrived, the starry-eyed admiration of German achievement passed and with it much pride in Japan's early
successes.   Above all, national self-interest drew
Japan to Asia and south-east Asia where Germany was
not welcome as a partner.

The attack on Pearl Harbor was arguably the most
dramatic event in world history.   It has exercised
a great fascination over documentary film-makers,
popular writers and academics.   It is, therefore,
natural for the historian of Japanese foreign policy
to wish to end his study with an account of the
breathtaking diplomatic activity of the Tōjō ministry
between October and December and then to conclude with
the Supreme Gamble in which the strategy of surprise
attack was given preference over the more difficult
way of diplomatic concession.   Yet we have tried to
resist the temptation to dwell on the well-travelled
exchanges of that period.

We have tried to avoid the notion that all roads
led to Pearl Harbor, to Singapore, to Rangoon or even
to the Coral Sea.   We have tried not to suggest that
the moves on the diplomatic chessboard led to an inevitable confrontation and that openings for conciliation were frittered away.   On the contrary, these
moves led to a host of genuine attempts to prevent
confrontation;   but the streamers of accommodation
that were exchanged grew taut and finally snapped on
7 December 1941.   Too great a preoccupation with the
origins of war can be a weakness.   To take an example
from European history, recent scholars have had to
undo the work of many carefully documented but slanted
studies which focused exclusively on the origins of
the First World War and hence ignored many of the most
illuminating aspects of European development in the
1890s and 1900s.   So it is with the Far East in the
1930s.   There comes a time when it is no longer

fruitful to be preoccupied with Pearl Harbor and what
led up to it. We have, therefore, been concerned in
this study to try to review the foreign policy of the
1930s without giving the story the perspective of an
inevitable war. (20)

We have tried to avoid distortion. The operation
at Pearl Harbor was Japan's bid for command of the
seas in the Pacific Ocean and was, therefore, a significant starting-point of the Pacific war. But the
so-called 'Pacific war' is an inadequate description
of the many-sided war in which the Japanese armies
were engaged in China and the tropics outside the
Pacific area. This land warfare was described by
contemporary Japanese as the Great[er] East Asia war,
the war to achieve their new order and to extend the
Great[er] East Asia Co-prosperity sphere. Although
much has been done to throw light on the Pacific war,
less has been done to illuminate the origins and
course of the Great[er] East Asia war. An account
of American-Japanese diplomacy may explain the former;
but it does not do much to explain Japanese preoccupation with China or the Asian mainland which are the
keys to an understanding of the latter.

On 16 July 1941 the reluctant Matsuoka passed out
of our story. Konoe remained at the helm in increasing bewilderment until October, when he was replaced.
Towards the end of the war, Konoe became associated
with the peace faction and was suggested by some for
a mission to Moscow to put out peace feelers. Matsuoka, on the other hand, was discarded like a spent
shot. He was never used during the war but was
allowed to go into retirement in the country to nurse
his illnesses and (as he thought) his grievances.
At the end of the war, Konoe as an ex-premier was
quite active but, when he learnt that he was going to
be arrested for war crimes, he committed suicide by
taking poison. Matsuoka was arrested and placed in
Sugamo prison in order to appear before the war crimes
tribunal. His physical condition and his mental
balance, whose derangement had long been suspected,
sharply deteriorated. He was after a few appearances
before the tribunal permitted to withdraw to hospital
where he died shortly after in 1946.

We have tried to see Japan's foreign policy through
the careers of some of the men who bore responsibility
for it. It is curious that Matsuoka who comes at the
end of these biographical sketches should be so un-
typical. Markedly different from his predecessors,
he did not belong to the Japanese establishment. In

family background, in education both at college and at
university, and in career pattern, he was dissimilar
to those who had been foreign ministers before him.
Both as diplomat and as political representative, his
career had not been without merit.   His work in China
and his international role in the solution of the
Shanghai imbroglio of 1932 had had elements of distinction.   For the Japanese his performance at the
League assembly in Geneva had had a heroic quality,
though the popular legend is far different from the
real thing.   But his moves in and out of politics
and his reckless expression of extremist views had by
1940 built up for him a notoriety which alienated
moderate opinion.   Despite his opinionated views, he
was invited by Konoe, who was in so many ways the
antithesis of Matsuoka, to join his Cabinet.   Two
things may be said of his twelve months in office:
he tried to build up the crumbling stature of the
Foreign Ministry according to his own lights; and
he did score some short-term successes in the art of
Great Power diplomacy.   Each of these credits had
its reverse side: the Foreign Ministry was 'revolu-
tionized' by Matsuoka and packed in the higher brackets
by his favourites; his diplomacy towards the United
States and China - which he might have been expected
to know most about - was signally unsuccessful.   His
performances on return from Moscow lost him the
support of those who had earlier befriended him.
His unwillingness to join in any consensus over policy
towards Washington of which he was not the originator
made him an impossible member of any Cabinet.   By
this time, his mind may have become unbalanced.   Be
that as it may, he had shown himself to be almost
too un-Japanese and was acceptable neither to the
army nor to the civilians any longer.

Postscript

In our concluding remarks, we must attempt to offer, however inadequately, some overall analysis of the Japanese Foreign Ministry, of Japan's foreign ministers and her foreign policy over the span of seventy years. All these changed many times during the period of this study; and there is not much evidence of continuity or of abiding long-term themes. In these years Japan was on the move but her progress as an expansive country was haphazard and interrupted. Her foreign relations also reflected this undulation of fortune.

We should not expect Japan to conform to a pattern which we find elsewhere in the diplomatic world. One of the distinctions which it is conventional to draw in looking at Europe is between the Old Diplomacy and the New Diplomacy which becomes apparent around 1919. This is basically the contrast between a pre-1914 diplomacy which was dealing with an assumedly peaceful world where wars of major dimensions had not occurred for a century and where the diplomat had, broadly speaking, a great voice in settling affairs in his own secretive ways and through private channels. After the war the old diplomatic methods were no longer acceptable, because Wilsonian ideals were in vogue and, more likely, because international relations were becoming infinitely more complex. The diplomat - and his class - was suspect; his 'web of alliances' was alleged to have been the main cause of the outbreak of war in 1914; and he was widely attacked for the lack of openness in his dealings. In Japan this distinction between the Old and the New is scarcely relevant. The nineteenth century was for her a period of struggle against countries assumed to be hostile and ready to attack her shores. It was

perhaps not unnatural for the Meiji constitution to
stress the rights of the military. The twentieth
century too was a time when the needs of defence were
never far away. Since the government never allowed
peace to be regarded as the expected order of things,
the Foreign Ministry had a smaller role than elsewhere
and was at most one voice among many in decision-
making.

More fundamentally one should not expect Japan's
method of making decisions on international issues to
correspond with that of other countries. During the
period of this study Japan entered international
society, for a time identified herself closely with
it and then pulled away from it. But did she really
adapt to the concept of inter-state diplomacy in
fundamentals? From the start Japanese diplomats
laboured under the difficulty of language in situations where distinctions of tone and nuance were
important. There were also equally formidable
barriers which derived from Japanese social customs.
There were the slow-moving methods of consulting all
officials affected by a particular item of business
before a decision was finally reached. While
decision-making by consensus is not now rare, Japan
was one of the few major countries who practised it
in the pre-war period. Second, since the need for
saving face comes as second nature to Japanese,
decisions were not subjected to rigorous, 'no holds
barred' debate before they were finally announced.
Since the degree of scrutiny of any project was sometimes shallow, the end-result was often clouded in
vagueness and deliberately ambivalent. Third, since
personal relationships were important among the
Japanese, there were often unexpected quirks in
decision-making. One which often embarrassed foreign
diplomats was the interventions of the genro, which
could be unpredictable and haphazard. After they
ceased to be a major force, there were still the
sallies into policy-making of groups and cliques,
such as the army and overseas business interests.
These features of Japanese life were not, of course,
peculiar to the operation of the Foreign Ministry,
whose officials were constitutionally servants of the
emperor. Nor are they mentioned here with any intention of passing judgment upon them. On the contrary,
decision-making by consensus would not be without its
advocates. But it remains a fact that the Japanese
became involved in a diplomatic process in which they
were operating on a different wavelength from foreign
diplomats.

Unquestionably this led on occasion to a lack of
communication with other countries in the course of
negotiations and, even when the 'system' was understood by foreigners, could lead to certain strains.
It was hard for Japanese to convince others that some
of the institutions they had adopted in name from the
West in the 1880s were being used differently by them.
Thus, the prime minister was merely one among several
foci of authority; the Cabinet and Diet were much
weaker bodies than their counterparts in the West.
In particular, the foreign minister and Foreign
Ministry lacked the standing which they sometimes
enjoyed in the West.

To add to the difficulty of comprehension, the
Foreign Ministry was a changing institution which
went through various phases of development. It is
important, therefore, to try to identify the turning-
points in its development which had seen both downs
and ups. In the early period down to 1900 a professional service had scarcely been formed. There
were many able men in the employment of Kasumigaseki
but its recruitment was until the 1890s haphazard and
the career pattern uncertain. On the other hand, the
foreign ministers were mainly distinguished sons of
the Restoration who enjoyed their own standing in
society and were personalities in their own right.
During the Sino-Japanese war the Foreign Ministry under
Mutsu was shown to be a really important institution
of government. Where Japan was lacking in this
period was in the capacity of her ministers in overseas capitals, many of whom were undistinguished and
reticent members of the diplomatic body. The
impression left is that of strong and influential
leadership at the top and unpredictable quality below.

Round about the turn of the century a new phase
began. By now the professional service was taking
root and there was a uniform quality of entrant.
It was from the cream of this service that Japan's
foreign ministers were to be drawn for four decades
as the new generation of politicians ceased to be
qualified to deal with diplomatic questions. As
Japan became recognized as one of the powers, so her
representatives abroad began to count and became
international figures, even if they were still shadowy
ones. In Japan herself, the advice of the Kasumigaseki bureaucrats became more influential in the
decisions reached by the Cabinet. The personality of
the foreign minister was, of course, paramount; and
during the tenure of personalities like Komura and

Katō Takaaki the influence of the office increased
enormously. But many foreign ministers did not match
the calibre of Katō or Komura.

At the same time, it has to be remembered that the
period from 1894 to 1918 was for Japan the period of
the three wars. In this atmosphere the Foreign
Ministry was often found alongside the military egging on
the nation to fight and to be expansionist. Thus,
as we tried to show, Mutsu played a large part in
conjunction with the military in using the Korean
issue to go to war with China in 1894; Komura was
anxious to overcome the Elder Statesmen's caution and
go to war with Russia in 1904; and Katō Takaaki had
a major role in bringing Japan in on the allied side
very early in the war in September 19194. It might
be said that these three statesmen-diplomats were
brought up in the climate of the 'diplomacy of
imperialism' and saw Japan as imitating the practices
of European Powers. After 1919 the diplomacy of
imperialism became unfashionable. When this notion
spread to east Asia after the Washington conference of
1921-2 and the diplomacy of post-imperialism became
the order of the day, the standpoint of the Foreign
Ministry changed slightly. More sensitive than
others to the appeal to bring territorial annexation
in China to an end, the Foreign Ministry became the
advocate within Japan of caution and restraint and
the peaceful settlement of disputes, while the army
and at times the navy pushed for continental expansion,
if necessary, by the use of force. As time went on,
this difference led to acute antagonism within
Japanese government circles in which the Foreign
Ministry, being divided against itself, was generally
the loser.

By the 1920s Kasumigaseki diplomacy seemed to be
riding high. This was for the Americans the 'age of
normalcy'; for some Japanese the 'liberal interlude'.
Yet many of the features which were to be more
dangerous for Japan in the 1930s were already present
in that decade. This was not, we have argued, primarily to be seen in any confrontation between
Shidehara and Tanaka in their China policies. Rather
it was discernible in the growing challenge of the
armed forces to the body politic. The partial
decline in Kasumigaseki's standing was not due to the
superior skills of the military or the faulty tactics
of the Foreign Ministry. It was a fact of life in
all countries in the 1920s that foreign offices had
to yield power to other ministries, whether the defence

ministries or the trading ministries (after 1929), and
that prime ministers were expected to take a larger
role. Japan was no exception here. On the contrary, the military, because of its constitutional
rights and its sense of grievance after the Washington
settlement of 1922, was especially well placed to
challenge the civilian government. The first serious
challenge was over the London naval treaty where the
government, with the support of the parties and the
evident approval of the newspapers, stressed the need
for economy and internationalism. But the navy was
able to appeal to a wider audience and to underscore
one of the shortcomings of Japan's rulers.

Throughout this period there was not a broad-based
public opinion on foreign relations. While there was
a small and expert band, mainly journalists, who
devoted their whole life to this study, there was not
much evidence of well-informed opinion. Very often,
as Kiyozawa Kiyoshi was to say, when public opinion
did assert itself, it did so against the more cautious
policies which the government was trying to pursue.
This is true of 1905, 1915 and 1932. Its influence
was not great, but, when it intruded, it was for a
hard line and against Kasumigaseki judgment. Perhaps
it showed up the failure of Kasumigaseki in the past
to take public opinion into account and to co-ordinate
public relations adequately. But, in circumstances
where journalistic freedom was limited, that was perhaps understandable. There was little attempt to
'educate' the public over foreign affairs or take the
public into the ministry's confidence.

In the world at large, the impression given by
Japan's representatives abroad was generally favourable. A typical reaction was that of the British
prime minister (1916-22), David Lloyd George, who had
close contact with Japan at the postwar international
conferences. He liked the Japanese, he said; 'the
reasons they gave very often for doing things were
quite unintelligible and they might have no conscience
but they did stand by those who stood by them.' (1)
So far as Britain was concerned, the reputation of
Japanese foreign policy was for loyalty, tinged with
a certain ambiguity. This impression still obtained
down to the time of the London Naval Conference in
1930. The assessment of the old Foreign Ministry
made in the United States was of course different.
But, if one may judge from the remarkable confidence
which Henry L. Stimson placed in Shidehara (and also
Debuchi) right down to his retirement in the midst of

the Manchurian crisis, one may conclude that he had a
remarkable regard for 'Kasumigaseki gaikō' and a
respect for Shidehara to a degree which was abnormal
in diplomatic circles. In both Britain and the
United States, there was the feeling that power in
Japan rested with the civilian Cabinet, which was
under the 'healthy' influence of the parties, but
that the parties and the civilians were under challenge and needed all the support they could get from
outside. Both countries had a clear impression that
the army could manipulate a crisis, as in 1914, 1918
and 1928, to its own ends but that it was still
possible for the civilians with the control of the
purse to cope with international crises in the end.

From the Manchurian crisis onwards the situation
changed again. Because of the success of the military in Japan during that crisis, it contrived to have
a greater say in policy-making thereafter. 'China
policy' which was a substantial aspect of Japan's
external relations was one in which the military insisted on having a major voice. Hence the Foreign
Ministry lost part of its conventional control over
national policy; and the 'national policy' that
emerged bore few of the hallmarks of 'Kasumigaseki
gaikō' in the past, such as the cautious balancing of
conflicting international interests.

This is not to say that the Foreign Ministry went
unrepresented in the major decisions of the 1930s.
The foreign ministers were physically present at
meetings of the Inner Cabinets at which so many of
the crucial government decisions of the 1930s were
formulated. But their officials could be by-passed -
and frequently were - over China and over Axis relations. In the decision-making process the voice of
the foreign ministers counted for less. The prevailing atmosphere of the country was less internationalist
and increasingly anti-foreign. The standing of
diplomats in society accordingly declined and their
superior, the foreign minister, often complained of
fighting an uphill struggle. It comes as no surprise
that General Tōjō said that the Foreign Ministry
should confine itself to observing protocol and
giving parties for foreign diplomats and leave the
real decisions to men with practical knowledge of
affairs, namely, the army. It was by no means an
uncommon complaint that the diplomats and the Kasumigaseki bureaucracy had become too professionalized and
had drifted away from the thinking of the people. It
is in this context that Tōjō contended that 'the

foreign minister was the mouthpiece of the national
will as debated and decided upon by the cabinet.' (2)
But 'the national will' was poorly formed and, such
as it was, tended to favour extreme measures.

The problems faced by the foreign ministers in
those days were twofold: how to sustain a ministry
which was declining in importance; and how to cope
with the challenge, both implicit and explicit, of
the military. These factors had been evident from
the 1920s onwards. They had been tackled in different ways. If one takes Shidehara as the dominant
figure of diplomacy in the 1920s, he responded to
military opposition by ignoring it and later from
December 1931 by retiring from the scene. If one
takes Hirota as a representative figure from the
1930s, he let the role of the ministry - perhaps
inevitably - diminish and allowed himself to collaborate with the military in the main. Matsuoka, the
maverick figure of 1940-1, sought to revitalize the
Foreign Ministry in his own particular way and,
despite many disagreements with the military, he must
be accounted as a collaborator of theirs. While
their attitudes were their own, each was still representative of a wider group of diplomats within the
ministry.

Nurtured in the internationalism of the Wilson
period and sorry for the current anti-foreign view,
the country's representatives overseas and the
Foreign Ministry bureaucracy had grown up over the
years with high standards. It was by the middle
1930s still the most internationally-minded sector of
the Japanese government but had become divided and
demoralized. The diplomats were demoralized in the
sense that they were conscious of serving in a
declining, second-string ministry; and that it was
not professional competence or even seniority which
was the criterion for promotion. This threw up
diverse responses to the problem of expansion and
dealing with the military. The ministry became divided
on this issue; or rather the divisions on this issue
which had been evident in the past became more manifest
in the 1930s. One can identify groups and cliques:
the Anglo-American clique; the Renovationist clique;
the traditional group. Each had its sponsors and its
adherents, its moments of power. One has, therefore,
to look at the ministry as comprehending a diverse
bundle of conflicting views.

There are two features of the foreign ministers of
the 1930s and their upper-echelon bureaucrats which

impress the outside observer.   One is that a premium
was placed on those with knowledge and experience of
China.   Remember that Shidehara, like his predecessors, had no direct knowledge or experience of China.
After his retirement in 1931, the post of foreign
minister often went to a China specialist.   At the
height of the Manchurian crisis, Inukai appointed
Yoshizawa, minister at Peking (1923-9); and Admiral
Saitō appointed Uchida, who had just served as president of the south Manchurian railway.   Hirota who
succeeded him was perhaps an exception but there can
be little doubt that his China policy for his first
period (1933-6) was in the hands of his vice-minister,
Shigemitsu, who had gained his first-hand knowledge as
consul-general, Shanghai and minister in Peking from
1930 to 1934.   The old-style Europe-oriented,
American-oriented foreign ministers had had their day.
In the lower reaches of the hierarchy a similar process was taking place.   The policy of regional
dominance - what later came to be called 'Great East
Asian policy' - tended to circumscribe the functions
of the established Foreign Ministry.   It did not
appeal to the majority of diplomats who had past
experience in, and enjoyable contacts with, the wider
world, though it naturally played into the hands of
those whose careers had tended to be limited to China
postings.   It was in this atmosphere that the Anglo-
American clique among diplomats declined, while the
China and Renovationist cliques prospered (Document 37).
    The second point concerns the late 1930s when the
qualities demanded of the foreign minister were
changing.   From 1900 down to the appointment of
General Ugaki in May 1938, the foreign minister had
always been a professional diplomat.   There had in
the past been occasions when a prime minister who was
a general or an admiral might assume the acting
appointment but it was brief except for Tanaka's case.
Ugaki's was the first case of a non-professional being
chosen.   Apart from his greater safety from the
assassin, it was intended to meet a practical need:
if Japan was to resolve the China issue, she would
have to employ someone who was not an established
diplomat.   Ugaki's appointment was a controversial
one but it set a new pattern.   He was followed in due
course by Admiral Nomura and Admiral Toyoda.
Strangely enough, these men, taken together, were
among the most liberal and conciliatory ministers of
the pre-war period.   But they had as little claim to
a popular or political following as had the career

diplomats. It is perhaps in this context that the
appointment of Matsuoka in July 1940 should be regarded. Matsuoka, though he was an Old China Hand with
a 'Manchurian mind' and had earlier been a diplomat
for twenty years, had more recently become a politician. Not a party politician, to be sure, but the
representative of an interest group who had a public
reputation. So after a half-century during which
the foreign minister had been a promoted diplomat,
the administrations of the late 1930s had found it
necessary to experiment with appointees from outside
the ministry. This was one of the factors which
damaged the esprit de corps of up-and-coming diplomats
and their promotion prospects. But it cannot be said
to have necessarily had adverse effects on the type of
policy that was evolved.

By 1940 enlightened leadership could not be expected from the Foreign Ministry. Relations with the
Powers were being injured by the military and the bulk
of the Foreign Ministry's work was to perform a mopping-
up operation for the work of the military. This led
to its becoming a sort of channel for covering up
actions of which it basically disapproved. This
meant that its Public Information Bureau (Jōhōbu)
came to assume greater and greater importance within
the bureaucracy. It was unfortunate that it was
manned by those who favoured the military: Shiratori
Toshio, Amau Eiji (though his loyalties are less
certain) and Kawai Tatsuo.

Since the ministry operated under conditions of
particular difficulty, it is well to record its
successes. During the Manchurian crisis, it succeeded
with the co-operation of the court in preventing the
capture by military operations in November 1931 of the
Chinese city of Chinchow, though in the long run it
only succeeded in postponing the attack for six weeks.
Later after the sinking of the American gunboat
'Panay' in December 1937 by the Japanese, it was left to
the Foreign Ministry to patch up some sort of agreement with the United States at a time when feelings
were very excited. In 1939 it was left to Ambassador
Shigemitsu in Moscow to work out a settlement over the
border disputes between Russia and Manchukuo, while
Foreign Minister Arita managed to work out a formula
with Ambassador Craigie to bring to a peaceful close
the bitter conflict over the British concession at
Tientsin. In these cases, the Foreign Ministry
inherited situations which were not of its creation
and was required to resolve them diplomatically and

sustain good relations with foreign Powers. While it
often performed difficult tasks skilfully, it lacked
the political muscle to push constructive policies of
its own.

After 1939 the Foreign Ministry had a particularly
tragic role. The successful diplomatic thrusts did
not take place in the late 1930s because the extent
of the concessions which Japan was prepared to offer
did not match those which her adversaries demanded.
That does not mean that there were not many individual
and worthy initiatives which did take place. But
clear-sighted central leadership was lacking in
decision-making in the search for a consensus. Much
too depended on the existence of a strong international
'thrust for peace'; but this was weak. Indeed the
foreigners' view of Japan had never been lower.
They had little confidence in the Japanese voices for
peace. Thus Sir George Sansom, engaged in an agonizing appraisal of Britain's role in August 1939,
summed up his perceptions thus:

> It is open to serious doubt whether in present con-
> ditions we have any really useful friends in Japan....
> The difference between the extremists and the
> moderates is not one of destination, but of the
> road by which that destination is to be reached and
> the speed at which it is to be travelled. There
> are certain elements comprising the so-called
> liberals and some bankers and industrialists who
> fear for their position under a full totalitarian
> regime and would like to stem the tide of totali-
> tarianism. These elements, though they are diverse
> and far from unified, could, it is true, in certain
> circumstances, be lined up in our favour and against
> the extremists. (3)

The Ministry has no mention among the 'so-called
liberals'.

The decline of the Foreign Ministry caused distress
at an individual level. Many of those most famous in
its service - Shidehara, Tokugawa Iemasa and Yoshida
Shigeru - proclaimed their distaste for Japan's
policies and resigned. They were fortunate in having
independent means which gave them the option of dissent.
Many others made clear their disapproval but, not
having financial independence, continued to serve.
Others again served the military, thinking that it was
perhaps the only way to keep the new rulers on the
rails.

The Foreign Ministry did have some residual powers
of resistance. It opposed to some purpose the setting

up of the Manchurian board, the Kō-A-in (East Asian
board) and the Great East Asia Ministry. Then there
was the Bōeki-shō crisis of 1939 when the elite of
the Foreign Ministry staff resigned en masse because
many of their functions were being taken away from
them. On occasion too, individuals could offer
their resignation - or threaten to do so - without
injuring their careers. The cases of Nishi Haruhiko
and Tōgō Shigenori are two in point. Yet these
protests were more against encroachments into their
vanishing privileges than against differences over
policy. Perhaps they were interested in keeping the
Ministry going as an institution, but less concerned
over policy (Document 37). Perhaps there is some
truth in Sansom's judgment quoted above that there was
no real difference among Japanese over the ultimate
objects for which Japan was striving, only over the
question of means. Put another way, while we know
that there were different perceptions circulating
within the Foreign Ministry, those who opposed the
policy-line in the 1930s either did not reach the
top or did not greatly influence the policies adopted.
The actual resistance of Kasumigaseki was comparatively small.

There were many grounds for this. We have not in
this study subscribed to the view that Japan in the
1930s saw a confrontation between a good Foreign
Ministry and a bad army-navy. This is too black and
white an interpretation; there is a blurred grey
area where truth is more likely to be found. The
officials of the Foreign Ministry, though their hearts
may have been in the right place, did not directly
oppose the actions of the expansionists because of
fear and despair. Fear, that is, of assassination,
of loss of career, of ostracism. Despair at the
difficulty of standing up against the rolling waves
of nationalism and of manoeuvring successfully against
a public opinion which had got seriously out of hand
and could not readily be held in check. The Ministry
lost the will to fight against the position which the
military had effectively grasped. Doubtless there
was also the moderates' hope of using their position
within the system, within the establishment, to
restrain expansion and add the occasional corrective
to policy. That there was some sense in this view
may be seen after the collapse of Japan's approach to
the axis countries with the signing of the Nazi-Soviet
pact in August 1939. But this was a case of external
forces liberalizing the diplomatic process in Japan,

rather than internal forces asserting themselves. In
general, such skirmishes as the Gaimushō had with the
military resulted in capitulation by the civilians,
who tended to be on the defensive.

The Foreign Ministry exists largely for the formulation and execution of foreign policy; and it is
fitting that we should at the conclusion of this
study try to draw together some of the aspects of
Japan's foreign policy. It seems that Japan's policy
has tended over the years to be hard-headed and mater-
ialistic rather than altruistic or ideological. Of
course, there were many ideologies which individual
Japanese had tried to impart to Chinese or Asians with
a remarkable lack of success. But they never featured
as part of government policy. When, after the war
with China began, the doctrine of Great East Asian Co-
prosperity was evolved, it was intended for export and
could not be ignored by the Gaimushō. It was essentially a military doctrine which pulled along the
civilians with it; and its tenets did not create much
opposition. Indeed, many like Shigemitsu were strong
defenders of its ideas. But, by and large, Japanese
government policy was remarkable for being non-ideolo-
gical, even on issues which were primarily racial.

On the other hand, there were, of course, continuing factors in the story of Japan's foreign relations.
But they were not very fundamental and tended to be
superficial. The continuities in Japanese foreign
policy were: economic and commercial, to obtain
access to supplies of raw materials and to remove
obstacles in the way of a profitable overseas trade;
defence, to secure Japan's own shores from attack and
to prevent the occupation by hostile countries of
territories likely to threaten the security of Japan;
diplomatic, to remain on good terms with other
countries and, where appropriate, to join international
bodies and thereby to improve Japan's standing in the
world. These objects are the stuff of which the
speeches of Japanese foreign ministers were made from
the 1870s to the 1940s. The questions which foreign
observers are more inclined to ask are: was there not
a continuity in Japan being harsh towards China? Or
in Japan being expansive on the Asian mainland? Or
in Japan being expansive in the Pacific area? These
propositions are as true as the earlier statements are
anodyne and unobjectionable. What we have sought to
show in this study is that there was probably no
single course which was mapped out and systematically
followed. Japan's foreign relations had many turning-

points and missed opportunities.   First they were
moulded by men of different types with different notions.
Had this study been broader, we could have affirmed this
by showing some of the smaller men who still left the
mark of their personality on policy like Foreign Minister Satō in 1936.   Second, foreign policy is not made
in isolation and often there was maladroitness on the
part of those with whom Japan had to deal.   There were
formidable problems of communication between Japan and
those with whom she conducted a dialogue.   But basically the dilemma of any author who touches the delicate
shell of Japanese foreign policy is that the Foreign
Ministry exercised only a partial grip on affairs - and
that a declining one.

Compared to other countries, there were not wide
variations in foreign policy.   Japan after all was
relatively stable during the long period of seventy
years which is being surveyed here.   Japan's foreign
ministers, vice-ministers and diplomats came from a
narrow group in class and education;   and only in one
case (that of Matsuoka) can it be said that they really
intended to rock the boat for political or other reasons.
Moreover the imperial institution had a stabilizing
effect.   The Meiji, Taishō and Shōwa emperors rarely
intervened and were rarely called upon to do so.   In
general, they interpreted their role as being to ensure
that issues which were referred to them had been ex-
haustively discussed by the parties concerned and a
consensus reached.   From time to time the emperor and
court would be partisan and let their views be known
as opposed to the course proposed.   Their interventions, therefore, tended to have a harmonizing purpose.
These are some of the reasons why there seem to have
been no wide swings in accordance with party or other
considerations as one would find in other countries.

It has been the argument of this study that, while
expansion was an important factor in Japan's foreign
policy over the years, it was not a continuous and un-
interrupted theme.   Thus, Japan's expansionism was
arrested, once in 1921 by the Powers at the Washington
conference and later on a smaller scale in 1939 by the
actions of Germany and Russia.   Moreover it was not
continuous in the sense that there are important distinctions to be drawn about the nature of Japanese
expansionism over the years.   For the first fifty
years of this study, the consensus among the policy-
makers (which included the Foreign Ministry) was 'Join
Europe and Ignore Asia'.   By the 1930s the consensus
was for 'joining Asia and being vigilant for Western

opposition' (a cause in which Kasumigaseki had not a
leadership role). By 1942 Japan had become an enormous expansive Power. But its expansion had been
haphazard and disordered.

We now come full circle to the point with which
the preface began: the place of personality in
Japanese foreign policy. Japan's great difficulty in
running a foreign policy lay in communication - which
was essentially a problem of personality. We do not
speak here of communication within the foreign service.
So far as we are aware, the reportage from diplomats
overseas was, on the whole, accurate, full and pains-
taking and their judgments of the foreign scene
realistic and perceptive. There was loyalty to
Tokyo regardless of the government there; and disloyalty or insubordination or indiscretions, though
examples can certainly be traced, were comparatively
rare. We refer rather to communication within Japan
and with foreign governments. Here there were three
problems: the Japanese penchant for secrecy, not to
say secretiveness; the difficulty of the Japanese
language; and the vagueness and politeness with which
it tends to be used. On the one hand, it is often
thought to be the object of governments to try to win
over and convince their own people of their foreign
policy. But the Japanese government's published
statements were often misleading, compromise documents,
which were less calculated to clarify than to confuse.
On the other, there is the long-standing problem of
communicating with foreign governments. By the 1930s
statements by Japanese diplomats, while they continued
to be courteous in tone, were often embarrassingly
ambiguous or evasive in substance. They were, of
course, tied to instructions from Tokyo where policy-
making was centralized; they lacked flexibility in
their responses, quite apart from linguistic competence.
There was of course an even larger complaint. It was
expressed in the words of the Japanophil British
ambassador, Sir Francis Lindley, in November 1931:
'foreign representatives [in Tokyo] found themselves
in the unpleasant position of seeking assurances from
a government which had not the power to make them
good.' (4) This was said of Shidehara; but the
phrase goes echoing down the 1930s in the archives of
London and Washington.

It is fitting to remember in conclusion the phrase
of Shidehara which forms the sub-title of this volume.
In his retirement in 1935 he wrote of his disgust at
seeing the serious loss of power sustained by the

Foreign Ministry: Kasumigaseki and Nagata-chō have both been taken over by Miyakezaka. (5)   According to his information, the army general staff had asserted its control over the Foreign Ministry and the prime minister's office in the matter of China policy.   The Foreign Ministry which had grown up with the Japanese nation-state and acquired a place of undisputed dignity and respect in international affairs in the 1920s, was now being attacked from inside Japan.   The prime minister's office which, in company with others throughout the world, had begun to take a larger role in foreign policy-making over the years, was similarly being challenged.   By infiltration and meddling in certain lines of diplomacy, the military had exposed unsuspected signs of weakness in these two institutions.   After six decades of apparent autonomy, the Foreign Ministry had become a second-class ministry, forced to make compromises, to stall and to fight rearguard actions. Worse was still to come.   But for Shidehara, who even in retirement embodied the Kasumigaseki ideal more than any other, it represented the destruction of his own life's work as he saw it.   The ultimate shame was that he could do nothing to arrest the drift of power from Kasumigaseki to Miyakezaka since he already saw himself as 'a mere private from a lost war'.

Documents

THE IWAKURA PERIOD, 1869-83

1 Vigilance abroad

Memorandum by Iwakura on Treaty Revision, February 1869
('Iwakura Tomomi Jikki', vol. 2, pp. 696-701 (extracts))

If one day disagreements develop with foreign countries,
we must consider the pros and cons with reason (jōri)
rather than emotion. If we judge that it is essential
to take up arms, we must be decisive in undertaking
hostilities. How have we time to ask whether our
military preparations are adequate or not? In normal
conditions, we can negotiate in good faith; in extraordinary conditions, it may be necessary to enter into
war after weighing the situation with reason. It is
necessary, therefore, to reconcile our views with
everyone in Japan; and, if we can fairly make friends
[with our former opponents here], then we should do so.
If we have to make war, then we must do so. It should
always be our great objective not to degrade the honour
of the Emperor or impair Japan's national rights....
After all, foreign countries are our enemies. They are
all striving to improve their position by comparison
with other countries.
   We must revise the treaties of commerce and navigation already concluded with Britain, France, Prussia
and the United States and thus protect the independence
of our country. Consular jurisdiction cannot be tolerated. If foreigners unreasonably refuse to revise
their treaties, we must argue with them on the basis
of reason. Foreigners have the spirit of the tiger
and the wolf; and, if we are afraid of their tyranny,
our country will become their slave. Whenever Japanese

and foreigners have been involved in fights with one
another, it was only Japanese who killed foreigners
that have in the past been required to pay compensation and not the foreigners.   The emperor's honour
is thereby impaired;   national rights are restricted;
this is intolerable to us.   We must devise laws to
govern relations with foreign countries.   If any
clash takes place between Japanese and foreigners from
now on, we should resolve it by these laws.

2   Iwakura on the Korean Expedition

*Iwakura's address to the emperor as acting minister of
the Right, 23 October 1873*
(Okubo Toshiaki (ed.), 'Kindaishi shiryō', Tokyo:
Yoshikawa, 1965, pp. 73-4)

It is only four or five years since the Meiji Restoration but the country's foundations are in my private
opinion not yet strong and the administration is not
yet in good order.   Though we seem to be accumulating
military weapons, it is difficult to assess how vul-
nerable we are.   At a time like the present we should
not take our foreign affairs lightly.
     If Korea, which has for some hundreds of years been
a friendly neighbour of ours, is insulting to us, why
should we take it lying down?   The proposal to send a
mission there has already been generally settled;   and
I agree with it.   But, in sending it, we must be clear
about our priorities and procedures.   If the Koreans,
being blind and ignorant people, do not show respect to
our mission, we will have to take steps to deal with
them.   If we do not take steps, we will forfeit our
national honour.   They have already shown the first
indications of disrespect.   Hence the day when the
mission is sent must be the day for us to decide on
war.   This is a grave decision for Japan;   and we must
think carefully about it and plan deeply.
     Let us observe the relative strengths of countries
in the world to-day.   In the east something may crop
up;   but in the background the west may sometimes be
associated with it.   Or there may be some European
factors involved in it.   It is not, therefore, enough
to assess the local situation at a superficial level.
Recently several incidents have occurred in Karafuto
(Sakhalin) and they are matters of extreme urgency over
which we must exercise great caution.   We must sort
out these problems first with the Russians in case they

become involved in Korean questions; and then we must decide on our objectives and be clear over our strategy, while preparing to preserve peace on other fronts.

Apart from that, we must well in advance of any action build warships, prepare to supply provisions for our forces, arrange funds and decide on procedure and objectives to the extent of tightening up a hundred aspects of our internal administration. Even if our mission to Korea is delayed a while by this, it will still not be too late. If we do not make adequate preparations and send this mission prematurely, there will be no back support if untoward things [war] result. Again, if other troubles arise, we should not be able to deal with them, regrettable as it may be. Thus I believe that it would be unwise to send a mission prematurely in these days while we are still unprepared. Even if it is inevitable [that we embark on hostilities], I think that it would really be unwise to get involved in war if we have not built solid foundations and made preparations for it.

I shall present the details of my case orally to the emperor. I respectfully request the emperor to study the fundamentals of the matter, to consider deeply the degree of urgency of the general situation and to give his verdict. (1)

Notes

1   Okubo's memorandum of October 1873 on the same theme will be found in Conroy, 'The Japanese seizure of Korea', pp. 47-9 and in Tsunoda (ed.), 'The Sources of the Japanese Tradition', pp. 658-62.

3   The Treaty Revision debate

Memorandum by Tani Kanjō, 3 July 1887
('Nihon Gaikō Bunsho', vol. 20, no. 26 (extracts))
[Foreign Minister Inoue Kaoru after many attempts over five years restarted conferences with foreign delegates in 1886. But the nature of the secret negotiations leaked out and aroused great opposition, notably from Agriculture Minister Tani, which led to Inoue's resignation in failure in September.]

Treaty revision which has been the much-desired goal of Japanese for many years recently came near to fruition. I understand that foreigners will not accept our juris-

diction because our laws are unsuitable for application
to them and that the government is ready to revise these
laws in order to satisfy their requirements.   Anyone
who thinks of reforming our laws for the sake of
foreigners has, in my view, lost all sense of independence....   I am unable to tell how the talks have been
going because I am an outsider....   It is not wise to
delegate the whole matter to the Foreign Ministry.   We
should do so only after all the ministers have discussed
the issues and expressed their views.   The Ministry of
Agriculture and Commerce under my charge has intense
interest in treaty revision because of the import
tariff prescribed.   Yet the Foreign Ministry will not
discuss matters with me....   My opinion is that treaty
revision will be achieved ultimately but it is not the
best policy to pursue at present.   We must be confident
enough to act boldly in our dealings with foreign
countries.   There must be few European nations who
would threaten to resist our proposals by force.   In
the present state of the powers, if any such country
existed, another would offer to make an alliance with
us.   Nothing will make a stronger impression on foreign
countries than public opinion.   Instead of keeping all
our talks secret, the government should marshal public
opinion by modifying the laws governing the press and
public meetings in order to persuade the countries of
Europe and America....   If, when our Parliament is
opened in 1890, the Foreign Ministry proposes treaty
revision, it will not be too difficult to secure the
adoption of our proposals abroad.   While no European
country would despatch its warships against us (for
reasons which I shall describe elsewhere), we have very
little hope of success, if we have not developed a
strong army and navy beforehand.

Foreign Minister Inoue's response, 9 July 1887
('Nihon Gaikō Bunsho', vol. 20, no. 26 (summary only))

The only independent countries left in the east are
Japan and China.   All countries of the west have
schemes for engulfing the east by force and we must
devise plans for defence against them.   To do this we
must set up a new 'civilized state' here and our countrymen must become people of knowledge and vigour by free
contact with people from the west.   It will do us no
harm to open our islands to foreigners because our
economy is strong.   It will have certain advantages:
it will lead to the investment of foreign capital in
Japan; it will assist us to imitate foreign industries.

Japanese industries like silk, tea and lacquerware are
not likely to be transferred to the hands of foreigners.
We need to build up a European civilization here on
a par with that of European civilized states. We
must inaugurate here a new-style 'European empire'.
To this end Japan will for the first time by treaty
occupy a position equal to the European Powers. For
us to revise the present treaties will mark the very
first step on the road to achieving this great purpose.
There are certain items on which we should make concessions in negotiating for treaty revision because
our present level of civilization is lower. Of course,
extraterritorial jurisdiction is harmful because of the
unlawful acts of foreigners and their possessing
'immovable property'. But Japan's law codes are
deficient; our courts are in their infancy. The time
is, therefore, appropriate for treaties to be revised.
Each minister has his responsibility for examining
detailed aspects of the revision of the treaties and
recommending whether to proceed. But, if it is difficult to bring about these treaties, let us break off
negotiations now.

THE MUTSU PERIOD, 1884-96

4 Aoki and the Revision of the British Treaties

Aoki (London) to Foreign Minister Mutsu, 19 July 1894
('Nihon Gaikō Bunsho', vol. 27/I, no. 56)

I informed you about our final discussions with the
British government on treaty revision in a separate
message to-day. Since I came here in February, I have
had about fifty official and private conversations and
have at long last clinched the talks and signed a satisfactory agreement. I hope that I have carried out
my emperor's instructions and justified the confidence
which you and the cabinet placed in me. During the
past year when various difficulties have arisen, you
have quickly disposed of them and thus enabled me to
pursue the negotiations. How could I with my feeble
talents otherwise have achieved this task? All my
thanks to you and my country for having brought this
to fulfilment.
In the treaty, and especially in the annexes, there
may be a number of clauses which do not meet with the
approval of Viscount Tani Kanjō and others but for the
most part it is an understanding which is not incon-

venient.   Under it we can discard the insults we have
suffered over the last thirty years and at one go
enter the 'Fellowship of Nations'.   Truly a matter
for great congratulation.   When we signed the treaty
two days ago, Lord Kimberley [British Foreign Secre-
tary] congratulated our cabinet and me, saying that
'the importance of this treaty for Japan far out-
weighs the defeat of the great armies of China'.
From now on we must try to make our government and
people act in accordance with 'the Laws of Nations'
and thereby cause civilization to flourish increasingly
in our land.

   ... From March onwards I have called the attention
of the British government to Korean affairs and tried
to prevent it from leaning towards China.   I have
listed the facts where it is difficult to credit Li
Hung-chang and the Peking government and disputed the
notions of Lord Kimberley and others.   I have
explained Japan's rights in Korea, that is to say,
our rights under the Tientsin treaty to protect and
educate her together with China.   When the incident
blew up recently, the foreign secretary tried to guess
my ideas from our most cordial conversations.   First
I succeeded in my efforts to separate China and
Britain and then I went so far as to argue that Japan
had the right to occupy Korea either individually or
together with China.   That is, it is an obligation
for us to keep Korea independent from a security point
of view, in the sense of 'protecting our national
existence'.   Lord Kimberley cordially accepted these
points.   On the one hand, I employed Siebold privately
to demolish the silly idea of the Foreign Office that
Britain should have confidence in China and should,
even in case of emergency, conclude a mutual agreement
with her.   On the other, I tried to educate British
public opinion using 'The Times', the 'Daily Telegraph' and the 'Daily Chronicle' and gained acceptance
for Japan's activities.   But your instructions on
this point were inadequate; and, while we could have
tried to net the big fish in one go, we have not yet
taken action and have held our hand.   I imagine that
you will have had a chance to glance at the protectorate proposals which I sent you last month.   If you
were to enter into an agreement on these lines with
the Chinese before or after war breaks out, would it
not quickly arrest the southward march of the Russians?
The London government did not indicate any disagreement with such a proposal....

   In retrospect, the importance of the present revised

treaty is great.   If a rescript on the lines of the
enclosed were issued on the occasion of the emperor's
ratification, it would give rise to unbounded grati-
fication at home and abroad and would certainly reap
exceptional benefits for the future.   Although there
are some who do not approve of the treaty, you wanted
to bring it to a positive conclusion and it has conferred a myriad of gifts on our country.

5   Mutsu on Japan's motives in Korea
('Kenkenroku', pp. 59-61)

On 1 June 1894 the Diet was in session and the lower
house as usual had a majority opposed to the government
[and wanted to create a climate of opinion in favour of
war in order to embarrass the government.]   But the
government had acted as broadmindedly as possible and
tried to avoid a collision.   The lower house voted in
favour of a petition to the throne criticizing the
cabinet's actions;   and the government, inevitably,
took the final step and asked for the issue of an order
suspending the Diet.   On 2 June when a cabinet meeting
was due to be held in the premier's residence, a telegram had just arrived from Sugimura [our chargé
d'affaires in Seoul], announcing that the Korean government had asked China for the help of her troops.
This was a difficult matter for us: if it were
ignored, the balance of power between China and Japan
in Korea which was already favourable to China, would
increasingly lean towards her;   Japan would have no
alternative but to leave China to do what she wanted
in Korea in future;   and there was the danger that the
spirit of the Korean-Japanese treaty would be violated.
I presented my cabinet colleagues with Sugimura's telegram and gave my view that, when it became clear that
China had sent troops to Korea without offering any
justification, we too should send a considerable force
there and provide against unforeseen eventualities, and
that we must maintain parity with the Chinese in the
Korean peninsula.   The cabinet agreed with this argument;   and Premier Itō immediately sent a messenger to
ask Prince Naruhito and General Kawakami, the chief
and deputy chief of the general staff, for their
presence.   When they arrived, we reached a secret
decision to send troops to Korea;   and the prime
minister called on the emperor without delay ... and
obtained the necessary sanction from him.

6 Origins of the Korean campaign, 1894
('Kenkenroku', p. 122)

When we enquire about the battle of Asan [Gazan, 29
July 1894] which started the Korean war, it broke out
on the surface because of the Japanese government
receiving an appeal from the Korean court and setting
out to drive the Chinese armies beyond Korea's frontiers. But in reality one cannot dispute the fact
that it was China's claim to suzerainty over Korea
which was the root cause of the trouble. When Tokyo
was first informed by the Chinese government that it
would send troops to Korea, I was on the point of
taking issue straightaway over the phrase 'tributary
country under our protection' which appeared in the
communication. But my cabinet colleagues would not
agree to a diplomatic wrangle between Japan and China
over the question of suzerainty at this juncture.
The reason was that the history of China's claims
over Korea was of long standing and over-ripe to be
made the excuse for a fresh dispute but was not
serious enough to attract the attention of the world.

7 Mutsu on Japan's wartime jingoism
('Kenkenroku', pp. 149-50)

The Japanese people who had been seriously worried
about the outcome of the war before the victories of
Pyongyang and the Yellow Sea [17 September 1894],
soon lost their doubts about ultimate success and
were only concerned about the date when the Japanese
flag would be carried through the gates of Peking.
The populace seemed to be carried away with patriotic
songs and their ambitions for the future knew no
bounds. As with the jingoism which engulfed the
British people before the Crimean war and spread to
the whole country, there were no voices to be heard
in Japan other than those calling 'on to victory'.
If a man of deep thought and far-sightedness spoke
of compromise or the appropriateness of the Middle
Way, he was condemned as lacking in patriotism.
Some countries congratulated us on our victories and
seem to have poured oil on troubled waters with our
people who were agog with vain ambitions.

THE AOKI PERIOD, 1896-1901

8 Afterthoughts on the Triple Intervention of 1895

*Speech by Foreign Minister Okuma to the 11th Diet,
December 1897*
(A. Stead (ed.), 'Japan by the Japanese', pp. 219-21)

... Foreign intercourse is a very difficult affair, not
to be regulated at will by a single country, and it has
now undergone gradual but great changes. Gentlemen,
the foreign intercourse of former years was really of
narrow limits, being concerned with the relations
between one country and another, or a few others. But
now, through the enormous development of facilities of
transportation and communication, and the close inter-
action of the world's interests foreign relations have
been greatly transformed.... In truth, the limits of
foreign intercourse have gradually widened to such an
extent that a very small affair becomes of concern to
the whole world. The war with China [in 1894-5]
originally concerned only Japan and China, and did not
touch other Powers in any way. But even this led, in
the latter year, to the interference of three of the
most influential Powers of Continental Europe. Thus
it also became a general international question. In
consequence of the war ·... it has come to pass that
whereas the expression 'Eastern Question' used to
apply only to the world-famed problem of Eastern
Europe, it now possesses the dual significance of the
Near-Eastern, or the Far-Eastern, Question. In a
word, the sphere of foreign intercourse has so greatly
widened that the slightest incident may affect the
interests of the whole world.
    Having devoted herself for years with ardour and
diligence to national progress, and having come to
enjoy the great friendship of the Powers of Europe and
America, Japan, which for forty years past has been
fettered with disadvantageous treaties, has now advanced
to such a position that [she], in conformity with international usage, is accorded the treatment of an equal.
This is, in fact, the result of her own progress, and
of England's consent, leading the rest of the world,
to a revision of the existing treaties....

9   Japan decides to take part in the rescue of the
Peking legations, 1900
('Aoki jiden', pp. 329-33)
[After the murder of Japan's chancellor of legation,
Sugiyama Akira, on 11 June, the Yamagata cabinet had
sent a force of 3000 troops to join the international
expedition.   Aoki in his memoirs deals with the China
problem as seen by the cabinet at the end of June.]

Our government with around 3000 troops under Major-
general Fukushima had co-operated with the soldiers
of other countries in the taking of Tientsin but
could not face the greater number of Chinese with a
small force of this kind and break the siege of Peking.
The governments of every country fully understood this
position.   Because it was extremely urgent to break
the siege of Peking and rescue the officials and other
nationals of foreign countries, the British government,
without waiting to consult other governments, asked us
several times to undertake the task of sending further
reinforcements and relieving Peking.   [23 June-5 July]
Since this was a major issue for the Japanese government which required cautious consideration from the
standpoint of political strategy, we could not respond
to these appeals immediately.   When I say that it
required cautious political consideration, it was
perfectly possible for Japan herself, without waiting
for other countries to send troops, to despatch more than
a division to Peking and thus suppress the Boxers.
There was little doubt that we would be successful.
But, if we alone sent a large force and exerted ourselves to the utmost, it goes without saying that we
would have to think, in the event of victory, of
demanding an indemnity from China of comparatively
large proportions in the light of the expenses incurred
by our expeditionary force and our wartime exploits.
For us to make a 'solo performance' in this way could
not fail to excite the deepest suspicion and jealousy
on the part of other countries and especially Russia;
and so we could not readily agree to send reinforcements.   Our government, therefore, intentionally
delayed matters by enquiring the attitude of the
various powers towards China.   It gave as reasons for
not sending reinforcements the fact that it could not
afford the money required to send troops and that it
was inappropriate for our country on its own to deal
with such an emergency.   On instructions from his
home government, J.B. Whitehead, the British chargé
d'affaires, proposed [8 and 14 July] that, if Japan

was in difficulties over affording the cost of sending troops, the British government would pay her one million pounds. This was, of course, not a proposal which I could accept but, since it was not something which I could decide arbitrarily on my own, I referred it straightaway to the cabinet. When my colleagues concluded that, if there was no alternative to sending further troops, we should accept the money which the British government was offering us, I was astonished at such an unexpected decision. I told Prime Minister Yamagata that there was the precedent in which Frederick II of Prussia had in the course of fighting the Seven Years war with five countries found himself very short of funds and had accepted a subsidy from Britain but that in this case the troops sent by Japan numbered only about 3000 men and we were hardly in the predicament of having what could be described as an empty treasury. The state already had a reserve of twelve divisions; and the expenditure incurred in preparing them to act in an emergency must be paid for from our own treasury. Such suggestions as receiving a subsidy from a foreign country were from the start unthinkable; and anything like the present British proposal should certainly not be accepted. The prime minister agreed with my arguments. But, when Genro Itō [Hirobumi] insisted that we should accept the British offer, the cabinet was split [on 9 July] and those in favour and against were about evenly divided. I asked them to leave this question to me as the foreign minister and dropped the British offer in order to avoid national disgrace for a hundred years.

In these circumstances, Britain was very impatient with our inability to decide on sending reinforcements and repeatedly urged the Japanese government to do so but I always replied that 'the suppression of the Boxers and the relief of Peking are matters for joint action by the Powers and our country cannot increase its forces by itself'.... [Most of the Powers then arranged to send small bodies of troops] but Japan, being nearest to the target area, could get her forces there in ten days or so, once the decision had been taken. She was closely observing the attitude of the powers. But there were those within the Tokyo cabinet, especially Navy Minister Admiral Yamamoto, who opposed the sending of troops. They held that the motive underlying the Boxer disturbances was the so-called 'expulsion of the foreigners' (jōi) but that the Japanese were not included among the 'foreigners'. But this was not true, as everyone could see from the

fact that Sugiyama Akira had been killed.   There was
one thing that worried me a lot.   It was that,
according to the newspapers, it seemed that the Powers
were intending to divide up China as soon as the
Boxers had been suppressed.   In the circumstances,
Japan asked the powers whether they would undertake
to withdraw their troops as soon as their object was
accomplished and told them that it depended on their
reply whether she would send large numbers of reinforcements.   When Britain and Germany replied
favourably, I asked Prime Minister Yamagata to issue
the mobilization order.   When it was finally produced,
all the Powers of Europe were greatly relieved
that Japan's attitude was clear.   They indicated
their appreciation to our government that it was
undertaking joint operations with them.
[The 5th mixed division under Lieutenant-general
Yamaguchi was sent to China, bringing the strength of
Japanese forces there to 22,000.   Japan did not accept
the subsidy from Britain and declined to send the extra
two divisions which London requested.]

THE KOMURA PERIOD, 1901-11

10   Russo-Japanese negotiations over Manchuria and Korea

*Komura's memorandum for the Imperial Conference and
Cabinet, 23 June 1903*
('Nihon Gaikō Bunsho', vol. 36/I, no. 1)

In thinking of the future in the light of the present
situation in east Asia, the policy which Japan should
adopt will be many-sided but can in brief concentrate
on her defence and economic activities.   In considering her political programme, Japan has a most intimate
connection with the [Asian] continent at two points,
Korea in the north and Fukien in the south.   Korea is
a peninsula which points from the continent to the
heart of Japan like a dagger and is separated from
Tsushima by a narrow girdle of water.   If Korea were
to be occupied by another power, it would always be a
threat to the safety of Japan.   This cannot be accepted; and it has been the essence of Japan's policy in
the past to prevent it.   [Here follows an account of
Japan's interests in Fukien.]   But problems relating
to Fukien are not at present of great urgency and
should not trouble us except in the remote future.   In
Korea the situation is quite different: Russia has not

only taken the lease of Port Arthur and Dairen in
Liaotung but is in reality occupying the whole of
Manchuria and is trying to establish herself in various
ways on the Korean frontier.   If we ignore her,
Russia will not only establish her position in Manchuria but will also quickly spread her influence to
the Korean peninsula and bring the court and government
there under her wing.   Because Russia acts selfishly,
she has no reason to preserve the powers and interests
which Japan has built up in the peninsula over long
years;   and there is no doubt that she will press to
the extent of putting Japan's existence there in
jeopardy.   From Japan's point of view it is very
important to attempt direct negotiations with Russia
and resolve the situation.   Now the time is ripe for
this.   If it is allowed to slip away, there will be
no similar opportunity again;   and this will be a
tragedy for long ages to come.

On this occasion we should decide on policy quickly
at a cabinet meeting and as a result open negotiations
with Russia.   Our prime object should be to safeguard
the security of Korea and try to restrict Russian
activities to the limits laid down in the existing
treaties, thus withdrawing the threat to Korean
security and fulfilling Japan's defence and economic
interests.   The basis of these talks should be as
follows: 1. we should observe the principles of the
independence of Korea and China and their territorial
integrity and of equal opportunity for commerce and
industry there; 2. Japan and Russia could recognize
mutually the rights that the two countries possess in
Korea and Manchuria respectively and take steps necessary to uphold them; 3. Japan and Russia should
mutually recognize that they have a right to send
troops when required to protect their above rights or
to suppress regional uprisings where there is any fear
of an international incident arising and should withdraw the troops as soon as they achieve their object
(this does not apply to police forces required for the
protection of railway and telegraph lines); 4. Japan
has the right to advise Korea over domestic reform and
to help her with it.

If Japan secures an agreement with Russia on these
lines, her rights and interests will be guaranteed.   I
think that it will be very difficult to get Russia to
accept this so it is most important for Japan, in
opening negotiations, to be resolute to attain her
objectives at whatever cost. (1)

Notes

1 For Komura's memorandum of 7 December 1901 on the
   Anglo-Japanese alliance, see Nish, 'The Anglo-
   Japanese Alliance', pp. 382-5.

11 Komura wants to break off the Portsmouth peace talks

Telegram from Komura (Portsmouth, New Hampshire) to
Katsura, 26 August 1905
('NGB', 37-8, vol. 5, no. 281)

As you may have gathered from my recent telegrams, the
peace negotiations have to-day ended in deadlock.
With the object of securing some agreement with Russia
and restoring peace, I was as careful as possible in
presenting our demands and in negotiations I offered
concessions wherever possible. Not only that but I
undertook at an appropriate moment to withdraw the
demands for the transfer of the Russian ships and for
limitation of the Russian fleet. I also submitted a
compromise plan to deal with the two prickly issues of
Sakhalin and the war indemnity and strove to secure a
satisfactory outcome to the talks. But on these two
points Russia has stuck to her guns and refused to
contemplate any concession. Judging from Witte's
remarks at to-day's secret session, there is no prospect that the Russian emperor will change his stand
[despite the intervention of President Theodore
Roosevelt]. He seems to have been convinced by the
reports of [General] Linievich that his armies in
Manchuria are superior and have a chance of changing
the fortunes of war. We have no alternative but to
believe that he is in no mood to make peace at this
juncture. But the two points [of the compromise plan]
have from the start generated much interest in the
world at large and I have at the last few encounters
done nothing else but argue over them. If therefore
we were now to give in on these points, our national
honour would suffer greatly. All will be well if we
arrange things generally in accordance with our compromise plan. Otherwise there is no path open to us
apart from breaking off the talks.
    Thus, when I receive the official Russian reply to
our compromise plan at our next sitting, I shall make
an appropriate statement in order to clarify Japan's
case and break off negotiations....

12   Overruled by Tokyo

Katsura to Komura, 28 August 1905
('NGB', 37-8, vol. 5, no. 284)

After close scrutiny at cabinet meetings and at an
Imperial Conference, we have obtained the emperor's
approval of the following course: after examining our
military and economic position and the fact that we
have by your efforts settled the more important
aspects of the Manchurian and Korean questions, which
were our main war aims, we have decided to clinch an
agreement now even if we have to give up our demands
for indemnity and territory....
    You should propose to Russia that we will as our
final concession abandon our indemnity demands provided that she recognizes Japan's occupation of
Sakhalin as a fait accompli.... Even if Russia's
delegates continue to refuse to agree, you should not
break off your talks straightaway.... If the American
president should decline to assume the role of media-
tor, you are instructed, in the last resort and as our
final concession, to withdraw the demand for territory
(Sakhalin). The Japanese government is convinced of
the need to reach a peace agreement during the present
negotiations by all available means.... (1)

Note

1   Japan amended this to incorporate the demand for
    half of Sakhalin; and Witte on 29 August agreed to
    make over Sakhalin south of the 50th parallel of
    latitude by supplementary articles of the treaty.

13   Komura's Foreign policy defined

*Memorandum by Komura to Cabinet as approved, 25 Septem-
ber 1908*
('NGB', 40/III, no. 2200, appendix 1 (extracts))

Bearing in mind Japan's progress and the situation
among the Powers, our policy for the future must be to
maintain peace and promote our national strength. In
accomplishing these two major objectives, it is necessary to lay down general policy on three matters: our
attitude towards the powers; overseas enterprise;
and treaty revision.

Our attitude towards the powers
[Here follows a study of the attitude to be taken to
Britain, Russia, China, United States, Germany, France -
omitted.]
Overseas Enterprises
To promote our trade and industry: we must develop our
overseas trade from now on, especially with our most
important markets in the United States and China.   But,
in expanding our trade, we cannot avoid the growth of
trade rivalry with foreign countries though we should
be cautious not to let it affect our political relations with them....
To encourage the expansion of merchant shipping....
To encourage joint enterprises between Japanese and
foreigners in order to meet the need of Japan for
foreign capital and advanced techniques....
Emigration policy: since it seems likely that Japan
will come into close contact with the two great
countries of the Asian continent, China and Russia, we
ought to concentrate our nationals in the east Asian
area and adopt a definite policy of 'refusing to budge'
(kakutei fudō).   It is necessary to avoid forcing
one's nationals on countries which are important for
trade.   There was the risk of political repercussions
and the fear of damaging commercial prospects, so
Japan should maintain the status quo over emigration,
especially to Anglo-Saxon countries like the United
States, Canada and Australia.
Treaty Revision
In 1910 when the time comes to denounce the present
commercial treaties we will recover completely the
right to impose tariffs and thus complete the return of
those national rights lost to us since the Meiji
Restoration....

THE KATŌ AND ISHII PERIODS, 1911-19

14   Japan's ultimatum to Germany

Katō to Count Rex, 15 August 1914
('NGNB', vol. 1, pp. 380-1)

We consider it highly important and necessary in the
present situation to take measures to remove the causes
of all disturbances of the peace in the Far East and to
safeguard general interests as contemplated in the
agreement of alliance between Japan and Great Britain.
In order to secure firm and enduring peace in eastern

Asia, the establishment of which is the aim of the said
agreement, the Imperial Japanese Government sincerely
believes it to be its duty to give advice to the
Imperial German Government to carry out the following
two propositions:
> 1 to withdraw immediately from Japanese and Chinese
> waters German men-of-war and armed vessels of all
> kinds, and to disarm at once those which cannot be
> withdrawn;
> 2 to deliver on a date not later than 15 September
> to the Imperial Japanese authorities, without con-
> dition or compensation, the entire leased territory
> of Kiaochow with a view to the eventual restoration
> of the same to China.

The Imperial Japanese Government announces at the
same time that, in the event of its not receiving by
noon of 23 August an answer from the Imperial German
Government signifying unconditional acceptance of the
above advice offered by the Imperial Japanese Government, Japan will be compelled to take such action as it
may deem necessary to meet the situation.

15   Promoting an alliance with Russia

Yamagata to Prime Minister Okuma, 21 February 1915
(Kobayashi (ed.), 'Yamagata Ikensho', pp. 345-8)
[Genro Yamagata prepared a memorandum in favour of
starting negotiations for an alliance with Russia and
obtained the approval of his fellow-genro before presenting it to the premier.]

If we desire the integrity and development of China in
order to strengthen the basis of Japan's prosperity,
it is necessary to make China trust Japan and also for
Japan to ally herself with some European powers.
This will prevent a situation arising in the struggle
of powers in China which is unfavourable to Japan.
It is extremely important, therefore, to take steps to
prevent the establishment of a white alliance against
the yellow peoples.... The British alliance is of
course already serving this purpose. It may seem
that there is no necessity to form another alliance so
long as this one holds good. But the European war
will change the balance of power. Reliance upon
Britain alone will probably not be a foolproof policy
for maintaining perpetual peace in east Asia. Is it
not, therefore, the urgent duty of Japan to conclude an
alliance with Russia side by side with the British

alliance so that we shall be able to attain this
purpose?

16   Japan's ultimatum to China

Hioki to Chinese minister of foreign affairs, 7 May 1915
('NGNB', vol. 1, pp. 402-3)

... From the commercial and military points of view,
Kiaochow is an important place, in the acquisition of
which the Japanese Empire sacrificed much blood and
money; and, after making the acquisition, the Empire
incurred no obligation to restore it to China.   But,
with the object of increasing the future friendly relations of the two countries, Japan went out of her way
to offer to restore the territory.   To her great
regret, the Chinese Government did not take into consideration the good intention of Japan or manifest any
appreciation of her difficulties.   Furthermore, the
Chinese Government ... even demanded its unconditional
restoration, insisted that Japan should bear the responsibility of indemnifying her for all the unavoidable
losses and damages resulting from Japan's military
operations at Kiaochow ... and declared that she had
the right of participation at any future peace conference to be held between Japan and Germany ... [Japan
cannot tolerate such demands and rejects the Chinese
reply as 'vague and meaningless'].
   As regards the articles [Group V] relating to the
employment of advisers, the establishment of schools
and hospitals, the supply of arms and ammunition, and
the establishment of an arsenal, and railway concessions in South China in the revised proposals, they
are either proposed with the proviso that the consent
of the Power concerned must first be obtained or merely
to be recorded in the minutes.   [Hence they] are not
in the least in conflict either with Chinese sovereignty, or her treaties with the Foreign Powers....   [Yet
Japan] will undertake to detach Group V from the present
negotiations and discuss it separately in the future.
Therefore, the Chinese Government [should immediately
accept], without any alteration, all the articles of
Groups I-IV and the exchange of notes in connection with
Fukien Province in Group V.

[The Chinese accepted on the revised basis on 8 May.]

17   Japan's commitment to the war

Statement by Katō, 1917, as leader of the Kensei
(opposition) party
(Tōyō Bunkō archives)
[In 1915-16 Japan came increasingly under attack abroad
for her limited contribution to the war and her
rumoured disloyalty to the Entente.   This led to
certain statements in defence of her stand.]

As one of the Entente Powers, Japan too is engaged in
the common struggle in conjunction with her allies.
Since the war started, she has not failed to confront
the enemy wherever it was feasible or to use every
opportunity to give aid to her partners.   Among her
most remarkable achievements may be cited the capture
of Tsingtao and of the German islands north of the
equator, the exploits of her navy in the Pacific and
Indian Oceans and the Mediterranean and, on another
front, her efforts in supplying arms and ammunition
and in raising loans for the allies.   But these have
more or less been the actions of the state, sponsored
either by the government or by industrialists and
financiers.   The Japanese people has, on the whole,
had no opportunity to show its fellow-feeling for
allied war objectives, its gratitude towards the
civilians and soldiers of the Entente nations for the
heroism they have displayed in protecting human lib-
erties or its deep sense of admiration for those
wounded and disabled.   To this end Japan has sent
detachments of Red Cross surgeons and nurses to
Britain, France and Russia and has accumulated a fund
for distribution among wounded soldiers and war-
victims in allied countries....
     I use the present occasion to urge the allies to
prosecute the war with ever-increasing vigour, for the
enemy will only give in under the pressure of strong
and repeated attacks.   As the allies pursue their
struggle successfully, I ask them to believe that
Japan has offered them her goodwill and assistance
since the beginning of the war and has fully exerted
herself in supplying their requirements as far as she
was able.

18   Japan's motives in the war

Statement by Inukai Tsuyoshi,leader of Kokumintō and member of Gaikō Chōsakai, 1917
(Tōyō Bunkō archives)

Japan's motives for participating in the war are different from those of the other allies.... To Japan the war in Europe is primarily a struggle between despotism and democracy, but Japan is fighting primarily for humanity and peace so as to ensure the progress of mankind. Of course the European allies are moved by the menace of absolute monarchy and militarism; but Japan, not being exposed to those dangers to the same extent, has not so much to fear from them. She is fighting against the principle of aggression no matter whence it comes.... There was absolutely no way by which the European allies could have avoided war and left their defences secure. There was no such necessity for Japan: she decided to enter the war purely from motives of humanity and peace.

It is consequently to be regretted that an opinion prevails abroad that Japan is participating in the European war only under the obligations imposed by the terms of the Anglo-Japanese alliance. I do not deny that even in Japan there are those who believe this to be the case; but when war begins we cannot expect all the people to know the reasons for it. Some are quite indifferent to accuracy and some merely accept rumours. In any case it must be admitted that the British Alliance did have some influence on Japan's attitude after the war broke out. The people of Japan do not admit that they are in this war because of any previous agreement with any nation; ... there is no provision in the alliance obliging Japan to participate in a European war or stipulating that Japanese ships have any obligation to patrol the waters of the Mediterranean Sea. These services Japan has undertaken purely for the sake of humanity and of her own free will.... What has Japan not done in this war, that she should have done?... It is very doubtful whether any other nation in the world, with so little interest in Europe, would have done as much as Japan has done for Europe in this dreadful war.

19   The Meaning of the Ishii-Lansing Declaration

Extracts from Ishii's diary after reading Lansing's
statement to the Senate Foreign Relations committee,
1919
(Ishii, 'Gaikō Yoroku', pp. 154-8)
[Having argued that, if the Ishii-Lansing Declaration
had not recognized Japan's political 'special interests'
in China, there would have been no point in signing it
in so far as the Root-Takahira note had previously
recognized her economic interests, Ishii proceeds:]

When I am asked what are Japan's 'special interests' in
China and how does Japan possess such interests, I will
amplify the statement which I made to Lansing during
the negotiations and reply: think of the eventuality
of a major natural disaster in China or an epidemic
spreading there or internal disturbances breaking out
with no hope of their being stopped or dangerous
thoughts circulating in China with the danger of their
spreading abroad....   In such cases Europe and America
could in the last resort dispose of their property and
leave China; but Japan alone could not be satisfied
with a simple solution of that sort.   While foreign
governments would not feel themselves endangered by
calamity, epidemic, civil war or bolshevism in China,
Japan could not exist without China and the Japanese
people could not stand without the Chinese.   All these
catastrophes could spread immediately to Japan and
make her a casualty like China.   This is the basis
for Japan's special interests there.   One could call
it an inter-dependent relationship: the two are inex-
tricably bound by geography....   While western
countries can help China in order to further the
general interests of civilization and within the limits
set by it, Japan must, in addition to these factors,
assist China from considerations of her own defence.
As Japan's interests grow in relation to those of
western countries, her responsibility for China's
problems and her right to express an opinion increase....
These 'special interests' can only be understood in
political terms.   Only when the Lansing-Ishii Declaration is interpreted in this way, does it have any
raison d'etre.

20   Japan's achievements at the Paris conference

Report to the emperor by Prince Saionji, 27 August 1919
(Itō Miyoji, 'Suisō nikki', Kobayashi Tatsuo (ed.),
pp. 691-2)

About the three problems which Japan declared to be her
'essential conditions for peace', her delegates gave
deep consideration to the timing of their presentation
and the ways of securing the agreement of the Powers.
I am sad that we could not accomplish our wishes in
total.   With respect to our obtaining possession of
the South Sea islands north of the equator belonging
to Germany, the American president proposed that the
peoples of the former German territories which were
under-developed should all be put under the control of
the League of Nations.   This proved to be a stumbling-
block.   But finally it was decided by compromise that
Japan would govern these islands as part of her own
territory under the authority of the League of Nations.
This was an inevitable outcome in view of the need for
us to keep on good terms with the Powers.
     Over racial equality, we had ten private discussions
with British and American delegates who had a great
stake in this question and exchanged opinions in a
spirit of compromise.   Although we put up a good fight
in the Committee on the League covenant, there was
persistent opposition from the British colonies and the
Anglo-American delegates finally went back on their
earlier acceptance.   What more could we do?   The
Japanese delegate announced that Japan would raise
this problem again at the 5th plenary Assembly, made
clear our standpoint and left the decision to a later
date.
     The transfer of German rights in Shantung to Japan
gave rise to very extreme difficulties because of the
opposition of the Chinese plenipotentiary and the
sympathy for China of part of the American delegation.
We met the representatives of other Powers in a
tolerant and friendly spirit to explain our just
policies and to correct any misunderstandings they had.
After long negotiations the other powers finally accepted our demands fully.   Then we were able to obtain
Germany's acceptance.   But the Chinese plenipotentiaries were continuously hostile and tried to sign
the peace treaty without the clause regarding Shantung
province.   When they failed in this object, they
finally did not sign the treaty.
     In presenting this outline of events at the peace

conference, I consider that the influence of the present
conference on Japan's standing among the Powers will be
very great. Japan stands among the five great Powers
in the world and has passed the threshold which allows
her to take part in the affairs of Europe. Again, we
have been granted an important place in the League of
Nations and acquired the right to take part in future
more and more in every aspect of the affairs of east
and west. This has been achieved by the inspiration
of our Emperor and the endeavours of our people. It
can be said that we can identify a new turning-point
in Japan's history. But the progress of the world
does not stop for a moment and international changes
cannot be foreseen. Japan must therefore endeavour,
internally, to make advances in civilization (bummei)
and develop her real power while she must always maintain a just attitude externally and thus gain the
confidence of others at all times. By taking initiatives in international affairs, we must acquire weight
among the Powers and improve in future the position to
which we have lately risen.

THE SHIDEHARA AND TANAKA PERIODS, 1920-31

21 A Replacement for the Anglo-Japanese alliance
('Shidehara Kijūrō', pp. 228-9)
[The aspect of the Washington Conference with which
Shidehara was most concerned was the negotiation over
China and the Anglo-Japanese alliance. This is his
account of his role in preparing a replacement treaty,
which was marred by a long period of illness.]

The draft Three-Power treaty which was sent by the
British plenipotentiary, Balfour, to our delegation
was a scheme of political association between Japan,
Britain and America which was tantamount to an alliance
between them. It struck me that it would be a difficult matter for the United States to accept because of
her past traditions. Among the instructions given to
the Japanese delegates attending the conference relevant to the Anglo-Japanese alliance, it was stated
that 'It is probable that the Anglo-Japanese alliance
will automatically be changed to bring it in line with
the disarmament agreement or any tripartite understanding between Japan, Britain and the United States.
We need not raise any objections if the alliance is
continued in a form which incorporates these changes.
If Britain wishes to convert the disarmament agreement

or the tripartite understanding into an alliance, there
would be no objection to agreeing.'   Let us consider
Japan's standpoint on this question.   The continuance
of the Anglo-Japanese alliance had previously not
obtained the unanimous approval of the [British] Imperial
Conference and it was clear that it was not liked in
the United States either.   In view of this, even if
the Japanese government were on this occasion to ask
strongly for the alliance to be kept going, it would
only cause the British government embarrassment and
therefore be purposeless and undignified.   [Even
though Australia and New Zealand had specially argued
in favour of continuing the alliance for motives of
their own], Japan was not too anxious for the alliance
to be continued in these circumstances.   I considered
Balfour's draft while I was confined to bed and tried
to draft in its place an understanding in the form of
a consultative pact rather than a military alliance.

22   Naval aspects of the Washington Conference

Admiral Katō Tomosaburō (Washington) to Navy Vice-
minister Ide (Tokyo), 27 December 1921
('Taiheiyō Sensō e no Michi', vol. 7, pp. 3-7)

Generally what has governed my thinking at the conference has been the need to improve the bad relations
which have until now existed between Japan and the
United States.   That is, I should like as far as
possible to set to rights the many anti-Japanese
opinions in America....   At the first plenary meeting
on 12 November we heard [naval] proposals which I had
not expected.   I was surprised and realized that
important developments were afoot.   Judging from the
prevailing atmosphere, there can be no denying that
Secretary Hughes' speech was very welcome to the
delegates.   [After a period of doubt] I concluded
that we could not in any circumstances oppose the
American proposals on principle.   If we were to oppose
them, Japan would pay dearly for it later.   We had to
accept the principles while we treated the details as
a separate issue.   So I assembled the important
people in our mission and announced my conclusions....
    Since the recent world war it would appear that the
feelings among politicians about defence have generally
been the same throughout the world.   That is to say,
security is not the exclusive preserve of soldiers and
war is not something which can be made by soldiers

only. It is difficult to achieve one's objectives if
one does not operate on the basis of total mobilization of the state.   Thus, however well one arranges
munitions, one cannot put them to practical use unless
one can exploit industrial power, encourage trade and
really maximize the national strength.   Frankly, one
has to admit that, if one has no money, one cannot
make war....   We cannot find any country apart from
the United States which can supply us with a loan ...
so there is no other course open to us but to avoid
war with her....

I felt that we had to agree in principle with the
American proposals.   What would happen if there was
no success over naval limitation and competition in
naval shipbuilding continued on the lines laid down
in the existing programmes?   Though Britain has not
the power any longer to expand her great navy, she
would certainly do something.   Although American
public opinion is opposed to expansion of armaments,
America has the power, if she once feels the need, to
expand as much as she wants.   On the other hand, if
we think about Japan, our 8-8 fleet will be completed
in 1924.   (Britain is a separate case at the moment.)
Despite the fact that Japan would continue her new
building between 1924 and 1927, the United States
would not ignore Japan's new building without herself
making a fresh plan.   Japan must make up her mind
that the United States would do this.   While Japan
was experiencing the greatest financial difficulties
in completing her own 8-8 programme, she could not
cope with further American naval expansion.   It would
be difficult for us to pursue a plan to expand the
8-8 fleet after 1927.   Thus, the gap between American
and Japanese naval strength would widen more and more
and we could do nothing to narrow it.   Japan would
therefore be seriously threatened.   Though we are
not satisfied with America's so-called 10.10.6 proposals, it would still be the best policy to accept
them when we consider what would happen if naval
limitation was not achieved.

It seems to me to be necessary to arrange for a
secret committee in the Diet on some occasion and to
explain to them the meaning of all this.   We should
not mention it in public session.   This view may seem
to be rather a cowardly course to take;   but there is
no alternative to it since it is an inevitable necessity for Japan....

In these circumstances Japan agreed on the 10.10.6
ratio.   If we had held to our original demands, we

might have accomplished our wishes; but, judging from
the state of opinion at the time, we could not hope to
get Britain and America to agree. If we had pressed
our views, they would merely have adopted the method
of referring the matter to the full public assembly.
I do not need to tell you the hostile attitude American
public opinion would have taken towards Japan.

23 Playing down the American immigration crisis

Shidehara to Hanihara (Ambassador in Washington), June
1924
('NGB' 'Tai-Bei Imin mondai keika gaiyō fuzokusho')

It has seemed evident to the Japanese Government that,
for the time being, any further exchange of correspondence between the two Governments in continuation of
the discussion on ... the Immigration Act of 1924
would only tend to arouse popular agitation in both
countries and to complicate further the situation without serving any useful purpose. For this reason they
have refrained from making a reply to the note of the
Secretary of State under date of 16 June.
The Japanese Government have not, at any stage of
the question, failed to appreciate the sentiments of
friendliness and sympathy consistently manifested by
the American Government, and they are gratified to find
reassuring proof of such sentiments in the last note of
the Secretary of State.
There is, however, nothing in the development of the
question that tends to dispel from the minds of the
Japanese people the painful impression that injustice
has been done them by the recent legislation. The
Act of Congress is admittedly mandatory upon the administrative branch of the American Government, but the
Japanese Government are unable to concede that the
incident in its international aspect is now closed.
They feel it their duty to maintain the protest filed in
the note of the Japanese Ambassador of 31 May, as long
as the grounds of that protest remain unadjusted. (1)

Note

1 Japan complained against the 'discriminatory clause
   embodied in the Act, namely Section 13(c), which
   provides for the exclusion of aliens ineligible to
   citizenship, in contradistinction to other classes

of aliens, and which is manifestly intended to apply
to Japanese.... Racial distinction in the Act is
directed essentially against Japanese, since persons
of other Asiatic races are excluded under separate
enactments of prior dates'. See also Shidehara's
speech to the Diet, 8 July 1924, in N. Bamba,
'Japanese diplomacy in a dilemma', p. 214.

24 Tanaka's Reflections on Disorder in China, July 1927
('Tanaka Giichi Denki', vol. 2, pp. 652-8)

During the present unstable situation in China, there
is no denying that the actions of lawless groups (futei
bunshi) are breaking down law and order and will cause
an unfortunate international incident. The Japanese
government expects the suppression of these 'gangster
elements' and the maintenance of order by the Chinese
authorities and by the awakening of the Chinese people.
At the same time when there is a danger that Japan's
rights and interests in China and the lives and
property of Japanese nationals are illegally attacked,
there is no alternative but to preserve them by taking
such firm measures of self-defence as the situation
requires. So far as those who establish an illegal
movement of anti-Japanese boycott based on unfounded
rumours about Sino-Japanese relations are concerned,
we must dispel these doubts and, of course, take
appropriate steps for the defence of our rights.
We use the phrase 'futei bunshi' to describe people
who are communists, stir up ignorant loafers and students and resort to terrorism with a view to building
up an anti-foreign movement which will destroy order
and break up the emperor system in Japan. At present
foreigners and especially Japanese are suffering direct
damage to life and property at their hands. This is
something that Japan cannot ignore.
As Consul-general Yada said at the Eastern Conference (Tōhō kaigi), the Chinese to-day despise the
Japanese. We believe that such thinking lay behind
the riots recently. It appears that the Chinese think
that Japan can do nothing over the boycott of Japanese
goods. We must drive into the heads of the Chinese
the message that we cannot ignore the damage done to
our national honour and our interests. As Minister
Yoshizawa said the other day, the sending and withdrawing of troops should be determined by the thinking of
Japan herself. It is quite unwise to do so only when
we are afraid of boycotts. We should decide our atti-

tude in the light of the overall situation and bring it home to the Chinese authorities.

25 Tanaka's case on China

Tanaka to special emissary Uchida Yasuya, 9 August 1928 ('NGNB', vol. 2, pp. 117-19)

The Japanese government is sending you to Paris in order to sign the No war treaty [i.e. the Kellogg-Briand pact]. Since the American Secretary of State Kellogg will go there with the same object as plenipotentiary for his government, the said gentleman may use the opportunity of his stay in Europe to embark on casual discussion of the China problem and the Pacific problem which centres on China with the various foreign ministers of important signatory states gathered in Paris. Considering the state of China to-day, we do not maintain that there should be nothing like a public debate over her. In that event we refer you to the outline of our policy towards China in the enclosed note. We should like you to make every effort to explain that the Japanese government consistently upholds the principles of peace in the Far East, the maintenance of good order, the Open Door and equal opportunity and to bring home to foreign countries the Japanese government's standing in view of its exertions for the development of China over many years. In particular, recognizing that it is essential that there should be no misunderstandings in Britain and the United States over our diplomatic policy and that we should for the future continue our attitude of accommodation and cooperation over China policy, we should like you to visit these countries and, if convenient, to negotiate with the authorities.

Enclosure

1 Manchuria is an 'outer enclosure' of Japan. The changing fortunes of that country - war or peace, rise or decline - have their influence on Japan and Korea and are important for our country. In the past we did not have the least intention of invading Manchuria territorially as a protectorate. So long as order was perfectly maintained in that territory and Chinese, Japanese and Koreans could carry on without hindrance there, Japan's requirements were realistically taken care of and we did not take a narrow view of things. That is to say, it was not a question of Japanese and Koreans alone but of nationals of every country living

and working freely. To this end we have loyally
observed the principles of the Open Door and equal
opportunity. We are hoping that the Three Eastern
provinces [Manchuria] will become a territory which
is genuinely peaceful for locals and foreigners alike
to live in and will be the safest in all China and
the most progressive.

2 In order to preserve law and order in the Three
Eastern provinces, it is essential to prevent communist
groups penetrating there. If these communists were
to infiltrate, order would break down and the economic
structure would be destroyed. Not only would Manchuria be dislocated but our rule in Korea would be
impaired to a not inconsiderable extent. There is
the further danger that it would have a bad influence
on our relations with Russia.

3 In present circumstances it would from Japan's
point of view be highly undesirable to reach a compromise with the south. Fortunately Chang Hsueh-
liang has thought deeply about the various factors from
his responsibility as commander-in-chief and has of
his own volition abandoned any thought of compromise,
a satisfactory outcome for Japan. If he continues in
this way of his own free will in the future, Japan
will do what she can for him behind the scenes. By
this means Manchuria can be made into the most developed
part of China. I believe that this can be done to the
advantage of Manchurians and Japanese but also of the
whole of China....

26 Shidehara on Tanaka's China policy

Shidehara in discussion with journalists, September 1928
('Shidehara Kijūrō', pp. 365-6)

In the 52nd Diet [1926-7] I explained Japan's policy
towards China clearly under two heads: non-intervention
in her domestic affairs and maintenance of Japan's
special rights and interests there. But Tanaka's
diplomacy which professes to be a 'positive policy'
towards China has unfortunately not yet been defined.
But it is being widely declared that Tanaka diplomacy
is not a matter of combining intervention in China's
domestic affairs and promotion of our economic rights
and interests. I doubt whether the actual course
which the government has adopted in its China policy is
true to that statement. And how much success has it
had in attaining friendship between Japan and China?

Its actions have always resulted in failure.   But it
is a great mistake for the government, in order to
conceal its failure, to make the irresponsible contention that, in dealing with China, a policy of upholding
Japan's interests cannot be reconciled with one of
non-intervention in China's domestic affairs.   On the
contrary, they can be reconciled.   To bring this
about is one of the real challenges of diplomacy.

   Although the policy which I pursued as foreign
minister is spoken of as being 'negative' by the
general public, quite on the contrary, I have no hesitation in describing mine as a 'positive policy' inso-
far as it was devoted to the objective of maintaining
Japanese interests....

27   Return to Shidehara's China policy

*Shidehara's foreign policy address to 57th Diet, 21
January 1930*
('Shidehara Kijūrō', pp. 389-91)

The recent civil strife in China has had very important
disadvantages for Japan in her political and economic
relationships with that country.   Two years ago, due
to the special exertions of the Nationalist government,
the great objective of national unification was partially accomplished;   and we are the first to welcome
it.   For historical, geographical and other reasons,
the peaceful unification of the whole country cannot
be expected in a day....   In the unsettled circumstances which may arise again from now on, there is no
other course for us but to offer our sympathy to those
who are trying to solve the present troubles and to
pray for their success.   Our concern is that, when
any country faces similar difficulties, the authorities
are inclined to divert the people's attention from
domestic problems to foreign problems;   and history
shows that the temptation to take an adventurous policy
in foreign relations is strong....   I can only hope
that China's statesmen will not succumb to this temptation and will prepare the way for their country's future
by means of steady and proper policies.   There are
various assessments of the state of Sino-Japanese relations in future.   There is the pessimistic view that,
however proper Japan may be, China can never match
this and, led on by internal factors, will increasingly
adopt a disrespectful attitude towards us and we may
expect relations to deteriorate further.   Then there

is the optimistic view that perhaps in their hearts the
Chinese people hold deep suspicions and misunderstandings
about Japan; but, when the roots are uncovered, there
is no ground for them; so if we could only bring home
adequately to the Chinese our true sentiments, the relationship between us would gradually improve.   Moreover,
as the domestic standing of the Kuomintang government
becomes stronger, its policy abroad will revert to the
middle way of moderation.

It is not for me to come down in favour of one or
other of these assessments.   But we have decided that,
however China treats us, we shall use every endeavour
to regulate relations between our two countries in
accordance with what we believe to be just and fair.
In various respects, Sino-Japanese relations have to
be particularly close; and it is inevitable that many
diplomatic issues should automatically arise between
us.   Some of these issues may irritate our people,
while others may irritate the Chinese.   But there can
be no doubt that, if we consider the fortunes of our
two nations in future, we both must go forward in co-
operation, even politically.   The fact that cases
where our true and permanent interests conflict with
one another do not exist while cases which confer
mutual benefits are many is a powerful guarantee that
the two countries will henceforth draw closer
together.

[When we turn to the question of the 'unequal'
treaties,] internal peace and order have not existed
in China for some time, central ordinances have not
been carried out at local level, the lives and property
of foreigners resident there have been increasingly
threatened and the provisions of the treaties in-
fringed.   One cannot fail to recognize that these
facts seriously weaken the grounds for the Chinese
people's claim for the abolition of the so-called unequal treaties.   It goes without saying that every
country must, as an ordinary duty, try to protect the
safety of its nationals abroad and their important
economic interests.   On the other hand, if one con-
siders the matter from China's point of view, one can
fully appreciate how painful the existence of the
unequal treaties is for the Chinese people.   The fact
that various eastern countries subject to similar
treaties have recently been released from their provisions, must plainly have given Chinese sensitivities
even greater offence.   For Japan to continue with
these treaties indefinitely in spite of the dissatisfaction of the Chinese people is certainly not a

constructive policy.   When Japan which had the same
experiences as China sees her being subjected to one-
sided limitations on her sovereignty, she should as
a friendly neighbouring state co-operate to remove
this slur without delay in some way....

THE UCHIDA PERIOD, 1931-3

28   Recognition of Manchukuo

*Foreign Minister Uchida's address to the Diet on
23 August 1932*
('Uchida Yasuya', pp. 353-4)

There are those who think that the creation of Manchukuo was the result of our military actions and
want to place the responsibility for it on Japan.
These people do not understand the facts and are
beyond our comprehension.   Again there are those who
see that there are many Japanese employed by the Manchukuo government and deduce that there must be some
connection between Japan and the founding of the new
state.   But there are many examples of a developing
country at its foundation making use of the skills of
foreigners.   Even Japan has employed many foreigners
as officials and advisers since the Meiji restoration,
the number around the year 1875 being over the 500
mark.   Those who draw these inferences from the fact
that individual Japanese are working for the Manchukuo
government are misconstruing the evidence.
     Manchukuo was set up as a result of separatist move-
ments in China herself.   But there are those who
claim that the recognition by Japan of the new state,
created in this way, is a violation of the terms of
the [Washington] Nine-Power treaty [of 1922].   I
find this argument very difficult to understand.   The
Nine-Power treaty does not prohibit separatist activities in China or, for that matter, prevent the
inhabitants of one part of China setting up an independent country of their own free will.   Thus, even
if Japan, which was a signatory of the Washington
Nine-Power treaty, recognized Manchukuo which has
been established in accordance with the desires of the
people of Manchuria and Mongolia, it would not be in
breach of the terms of that treaty.   But it would be
quite another matter if we assumed that Japan had in
mind to annex Manchuria and Mongolia or perhaps to
satisfy her territorial appetites in that area.

There is no need to reiterate here once again that
Japan has no territorial designs on Manchuria and
Mongolia.   On all this evidence I believe that Japan's
attitude towards China and especially the steps taken
since the episode of 18 September [1931] have been
just and lawful.

29   Japan's case before the League of Nations
(Digest of the Japanese government's observations on
the Lytton Commission report, an extract from the conclusion, 20 November 1932.)
Among foreign nationals in China the Japanese have
sustained the greatest damage from the anarchy in the
country and its anti-foreign policy.   In Manchuria
Japan's special position, economically, politically
and strategically (in so far as her own security is
concerned), is quite exceptional and is unprecedented
in other parts of the world.   But a number of intrigues have come to light in recent years, especially
after Marshal Chang Hsueh-liang threw in his lot with
Nanking, in order to undermine Japan's special position in Manchuria.   Despite Japan's efforts to
improve the situation, the flagrant challenge to her
rights and interests created an alarming state of
tension in the country.
   The events of 18 September [Mukden incident] took
place in these tense circumstances;   and the measures
which Japanese troops took at that time and later were
not excessive from the standpoint of self-defence.
A movement calling for maintaining the frontier
against China and ensuring peace grew out of the situation of Manchuria which has always been geographically
and historically separated from China and out of the
widespread opposition to the autocracy of Chang Tso-lin
and Chang Hsueh-liang.   This movement and that for
the restoration of the Manchus brought about the
creation of Manchukuo with the spontaneous support of
the population.   The attitude of Japan to the new
state and her formal recognition of it do not violate
any international engagements.
   The Lytton Commission recognized the abnormal nature
of the problem: 'a mere restoration of the status quo
ante (before 18 September) would be no solution'; 'to
restore these conditions would merely be to invite a
repetition of the trouble'.   Yet it considered 'the
maintenance and recognition of the new regime in Manchuria equally unsatisfactory' as a solution.   The
Japanese government, for its part, is convinced that

the recognition of Manchukuo contravenes none of the
principles of international obligation, satisfies the
aspirations of the Manchurian people and could probably in the future gain the acquiescence of China
herself.   Japan, because of her special position in
Manchuria, cannot afford to leave her in a state of
instability and concludes that the recognition of Manchukuo [by all powers] is the only way of stabilizing
the situation in Manchuria and ensuring peace in the
far east.

30   Japan's Withdrawal from the League of Nations

*Uchida to Secretary-general of the League of Nations,
27 March 1933 (as approved by the Privy Council)*
('League of Nations Official Journal', 14 of no. 5
(May 1933), pp. 657-8.   'NGNB', vol. 2, pp. 268-9.)

It is and has always been the conviction of the
Japanese Government that, in order to render possible
the maintenance of peace in various regions of the
world, it is necessary in existing circumstances to
allow the operation of the Covenant of the League to
vary in accordance with the actual conditions prevailing in each of those regions.... Acting on this
conviction, the Japanese Government, ever since the
Sino-Japanese dispute was, in September 1931, submitted to the League, have, at meetings of the League
and on other occasions, continually set forward a
consistent view: [namely that the League] should
acquire a complete grasp of the actual conditions in
this quarter of the globe and apply the Covenant of
the League in accordance with these conditions.   They
have repeatedly emphasized and insisted upon the
absolute necessity of taking into consideration the
fact that China is not an organized state;   that its
internal conditions and external relations are charac-
terized by extreme confusion and complexity and by
many abnormal and exceptional features;   and that,
accordingly, the general principles and usages of
international law which govern the ordinary relations
between nations are found to be considerably modified
in their operation so far as China is concerned,
resulting in the quite abnormal and unique international
practices which actually prevail in that country.
    The report adopted by the [League] Assembly at the
special session of 24 February last, entirely mis-
apprehending the spirit of Japan, pervaded as it is by

no other desire than the maintenance of peace in the
Orient, contains gross errors both in the ascertain-
ment of facts and in the conclusions deduced.   In
asserting that the action of the Japanese army at
the time of the incident of 18 September and subsequently did not fall within the just limits of self-
defence, the report assigned no reasons and came to
an arbitrary conclusion, and in ignoring alike the
state of tension which preceded, and the various
aggravations which succeeded, the incident - for all
of which the full responsibility is incumbent upon
China - the report creates a source of fresh conflict
in the political arena of the Orient.   By refusing to
acknowledge the actual circumstances that led to the
foundation of Manchukuo, and by attempting to challenge
the position taken up by Japan in recognizing the new
State, it cuts away the ground for the stabilization
of the Far Eastern situation.   Nor can the terms laid
down in its recommendations - as was fully explained
in the statement issued by this Government on 25
February last - ever be of any possible service in
securing enduring peace in these regions.

The conclusion must be that, in seeking a solution
of the question, the majority of the League have
attached greater importance to upholding inapplicable
formulas than to the real need of assuring peace, and
higher value to the vindication of academic theses
than to the eradication of the sources of future conflict.   For these reasons, and because of the profound
differences of opinion existing between Japan and the
majority of the League in their interpretation of the
Covenant and of other treaties, the Japanese Government
have been led to realize the existence of an irreconcilable divergence of views, dividing Japan and the
League on policies of peace, and especially as regards
the fundamental principles to be followed in the
establishment of a durable peace in the Far East.
The Japanese Government, believing that, in these
circumstances, there remains no room for further co-
operation, hereby gives notice, in accordance with the
provisions of Article I, paragraph 3, of the Covenant,
of the intention of Japan to withdraw from the League
of Nations.

THE HIROTA PERIOD, 1933-7

31 Japan approaches the end of Naval Limitation

Cabinet resolution of 7 September 1934
('Taiheiyō sensō e no michi', vol. 1, pp. 157-8.)
[Admiral Okada who became prime minister on 8 July,
was immediately asked to authorize naval building.   In
a statement of government policy on 20 July, he declared:
'Since national defence is an essential factor in the
survival of a state, we plan to improve ours in keeping
with the requirements of the period.   At the naval
limitation conference which will be opened shortly, we
shall take as our first principle the maintenance of
national security and endeavour to accomplish it
through fair and appropriate policies.'   After discussion on 7 September, the cabinet resolved to
instruct their delegates to the London preparatory conference as follows:]

1 Under the principle of ratios which prevails at
present, the countries with lower ratios [i.e. France,
Italy and Japan] are threatened by countries with
higher ratios; hence we should denounce the ratios;
2 In replacement of the ratio principle, we should
advocate the principle of uniform aggregate naval tonnage [which later came to be referred to at the conferences as 'the common upper limit on overall
tonnage'];
3 In conformity with the spirit of disarmament, we
should limit the forces possessed by all countries to
what is enough for their defence but not enough for
them to make attacks and we should concentrate on arms
for defence while at the same time abolishing arms for
attack [by this Japan appears to have meant 'aircraft
carriers and battleships'];
4 We should get rid of, and extricate ourselves from,
the Washington, London and other treaties which are not
of advantage to us.   [The cabinet agreed to negotiate
before abrogating.]

32 Revised 'Fundamentals of National Policy', 7 August
1936 (as approved at the five-minister conference)
('NGNB', vol. 2, pp. 344-5, Yoshii; 'Shōwashi gaikōshi',
p. 245.)

I The basis of national policy is the need to consolidate national development internally and increase our

prestige internationally through fairness and justice. Japan as the force for stability in east Asia in name and in fact must ensure the peace of the area and contribute to the well-being of men throughout the world, thereby living up to the ideals of the founding of our nation. Considering Japan's situation at home and abroad, the basic policies which she must adopt are to secure her position on the east Asian continent both diplomatically and militarily. The fundamental principles are as follows:

1 Japan must endeavour to eliminate the aggressive policies of the Powers in east Asia and share with people there cordial relations which are founded on the principles of co-existence and co-prosperity. This will be a manifestation of the spirit of the Imperial Way and a guiding light which we must use in pursuing our foreign policy.

2 Japan must complete her defence and armament programmes in order to guarantee her security and progress. Only thus can her position as a force for stability in east Asia be accomplished in name and in fact.

3 The basis of our continental policy must be to cope with the threat from the Soviet Union in the north in order to assure healthy development in Manchukuo and Japan-Manchukuo defence and, meanwhile, to plan our economic expansion by creating a strong coalition between Japan, Manchukuo and China against Britain and the United States. In bringing this about, we must bear in mind the need for cordial relations with other Powers.

4 We plan social and economic developments in the South Seas (Nampō Kaiyō), especially in the Outer Nanyō area, and contemplate the extension of our power by modest and peaceful means, avoiding clashes with other Powers. Thereby, we may anticipate the coming to fruition of Japan as a nation and the full development of Manchukuo.

II Adopting these fundamentals as our criteria, we must reconcile our internal and external policies and bring our administration into line with present day needs in the following ways:

1 In tackling Japan's security and armaments, the army must aim at dealing with the forces which Soviet Russia can deploy in the far east and increasing its garrisons in Kwantung and Korea so as to strike the first blow in the event of war breaking out with Soviet far eastern forces.

2 The navy must aim at building up forces adequate to maintain ascendancy in the west Pacific against the American fleet.

With a view to the harmonious application of these
fundamental policies, our foreign policy must be co-
ordinated and amended.   In order to enable beneficial
and smooth progress to be made over diplomatic activities, the military should try to help through private
channels, without assuming any public role [Part III,
covering in the main financial and commercial policies,
is omitted].

THE KONOE AND MATSUOKA PERIODS, 1937-41

33   Konoe's Thoughts on his cabinet experiences, 1938
(Yabe Sadaji, 'Konoe Fumimaro', Tokyo: Kōbundō, 1952,
2 vols, vol. 2, pp. 74-5)

The conclusions that I draw from my experience as
prime minister, especially during my first administration, are that my cabinet was predestined to be a
fence-sitting one and was not backed by public opinion.
The rights of the state [kokumuken] and the rights of
the military [tōsuiken] were entirely separate as if
they were distinct phenomena;   what brought the two
together was the link supplied by the presence of the
army minister in the cabinet.   Moreover, the army
minister, who was very vague [Sugiyama], had the power
to bring down the cabinet at any time.   Government
and the formulation of national policies could only
be conducted weakly under the shadow of military intervention.   Domestic and foreign policy was decided
upon, amended and rejected at the whim of the military
which was by this time totally alienated from public
opinion.   Because of my desire to act as far as
possible within the context of political responsibility,
I often asked the service ministers for some elucida-
tion of the truths behind the will of the military
which were so hard to grasp.   In order to bring about
a change in policy towards China, I appointed General
Ugaki Kazushige as foreign minister [May to September
1938] but his approach to the China question was again
destroyed by military intervention.
      Eventually I cleared my cabinet of its reputation
for fence-sitting by taking responsibility for the enlargement of the China Incident.   I tried to restrain
the military by an appeal to public opinion.   In
January 1938 when I issued the 'Aite ni sezu' declaration, it was my hope to overcome the charge of fence-
sitting.   Meanwhile, the political parties having
been in decline since the Incidents of 15 May 1932 and

26 February 1936, it was not possible to control the
military by the strength of any one party by itself.
I thus concluded that it would only be possible to
restrain the military and solve the China Incident
when we could form a cabinet whose strength depended
on something more than the existing political parties,
on some organization with its roots penetrating the
whole Japanese nation.   It was my greatest desire
when my first cabinet resigned [January 1939] and
when my second cabinet was being formed [July 1940] to
see how our nation could be re-styled in some such
way.   [In order to realize this New Order through
this 'organization of the people', I set out to
organize the Imperial Rule Assistance Association
(Taisei Yokusankai).]

34   New Order in East Asia, 1938
(Extract from the conclusion to Kawai Tatsuo, 'Hatten
Nihon no Mokuhyō', Tokyo: Chūō Koronsha, February
1938, pp. 151-6)
[Kawai was head of the Information Bureau of the
Foreign Ministry and a member of the Renovationist
clique, which, while not typical, was growing in
influence.]

Japan's power of stabilizing east Asia will lead inevitably to the collapse of the Washington Nine Power
treaty and thus serve an important purpose in world
history.   Between 1922 when the treaty was signed and
to-day when Japan has built up her own axis in the
east, the world has radically changed and no Asian
problem can be solved without recognizing Japan's axis
in the north Pacific.   This axis will not permit
Japan morally to leave China permanently in the turmoil created by the Powers or to let her continue in
a feudal backwater as a semi-colony being systematically exploited....   The spirit of Asia which has
rested in a deep sleep for centuries first arose as
a fresh living force in Japan by her contacts with
western civilization.   Truly the China Incident opens
the main chapter in the story of the Asiatic race....
    The Asian peoples must turn their backs on the self-
centred individualistic materialism of Europe, accept
the common ideals of Asia and devote themselves to
lives rooted in Asia.   Confucian doctrines that were
evolved in China and perfected in Japan have supplied
the raison d'etre for the union of Japan, Manchukuo and
China by their awesome message of 'self-control and

mutual civility' which might be regarded as applying equally to our needs in these times.

35   Matsuoka's conception of Japan's mission

Matsuoka's letter to Winston Churchill, 22 April 1941
(Tokyo: Ministry of Foreign Affairs archives)
[This is written in reply to Churchill's letter of 12 April in 'NGNB', vol. 2, pp. 489-90 which suggests 'a few questions which deserve the attention of the Imperial Japanese government and people', notably:
'(4) If the United States entered the war at the side of Great Britain and Japan ranged herself with the Axis Powers, would not the naval superiority of the two English-speaking nations enable them to deal with Japan while disposing of the Axis Powers in Europe?...
From the answers to these questions may spring the avoidance by Japan of a serious catastrophe and a marked improvement in the relations between Japan and Great Britain, the great sea Power of the West.'
Churchill, 'The Second World War', vol. 3, pp. 167-71.]

I have just come back from my trip [to Europe] and hasten to acknowledge the receipt of a paper, handed to me at Moscow on the evening of the 12th instant by Sir Stafford Cripps ... I wish to express my appreciation for the facilities with which your Government made efforts to provide our Ambassador [Shigemitsu] when he wanted to meet me on the [European] continent. I was keenly disappointed when I learned that he could not come.
    Your Excellency may rest assured that the foreign policy of Japan is determined upon after an unbiased examination of all the facts and a very careful weighing of all the elements of the situation she confronts, always holding steadfastly in view the great racial aim and ambition of finally bringing about on earth the conditions envisaged in what she calls 'Hakkō Ichiu', the Japanese conception of a universal peace under which there would be no conquest, no oppression, no exploitation of any and all peoples.   And, once determined, I need hardly tell Your Excellency, it will be carried out with resolution but with utmost circumspection, taking in every detail of the changing circumstances.

36 Japan's motives for war

Imperial Rescript on the declaration of war, 8 December 1941
(Official translation from 'Osaka Mainichi Shimbun')

We hereby declare war on the United States of America and the British Empire.... The entire nation with a united will shall mobilize its total strength so that nothing will miscarry in the attainment of our war aims: to insure the stability of East Asia and to contribute to world peace is the farsighted policy which was formulated by our Great Illustrious Imperial Grandsire and Our Great Imperial Sire succeeding Him, and which we lay constantly to heart; to cultivate friendship among nations and to enjoy prosperity in common with all nations has always been the guiding principle of Our Empire's foreign policy. It has been truly unavoidable and far from Our wishes that Our Empire has now been brought to cross swords with America and Britain.

More than four years have passed since China, failing to comprehend the true intentions of Our Empire, and recklessly courting trouble, disturbed the peace of east Asia and compelled Our Empire to take up arms. Although there has been reestablished the National Government of China, with which Japan has effected neighbourly intercourse and co-operation, the regime which has survived at Chungking, relying upon American and British protection, still continues its fratricidal opposition.

Eager for the realization of their inordinate ambition to dominate the Orient, both America and Britain, giving support to the Chungking regime, have aggravated the disturbances in east Asia. Moreover, these two Powers, inducing other countries to follow suit, increased military preparations on all sides of Our Empire to challenge us. They have obstructed by every means our peaceful commerce, and finally resorted to a direct severance of economic relations, menacing gravely the existence of Our Empire.

Patiently have We waited and long have We endured in the hope that Our Government might retrieve the situation in peace, but Our adversaries, showing not the least spirit of conciliation, have unduly delayed a settlement; and in the meantime, they have intensified the economic and political pressure to compel thereby Our Empire to submission....

37 Limitations on the Foreign Ministry's role
(Nishi Haruhiko, 'Kaisō no Nihon gaikō', pp. 114-15;
pp. 126-8.)

[The Foreign Ministry fitted badly into the Japanese
state as it was developing in the late 1930s. In
this extract from Vice-minister Nishi's autobiography,
he illustrates the attempts made by Tōjō and others
to limit the role of the Foreign Ministry which did
not enjoy their confidence.]

After the resignation of the Konoe cabinet on 16 October
1941, Tōjō was instructed to form its successor and
Tōgō Shigenori entered the cabinet as foreign minister.
At his request I became his vice-minister. Since
Tōgō was not a man who belonged to the mainstream of
the Foreign Ministry, those who knew him intimately
were few. I was a person from the same prefecture
as Tōgō [Kagoshima]; I had as head of the first
section during Tōgō's tenure as head of the European
and Asian section [O-A kyokuchō] conducted the negotiations for purchasing the North Manchurian railway;
and I had held the fishery talks in Moscow during
Tōgō's period as ambassador there [1938-40]. In
these ways I was relatively close to him. I thought
that, since Tōgō was inclined to take a severe attitude towards everyone, it would be good if I could act
as a cushion between him and the departmental heads
in the ministry in order not to alarm them. But I
felt that, if there was someone that Tōgō wanted to
choose as vice-minister, it was better that he should
make the necessary approaches. So I did not call on
him to offer my congratulations even when he took up
his appointment. But a messenger came from Tōgō and
asked whether I would become his vice-minister. I
replied that I was ready to do my utmost to serve him
and that I left the decision to the minister. At the
moment I became vice-minister, I knew absolutely
nothing about the course of the talks which were then
going on with the Americans. Since they were a state
secret and were certainly not discussed outside the
circle of those involved, Tōgō himself entered the
cabinet with only a fragmentary knowledge of them....
    [After the war began, the campaigns in south-east
Asia got under way.] Since the consequences of the
start of hostilities were great, we set up a Greater
East Asian Establishment Enquiry Commission [Dai Tō-A
kensetsu shingikai] and obtained the services of

Fujiyama Aiichirō and other civilians and discussed
fairly often whether to grant the occupied territories
their independence, how to deal with them etc.   It
was decided to send a civilian commissioner to the
occupied territories; we secured the appointment in
connection with the Foreign Ministry of Hayashi
Kyūjirō as commissioner to the army in Java and of
Inoue Kōjirō as commissioner to the navy in Borneo.

In August 1942 arose the problem of setting up the
Greater East Asian Ministry.   That is to say, a
Greater East Asian Ministry was to be established and
the various territories of east Asia which were almost
all territories occupied by Japan were to be placed
under its jurisdiction, while they were to be excluded
from the purview of the Foreign Ministry.

Our ministry opposed this plan strongly on the two
grounds that for Japan to deal with east Asian countries
through a different ministry from other countries would
destroy the essential unity of her diplomacy and that
the peoples of east Asia who were seeking their independence would feel that they were being regarded in
this proposal as dependencies so that Japan would not
be able to procure their cooperation in the war effort.
It resembled the [abortive] attempt in 1939 to set up
a Trade Ministry [Bōekishō].   But this time it was
during the war and there was even a rumour that, if
there was any repetition of our previous opposition,
the army would surround the Foreign Ministry.   On
this occasion those in the ministry did not stand up
for their views as a united body and left the matter
to be resolved in ordinary negotiations.

But the discussions did not go well.   Eventually
Foreign Minister Tōgō sparred with Premier Tōjō for
about three hours at a cabinet on 1 September 1942,
arguing forcefully as he had already done that diplomacy would become impossible under the new arrangements
and that they would have a bad influence on the
peoples of east Asia.   The other ministers hardly
said a thing.   No agreement was reached.   During an
interval the foreign minister returned to his official
residence nearby.   It appears that the prime minister
had called for his personal resignation and Tōgō had
refused.

Before Tōgō had set off for this cabinet, two or
three of us had gone to his residence and recommended
that, even if his individual resignation were called
for, he should not accept but should stick to his guns.
At that Tōgō made a gloomy face; but things worked
out that way in the end.   Finance Minister Kaya Okinori

called on Tōgō at his residence and recommended him to resign; but he took no notice. General Mutō Akira, the head of the army Military Affairs Bureau [gummu kyokuchō], also visited him but did not alter his resolve. After that the navy minister, Admiral Shimada Shigetarō, finally came and said that the palace did not want a cabinet crisis at this moment. When it came to this, it was unbearable for Tōgō to trouble the emperor more than he had already been troubled though it was also highly regrettable to resign. So Tōgō gave up as foreign minister and I simultaneously resigned as vice-minister.

The complexities of this episode will be found in the diary of Marquis Kido Kōichi ['Kido nikki']. Probably Tōjō went to the palace when the cabinet was in recess and told the emperor that there was no alternative but to offer the resignation of the full cabinet. The emperor was taken aback and replied that he would be in difficulties. The emperor thought that this was a critical juncture but did not know in detail about the proceedings of Tōjō's administration.

[After the resignations, Tōjō set up in November the Greater East Asian Ministry which ate into many of the traditional functions of the Foreign Ministry and furthered the notion of Greater East Asian co-prosperity.]

Notes

INTRODUCTION

1 'Shidehara Kijūrō' (Tokyo: Shidehara Heiwa Zaidan, 1955), p. 497. Shidehara to Ohira, 4 June 1935.
2 Hagihara Nobutoshi (ed.), 'Mutsu Munemitsu' in 'Nihon no meicho, 35 (Tokyo: Chūō Kōronsha, 1973), p. 58.
3 M.D. Kennedy, 'The estrangement of Great Britain and Japan, 1917-35' (Manchester, 1969), p. 7.

CHAPTER 1 THE IWAKURA PERIOD

1 The main source on Iwakura's own writing is Tada Komon (ed.), 'Iwakura Kō Jikki' (Tokyo, 1927-35, 3 vols) [Hereafter 'Iwakura Jikki']. 'Meiji Japan through Contemporary Sources' (Tokyo: Tōyō Bunko, 1969-72, 3 vols) gives a wide range of translations of Japanese writings in domestic and foreign affairs. The main studies in English are the various works of Marlene Mayo; E. Soviak, On the nature of western progress: the Journal of the Iwakura Embassy, in D.H. Shively, 'Tradition and Modernization in Japanese Culture' (Princeton, 1972), pp. 7-34; and, an older work, J. Morris, 'Makers of Japan' (London, 1906), pp. 154-62.
2 'Iwakura Jikki', vol. 2, pp. 68-9.
3 Ibid., vol. 1, pp. 383-7; also vol. 2, pp. 68-9. W.G. Beasley, 'Select Documents on Japanese Foreign Policy, 1853-68' (London, 1955), no. 31.
4 Quoted in Marlene Mayo, Rationality in the Meiji restoration: the Iwakura embassy, in H. Harootunian and B. Silberman, 'Modern Japanese Leadership' (Tucson, 1966), p. 339. 'Iwakura Jikki', vol. 2, pp. 696-701.
5 'Nihon Gaikō nempyō narabi ni shuyō bunsho' (Tokyo:

Foreign Ministry, 2 vols, 1955) vol. 1, documents, 10 January 1868 [Hereafter 'NGNB'].

6 'Gaimushō no 100-nen' (Tokyo: Hara Shobō, 1969, 2 vols) vol. 1, p. 87. The designations, gaimu daijin (foreign minister) and Gaimushō (Foreign Ministry), were not adopted till 1885.

7 Jōyaku kaisei torishirabe gakari, the official in charge of examining treaty revision.

8 I.P. Hall, 'Mori Arinori' (Cambridge, Mass., 1972), chs 8-9.

9 Like Shinagawa Yajirō (1843-1900), who was consul in Germany (1874-6) and minister (1886-7). Another case is Hatoyama Kazuo (1856-1911), who studied at Yale (1875-80) and was put in charge of Treaty Revision (chōsakyokuchō) under Foreign Minister Inoue. Turning more to politics, he became speaker of the house of representatives in 1896 and foreign vice-minister (1898), before becoming president of Waseda university.

10 F.V. Dickins and S. Lane-Poole, 'The life of Sir Harry Parkes' (London, 1894, 2 vols), vol. 2, p. 183.

11 'Iwakura jikki', vol. 2, pp. 68-9.

12 Tsunoda Ryūsaku (ed.), 'Sources of the Japanese tradition' (New York, 1958), pp. 658-62.

13 Mayo, Rationality in the Meiji Restoration, in Harootunian and Silberman, pp. 323-62.

14 For interesting extracts from the Iwakura report, Soviak, Journal of the Iwakura embassy in Shively, pp. 7-34.

15 S. Mossman, 'New Japan' (London, 1873), p. 443. Remember his observation: 'What did we learn regarding their country? ... little or nothing.'

16 Ibid., 'New Japan', p. 433.

17 Marlene Mayo, The Korean crisis of 1873 and early Meiji foreign policy,in 'Journal of Asian Studies', 31 (1972), pp. 795-7 [Hereafter 'JAS'].

18 Ibid., p. 818.

19 J.J. Stephan, 'Sakhalin: a history' (London, 1971), pp. 62-4.

20 Tokutomi Iichirō, 'Kōshaku Yamagata Aritomo den' (Tokyo, 1933, 3 vols), vol. 1, p. 302.

21 F.H. Conroy, 'The Japanese Seizure of Korea, 1868-1910' (Philadelphia, 1960), ch. 2.

22 M. Iwata, 'Okubo Toshimichi: the Bismarck of Japan' (Berkeley, 1964), pp. 163-73; A. Iriye, 'Pacific Estrangement' (Cambridge, Mass., 1972), pp. 17-18.

CHAPTER 2   THE MUTSU PERIOD

1   Mutsu's writing, Kenkenroku [Record of an uphill
    struggle], appeared in Mutsu Hirokichi (ed.),
    'Hakushaku Mutsu Munemitsu ikō' (Tokyo: Iwanami,
    1929);   as 'Kenkenroku' (Tokyo: Iwanami, 1939);
    and in Hagihara Nobutoshi (ed.], 'Mutsu Munemitsu'
    in the series, 'Nihon no Meicho, 35' (Tokyo: Chūō
    Kōronsha, 1973).   It had earlier been banned from
    publication.   Mutsu is the subject of a number of
    essays, including M.B. Jansen, Mutsu Munemitsu, in
    A.M. Craig and D.H. Shively (eds), 'Personality in
    Japanese history' (Berkeley, 1970), pp. 309-34;
    Hagihara Nobutoshi, Mutsu Munemitsu, in Kamishima
    Jirō (ed.], 'Kenryoku no Shisō' (Tokyo: Chikuma
    Shobō, 1965), pp. 123-57;   and Shinobu Seizaburō,
    'Mutsu Gaikō: Nisshin sensō no gaikō shiteki
    kenkyū' (Tokyo: Sobunkaku, 1935) and 'Mutsu
    Munemitsu' (Tokyo: Hakuyōsha, 1938).
2   D.H. Shively, 'The Japanization of the middle
    Meiji' in Shively (ed.), 'Tradition and Moderniza-
    tion' (Princeton, 1972), pp. 89-100;   117-19.
3   The system here described held good in the main
    until the new constitution was introduced in 1947.
4   The leading studies of treaty revision are to be
    found in the various writings of Inō Tentarō,
    Hirose Shizuko, Shimomura Fujio, and the older work
    of Yamamoto Shigeru.   The leading authority in
    English is F.C. Jones, 'Extraterritoriality in
    Japan and the diplomatic relations resulting in its
    abolition, 1853-99' (New Haven, 1931), whose work
    has never been superseded.
5   For more detail about the diplomatic implications
    Nish, Japan reverses the unequal treaties, 'Journal
    of Oriental Studies' (Hongkong), 3 (1975), pp. 137-
    45.
6   On the Sino-Japanese war, there are the older
    Japanese works like Tabohashi Kiyoshi, 'Nisshin
    seneki gaikōshi no kenkyū' (Tokyo: Tōkō, 1951) and
    Shinobu Seizaburō, 'Mutsu gaikōshi';   but the most
    recent account will be found in 'Gaimushō no 100-
    nen' (Tokyo: Hara Shobō, 1969, 2 vols), vol. 1,
    ch. 2(2).   In English, there is, in addition to
    Conroy, 'The Japanese Seizure of Korea, 1868-1910'
    (Philadelphia, 1960), chs 5-6, F.W. Ikle, Triple
    Intervention: Japan's lesson in the Diplomacy of
    Imperialism, 'Monumenta Nipponica', 22 (1967),
    pp. 122-30.
7   Conroy, p. 222.

8 'Gaimushō no 100-nen', vol. 1, pp. 309-10.
9 Ibid., vol. 1, p. 319.
10 N. Rich and M.H. Fisher (eds), 'The Holstein papers'
    (London, 1955-63, 4 vols), nos 470 and 458.
11 Hagihara, 'Mutsu (Kenkenroku)', pp. 258-9.
12 'Gaimushō no 100-nen', vol. 1, pp. 288 ff and 350 ff.
    A.M. Pooley (ed.), 'The secret memoirs of Count
    Tadasu Hayashi' (London, 1915), p. 43.

CHAPTER 3   THE AOKI PERIOD

1 'Aoki Shūzō jiden' (Tokyo: Heibonsha, 1970) edited
   by Sakane Yoshihisa, p. 111.   Professor Sakane has
   also written of 'Aoki Shūzō' in 'Kokusai Seiji', 1
   (1966), pp. 10-26.   Undoubtedly the 'jiden' is a
   most important work and is one of the rare works on
   Aoki but the coverage of the later 1890s is thinner
   than for earlier periods.
2 'Nihon Gaikō Bunsho' (Tokyo: 1936-), vol. 23,
   p. 539 [Hereafter 'NGB'].   R.F. Hackett, 'Yamagata
   Aritomo in the Rise of Modern Japan, 1838-1922'
   (Cambridge, Mass., 1972), pp. 145-6.
3 Barbara Teters, The Otsu affair: the formation of
   Japan's judicial conscience, in D. Wurfel (ed.),
   'Meiji Japan's centennial: aspects of political
   thought and action' (Lawrence, Kansas, 1971),
   pp. 36-60.
4 'Aoki jiden', pp. 272-6.
5 On Aoki's relations with Mutsu and others, 'Gaimushō
   no 100-nen' (Tokyo: Hara Shobō, 1929, 2 vols), vol.
   1, pp. 335-50, which shows Aoki's poor reading of
   the German mind.
6 The treaties in general came into operation on 17
   July but those for France and Austria only took
   effect on 4 August.
7 'Aoki jiden', pp. 329-35; Tokutomi Iichirō,
   'Kōshaku Yamagata Aritomo den' (Tokyo, 1933, 3 vols),
   vol. 3, p. 407; Nish, Japan's indecision during
   the Boxer disturbances, 'JAS', 20 (1961), pp. 449-
   61.
8 Ibid., pp. 333-4.
9 G.A. Lensen, 'The Russo-Chinese war' (Tallahassee,
   Florida, 1967).
10 'NGB', 31/I, no. 437.
11 'NGB', 33, bekkan, 'Hokushin jihen', i, no. 2370.
12 Kamikawa Hikomatsu (ed.), 'Nikkan gaikō shiryō
    shūsei', vol. 8, pp. 406-7.
13 'Aoki jiden', pp. 337-8.

14 A more detailed account is given in Nish, 'JAS', 20 (1961), pp. 456-61 and Kawamura Kazuo, Aoki gaisō no Kankoku ni kanren suru tai-Ro kyōkō seisaku, in 'Chōsen Gakuhō', 63 (1972), pp. 129-38.
15 'NGB', 33, no. 930. Aoki to Inoue (Berlin), 5 October 1900.
16 Nish, 'Alliance in Decline, 1908-23' (London, 1972), pp. 32-6.
17 Pooley (ed.), 'The Secret memoirs of Count Tadasu Hayashi' (London, 1915), p. 8.
18 'Aoki jiden', pp. 356-7. For a suggestive study on Aoki's propensity to work the press, see R.B. Valliant, The Selling of Japan, 1900-5, 'Monumenta Nipponica', 29 (1974), pp. 415-21.

CHAPTER 4 THE KOMURA PERIOD

1 The central works in Japanese are 'Komura gaikōshi' (Tokyo: Foreign Ministry, 1953, 2 vols) and Tsunoda Jun, 'Manshū mondai to kokubō hōshin' (Tokyo: Hara Shobō, 1967). The central work in English is 'The Japanese Oligarchy and the Russo-Japanese War' by Okamoto Shumpei (London, 1970), who is understood to be preparing a more detailed work on Komura.
2 Shinobu Jumpei, 'Nidai gaikō no shinsō' (Tokyo: Banrika, 1928).
3 Takahashi Masao (ed.), 'Nihon kindaika to Kyūshū' (Tokyo: Heibonsha, 1971); M.B. Jansen, 'The Japanese and Sun Yat-sen' (Cambridge, Mass., 1954), pp. 34-41.
4 'Gaimushō no 100-nen' (Tokyo: Hara Shobō, 1969, 2 vols), vol. 1, pp. 236-53; P. Duus, 'Party Rivalry and Political Change in Taishō Japan' (Cambridge, Mass., 1968), pp. 73-6.
5 Katsura was so determined to appoint Komura as foreign minister that he waited until Komura had completed his part in the crucial negotiations leading up to the signing of the Peking protocol (September 1901) to secure his services.
6 Scepticism about the divergent views of the Japanese leaders has been expressed in the writings of Imai Shōji, Murashima Shigeru and Nish. A thorough and more conventional account is given in Kuroha Shigeru, 'Nichi-Ei dōmei no kenkyū' (Sendai: Tōhoku Kyōiku Tosho, 1968).
7 I.H. Nish, 'The Anglo-Japanese Alliance, 1894-1907' (London, 1966), pp. 111-20.

8 Yale archives on bicentenary. Itō was not the only Japanese invited but he appears to have been the only national leader approached. Hatoyama Kazuo, a Yale alumnus, bureaucrat and university administrator, also attended.

9 'Aoki jiden', pp. 83-5; 111-15. Kawamura, Nichi-Ei dōmei no genin, in 'Chōsen Gakuhō', 63 (1972), pp. 134-6; Tsunoda, 'Manshū mondai' (Tokyo: Hara Shobō, 1967), pp. 36-8.

10 Papers of Sir John Jordan (Public Record Office, London) 3, Jordan to Admiral Bridge, 31 March 1902.

11 In March 1902 Russia had made her joint declaration with France in answer to the Anglo-Japanese alliance. Tsunoda, 'Manshū mondai', chs 1-2, is the best account.

12 Okamoto, pp. 72-6.

13 Ibid., pp. 98-9.

14 'Shidehara Kijūrō' (Tokyo: Shidehara Heiwa Zaidan, 1955), p. 50.

15 Okamoto, pp. 216-17.

16 Ibid., pp. 112-25.

17 J.A. White, 'The Diplomacy of the Russo-Japanese War' (Princeton, 1964), ch. 18

18 'Komura gaikōshi', vol. 2, pp. 285-413.

19 'Documents on British Foreign Policy, 1919-39' (London, 1949-), 2(ix), no. 43, letter by Sir Francis Lindley, 31 December 1931 [Hereafter 'DBFP'].

20 The raising of the Rome legation in 1906 was deferred by Japan for financial reasons. 'Gaimushǒ no 100-nen', vol. 1, pp. 488-96.

21 See, for example, the standard works by C.E. Neu, 'An Uncertain Friendship, 1906-9' (Cambridge, Mass., 1967); R.A. Esthus, 'Theodore Roosevelt and Japan' (Seattle, 1966); C. Vevier, 'The United States and China, 1906-13' (New Brunswick, 1955); and, more recently, A. Iriye, 'Pacific Estrangement 1897-1911' (Cambridge, Mass., 1972).

22 'NGNB', vol. 1, pp. 305-9; 'NGB', 40/III, no. 2200; 'Komura gaikōshi', vol. 2, pp. 292-7.

23 'Gaimusho no 100-nen', vol. 1, p. 414; 'Japan Weekly Mail', 3 October 1914.

24 Archives of the [British] Foreign Office (Public Record Office, London) 371/1145/51951, MacDonald to Grey, 9 December 1911.

CHAPTER 5   THE KATŌ PERIOD

1   Biographical studies of Katō are to be found in
    Itō Masanori, 'Katō Takaaki' (Tokyo, 1929, 2 vols)
    and Nagaoka Shinjirō, Katō Takaaki Ron in 'Kokusai
    Seiji', 1 (1966), pp. 27-40.   In English, a
    detailed account will be found in P. Duus, 'Party
    Rivalry' (Cambridge, Mass., 1968).

2   Komura had left the Foreign Ministry in August 1911.
    In order to focus on Katō, we have left out of
    account several important foreign ministers:
    Hayashi Tadasu, Uchida Yasuya and Katsura Tarō
    (temporarily, while holding the office of premier).
    Between Katō's last two phases at Kasumigaseki, the
    foreign minister was Makino, who was his good
    friend.

3   Nish, 'The Anglo-Japanese alliance: the diplomacy
    of two island empires, 1894-1907' (London, 1966),
    pp. 63-6.

4   [British] Foreign Office, Japan 593, MacDonald to
    Lansdowne, 10 September 1905.

5   'Japan Weekly Mail', 3 October 1914.

6   [British] Foreign Office, Japan 593, MacDonald to
    Lansdowne, 27 August 1905.

7   Pooley, 'The secret memoirs of Count Tadasu Hayashi'
    (London, 1915), pp. 20-1.

8   Nish, 'The Anglo-Japanese alliance', p. 101.

9   Nish, 'Alliance in Decline: a study in Anglo-
    Japanese relations, 1908-23' (London, 1972), p. 92.

10 Itō, 'Katō', vol. 1, pp. 582 ff.

11 'Gaimushō no 100-nen' (Tokyo: Hara Shobō, 1969,
    2 vols), vol. 1, pp. 500 ff.

12 'NGNB', vol. 1, documents, pp. 356-7.

13 'NGB', 44/45, no. 535;   Tokutomi Iichiro, 'Kōshaku
    Yamagata Aritomo den' (Tokyo, 1933, 3 vols), vol.
    3, p. 778.

14 Jansen, 'Japanese and Sun Yat-sen', ch. 7;   A.M.
    Pooley, 'Japan's Foreign Policies' (London, 1920),
    ch. 4.

15 'Gaimushō no 100-nen', vol. 1, pp. 586-92 for
    Foreign Minister Makino's address of January 1914.

16 Kurihara Ken, 'Tai Man-Mō seisakushi no ichimen'
    (Tokyo: Hara Shobō, 1966), pp. 139-59.

17 Japan's entry into the world war is well covered in
    Uchiyama Masakuma, 'Gaikō to kokusai seiji' (Tokyo:
    Keio, 1960), pp. 263-329;   and P.C. Lowe, 'Great
    Britain and Japan, 1911-15' (London, 1969).

18 Itō, 'Katō', vol. 2, pp. 78-81.

19 The details were worked out at a meeting held at

Katō's private residence at 8 p.m. on 8 August at which his own particular Dōshikai supporters within the cabinet attended. These were the finance minister, Wakatsuki Reijirō, the education minister, Ichiki Kitokurō and the chief cabinet secretary, Egi Yoku - an odd assembly to discuss Japan's first steps into the war.

20 'NGB' T. 3/III, pp. 1-50.
21 'Segai Inoue kō den' (Tokyo: Naigai Shoseki, 1933-4, 5 vols), vol. 5, pp. 367-9 [Hereafter 'Inoue-den'].
22 Nish, 'Alliance', pp. 362, 377; 'Alliance in Decline', pp. 126-31.
23 Itō, 'Katō', vol. 2, pp. 78-80.
24 'NGB' T. 3/III, nos 181 and 184.
25 'NGB' T. 3/III, no. 429.
26 'Inoue-den', vol. 5, pp. 390-1.
27 The text of the demands is given in Lowe, pp. 258-62. The subject is well covered in the standard works of R.H. Fifield, T.E. La Fargue, Madeleine Chi, M.B. Jansen and a host of Japanese writers.
28 B.L. Simpson (Putnam Weale), 'An Indiscreet Chronicle from the Pacific' (London, 1923), pp. 308-10. This is confirmed by 'Inoue-den', vol. 5, pp. 397-405; and also in the same work, 'Inoue Katsunosuke-den', p. 224.
29 Lowe, ch. 7.
30 'Gaimushō no 100-nen', vol. 1, pp. 613-14.
31 For a defence of many aspects of Japan's policy, Kajima Morinosuke, 'Emergence of Japan as a World Power 1895-1925' (Tokyo: Tuttle, 1968), pp. 377-8: 'The articles ... reveal no aggressive intent.'
32 Ishii, who was not one of Katō's intimates, describes him as prudent and cautious to a fault.
33 Katō Takaaki, Preface, in Matsumoto Tadao, 'Nisshi shinkōshō ni yoru teikoku no riken' (Tokyo, 1915).

CHAPTER 6 THE ISHII PERIOD

1 'Diplomatic Commentaries' (Baltimore, 1936) is a translation by W.R. Langdon of parts of 'Gaikō yoroku' (Tokyo: Iwanami, 1930). Other works by Ishii are 'Gaikō kaisō dampen' (Tokyo: Kinseidō, 1939); 'Gaikō zuisō' (Tokyo: Kajima, 1967); and (in English) an essay on Japan in J.M. Cambon (ed.), 'The Foreign Policies of the Powers' (New York, 1935).
2 [British] Foreign Office, Japan 593, MacDonald to Lansdowne, 27 August 1905; FO 371/3816 [158392], Alstin to Curzon, 30 October 1919.

3 Ishii, 'Diplomatic Commentaries', p. 87, describes
   Japan's return to China of Manchuria (1905) and
   Shantung (1915) as 'acts of generosity without
   parallel in history'.
4 Ishii, 'Gaikō yoroku', pp. 120-1.
5 Nish, 'Alliance in decline: a study in Anglo-
   Japanese relations, 1908-23' (London, 1972), pp.
   178-83.
6 This subject has been dealt with in P. Berton,
   Secret Russo-Japanese Alliance of 1916, PhD thesis,
   Columbia University, 1956, and G.D. Malone, War
   Aims towards Germany, in D. Dallin, 'Russian Diplomacy and Eastern Europe' (New York, 1963), pp.
   124-62. It is linked with German diplomacy in
   M. Miyake, Dai 1-ji sekai taisen ni okeru Nichi-
   Doku kankei to Nichi-Ro kankei, 'Kokusai Seiji',
   3 (1967), pp. 105-33. Japanese materials are to
   be found in 'NGB' T. 5/I, pp. 383-402, and in a
   useful summary 'Nichi-Ro dōmei kankei chōsho'
   (Makino papers, 404).
7 E.B. Price, 'The Russo-Japanese Treaties concerning
   Manchuria and Mongolia' (Baltimore, 1933), pp.
   121-3.
8 D.I. Abrikossow, 'Revelations of a Russian Diplomat', edited by G.A. Lensen (Seattle, 1964), pp.
   243-4.
9 Ishii, 'Diplomatic Commentaries', pp. 104-5;
   'Gaikō yoroku', pp. 126-8.
10 Makino papers 404.
11 The council debates are available in 'Suiusō nikki'
   (edited by Kobayashi Tatsuo, Tokyo: Hara Shobō,
   1966), the record kept by one of its members, Itō
   Miyoji.
12 Ishii, 'Diplomatic Commentaries', p. 92.
13 The industrialist, Shibusawa, had urged American-
   Japanese co-operation, especially in financial
   spheres, during an American visit in 1916.
   Shibusawa Eiichi denki shiryō (Tokyo: Shibusawa
   Kinen Zaidan, 1955-65, 58 vols), 33.
14 'Gotō Shimpei', edited by Tsurumi Yūsuke (Tokyo,
   1937-8, 4 vols), vol. 3, p. 811; Nish, 'Alliance
   in Decline', p. 236.
15 For more detail, Nish, 'Alliance in Decline', p. 200.
16 These conversations are recorded in 'NGB' T. 6/III,
   pp. 705-874 and in 'Foreign Relations of the United
   States, The Lansing Papers, 1914-20', vol. 2, pp.
   432-51 [Hereafter FRUS]. Ishii left a personal
   account in 'Gaikō yoroku', pp. 135-61 ('Commentaries',
   pp. 111-35), while Lansing gave his views in 'War

Memoirs', pp. 290-306. Another American contemporary account is T.F. Millard, 'Democracy and the Eastern Question' (New York, 1919), chs 6-7; a Japanese version is Kajima, 'Emergence of Japan as a world power' (Tokyo: Tuttle, 1964), pp. 244-58.

17 Kajima, 'Emergence of Japan', pp. 256-8; Ishii, 'Gaikō yoroku', p. 163; Kajima, 'Nichi-Bei gaikōshi' (Tokyo: Kajima, 1958), appendix.

18 Miwa Kimitada, 'Matsuoka Yōsuke' (Tokyo: Chūō Kōronsha, 1971), pp. 56-9. Also Miwa, Japanese opinions on Woodrow Wilson in War and Peace, 'Monumenta Nipponica', 22 (1967), pp. 368-89.

19 'Shidehara kijūrō' (Tokyo: Shidehara Heiwa Zaidan, 1955), p. 148.

20 R.H. Fifield, 'Woodrow Wilson and the Far East' (Hamden, 1965), p. 162.

21 'Gaimushō no 100-nen' (Tokyo: Hara Shobō, 1969, 2 vols), vol. 1, pp. 702-4.

22 S.W. Roskill, 'Hankey: Man of Secrets' (London, 1972, 3 vols), vol. 2, p. 133.

23 Nish, 'Alliance in Decline', pp. 274-6.

24 'FRUS, 1919', vol. 1, pp. 556-66. So far as I can find, there is no mention of this in Ishii's writings or in 'NGB' T. 7 or T. 8.

25 Papers of Frank L. Polk (Sterling library, Yale University), Breckinridge Long to Polk, 17 April 1919.

CHAPTER 7 THE SHIDEHARA PERIOD

1 Shidehara's career is covered in many writings, notably 'Shidehara Kijūrō' (Tokyo: Shidehara Heiwa Zaidan, 1955); 'Gaikō 50-nen' (Tokyo: Yomiuri, 1951); and Ujita Naoyoshi, 'Shidehara Kijūrō' (Tokyo: Jiji Tsushinsha, 1958). In English, the best treatments are A. Iriye, 'After Imperialism' (Cambridge, Mass., 1965); Bamba Nobuya, 'Japanese Diplomacy in a dilemma' (Kyoto: Minerva, 1972); and S. Brown, Shidehara Kijūrō; The Diplomacy of the Yen, in R.D. Burns and E.M. Bennett, 'Diplomats in Crisis' (Oxford, 1974), pp. 201-25.

2 Bamba, p. 153.

3 Nish, 'Alliance in Decline: a study in Anglo-Japanese relations, 1908-23' (London, 1972), pp. 272-6.

4 'Gaimushō no 100-nen' (Tokyo: Hara Shobō, 1969, 2 vols), vol. 1, pp. 586-92.

5 Hara Keiichirō (ed.), 'Hara Kei nikki' (Tokyo: Kengensha, 1950-1, 9 vols), vol. 9, p. 214.

6   'Gaimushō no 100-nen', vol. 1, p. 807.
7   Ibid., pp. 820-1; 'Shidehara', pp. 208-15.
8   Nish, 'Alliance in Decline', chs 22-3; 'Shidehara', pp. 226-31.
9   Ichihashi Yamato, 'Washington conference and after' (Baltimore, 1928), p. 285.
10 Ichihashi, p. 343, argues that by the Shantung agreement China acknowledged the validity of the Sino-Japanese treaties of 1915 and 1918 and the Versailles treaty.
11 Ibid., ch. 7.   Nish, Japan and Naval Aspects of the Washington Conference, in W.G. Beasley (ed.), 'Modern Japan: Aspects of history, literature and society' (London, 1975), pp. 67-80.
12 Shidehara's account of the naval issue in his 'Inside view (Rimenkan) of the Washington Conference' is slight.   'Shidehara', pp. 218-20.
13 For the advantages which the Japanese delegates thought they had secured from the settlement, see Admiral Katō's memorandum, Document 22.
14 [British] Foreign Office 410/74 [F. 675], Eliot to Curzon, 31 January 1923.
15 'NGB', Tai-Bei imin mondai keika gaiyo fuzokusho (Tokyo, 1973), pp. 561-678.
16 'Shidehara', pp. 123-5.
17 On the theme of this section, the following books are helpful: Tsurumi Yūsuke (ed.), 'Gotō Shimpei' (Tokyo, 1937-8, 4 vols), vol. 3, pp. 876-952; J.W. Morley, 'The Japanese Thrust into Siberia, 1918' (New York, 1957); and Hosoya Chihiro, 'Shiberia shuppei no shiteki kenkyū' (Tokyo: Yūhikaku, 1955).   On later Soviet-Japanese relations, Gaimushō, 'Nisso kōshōshi' (Tokyo, 1942, reprinted, 1971) and G.A. Lensen, 'Japanese Recognition of the U.S.S.R.' (Tallahassee, 1970).
18 Stephan, 'Sakhalin: a history' (London, 1971), p. 99; 'Gaimushō no 100-nen' (Tokyo, Hara Shobō, 1969, 2 vols), vol. 1, pp. 691-3, says 7,500 were killed.
19 Hora Tomio, 'Dai-1-ji sekai taisen' (Tokyo: Jimbutsu Oraisha, 1966), p. 278, says Nikolaievsk offered a good opportunity to do what Japan had long wanted to do.
20 'Shidehara', pp. 178-9.
21 Ibid., pp. 324-5.
22 Lensen, p. 162; Stephan, 'Sakhalin', pp. 106-7.
23 'Gaimushō no 100-nen', vol. 1, pp. 851-6.
24 Ibid., pp. 704-14; 'Shidehara', pp. 136-7; 281.

CHAPTER 8 THE TANAKA PERIOD

1 On Tanaka, the main source is Takakura Tetsuichi
(ed.), 'Tanaka Giichi denki' (Tokyo, 1958-60, 3
vols). In addition to Iriye and Bamba mentioned
in the last chapter, there are important studies:
Usui Katsumi, 'Nitchū gaikōshi: Hokubatsu no
jidai' (Tokyo: Hanawa Shobō, 1971); and Etō
Shinkichi, Shidehara gaikō kara Tanaka gaikō e,
'Sekai keizai', 82 (1963), pp. 2-12.
2 Bamba Nobuya, 'Japanese Diplomacy in a dilemma'
(Kyoto: Minerva, 1972), pp. 130-1.
3 Iriye, 'After imperialism' (Cambridge, Mass., 1965),
p. 164.
4 'Tanaka denki', vol. 2, p. 910.
5 Inoue Junnosuke, 'Problems of the Japanese exchange
1914-26' (translated by E.H. de Bunsen, London,
1931), pp. 184-5.
6 'Shidehara Kijūrō' (Tokyo: Shidehara Heiwa Zaidan,
1955), pp. 331-2 (excerpt from Ishii Itarō diary).
7 Bamba, p. 261; 'Shidehara', p. 297; Iriye, 'After
imperialism', p. 79.
8 Usui, 'Nitchū gaikōshi' (Tokyo: Hanawa Shobō,
1971), pp. 52-9.
9 On the Tōhō kaigi, Bamba, pp. 293-303; and Iriye,
'After imperialism', pp. 151-6.
10 Iriye, 'After imperialism', p. 201.
11 Lytton report, para. 41.
12 Yoshizawa Kenkichi, 'Gaikō 60-nen' (Tokyo: Jiyū
Ajiasha, 1958), p. 8.
13 J.J. Stephan, The Tanaka memorial (1927): authentic
or spurious?, 'Modern Asian Studies', 7 (1973),
pp. 647-76. Inou Tentarō, 'Nihon gaikōshi no sho-
mondai' (Tokyo: Yūhikaku, 2 vols), vol. 1, pp. 72-87.
14 'Gaimushō no 100-nen' (Tokyo: Hara Shobō, 1969, 2
vols), vol. 1, pp. 894-906.
15 The best English account is in Iriye, 'After imperialism', ch. 8.
16 British Foreign Office 371/15508 [F. 5633], M.
Lampson (Peking) to A. Henderson, 23 July 1931.
17 'Taiheiyō sensō e no michi' (Tokyo: Asahi Shimbunsha, 1963, 7 vols), vol. 1, pp. 58-9 [Hereafter
TSM].
18 On the London naval conference, T.F. Mayer-Oakes,
'Fragile Victory: Prince Saionji and the 1930
London naval treaty, from the memoirs of Baron
Harada Kumao' (Detroit, 1968); S.E. Pelz, 'Race to
Pearl Harbor' (Cambridge, Mass., 1974).
19 'TSM', vol. 1, pp. 69-70.

20 'Matsudaira Tsuneo Tsuisōroku' (Tokyo, 1961),
    p. 254.
21 'DBFP', 2(i), no. 156.
22 'TSM', vol. 1, pp. 73-4.
23 'Katō Kanji den' (Tokyo, 1941), p. 896.
24 A good account is given in J.B. Crowley, 'Japan's
    Quest for Autonomy' (Princeton, 1966), pp. 66-81.
    For a recent interpretation, D.A. Titus, 'Palace
    and Politics in prewar Japan' (New York, 1974),
    pp. 150-6.
25 Shidehara acted as prime minister from 15 November
    1930 until 9 March.   Wakatsuki took over on 14
    April when Hamaguchi resigned.
26 Asada Sadao, The Japanese navy and the United States,
    in Dorothy Borg and Shumpei Okamoto, 'Pearl Harbor
    as History' (New York, 1973), p. 239 [Hereafter
    'Borg/Okamoto'].
27 'Gaimushō no 100-nen', vol. 1, pp. 924-5.
28 Iriye, 'After imperialism', p. 159.
29 Ibid., p. 111.   Other discussions of this problem
    will be found in Bamba and the studies by Hosoya
    and Iriye in J.W. Morley (ed.), 'Dilemmas of Growth
    in Prewar Japan' (Princeton, 1972).
30 'Shidehara', p. 497.   Shidehara to Ohira, 30 June
    1935.
31 Ibid., p. 508.   Shidehara to Ohira, 25 October
    1938.

CHAPTER 9   THE UCHIDA PERIOD

1 On the role of Uchida in the Manchurian crisis,
   there are two important studies: 'Uchida Yasuya'
   (Tokyo: Kajima Kenkyūjo, 1969), pp. 307-88; and
   Uchiyama Masakuma, 'Gendai Nihon Gaikōshiron'
   (Tokyo: Keio, 1961), pp. 139-211.   In English,
   there is the considerable monographic literature
   on the Manchurian crisis (J.B. Crowley, Ogata
   Sadako, G.R. Storry, C.G. Thorne, Yoshihashi
   Takehiko and M.R. Peattie).
2 'DBFP' 2(x), no. 272.
3 M. Shigemitsu, 'Japan and her destiny' (London,
   1958), pp. 59-65.
4 Yoshihashi Takehiko, 'Conspiracy at Mukden' (New
   Haven, 1963), p. 213.
5 G.A. Lensen, Ambassador Forbes's Appraisal of
   American Policy toward Japan in 1931-2, 'Monumenta
   Nipponica', 23 (1968), pp. 83 f.
6 'Uchida', pp. 307-24.

7 Ibid., pp. 326.
8 Ibid., pp. 329-33.
9 'DBFP' 2(x), no. 272.
10 'Uchida', pp. 334-8.
11 Ibid., pp. 342-50.
12 'DBFP' 2(x), no. 445; 'NGNB', vol. 2., p. 512.
13 M.D. Kennedy, 'The Estrangement of Great Britain and Japan, 1917-35' (Manchester, 1969), p. 248.
14 'Uchida', pp. 378-9.
15 Ibid., p. 359 and, for the whole speech, pp. 350-62.
16 K. Sansom, 'Sir George Sansom and Japan' (Tallahassee, 1972), p. 52. On the role of Dr T. Baty, Uchiyama, 'Gendai Nihon gaikōshiron', pp. 187-97.
17 Miwa, 'Matsuoka' (Tokyo: Chūō Kōronsha), pp. 99-100. I have benefited from discussions with Professor David J. Lu who is preparing a new biography of Matsuoka.
18 'Uchida', pp. 384-6; 'The Times' (London), 25 February 1933.
19 'Uchida', pp. 384-6.
20 Miwa, 'Matsuoka', pp. 105-6.
21 'Uchida', p. 387.
22 Ibid., p. 386; Usui, The Role of the Foreign Ministry in Borg/Okamoto, pp. 133-4.
23 Usui Katsumi, 'Manshū Jihen' (Tokyo: Chūō Kōronsha, 1974), pp. 211-12.
24 'Uchida', pp. 367-9; Hata Ikuhiko,'Reality and Illusion, 1932-4' (New York, 1967), pp. 15-17.
25 G.A. Lensen, 'The damned inheritance: The Soviet Union and the Manchurian crises, 1924-35' (Tallahassee, 1975), chs 7-10.
26 H. Von Dirksen, 'Moscow, Tokyo, London' (London, 1951), p. 144.
27 Ann Trotter, 'Britain and East Asia, 1933-37' (London, 1975), chs 7 and 9. On American interest in Manchukuo, Chō Yukio, An inquiry into the problem of importing American capital into Manchuria: a note on Japanese-American relations, 1931-41, in Borg/Okamoto, pp. 377-92.

CHAPTER 10   THE HIROTA PERIOD

1 The standard biography is 'Hirota Kōki' (Tokyo, 1966). Short biographical studies are to be found in Usui Katsumi, Hirota Kōki ron, in 'Kokusai Seiji', 1 (1966), pp. 41-53; and L. Farnsworth, Hirota Kōki, in Burns and Bennett, 'Diplomats in Crisis', pp. 227-46. Indirectly relevant to

Hirota are Shigemitsu, 'Japan and her Destiny' and Matsumoto Shigeharu, 'Jōkai jidai: Jānaristo no kaisō' (Tokyo: Chūō Kōron, 1974).

2 R.L. Craigie, 'Behind the Japanese Mask' (London, 1946), p. 60.

3 Shigemitsu, 'Japan and her Destiny', p. 111.

4 'Hirota Kōki', p. 175 (on Hirota's cabinet). But see also pp. 151 and 115-23.

5 Usui in Borg/Okamoto, pp. 132-4.

6 Ibid., pp. 135-7.

7 Ibid., pp. 146-8.

8 E.O. Reischauer, What went wrong?, in J.W. Morley, 'Dilemmas' (Princeton, 1972), p. 504.

9 R.M. Spaulding, The Bureaucracy as a Political Force, 1920-45 in Morley, 'Dilemmas', p. 72.

10 Archives of the [British] Premier (Public Record Office, London), 1/330, Drummond to Vansittart, 5 March 1937.

11 F. Leith-Ross, 'Money Talks' (London, 1968), pp. 221-2; Matsumoto, 'Jōkai jidai', pp. 143-52.

12 G.M. Wilson (ed.), 'Crisis Politics in prewar Japan' (Tokyo: Sophia, 1970), pp. 51-70; and B. Shillony, 'Revolt in Japan' (Princeton, 1973).

13 Usui in Borg/Okamoto, p. 127.

14 The most accomplished treatments of this subject are Asada, The Japanese Navy and the United States, in Borg/Okamoto, pp. 225-59; and Pelz, 'Race to Pearl Harbor' (Cambridge, Mass., 1974), pp. 18-20.

15 Admiral Enomoto in 'Matsudaira Tsuneo tsuisōron' (Tokyo, 1961), pp. 115-9.

16 Kennedy, 'Estrangement' (Manchester, 1969), p. 327.

17 'TSM', vol. 1, pp. 155-60.

18 Ibid., p. 158.

19 Enomoto, op. cit., p. 117.

20 An important documentary account of the second London conference is in 'DBFP, 1919-39' 2(xiii), Naval policy and defence requirements, July 1934-March 1936 (London, 1973).

21 Craigie, p. 17.

22 'DBFP', 2(xiii), no. 638.

23 Ibid., nos 671 and 608.

24 Yoshida Shigeru, 'Kaisō 10-nen' (Tokyo: Shinchōsha, 1957, 4 vols), vol. 4, p. 113, comments favourably on Shiratori's competence in English.

25 Usui Katsumi, 'Nitchū sensō' (Tokyo: Chūō Kōron, 1967), pp. 14-16.

26 Iriye Akira, Japan's foreign policies between the world wars, in E.M. Robertson (ed.), 'The origins of the second world war' (London, 1971), pp. 265-6.

27 Usui, 'Nitchū sensō', p. 19.
28 Leith-Ross, 'Money Talks', ch. 15.
29 Usui, 'Nitchū sensō', p. 18.
30 Trotter, 'Britain and East Asia' (London, 1975),
    ch. 9; Matsumoto, 'Jōkai jidai', pp. 74-80.
31 'NGNB', vol. 2, documents, pp. 334-40.
32 R.H. Akagi, 'Japan's Foreign Relations, 1542-1936'
    (Tokyo: Hokuseidō, 1936), p. 514.
33 Ibid.
34 Satō Naotake, 'Kaiko 80-nen' (Tokyo: Jiji
    Tsūshinsha, 1963), p. 366.
35 Usui in Borg/Okamoto, p. 135.

CHAPTER 11 THE KONOE PERIOD

1 Konoe's own writings are 'Heiwa e no dōryoku'
   (Tokyo: Nihon Dempō, 1946) and 'Ushinawareshi
   seiji' (Tokyo: Asahi Shimbun, 1946). The standard
   biographies are Yabe Teiji (Konoe's secretary),
   'Konoe Fumimaro' (Tokyo: Kōbundō, 1952, 2 vols)
   and Oka Yoshitake, 'Konoe Fumimaro: ummei no
   seijika' (Tokyo: Iwanami, 1972). On Konoe's
   early career, see G.M. Berger, Japan's Young
   Prince, 1916-31, 'Monumenta Nipponica', 29 (1974),
   pp. 451-76.
2 J.B. Crowley, Intellectuals as visionaries of the
   New Asian Order, in Morley, 'Dilemmas' (Princeton,
   1972), p. 321 ff.
3 Titus, 'Palace and Politics in Prewar Japan' (New
   York, 1974), p. 190.
4 Ei-Bei honi no heiwa shugi wo hai su. Miwa,
   'Matsuoka Yōsuke: Sono ningen to gaikō' (Tokyo:
   Chūō Kōronsha, 1971), pp. 59-62.
5 Hosoya in Morley, 'Dilemmas', pp. 95-6: Ike
   Nobutaka, 'Japan's Decision for War' (Stanford,
   1967), p. xviii.
6 Konoe, 'Heiwa e no dōryoku', p. 101.
7 Nishi Haruhiko, 'Kaisō no Nihon gaikō' (Tokyo:
   Iwanami, 1965), p. 98.
8 Hosoya in Morley, 'Dilemmas', pp. 99-105.
9 T. Kase, 'Eclipse of the Rising Sun' (London, 1951),
   pp. 17-19.
10 Yabe, 'Konoe', vol. 2, p. 75.
11 'Gaimushō no 100-nen' (Tokyo: Hara Shobō, 1969, 2
    vols), vol. 1, pp. 991-3.
12 F.W. Ikle, 'German-Japanese relations, 1936-40 (New
    York, 1956), pp. 62-7.
13 Yabe, 'Konoe', vol. 2, p. 75.

14 i.e., if one excludes Tanaka. Cf. 'Ugaki Kazushige
    nikki' (Tokyo: Misuzu Shobō, 1968, 3 vols).
15 Craigie, 'Behind the Japanese mask' (London, 1945),
    p. 61.
16 It was 1940 before the beleaguered Wang made his
    Shanghai declaration and established his new govern-
    ment at Nanking on 30 March. On 30 November,
    once again the time of the Konoe ministry, Wang
    signed a treaty with Japan and a joint declaration
    with Japan and Manchukuo.
17 J.H. Boyle, 'China and Japan at war, 1937-45'
    (Stanford, 1970), p. 286. Also G.E. Bunker, 'The
    Peace Conspiracy' (Cambridge, Mass., 1971).
18 Oka, 'Konoe', pp. 100-3.
19 Usui in Borg/Okamoto, pp. 142-6.
20 Katsu Young, The Nomonhan Incident, 'Monumenta
    Nipponica', 22 (1967), p. 100.
21 'Gaimushō no 100-nen' vol. 2, pp. 85-146.

CHAPTER 12   THE MATSUOKA PERIOD

1 Matsuoka wrote several pamphlets but these belong
   not to his Foreign Ministry period but to his years
   as politician and Manchurian railway executive.   A
   good summary of his career is given in Miwa Kimitada,
   'Matsuoka Yōsuka' (Tokyo: Chūō Kōron, 1971), who
   also contributed The case for Matsuoka to 'Monumenta Nipponica', 16 (1960), pp. 402-6.   Barbara
   Teters wrote a valuable short essay, Matsuoka
   Yōsuke: the diplomacy of bluff and gesture, for
   Burns and Bennett, 'Diplomats in Crisis', pp. 275-
   93.   Other sources are F.H. Conroy on Nomura in
   the same collection and the standard works by
   R.J.C. Butow, F.C. Jones, D. Lu, J.C. Grew and
   R.L. Craigie.
2 Oka, 'Konoe' (Tokyo: Iwanami, 1972), pp. 135-6.
3 Miwa, 'Matsuoka', pp. 72-80.   In 1929 Matsuoka had
   been one of the Japanese delegates at the Kyoto
   conference of the Institute of Pacific Relations
   where he made impassioned speeches implying his
   support for a tough line towards the Chinese.
4 Oka, 'Konoe', p. 119; Miwa, 'Matsuoka', pp. 136-8.
5 Hosoya in Morley, 'Dilemmas' (Princeton, 1972),
   pp. 92-3.
6 Asada in Borg/Okamoto, pp. 248-9.
7 'Documents on German Foreign Policy, 1919-45',
   Series D (xi), September 1940-January 1941 (London,
   1962), no. 156, p. 265.   Amau was recalled since

he opposed the Tripartite Pact and Japanese diplomats were seriously divided over it.

8 L.N. Kutakov, 'Japanese Foreign Policy' (Tallahassee, 1972), pp. 128-98. Also Nishi, 'Kaisō' (Tokyo: Iwanami, 1965), p. 101f; Miwa, 'Matsuoka', pp. 174-9.

9 Nishi, 'Kaisō', p. 109.

10 Kutakov, 'Japanese foreign policy on the eve of the Pacific war' (Tallahassee, 1972), pp. 193-4.

11 Toshikazu Kase, 'Watashi no gendai gaikōshi' (Tokyo: Shinchosha, 1971), p. 171; Ike, 'Japan's decision for war' (Stanford, 1967), p. 58.

12 'Gaimushō no 100-nen' (Tokyo: Hara Shobō, 1969, 2 vols), vol. 2, pp. 575-6. Young, 'Monumenta Nipponica' 22 (1967), p. 101.

13 Oka, 'Konoe', pp. 161-3; Miwa, 'Matsuoka', pp. 184-5.

14 Imai Seiichi, Cabinet, Emperor and Senior Statesmen in Borg/Okamoto, p. 76.

15 Shigemitsu, 'Japan and her Destiny' (London, 1958), p. 238.

16 'Akten zur deutschen auswärtigen Politik, 1918-45', Serie E, 1941-5, Band I (Göttingen, 1969), no. 145 and Band II (1972), no. 48.

17 F.C. Jones, 'Japan's New Order' (London, 1954), p. 401; Nishi, 'Kaisō', pp. 125-6; B. Martin, 'Deutschland und Japan in 2. Weltkrieg (Göttingen, 1969), ch. 1.

18 F.W. Deakin and G.R. Storry, 'The case of Richard Sorge' (London, 1966), pp. 331-2.

19 Satō, 'Kaiko 80-nen' (Tokyo: Jiji Tsushin, 1963), ch. 14.

20 Nish, Japan and the Outbreak of war in 1941, in A. Sked and C. Cook (eds), 'Crisis and Controversy' (London, 1976), pp. 130-46.

21 To add to the confusion, the Japanese have translated 'Dai Tō-A' as 'Greater East Asia' and 'Great East Asia', two phrases which have different implications for foreign readers but not for Japanese.

POSTSCRIPT

1 Nish, 'Alliance in Decline' (London, 1972), p. 330.

2 R.J.C. Butow, 'Tojo and the Coming of the War' (Stanford, 1961), p. 133.

3 'DBFP' 3(ix), Appendix I, note by Sansom, 3 August 1939.

4 'DBFP' 2(ix), no. 43.

5 'Shidehara' (Tokyo: Shidehara Heiwa Zaidan, 1955),
   p. 497.   Shidehara to Ohira, 4 June 1935.

Select Bibliography

ABRIKOSSOW, D.I. (1964), 'Revelations of a Russian diplomat', G.A. Lensen (ed.), Seattle.
AOKI SHŪZŌ (1970), 'Aoki Shūzō jiden', Sakane Yoshihisa (ed.), Tokyo: Heibonsha.
ARITA HACHIRŌ (1959), 'Baka Hachi to hito wa iu: gaikōkan no kaisō', Tokyo: Kōwasha.
BAMBA NOBUYA (1972), 'Japanese diplomacy in a dilemma: new light on Japan's China policy, 1924-9', Kyoto: Minerva.
BEASLEY, W.G. (1955), 'Select documents on Japanese foreign policy, 1853-68', London.
BEASLEY, W.G. (1973), 'The Meiji restoration', Stanford.
BEASLEY, W.G. (ed.) (1975), 'Modern Japan: aspects of history, literature and society', London.
BERGER, G.M. (1974), Japan's young prince: Konoe Fumimaro's early political career, 1916-31, 'Monumenta Nipponica', 29, 451-76.
BISSON, T.A. (1973), 'Yenan in June 1937: talks with the communist leaders', Berkeley.
BORG, DOROTHY and SHUMPEI OKAMOTO (1973), 'Pearl Harbor as history: Japanese-American relations, 1931-41', New York.
BOYLE, J.H. (1972), 'China and Japan at war, 1937-45: the politics of collaboration', Stanford.
BUNKER, G.E. (1971), 'The peace conspiracy: Wang Ching-wei and the China war, 1937-41', Cambridge, Mass.
BURNS, R.D. and BENNETT, E.M. (eds) (1974), 'Diplomats in crisis: United States-Chinese-Japanese relations, 1919-41', Oxford.
BUTOW, R.J.C. (1961), 'Tōjō and the coming of the war', Stanford.
BUTOW, R.J.C. (1974), 'The John Doe Associates: back-door diplomacy for peace, 1941', Stanford.
CALVOCORESSI, P. and WINT, G. (1972), 'Total war: causes and courses of the second world war', London.
329

CHANG, R.T. (1975), The Chishima case, 'Journal of Asian Studies', 24, 593-612.

CHŌ YUKIO (1973), 'Shōwa no kyōkō', Tokyo: Iwanami.

CONROY, F.H. (1960), 'The Japanese seizure of Korea, 1868-1910', Philadelphia.

CRAIG, A.M. and SHIVELY, D.H. (eds) (1970), 'Personality in Japanese history', Berkeley.

CRAIGIE, R.L. (1945), 'Behind the Japanese mask', London.

CROWLEY, J.B. (1966), 'Japan's quest for autonomy: national security and foreign policy, 1930-8', Princeton.

CROWLEY, J.B. (ed.) (1970), 'Modern East Asia: essays in interpretation', New York.

DALLIN, D. (1963), 'Russian diplomacy and eastern Europe', New York.

D'ANETHAN, A. (1967), 'The D'Anethan despatches from Japan, 1894-1910', G.A. Lensen (ed.), Tokyo: Sophia.

DANIELS, G. (1968), The British role in the Meiji restoration: a reinterpretation, 'Modern Asian Studies', 11, 291-313.

DEAKIN, F.W. and STORRY, G.R. (1966), 'The case of Richard Sorge', London.

DIRKSEN, H. von (1951), 'Moscow, Tokyo, London', London.

'Documents on British Foreign Policy, 1919-39', E.L. Woodward et al. (eds), London, 1949- .

DUUS, P. (1968), 'Party rivalry and political change in Taishō Japan', Cambridge, Mass.

ENDICOTT, S.L. (1975), 'Diplomacy and enterprise: British China policy, 1933-7', Manchester.

FIFIELD, R.H. (1952), 'Woodrow Wilson and the far east: the diplomacy of the Shantung question', New York.

FOX, GRACE (1969), 'Great Britain and Japan, 1858-83', London.

FUJIMURA MICHIO (1973), 'Nisshin sensō: Higashi Ajia kindaishi no tenkanten', Tokyo: Iwanami.

FUKUDA SHIGEO (1967), 'Amerika no tai-Nichi sansen', Kyoto: Minerva.

'Gaimushō no 100-nen', Tokyo: Hara Shobō, 2 vols, 1969.

GALPERIN, A.L. (1947), 'Anglo-Iaponskii soiuz, 1902-21', Moscow.

GOODMAN, G.K. (ed.) (1967), 'Imperial Japan and Asia: a reassessment', New York.

GORE-BOOTH (Lord) (1974), 'With great truth and respect', London.

GREW, J.C. (1944), 'Ten years in Japan', London.

HACKETT, R.F. (1971), 'Yamagata Aritomo in the rice of modern Japan, 1838-1922', Cambridge, Mass.

HAGIHARA NOBUTOSHI (1968), Mutsu Munemitsu, in Kamishima Jirō (ed.), 'Kenryoku no shishō', Tokyo: Chikuma Shobō, pp. 123-51.

HAGIHARA NOBUTOSHI (1973), 'Mutsu Munemitsu', vol. 35 in
Nihon no meicho, Tokyo: Chūō Kōronsha.
'Hakushaku Mutsu Munemitsu ikō', Mutsu Hirokichi (ed.),
Tokyo: Iwanami, 1929.
HALL, I.P. (1972), 'Mori Arinori', Cambridge, Mass.
HARA KEI (1950), 'Nikki', Tokyo: Kangensha, 9 vols.
HAROOTUNIAN, H.D. and SILBERMAN, B.S. (eds) (1966),
'Modern Japanese leadership: transition and change',
Tucson.
HAROOTUNIAN, H.D. and SILBERMAN, B.S. (eds) (1974),
'Japan in crisis: essays on Taishō democracy',
Princeton.
HAVENS, T.R.H. (1974), 'Farm and nation in modern Japan:
agrarian nationalism, 1870-1940', Princeton.
HIROSE SHIZUKO (1975), Nisshin sensōzen no Igirisu
kyokutō seisaku no ichikōsatsu, 'Kokusai Seiji', 51,
129-54.
'Hirota Kōki', Tokyo, 1966.
HORA TOMIO (1966), 'Dai 1-ji sekai taisen', Tokyo:
Jimbutsu Oraisha.
HOSOYA CHIHIRO (1955), 'Shiberia shuppei no shiteki
kenkyū', Tokyo: Yūhikaku.
HOSOYA CHIHIRO with SAITO MAKOTO, IMAI SEIICHI and ROYAMA
MICHIO (1971), 'Nichi-Bei kankeishi: Kaisen ni itaru
10-nen, 1931-41', Tokyo, Tōdai Shuppankai, 4 vols.
ICHIHASHI YAMATO (1928), 'The Washington conference and
after', Stanford.
IKE NOBUTAKA (1967), 'Japan's decision for war: records
of the 1941 policy conferences', Stanford.
IKEI MASARU (1966), Japan's response to the Chinese
revolution of 1911, 'Journal of Asian Studies', 25, 213-
27.
IKEI MASARU (1973), 'Nihon gaikōshi gaisetsu', Tokyo:
Keio Tsūshin.
IKLE, F.W. (1956), 'German-Japanese relations, 1936-40',
New York.
IKLE, F.W. (1967), The Triple Intervention: Japan's
lesson in the diplomacy of imperialism, 'Monumenta
Nipponica', 22, 122-30.
IMAI SHŌJI (1957), Nichi-Ei dōmei kōshō ni okeru Nihon
no shūchō, 'Kokusai Seiji', 119-36.
INO TENTARO (1966-7), 'Nihon gaikō shisōshi ronkō',
Tokyo: Komine Shoten, 2 vols.
INOUE JUNNOSUKE (1931), 'Problems of the Japanese
exchange, 1914-26', trans. E.H. de Bunsen, London.
INOUE KIYOSHI (1955), 'Jōyaku kaisei', Tokyo: Iwanami.
'(Segai) Inoue-kō den', Tokyo: Naigai shoseki, 5 vols,
1934.
IRIYE AKIRA (1965), 'After imperialism', Cambridge,
Mass.

IRIYE AKIRA (1967), 'Across the Pacific', New York.
IRIYE AKIRA (1972), 'Pacific estrangement: Japanese
and American expansion, 1897-1911', Cambridge, Mass.
ISHII KIKUJIRŌ (1930), 'Gaikō yoroku', Tokyo: Iwanami.
Trans. F.C. Langdon as 'Diplomatic commentaries',
Baltimore, 1936.
ISHII KIKUJIRŌ (1939), 'Gaikō kaisō dampen', Tokyo:
Kinseidō.
ISHII KIKUJIRŌ (1967), 'Gaikō zuisō', Tokyo: Kajima.
ITŌ MASANORI (1929), 'Katō Takaaki', Tokyo, 2 vols.
ITŌ TAKASHI (1969), 'Shōwa shoki seijishi kenkyū',
Tokyo: Tōdai Shuppankai.
ITŌ TAKASHI (1970), Conflicts and coalitions in Japan,
1930: political groups and the London naval conference,
in S. Groennings and E.W. Kelley (eds), 'Study of
coalition behaviour', New York, pp. 160-76.
IWATA MASAKAZU (1964), 'Okubo Toshimichi: the Bismarck
of Japan', Berkeley.
JANSEN, M.B. (1954), 'The Japanese and Sun Yat-sen',
Cambridge, Mass.
JONES, F.C. (1931), 'Extraterritoriality in Japan and
the diplomatic relations resulting in its abolition,
1853-99', New Haven.
JONES, F.C. (1954), 'Japan's new order in east Asia:
its rise and fall, 1937-45', London.
KAJIMA MORINOSUKE (1957), 'Nichi-Ei gaikōshi', Tokyo:
Kajima.
KAJIMA MORINOSUKE (1958), 'Nichi-Bei gaikōshi', Tokyo:
Kajima.
KAJIMA MORINOSUKE (1964), 'The emergence of Japan as a
world power', Tokyo: Tuttle.
KAMIKAWA HIKOMATSU (ed.) (1962-6), 'Nik-kan gaikōshiryō
shūsei', Tokyo: Gannandō, 8 vols.
KASE TOSHIKAZU (1951), 'Eclipse of the rising sun',
London.
KASE TOSHIKAZU (1971), 'Watashi no gendai gaikōshi:
Taiketsu kara taiwa e no chōryū', Tokyo: Shinchōsha.
'Katō Kanji Taishō den', Tokyo, 1941.
KAWAMURA KAZUO (1972), Aoki Gaisō no Kankoku ni kanren
suru tai-Ro kyōkō seisaku no hatten to Nichi-Ei dōmei
no seiritsu to no kankei, 'Chōsen Gakuhō', 63, 129-38.
KENNEDY, M.D. (1969), 'The estrangement of Great
Britain and Japan, 1917-35', Manchester.
KIYOZAWA KIYOSHI (1942), 'Nihon gaikōshi', Tokyo:
Tōyō Keizai, 2 vols.
'Komura gaikōshi', Tokyo: Nihon gaikō bunsho hampukai,
2 vols, 1953.
KONOE FUMIMARO (1946), 'Heiwa e no dōryoku', Tokyo:
Nihon Dempō Tsūshin.

KURIHARA KEN (1955), 'Tennō: Shōwashi oboegaki', Tokyo: Yūshindō.
KURIHARA KEN (1966), 'Tai Man-Mō seisakushi no ichimen', Tokyo: Hara Shobō.
KUROHA SHIGERU (1968), 'Nichi-Ei dōmei no kenkyū', Sendai: Tōhoku Kyōiku Tosho.
KUTAKOV, L.N. (1972), 'Japanese foreign policy on the eve of the Pacific war: a Soviet view', G.A. Lensen (ed.), Tallahassee.
LAFARGUE, T.E. (1937), 'China and the world war', Stanford.
LANE-POOLE, S. and DICKINS, F.V. (1894), 'The life of Sir Harry Parkes', London, 2 vols.
LEBRA, JOYCE (1973), 'Okuma Shigenobu: Statesman of Meiji Japan', Canberra.
LEBRA, JOYCE (1975), 'Japan's Greater East Asia Co-prosperity Sphere in world war II', London.
LEE, B.A. (1973), 'Britain and the Sino-Japanese war, 1937-9', Stanford.
LEITH-ROSS, F. (1968), 'Money talks', London.
LENSEN, G.A. (1967), 'The Russo-Chinese war', Tallahassee.
LENSEN, G.A. (1968), Japan and Manchuria: Ambassador Forbes's appraisal of American policy toward Japan in 1931-2, 'Monumenta Nipponica', 23, 66-89.
LENSEN, G.A. (1970), 'Japanese recognition of the U.S.S.R.: Soviet-Japanese relations, 1921-30', Tallahassee.
LENSEN, G.A. (1972), 'The strange neutrality: Soviet-Japanese relations during the second world war, 1941-5', Tallahassee.
LENSEN, G.A. (1974), 'The damned inheritance: the Soviet Union and the Manchurian crises, 1924-35', Tallahassee.
LO HUI-MIN (ed.) (1976), 'The correspondence of G.E. Morrison', vol. 1, 1895-1912, Cambridge.
LU, D.J. (1961), 'From the Marco Polo Bridge to Pearl Harbor: Japan's entry into world war II', Washington.
MARTIN, B. (1969), 'Deutschland und Japan in 2 Welt-Krieg', Göttingen.
'Matsudaira Tsuneo tsuisōroku', Tokyo, 1961.
MATSUMOTO SHIGEHARU (1974), 'Jōkai jihen: Jānaristo no kaisō', Tokyo: Chūō Kōronsha.
MAY, E.R. and THOMSON, J.C. (eds) (1972), 'American-East Asian relations: a survey', Cambridge, Mass.
MAYER-OAKES, T.F. (1968), 'Fragile Victory: Prince Saionji and the 1930 London naval treaty from the memoirs of Baron Harada Kumao', Detroit.
MAYO, MARLENE J. (1967), A catechism of western

diplomacy: the Japanese and Hamilton Fish, 1872, 'Journal of Asian Studies', 26, 389-410.

MAYO, MARLENE J. (1972), The Korean crisis of 1873 and early Meiji foreign policy, 'Journal of Asian Studies', 31, 793-819.

MESKILL, JOANNA (1966), 'The hollow alliance: Hitler and Japan', New York.

MILLARD, T.F. (1919), 'Democracy and the eastern question', New York.

MITANI TAICHIRŌ (1967), 'Nihon seitō seiji no keisei', Tokyo: Tōdai shuppankai.

MIWA KIMITADA (1960), The case for Matsuoka, 'Monumenta Nipponica', 16, 402-6.

MIWA KIMITADA (1967), Japanese opinions on Woodrow Wilson in war and peace, 'Monumenta Nipponica', 22, 368-89.

MIWA KIMITADA (1971), 'Matsuoka Yōsuke: Sono ningen to gaikō', Tokyo: Chūō Kōronsha.

MORLEY, J.W. (1957), 'The Japanese thrust into Siberia, 1918', New York.

MORLEY, J.W. (ed.) (1972), 'Dilemmas of growth in prewar Japan', Princeton.

MORLEY, J.W. (ed.) (1974), 'Japan's foreign policy, 1868-1941: a research guide', New York.

MOSSMAN, S. (1873), 'New Japan', London.

MUTSU MUNEMITSU (1939), 'Kenkenroku', Tokyo: Iwanami.

NAGAOKA SHINJIRŌ (1966), Kātō Takaaki ron, in 'Kokusai Seiji', 1, 27-40

'Nihon gaikō bunsho', Tokyo: Gaimushō, 1936- .

'Nihon gaikō nempyō narabi ni shuyō bunsho', Tokyo: Gaimushō, 2 vols, 1955.

NISH, I.H. (1961), Japan's indecision during the Boxer disturbances, 'Journal of Asian Studies', 20, 449-61.

NISH, I.H. (1966), Korea, focus of Russo-Japanese diplomacy, 1898-1903, 'Asian Studies', 4, 70-84.

NISH, I.H. (1966), 'The Anglo-Japanese alliance: the diplomacy of two island empires, 1894-1907', London.

NISH, I.H. (1972), 'Alliance in decline: a study in Anglo-Japanese relations, 1908-23', London.

NISH, I.H. (1975), Japan reverses the unequal treaties: the Anglo-Japanese commercial treaty of 1894, 'Journal of Oriental Studies (Hongkong)', 13, 137-45.

NISHI HARUHIKO (1965), 'Kaisō no Nihon gaikō', Tokyo: Iwanami.

NISHIHARA KAMEZŌ (1949), 'Yume no 70-yo nen: Nishihara Kamezō jiden', Murashima Nagisa (ed.), Kyoto.

'Nisso kōshōshi', Tokyo: Gaimushō, 1942 and 1971.

OGATA SADAKO (1964), 'Defiance in Manchuria: the making of Japanese foreign policy, 1931-2', Berkeley.

OHATA TOKUSHIRŌ (1966), 'Kokusai kankyō to Nihon gaikō', Tokyo: Higashi.

OKA YOSHITAKE (1972), 'Konoe Fumimaro: Ummei no seijika', Tokyo: Iwanami.

OKAMOTO SHUMPEI (1970), 'The Japanese oligarchy and the Russo-Japanese war', London.

PEATTIE, M.R. (1975), 'Ishiwara Kanji and Japan's confrontation with the west', Princeton.

PELZ, S.E. (1974), 'Race to Pearl Harbor: the failure of the second London naval conference and the onset of world war II', Cambridge, Mass.

POOLEY, A.M. (ed.) (1915), 'The secret memoirs of Count Tadasu Hayashi', London.

POOLEY, A.M. (1920), 'Japan's foreign policies', London.

PRESSEISEN, E.L. (1958), 'Germany and Japan: a study in totalitarian diplomacy, 1933-41', The Hague.

PRICE, E.B. (1933), 'The Russo-Japanese treaties of 1907-16 concerning Manchuria and Mongolia', Baltimore.

PU YI, H. (1964-5), 'Autobiography: from emperor to citizen', Peking, 2 vols.

ROSKILL, S. (1972-4), 'Hankey: man of secrets', London, 3 vols.

SAKANE YOSHIHISA (1966), Aoki Shūzō, in 'Kokusai Seiji', 1, 10-26.

SANSOM, KATHERINE (1972), 'Sir George Sansom and Japan', Tallahassee.

SATŌ NAOTAKE (1963), 'Kaiko 80-nen', Tokyo: Jiji Tsūshin.

SATOW, E.M. (1966), 'Korea and Manchuria between Russia and Japan: observations, 1895-1904', G.A. Lensen (ed.), Tokyo: Sophia.

'Shidehara Kijūrō', Tokyo: Shidehara Heiwa Zaidan, 1955.

SHIGEMITSU MAMORU (1958), 'Japan and her destiny: my struggle for peace', F.S.G. Piggott (ed.), London. Taken from 'Shōwa no dōran', Tokyo, 1952.

SHILLONY, B. (1973), 'Revolt in Japan: young officers and the February 26, 1936 incident', Princeton.

SHIMOMURA FUJIO (1962), 'Meiji shonen jōyaku kaiseishi no kenkyū', Tokyo: Yoshikawa Kōbunkan.

SHINOBU SEIZABURŌ (1934 and 1972), 'Mutsu gaikō: Nisshin sensō no gaikō shiteki kenkyū', Tokyo: Sobunkaku.

SHINOBU SEIZABURŌ (1933), 'Mutsu Munemitsu', Tokyo: Hakuyōsha.

SHINOBU SEIZABURŌ and NAKAYAMA JIICHI (eds) (1951), 'Nichi-Ro sensōshi no kenkyū', Tokyo: Kawade.

SHINOBU SEIZABURŌ and NAKAYAMA JIICHI (eds) (1974), 'Nihon gaikōshi', Tokyo: Mainichi, 2 vols.

SHIVELY, D.H. (ed.) (1972), 'Tradition and moderniza-
tion in Japanese culture', Princeton.
SKED, A. and COOK, C. (1976), 'Crisis and controversy:
essays in honour of A.J.P. Taylor', London.
STEPHAN, J.J. (1971), 'Sakhalin: a history', London.
STEPHAN, J.J. (1973), The Tanaka memorial, 1927:
authentic or spurious?, 'Modern Asian Studies', 7,
647-76.
STEPHAN, J.J. (1974), 'The Kuril islands: Russo-
Japanese frontiers in the Pacific', London.
STORRY, G.R. (1957), 'The double patriots: a study of
Japanese nationalism', London.
TABOHASHI KIYOSHI (1951), 'Nisshin seneki gaikōshi no
kenkyū', Tokyo: Tōkō Shoin.
TADA KŌMON (ed.) (1927-35), 'Iwakura-kō jikki', Tokyo, 3
vols.
'Taiheiyō sensō e no michi', Tokyo: Asahi Shimbunsha,
8 vols, 1962.
TAKAHASHI MASAO (ed.) (1971), 'Nihon kindaika to
Kyūshū', Tokyo: Heibonsha.
TAMURA KŌSAKU (1944), 'Genesis of the Pacific war',
Tokyo: Taiheiyō Kyōkai.
'Tanaka Giichi denki', Takakura Tetsuichi (ed.), Tokyo,
3 vols, 1958.
THORNE, C. (1972), 'The limits of foreign policy: the
west, the League and the far eastern crisis of 1931-3',
London.
TITUS, D.A. (1974), 'Palace and politics in prewar
Japan', New York.
TŌGŌ SHIGENORI (1956), 'The cause of Japan', New York.
Translates part of 'Jidai no ichimen', Tokyo, 1952.
TROTTER, ANN A. (1974), Tentative steps for an Anglo-
Japanese rapprochement in 1934, 'Modern Asian
Studies', 8, 59-83.
TROTTER, ANN A. (1975), 'Britain and East Asia, 1933-7',
London.
TSUNODA JUN (1967), 'Manshū mondai to kokubō hōshin',
Tokyo: Hara Shobō.
TSUNODA RYŪSAKU (ed.) (1958), 'Sources of the Japanese
tradition', New York.
TSURUMI YŪSUKE (1937), 'Gotō Shimpei', Tokyo, 4 vols.
'Uchida Yasuya', Tokyo: Kajima Kenkyūjo, 1969.
UCHIYAMA MASAKUMA (1968), 'Gaikō to kokusai seiji:
Riron to rekishi', Tokyo: Keio Tsūshin.
UCHIYAMA MASAKUMA (1971), 'Gendai Nihon gaikōshiron',
Tokyo: Keio Tsūshin.
UGAKI KAZUSHIGE (1954), 'Ugaki nikki', Tokyo: Asahi
Shimbunsha.
USUI KATSUMI (1967), 'Nitchū sensō', Tokyo: Chūō
Kōronsha.

USUI KATSUMI (1971), 'Nitchū gaikōshi: Hokubatsu no jidai', Tokyo: Hanawa Shobō.

USUI KATSUMI (1974), 'Manshū jihen: Sensō to gaikō to', Tokyo: Chūō Kōronsha.

VALLIANT, R.B. (1974), The selling of Japan: Japanese manipulation of western opinion, 1900-05, 'Monumenta Nipponica', 29, 415-38.

WHITE, J.A. (1964), 'The diplomacy of the Russo-Japanese war', Princeton.

WILSON, G.M. (ed.) (1970), 'Crisis politics in prewar Japan', Tokyo: Sophia.

WURFEL, D. (ed.) (1971), 'Meiji Japan's centennial: aspects of political thought and action', Lawrence, Kansas.

YABE SADAJI (TEIJI) (1952), 'Konoe Fumimaro', Tokyo: Kōbundō, 2 vols.

YAMABE KENTARŌ (1966), 'Nik-Kan heigō shoshi', Tokyo: Iwanami.

'Yamagata Aritomo ikensho', Oyama Azusa (ed.), Tokyo: Hara Shobō, 1966.

YAMAMOTO SHIGERU (1943), 'Jōyaku kaiseishi', Tokyo.

YASUOKA AKIO (1974), Gaikōka to shite no Mori Arinori, 'Shigaku Ronshū', 3, 331-57.

YOSHIDA SHIGERU (1962), 'The Yoshida memoirs', London. Partly translates 'Kaisō 10-nen', Tokyo, 4 vols, 1957.

YOSHIHASHI TAKEHIKO (1963), 'Conspiracy at Mukden', New Haven.

YOSHII HIROSHI (1971), 'Shōwa gaikōshi', Tokyo: Nansōsha.

YOUNG, A.M. (1928), 'Japan under Taishō Tennō, 1912-26', London.

YOUNG, A.M. (1938), 'Imperial Japan, 1926-38', London.

YOUNG, J.W. (1972), Hara cabinet and Chang Tso-lin, 1920-1, 'Monumenta Nipponica', 27, 125-42.

YOUNG, KATSU (1967), The Nomonhan incident: Imperial Japan and the Soviet Union, 'Monumenta Nipponica', 22, 82-102.

Index